ONLY FOR LIFE

For Ray & Audrey
with best wishes

Peter Mimms

JUN 1997.

Only for Life

A labouring family from Civil War to Second World War

by

Peter Mimms

with illustrations by

Audrey Appleby

BREWIN BOOKS

First published in 1995 by
Brewin Books, Studley, Warwickshire B80 7LG

ISBN 1 85858 065X

British Library Cataloguing in Publication Data.
A Catalogue record for this book is available from the
British Library

Typeset by Avon Dataset, The Studio, Bidford on Avon B50 4JH
Printed in Great Britain byWBC Book Manufacturers Ltd, Bridgend, Glamorgan

"Sometimes we seems to be gettin' on a little, and then you has bad luck, and there you are again where you were before. It's like gettin' part way up a hill and fallin' down to the bottom again, and you got it all to begin over again."

I said something – some platitude -turning to go away. Then she managed to smile – a shining-eyed smile – saying: "Well, 'tis only for life. If 'twas for longer than that I don't know if we should hardly be able to bear it."

– George Sturt, 'Change in the Village'
Duckworth, 1912 (1955 edn. p.42)

for Jean

ACKNOWLEDGEMENTS

I would like to acknowledge my debt to the authors and publishers of the works listed in the Bibliography at the end of this book and, in particular, to those who have so freely given me permission to quote from works still subject to copyright. Unfortunately, all attempts to trace the copyright holder of 'TEN LEAN YEARS' by Wal. Hannington, published by Victor Gollancz Ltd. have been unsuccessful. Chapters Four and Seven could not have been written in such depth had it not been for a detailed local history of St Neots and Eynesbury, and I am indebted to Phillimore & Co Ltd. of Chichester for permission to quote from 'ST NEOTS: THE HISTORY OF A HUNTINGDONSHIRE TOWN' by C F Tebbutt, first published in 1978 and reprinted in 1984.

I am deeply grateful also to the Archivists and staff of those record offices and repositories I have used, most especially those of the Cambridgeshire and Northamptonshire Record Offices, the Corporation of London Greater London Record Office, the County Record Office of Huntingdon, Southwark Local Studies Library, the Clerk of the Records at the House of Lords Record Office, the Public Record Office Census Room and the County Archivist for permission to quote from material held in the Bedfordshire County Record Office. I have never found keepers of records to be less than wholly committed, unfailingly courteous and indispensably helpful. My gratitude to them is boundless.

Parish registers and records from which I have extracted material are far and away too many to quote individually; they are all identified in the References and I am most grateful for having had the opportunity to study them. I must, however, express my especial thanks to the Parochial Church Councils of Ampthill, Eaton Socon and Shillington (Bedfordshire), Eynesbury (Huntingdonshire) and Wellingborough (Northamptonshire) whose archives I have employed extensively.

The Chartered Insurance Institute gave me permission to quote prolifically from original material relating to the Tooley Street fire and the Headteacher of Riverside Primary School, Southwark, kindly made the Farncombe Street Infants' School log available to me – my thanks to them both.

I must also record my admiration for the efficiency of the Lansdowne Library, Bournemouth, whose cheerful staff never once failed to find me a copy of the hundred or so books, however obscure, which I ordered through the library loan service.

In conclusion, my deepest thanks are due to my aunt, Alice Humphreys (Cis Jarman), without whose memories of Bermondsey and Exmouth during the first half of the present century the final chapters of this book would have been substantially less complete.

CONTENTS

INTRODUCTION

"Poverty preserves the Purity of the Body, by keeping it at a Distance from Pleasure"

– Robert Nelson (1715)[1]

' "I'm ashamed of my state if you aren't. Paupers – we're nothing else. And that man will come tomorrow and sit there and say 'Fetch the rent book', 'Fetch the bank book', Fetch the insurance policies', 'Fetch the sick-club cards', Bank book!" – she laughed cynically – "bank book! Two pound in." '

– Walter Brierley (1935)[2]

'Most are accepters, born and bred to harness, and take things as they come.'[3] Louis MacNeice's lines could be said to summarise the lives of nine generations of my family whose story is told here. They inherited nothing, bequeathed nothing and influenced no one. They acquired few skills and, for the most part, described their occupations simply as 'labourer'. Their fortunes were dictated by others: they did what they were told, or starved. Their history, and that of the millions who shared their experiences, has been written by others since they were mostly illiterate and, in any case, were more than fully occupied in the struggle to survive.

Their story is reconstructed from parish maps and registers, Poor Law records, Parliamentary papers, Board school logs and accounts written by those of their contemporaries who had benefitted from some education. It tells of the homes they lived in, the wages they earned, the work they did on Midland farms and on London's waterfront, of how they were cared for when no employment offered and when they became too sick or old to work. It is a story of survival against the odds.

Charles Masterman has said that each generation stands 'in the roll-book of the centuries, not as it appears to itself but as it appears to observers gazing, as from a distance, over a gulf of time.'[4] That gulf is hard to cross when one is loaded down with the heavy baggage of late twentieth century hindsight, and Dr. M.A. Crowther has warned that any book which deals 'with the most helpless members of a past society, runs the risk of turning them into an abstraction, of stripping them of their humanity', and that 'historians have tended either to search for working class heroes, or to turn the whole class into a heroic figure ennobled by endurance and achievement.'[5] This story, though, is about real people; they actually lived when and where the pages say they did. They all belonged to one family, son following father, for three hundred years. Only in fiction would it be possible to glamourise them, whereas the harsh realities of their lives invites compassion not heroics.

This book attempts to portray the lives lived by the poor over a period of three centuries through the medium of one particular family, but, whilst this is their story, it could, with minor variations of geography, be the story of hundreds of thousands of families who worked the land until they lost any rights over it, who fled to the towns for work to find filth, squalor and ill-paid casual employment, but survived only to become twentieth century paupers in the slump of the 1930s. I have tried to write their story as it might have seemed to those living at the time near the bottom of the social heap. If a degree of objectivity has been lost in so doing, I can only plead that *they* were unaware of the ultimate benefits of field enclosure, of industrialisation, of railway construction and slum clearance schemes, nor did they understand why the world went bankrupt after 1929; they only knew the price which, in large measure, was paid only by them.

The detail of their lives is lost forever, in its place is a record of what those lives were like at the times and in the places where they lived. I should like to think that should they read what I have written my ancestors would recognise most of it as a fair description of at least parts of their lives. I hope they will not be able to say, "It wasn't like that at all."

'And some there be', Ecclesiasticus tells us, 'which have no memorial; who are perished, as though they had never been; and are become as though they had never been born.' – They were my family, and this is their memorial.

References

[1] Nelson, R., 'An Address to Persons of Quality and Estate' (1715) p.39: quot. in Malcolmson, 'Life and Labour in England', p.17.
[2] Brierley, 'The Means Test Man', p.237.
[3] MacNeice, L., 'Autumn Journal', (1939)
[4] Masterman, 'The Condition of England', p.6.
[5] Crowther, 'The Workhouse System', p.1.

PART ONE

Country Life, 1640 - 1830

CHAPTER ONE

WELLINGBOROUGH

> 'But rich men receive all they have from the labourer's hand, and when they give they give away other men's labours, not their own.'
>
> Gerrard Winstanley[1]

> 'Behold them, leaning on their scythes, look o'er
> The labour past, and toils to come explore;
> See them alternate suns and showers engage,
> And hoard up aches and anguish for their age;'
>
> George Crabbe[2]

A performing bear lumbered along the Northampton road carrying Thomas Jones on his back. Jones was not the town drunk, but the ordained minister of All Saints, Wellingborough; and the mob goading the bear, a detachment of three hundred soldiers loyal to the cause of Parliament, most probably a Trained Band of the London militia.

The Reverend Thomas Jones was over seventy years of age and had been Wellingborough's vicar for thirtyfour years. King Charles had worshipped at his church when he and his queen, Henrietta Maria, visited the town with Archbishop William Laud to take the spa waters. The Bishop of Peterborough had conferred on the Revd. Jones the honour of attending Archbishop Laud's translation to Canterbury. Thomas Jones, then, was a strong supporter of the monarchy and of William Laud's church reforms which Puritans condemned as 'Popish practices'. When the struggle for dominance between the King

'A performing bear lumbered along the Northampton road carrying Thomas Jones on his back.'

and his Parliament degenerated into violence in 1642, it was, therefore, scarcely surprising that so staunch a royalist as Thomas Jones, preaching in so predominantly Parliamentarian an area as Northamptonshire should be taken prisoner and marched ten miles to gaol in the county town.

The troopers had stolen the performing bear from a barber whom they had murdered and, because Thomas Jones could not walk fast enough, a Lieutenant Grimes 'forceth the bear upon him, which running between his legs took him upon her back and . . . to the astonishment of the beholders carried him quietly.' This could not have provided quite the sport the soldiers had intended, and Jones was shortly removed and put on a horse instead. One of the troop, assuming that the bear had been trained to the saddle, attempted to ride her but, in the words of the royalist pamphleteer, the bear 'as if she had been robb'd of her whelps did so mangle, rend and tear him with her teeth and paws, that the presumptuous wretch died of those hurts suddenly after.' Thomas Jones fared little better. He was released from gaol after a few months and returned to Wellingborough where he continued to observe Laud's High Church liturgy and to preach against the rebellion so that he was once again imprisoned and died of his privations in Northampton gaol. He was not replaced as vicar until Charles I was beheaded in Whitehall seven years later.[3]

The Civil Wars divided families. Cousins, and even brothers, fought on different sides. Fathers and their sons were separated by their allegiance to the King or Parliament. Towns, however, tended to declare for one side or the other, but Wellingborough, the second largest town in Northamptonshire, was not united. Its two leading landowners supported opposite sides at the outbreak of war. Sir Christopher Hatton, a royalist, owned the manor of Wellingborough-Hatton until impoverishment obliged him to sell it. The purchaser was another royalist, Francis Gray, a Clerk of the Peace of the county. In the same year as Thomas Jones's abduction Gray had been attacked by Roundhead soldiers, his possessions thrown into the street and burned, and Gray himself arrested for failing to contribute to the defence of the kingdom (i.e. Parliament's coffers). In his defence the townsfolk attacked the soldiers and reinforcements had to be rushed from Northampton to quell the riot.[4] Robert Greville, Lord Brooke, a supporter of Parliament, owned the other manor of

Wellingborough proper and with it the right to nominate its vicar. It is perhaps ironic that so convinced a puritan as Brooke who encouraged preaching by untutored laymen amongst other heresies, should have been saddled with as unrepentant a royalist as the Revd. Thomas Jones whose installation as vicar long predated Brooke's inheritance of the lordship of Wellingborough manor. Brooke was the highly regarded commander of Parliament's Midlands Association army but was shot and killed by 'Dumb Dyott' whilst leading an assault on Lichfield, his troops storming the cathedral as they chanted the 149th psalm:

> '. . . Let the praises of God be in their mouth:
> and a two-edged sword in their hands:[5]

Despite the strong support given to the Parliamentary side throughout Northamptonshire and the dominant influence of the Puritan Brooke family, Wellingborough appears to have suffered more from the depredations of Roundheads than from the King's Cavaliers. In the year leading up to the battle of Naseby, a force of Parliament's men under the command of Lord Grey ransacked the town and, as a royalist reporter put it, 'what they could not carry away, they spoile, so that the losse sustained by the towne is valued at six thousand pounds.'[6] And yet shortly afterwards Wellingborough played host, probably reluctantly, to General Sir Thomas Fairfax's New Model Army mustering to fight the King at Naseby some fifteen miles away.[7]

It was amidst all the confusion of war that Gregory Mims first settled in Wellingborough where his numerous descendants were to remain for a century. Where he came from remains a mystery: certainly not from any nearby parish. At his death in 1702 he was described simply as a 'labourer', so that in 1650 when his first child, Judith, was baptised at All Saints church in the town he would have been a young man in his twenties with no land of his own to farm. In the middle of the seventeenth century there were many like him. A doubling of the population in the preceding century had led to a land shortage and decreasing opportunities for employment in agriculture on which some 70 per cent of the population depended. The East Midlands appears to have been particularly badly affected. In Northamptonshire it was suggested that the state should determine the optimum size of the population and ship the surplus to fight in the continental wars or to develop the overseas colonies. Given these circumstances 'displaced villagers either swelled the bands of vagabonds and sturdy beggars or settled wherever they could scrape together a meagre living.'[8] In the months before the first Civil War broke out a petition from Northamptonshire was delivered to the House of Lords by 'gentlemen of quality' begging their Lordships 'to take into consideration the distressed state of the poorer sort of people, who, for want of trade and employment, are brought to extremity, which (without timely prevention) may prove of dangerous consequence.'[9] The 'dangerous consequence' they feared was, at worst, a popular insurrection or, at the very least, an outbreak of food rioting. Already there had been an alarming growth of begging especially in the towns, and of the vagrant poor wandering the countryside with evil intent. Bands of such 'masterless men' under no-one's control had become a threat to a society which was none too stable at the best of times.[10] Had Gregory Mims in his wanderings been found guilty of begging he would first have been whipped by order of a Justice of the Peace or a parish official and then given a pass to return to his birthplace. For the more serious offence of being an 'incorrigible and dangerous rogue' the punishment for a first offence was branding 'on the left shoulder with a hot iron of the breadth of a shilling having a Roman R upon it.'[11] Presumably in an attempt at reforming such people the Puritan legislators of 1644 laid it down that rogues, vagabonds and beggars should be compelled to attend church every Sunday.[12]

If he had not been travelling in search of work, Gregory might well have been a foot-soldier demobilised far from home from one or other of the opposing armies, or, equally likely, a deserter of whom there were thousands especially amongst the lower ranks of pressed men. Colonel John Venn, the Parliamentarian Governor of Windsor Castle, had little time for them: 'Most counties press the Scum of all their Inhabitants,' he complained, 'men taken out of prison, Tinkers, Peddlers and Vagrants that have no dwelling and such as whom no account can be given: It is no marvel if such run away.'[13] Gregory's attitude to the wars, like that of most men whose main preoccupation was to secure the next meal, probably echoed the reaction of the apocryphal farmhand ploughing on Marston Moor who, when told to clear off as the King and Parliament were to fight a battle there that afternoon, incuriously exclaimed, "What! Has them two buggers fallen out?"[14] The outcome of the Civil Wars, which occupied the greater part of a decade, were to make no difference to his standard of life. Whether the authority of the state was vested in King Charles, assumed by the Commonwealth, or imposed by Lord Protector Cromwell, a labourer's lot ultimately depended on a good harvest or the generosity of parish relief and private charity.

Three successive disastrous harvests, which more than doubled the price of corn and brought about widespread misery, ended the 1640s.[15] By March of 1650, six months before Gregory's daughter Judith was born, 1169 of Wellingborough's inhabitants were in receipt of alms. The town's population was little more than two thousand souls and half of them were destitute. So desperate had they become that they took matters into their own hands. Following the example set by the famous Digger colony which had been set up the year before at Cobham in Surrey, they appropriated a stretch of common and waste land of about 140 acres called Bareshanks Leys two miles west of the town on which to grow their own food, publishing a Declaration giving reasons for their actions. The county's Justices, they claimed, knew of their plight and had ordered the town to create work for them, 'but as yet we see nothing is done, nor any man that goeth about it.' Describing their circumstances, they declared, ' . . . we have spent all we have, our trading is decayed, our wives and children cry for bread, our lives are a burden to us, divers of us having 5. 6. 7. 8. 9 in Family, and we cannot get bread for one of them by our labor . . . ' As if their readers were unaware of the severe penalties for unlawful action, they added ' . . . rich mens hearts are hardened, they will not give us if we beg at their doors; if we steal, the Law will end our lives', but added a defiant challenge, ' . . . divers of the poor are starved to death already, and it were better for us that are living to dye by the Sword than by the Famine.' In their Declaration the Wellingborough men acknowledged the support they had received from some local landowners who had waived their rights over Bareshanks Commons and of farmers who had given them seedcorn to plant.[16]

Three-fifths of England was still farmed as common land at this time and large areas were still uncultivated 'wastes'. Bareshanks Leys was a mixture of both and its acreage would scarcely seem to have been crucial to the economy of a parish of over 4,000 acres, but in their Declaration the Wellingborough Diggers had made the dangerous political assertion that 'the common and waste Grounds belong to the poor, and that we have a right to the common ground both from the Law of the Land, Reason and Scriptures; and therefore we have begun to bestow our righteous labor upon it.' Perhaps that was the reason why the colony was eventually suppressed, possibly under the influence of Oliver Cromwell who, whilst prepared to execute a king, was otherwise rigidly conservative when it came to the rights of property and the established social order. Certainly their fellow Diggers at Cobham under their leader Gerrard Winstanley were consciously setting an example of common ownership of the land and its produce. 'Work together; eat bread together,' urged Winstanley, 'he that works for another, either for wages or to pay him rent, works unrighteously . . . but they that are resolved to work and eat together, making the earth a common treasury, doth join hands with Christ to lift up the creation from bondage . . .'[17]

After the Surrey Diggers had begun to cultivate St George's Hill at Cobham, and before the houses they had built and the crops they had grown were destroyed by their opponents, Winstanley claimed that 'England is not a Free People, till the Poor that have no Land, have a free allowance to dig and labor the Commons, and so live as Comfortably as the Landlords that live in their Inclosures.'[18] Not content merely to challenge the rights of landowners, Winstanley attacked ministers who preach the Scriptures and who 'lay claime to Heaven after they are dead, and yet they require their Heaven in this World too, and grumble mightily against the People that will not give them a large temporal maintenance. And yet they tell the poor People, that they must be content with their Poverty, and they shall have their Heaven hereafter. But why may we not have our Heaven here (that is, a comfortable livelihood in the Earth) And Heaven hereafter too, as well as you, *God is no respecter of Persons*.'[19]

Robert Coster's 'The Diggers' Song' expressed these sentiments more crudely:

> 'Your houses they pull down, stand up now, stand up now,
> Your houses they pull down, stand up now,
> Your houses they pull down to fright poor men in town,

> But the gentry must come down, and the poor shall wear
> the crown.
> STAND UP NOW, DIGGERS ALL.[20]

Such dangerously revolutionary thoughts could not be tolerated by a Parliament composed largely of landed gentry, and none of the Digger colonies survived for very long. For a brief period in the middle of the seventeenth century 'ordinary people were freer from the authority of church and social superiors than they had ever been before, or were for a long time to be again.'[21] But even then subversive acts which threatened to undermine the settled order of society had to be suppressed by those who had the most to lose in a world which they feared might be turned upside down.

Ten years later Parliament restored the monarchy and, with the return of the king in the person of Charles II, everyone once again knew where they stood in the great scheme of things. In his remarkable population survey based on the new Hearth Tax returns, Gregory King, the herald and genealogist, firmly placed Gregory Mims' family one notch above gipsies, thieves and beggars together with that half of the people of England (labourers, common soldiers and seamen, cottagers and paupers) who, however hard they worked, could never earn enough to keep themselves and their dependants from destitution without recourse to charity or a parish handout. They, 'the poor', Gregory King dismissed as 'those who decrease the wealth of the Kingdom.' It was a strange phrase to use particularly in an era when working the land was so highly labour-intensive. Whilst parts of Wellingborough had been enclosed, some 4,000 acres of the parish were still laid out in large open fields which the owners or tenants cultivated in common.[22] Those villagers with insufficient land of their own or none at all, which would seem to have been Gregory Mims' lot, hired themselves out as day-labourers to work on land owned by their wealthier neighbours. When Charles II first imposed the Hearth Tax, 440 families in the town were required to pay it. Gregory and Frances were amongst that quarter of the population considered too poor to find two shillings a year for each chimney. In Northamptonshire as a whole 35 per cent of families were exempt.[23] For a labouring family any time which could be spared from working in the fields would have been devoted to one or both of the town's cottage industries, shoe- and lace-making. These part-time occupations helped to supplement the meagre earnings from agriculture which, of course, was the major employer of labour in the rich and fertile lands of the Midlands Plain.

Wellingborough was known as a 'town' only because King John had granted it a charter to hold a market every Wednesday.[24] In reality it was little more than a village. During the reign of Charles II it was described as 'a borough containing a great number of houses, all built of stone, and a considerable population,'[25] but even forty years later it still housed only six hundred families, or a little over two thousand people.[26] The town itself stood on a hill with three of its long main streets, High Street, Silver Street and Sheep Street, sloping gently down in more or less of a straight line from the Green at the top to the Swanspool rivulet at the foot. At the junction of Silver Street and Sheep Street stood the Borough or Market Cross from where the town's fourth major thoroughfare, Market Street, lying south of the church ran eastwards to Hog Hill. The whole built-up area was less than a mile long from north to south and only half that in width, and the streets themselves were of hard-packed earth; they were not paved until well into the nineteenth century.[27]

It was in this busy little market town that Gregory and Frances brought up their family of three girls and three boys. We do not know if the couple ever went through a form of church marriage, but, if so, it was not in Wellingborough or its neighbouring parishes. In the seven years prior to the birth of their first child Wellingborough had no appointed vicar after the death of Thomas Jones. During the Commonwealth period banns were simply announced from the Cross on market days and the marriage solemnized before a magistrate.[28] In fact the parish register records such a marriage in these words:

> 'Thomas Tebutt of Hanninton & Jant Darvis of Hardwick widow were published at the market place Wellingborow March 4, 11 & 18 1656 & married by Mr Browne March 19 at Kettring.'

It had already become a criminal offence to use the Book of Common Prayer or to celebrate any of the old festivals of Christmas, Easter, Whitsun or saints' days.[29] Churchwardens had been ordered to remove the communion table from the east end of the church, take away the altar rails, candlesticks and crucifixes, destroy stone statues and stained glass and whitewash over wall paintings.[30] Anything which smacked of Catholic idolatry or which otherwise could distract the congregation's attention from the words of the sermon were to be destroyed. King Charles abolished these harsh regulations but Puritan influence long outlasted his restoration to the throne. The church register of Wellingborough's neighbour, Hardwick, records the case of Charles and Hannah Tear who were required to perform a public penance in 1696 for engaging in pre-marital sex. Four years earlier in the same church Elizabeth Law confessed her sin to the whole congregation at Morning Prayer:

> 'I Elizabeth Law having not the fear of God before my eyes nor yet regarding my own Souls health have been guilty of the filthy sin of Adultery and have lately been delivered of a bastard child to the great displeasure of Almighty God the danger of my own Soul and the Evil Example of others . . .'

As she spoke those words 'in a penitent manner and with an audible voyce' she was required to stand in full view of the congregation clothed in white, carrying a white sheet, bare-headed, bare-legged and bare foot.[31]

Gregory's three sons were all labourers, as were three of his five surviving grandsons, their working lives dominated by the weather, the seasons and agricultural methods which, in the first half of the eighteenth century, had not changed since biblical times. The church's year began with Advent, the four weeks leading up to Christmas; The secular year, at least until the middle of the century, began on Ladyday, March 25th, but the agricultural year began with Plough Monday - the first working day after Christmas when the seasonal cycle of arable work in the fields really started. The cycle followed the invariable and immemorial pattern of ploughing, sowing, hoeing, mowing (hay-making), reaping (corn harvest) and threshing: ending at mid-winter with a Christmas celebration. No matter what the church or state decreed, this was how country people saw the year.

Plough Monday was, therefore, an important day especially in the East Midlands where it was particularly celebrated. The day itself was either the second Monday in January or the first Monday after Twelfth Day so that it could fall anywhere between January 7th and 14th. Although supposedly the first working day, it was celebrated as a holiday by farm labourers, who had probably been at work since the day after Christmas anyway. Labourers would dress up, blacken their faces with burnt cork and drag a plough from door to door soliciting 'plough-money' to pay for feasting, drinking and dancing in the evening. A contributor to the Gentleman's Magazine complained that 'the young men yoke themselves, and draw a plough about with musick, and one or two persons, in antic dresses, like jack-puddings, go from house to house to gather money to drink; if you refuse them, they plough up your dung-hill.'[32] One of the songs sung by the ploughboys, 'Plough Witches' or 'Plough-Bullocks' as they were variously called, ran:

> 'Think of the poor old ploughboys
> When the dirt sticks like glue.
> No-one knows what the poor old ploughboy
> Has to go through.'[33]

Midlands clay called for a large team of horses or oxen to drag the plough through the sticky soil for as many as six ploughings and five harrowings to produce a seed bed. In wet weather the land was unworkable, the teams stood idle and the men laid off. Harrows were often no more than bushes tied to a wooden frame. Large logs or stone rollers were used to flatten the earth until cast iron rollers became available at the end of the century.[34] Most sowing was still done by the biblical method of broadcasting, throwing a handful of seed from a basket in an arc, whilst walking across the ploughed and harrowed field, and following the old country lore of using four times as much seed as one expected to grow:

> 'One for the sparrow, one for the crow,
> One to rot, and one to grow.'

Candlemas is a church festival celebrating the Purification of the Blessed Virgin Mary when the candles to be used on the altar were traditionally blessed. For country folk, however, February 2nd had another, and more important, significance as its weather was commonly believed to foretell the weather for the rest of the winter:

> 'If Candlemas be clear and bright
> Winter shall have another flight:
> If Candlemas be dull and rain
> Winter shall not come again.'[35]

It is easy to understand how these items of folklore, based on observation over many generations from pre-Christian times, became entwined with important dates in the church calendar as early Christian missionaries acknowledged deeply held superstition and popular belief and grafted their own festivals and feasts on to celebrations of pagan origin, Easter and Christmas being prime examples. One pagan festival, however, was never successfully absorbed into the church calendar. Instead, serious attempts were made to suppress its celebration. This was May Day, a pre-christian celebration of fertility, both of the land and humankind. Christopher Fetherstone, a Puritan divine, in his 'Dialogue against light, lewde and lascivious dauncing', condemned May Day celebrations in which young men ' . . . doe use commonly to runne into woodes in the night time, amongst maidens, to set bowes (bowers), in so muche, as I have hearde of tenne maidens whiche went to set May, and nine of them came home with childe.'[36] Little wonder, then, that the priesthood disapproved of all this cavorting. Matthew Stevenson recognised what the celebration was really about when he acknowledged that ' . . . if any kind Sweet-heart left her Maidenhead in a Bush, she has good luck if she finde it again next May-day.'[37] A central feature of this spring fertility rite was the maypole: 'The maypole, 100 feet high, the tallest and straightest tree in the wood, brought in with the may and with a special song, was a phallic symbol, and the Morris dancers stamped to awaken the earth-goddess and jumped high for growing corn.'[38] To the Puritans the maypole was 'a heathenish vanity' and their influence prompted Parliament to order its destruction in every parish in England.[39] The maypole survived this persecution but it had been stripped of its potency and the English peasantry had lost its celebration of spring and of new life.

Haymaking in the popular imagination has always been seen as a joyous time with the midsummer sun shining down on happy mowers, their leader at the head and his team strung out in staggered line behind him, their sweeping scythes swinging in rhythm to a jovial rustic tune sung with bucolic gusto as the long grass falls in sinuous lines across the meadow. Doubtless it was a happier task than pulling turnips in the winter mud, but Stephen Duck caught the weariness of the mowers' seemingly endless toil:

> 'But when the scorching Sun is mounted high,
> And no kind Barns with friendly Shade are nigh:
> Our weary Scythes entangle in the Grass,
> While Streams of Sweat run trickling down apace,

then, after a midday snack in the shade of a hedge eating the hunk of bread with bacon or cheese brought from home and washed down with some of the farmer's ale:

> '. . . Again we rise from off the Grass:
> Again each Mower takes his proper Place:
> Not eager now, as late, our Strength to prove:
> But all contented regular to move.

until dusk when the sun

> '. . . bids the weary Labourer, Good Night.
> Homewards we move, but spent so much with Toil,
> We slowly walk, and rest at ev'ry Stile.'[40]

After haymaking the next major task was the corn harvest for which every available hand was needed. It was the one time in the agricultural year when a labourer could be guaranteed extra earnings on which he relied to pay his rent at Michaelmas and buy more expensive items such as clothes and shoes which could rarely be afforded out of his normal weekly earnings. His wife could also earn money as a binder, one to every three or four reapers, following them as they cut the corn, binding each sheaf with straw and setting them together into shocks or stooks to stand in the fields to dry.

At Wellingborough each day began with the ringing of the harvest bell to encourage everyone to reach the fields as early as possible: those who arrived before the bell had stopped its ringing were given free beer to start the day.[41] The quantity of beer drunk during the working day was quite prodigious and particularly so at harvest time:

> 'In the midland counties, the improvident consumption of malt liquor is no less remarkable (than in Gloucestershire) . . . In hay and corn harvest the customary allowance is a gallon of beer a man (in hot weather they drink more) and besides this, the mowers expect two quarts of ale, and never have less than one.'[42]

If some men regularly drank at least one and half gallons a day it is not surprising to find the Shefford (Beds.) overseers paying 'four men to hold Jem Smith till he got sober.'[43]

After the last sheaf had been gathered, the poor of the parish could glean in the stubble for ears of wheat, oats or barley left by the reapers. There does not seem to have been any right in common or statute law for this practice, but by long-standing custom this perquisite was claimed as a right 'from time immemorial'. In the common fields it seems to have been accepted that the women and children could glean for seven days before the cattle were let loose to pasture in the stubble fields.[44]

Once the corn was in, and especially if it had been a good harvest, there was great rejoicing, partly in relief that the wearying work was over, partly in pride at a job well done, but also because they all knew that the price of bread throughout the next winter would not rise out of a labourer's reach as was always the case following a poor harvest.

'It was always arranged that the last load of corn should be carried on a waggon, and not many sheaves on it. All the youth of the village used to climb on to this as it left the field, and with odd bits of bunting and boughs of hedgerow ash stuck all around . . . On arrival at the farm where everybody had collected, a barrel of beer had been set up and tapped earlier in the day to allow it to settle, and great quartern loaves were cut up, with slices of cheese cut from a whole cheese that stood there. Everyone looked after himself; man, woman and child had as much as they could eat and drink, often more than they wanted, and when their holding capacity was reached all quietly went home. No speeches, no songs, no health drinking, just a solemn 'fill up', no more except 'goodnight'. Speeches, songs etc. were out of place when no-one had anything but just working clothes on.'[45]

> 'In noisy Triumph the last Load moves on,
> And loud Huzza's proclaim the Harvest done.
> Our Master, joyful at the pleasing Sight,
> Invites us all to feast with him at night.
> A Table plentifully spread we find,
> And jugs of huming Ale to Chear the Mind;
> Which he, too gen'rous, pushes round so fast,
> We think no Toils to come, nor mind the past.'

Stephen Duck was a poet who understood the reality of eighteenth century rural life and declined to glamourise even its genuine occasions for joyful celebration, knowing that the harvest feast was only a brief respite in the unremitting grind involved in working the land:

> 'But the next morning soon reveals the Cheat,
> When the same Toils we must again repeat;
> To the same Barns must back again return,
> To labour there for Room for next Year's Corn.'

To make room for next year's corn, this harvest had to be threshed; back-breaking work with the hand-flail and winnowing fan to separate the grain from the husks and chaff. This was the main winter work for labourers in the arable areas lasting from harvest until well after Christmas. Not only corn but field peas, which could grow to the height of a man, had to be threshed:

> 'When sooty Pease we thresh, you scarce can know
> Our native Colour, as from Work we go:
> The Sweat, the Dust, and suffocating Smoke,
> Make us so much like *Ethiopians* look, . . .
> Week after Week, we this dull Task pursue . . . '[46]

There were, of course, occasional respites from the fields and threshing barns, The parish feast, sometimes called a 'wake' or 'revel', was celebrated usually at the anniversary of the dedication of the parish church. All Hallows, Wellingborough was until the nineteenth century, dedicated to All Saints and its patronal festival, therefore, fell on November 1st.[47] The parish feast would have started on that day, or on the nearest Sunday, and continued for as long as a week with country sports, drinking and a travelling fiddler to accompany the dancing. It was a time for family get-togethers from all the surrounding areas.

By no means everybody approved of even the limited leisure time available to labouring people or of the holidays afforded by fairs, wakes and festivals: 'The only way to make them temperate and industrious,' recommended one, 'is to lay them under the necessity of labouring all the time they can spare from meals and sleep, in order to procure the common necessaries of life.'[48] Another, who described himself as a 'Well-Wisher of Mankind', commented, 'The poor know nothing of the motives which stimulate the higher ranks to action – pride, honour, and ambition. In general it is only hunger which can spur and goad them on to labour.'[49]

'Leisure in a poor man,' wrote Charles Hall a few years later and with tongue firmly in cheek, 'is thought quite a different thing from what it is to a rich man, and goes by a different name. In the poor it is called idleness, the cause of all mischief.'[50]

References

[1] Brockway, 'Britain's First Socialists', p.128
[2] Poster, 'George Crabbe, Selected Poetry', p.21
[3] Cole, 'Wellingborough', pp.xi, 157/8 and 255/6: Victoria County history, vol.4. p.144: Matthews, A.G., 'Walker revised', Clarendon Press, Oxford (1948), p.281: Evans, 'Highways and Byways in Northamptonshire', pp.37–39.
[4] Palmer, J. and M., 'Wellingborough', p.341: Victoria County History, vol.4., p.139.
[5] Hill, C., 'Society and Puritanism', p.452.: Carlton, 'Going to the Wars' pp.83 and 160: Kenyon, 'The Civil Wars of England', p.66.
[6] Mercurius Rusticus, Part I p.57: quot. Sherwood, 'Civil Strife in the Midlands', pp.170/1.
[7] Palmer, J. and M., 'Wellingborough', p.74
[8] Pettit, 'The Royal Forests of Northamptonshire', p.147.
[9] Manning, 'The English People and the English Revolution', pp.171 and 173.
[10] Kenyon, 'The Civil Wars of England', p.160: Morrill, 'The Impact of the English Civil War', p.104.
[11] Eden, 'The State of the Poor', vol.I, Book I, ch.2.
[12] Hill, C., 'The World Turned Upside Down', p.40
[13] Carlton, 'Going to the Wars', p.68
[14] ibid., p.291
[15] Kenyon, 'The Civil Wars of England', p.160

[16] Sabine, 'The Works of Gerrard Winstanley', pp.649/650: Hill, C., 'The World Turned Upside Down.' pp.124/7: Brockway, 'Britain's First Socialists', pp.124 and 130/2: Palmer, J. and M., 'Wellingborough', pp.131 and 142.
[17] Hill, C., 'The World Turned Upside Down', p.129.
[18] Sabine, 'The Works of Gerrard Winstanley', p.260.
[19] ibid. p.409
[20] Brockway, 'Britain's First Socialists' p.140
[21] Hill, C., 'The World Turned Upside Down' p.361.
[22] Palmer, J. and M., 'Wellingborough' p.123.
[23] Wrightson, 'English Society', p.148: PRO, E 179/157/468
[24] Victoria County History, vol. 4. p.141.
[25] ibid. p.138
[26] Morton, J., 'Natural History of Northamptonshire' (1772): quot. Palmer, J. and M., 'Wellingborough' p.175/6.
[27] Cole, 'Wellingborough' pp.8/9
[28] ibid. p.243/4
[29] Morrill, 'The Impact of the English Civil War' p.57.
[30] ibid., p.54: Manning, 'The English People and the English Revolution', p.88.
[31] Hibbert, 'The English, A Social History', p.260.
[32] Malcolmson, 'Popular Recreations', p.28.
[33] Godber, 'History of Bedfordshire', p.523.
[34] Chambers and Mingay, 'The Agricultural Revolution', pp.58 and 70.
[35] Tebbutt, 'Hunts. Folklore', p.56.
[36] Malcolmson, 'Popular Recreations', p.10.
[37] Stevenson, J., 'The Twelve Monthes' (1661): quot. Malcolmson, 'Popular Recreations' p.77.
[38] Godber, 'History of Bedfordshire', p.169.
[39] Hill, C., 'Society and Puritanism' pp.180/1
[40] Duck, S., 'The Thresher's Labour' (1736): quot. Barrell and Bull, 'English Pastoral Verse'.
[41] Cole, 'Wellingborough' pp.98/9.
[42] Eden, 'The State of the Poor', vol. I. p.547.
[43] Bedfordshire Record Office, P.70/12/2 (1821)
[44] Ault, 'Open-field Husbandry' p.14.
[45] Tebbutt, 'Hunts, Folklore' p.72.
[46] Duck, S., 'The Thresher's Labour' (1736): quot. Barrell and Bull, 'English Pastoral Verse'.
[47] Palmer, J. and M. 'Wellingborough' p.54.
[48] Temple, W., 'A Vindication of Commerce and the Arts' (1758): quot. Malcolmson, 'Popular Recreations' p.97
[49] Townsend, J., 'Dissertation on the Poor Laws by a Well- Wisher of Mankind', (1780): quot. Hobsbawm, 'Labouring Men' p.352.
[50] Cunningham, H., 'Leisure in the Industrial Revolution' p.12.

CHAPTER TWO

LEAVING HOME

> 'For more than two centuries a civil war was waged between the separate parishes of England and Wales. The military commanders were the owners and occupiers of land, their adjutants were the parish overseers, and the casualties in the front line were the labouring poor.'
>
> Anne Digby[1]

The return of the king from exile released a pent-up demand for what were supposed to be his unique healing powers. Scrofula, a tubercular disease affecting the lymph glands causing disfiguring and chronic swellings of the face, neck and arms, was known as the 'King's Evil' because people believed that if the king touched the affected part it would bring about a miraculous cure. So wide-spread was this belief that parishes were instructed to maintain a register of their inhabitants who were granted a certificate by the minister or churchwarden to travel to London to be 'touched'. Charles II was said to have 'touched' 92,000 sufferers during his reign, no fewer than 6,700 of them in the first eight months following his return to the capital. The Wellingborough Town Book records the payment of £1 to Widow Gunnell and Roger Bretton 'to convey their children to London to get cured for the Evil'.[2]

In a newspaper advertisement attesting to the efficacy of Leake's Patent Pills in effecting a cure for this illness, a father described his eleven years old son's symptoms as a lump under the skin, on the side of the face and neck. 'I took an opportunity, while he was sleeping', wrote the father, 'to cut off a good lump of it with a sharp pair of scissors; it discharged blood and water with little pain: some time after this his arm and elbow became stiff and swelled.' Later, another lump in the child's throat swelled up threatening to suffocate him.'[3] Leake's Patent Pills, one suspects, were no more efficacious than the father's ministrations with the scissors. Equally certainly, the monarch's touch would have produced no better cure, but, at least, it could have done no harm. That is more than can be said about most early eighteenth century medical practices which, herbal remedies apart, were an amalgam of superstition, quackery and butchery in more or less equal proportions. Even a century later George Crabbe could write approvingly of the parish doctor 'whose most tender mercy is neglect.'[4] Mrs Deakins of Dartford who had lost the use of her limbs in 1736 might well have benefitted from that benign neglect. Instead, she 'was advis'd to be Sweated in a Horse-Dunghill, where she continued 2 Hours and a half, but fainting was taken out Dead.'[5]

Smallpox epidemics ravaged eighteenth century England. The disease was highly infectious and fatal in one case out of every five or six. Those it did not kill could find themselves severely weakened, permanently scarred on the face or blinded. Until effective inoculation was developed in the middle of the century the disease was greatly and understandably feared.[6] Market towns suffered considerable loss of trade when an epidemic raged. St Neots in Huntingdonshire was especially vulnerable, sited as it is beside the Great North Road with its constant flow of travellers. During one of the most serious epidemics its vestry felt impelled to pay for the insertion of an advertisement in a regional newspaper on three successive weeks announcing that no outbreak had occurred in their town.[7] It was mainly for this reason, and to reduce the impact on the poor rates should an outbreak occur, that parishes went to the considerable expense of inoculating every one of the parish poor who wished it – the cost varied between 2s. 6d. and 5 shillings a head. One family alone in Eaton Socon in Bedfordshire cost the parish more than £8 for medicine, food and nursing, equivalent to one-twentieth of the total annual poor rate. The worst epidemic in that parish carried off the master, the matron and six of the workhouse inmates within a few weeks.[8]

The Wellingborough burial register clearly illustrates the effect on the inhabitants of an infected visitor to the town. On

September 27th 'John Towson (Stranger)' died of the smallpox. Almost exactly one month later the first of a spate of smallpox deaths is recorded – thirteen by the year end, and all but one of them young children. John Towson must have been responsible for infecting about eighty people within three months of his arrival in the town.

The death of a child was no rare event in eighteenth century England. Amongst labouring families about three in every ten children died before reaching the age of five.[9] Between 1680 and 1780 forty-one children were born to Mims families in Wellingborough: only twenty of them survived to attain their majority. Eighteen, or 44 per cent, of them died before their fifth birthday. Dr Isaac Watts, best known for his hymn, 'O God, our help in ages past', saw nothing incongruous about including in his collection of hymns for children:

> 'There is an hour when I must die.
> Nor do I know how soon 'twill come:
> A thousand children young as I,
> Are called by death to hear their doom.'[10]

The break up of a marriage brought about by the early death of one of the partners before all their children had grown up was quite common. In this respect the Mims families seem to have been more fortunate than most. There were seven marriages in that century where we can be reasonably certain of their duration. On average they lasted 36 years before the death of one of their partners, as compared with a national average of about 23 years.[11] In part this was owing to the longevity of the husbands whose average life-span exceeded 70 years. Thomas Mims, Gregory and Frances's second son, was not baptised until 1729 when, according to the parish register he was 'about 75 years old'.

One of Gregory's grandsons was the first of the, by now extended, family to leave Wellingborough. He married and settled eight miles away at Sharnbrook in north Bedfordshire. The next to leave in the 1750s were two brothers, John and William Mims, both labourers, two years apart in age, who, doubtless, set out together to look for work in Bedfordshire. By the end of the century the only ones left in Wellingborough bearing that surname were a widow and a pair of spinster sisters, lacemakers, who died in the town in the middle of the nineteenth century.

Leaving one's home parish was not always an easy thing to do. A labourer 'was not free to roam over England, and try his luck in some village or town when his circumstances became desperate at home. He lived under the capricious tyranny of the old law of settlements.'[12] In theory every person had one parish in which he or she was entitled to receive poor relief. Every parish was expected to look after its own poor – sick, old, disabled, destitute or unemployed – and another parish would not welcome any newcomer who might become a charge on their poor rates.

John and William would have established their legal settlement in Wellingborough as three generations of their family had been both born and employed there for a hundred years. It was, of course, possible to establish a new settlement elsewhere or people would never have moved at all. The most common method for unmarried, able-bodied men was to be hired by a new master for an uninterrupted twelve-month period as a live-in farm servant. A new settlement could also be acquired by serving one's apprenticeship in a new parish, by paying parish taxes or holding an annual parish office – churchwarden, overseer etc. – but these were methods normally available only to men of property or with a skilled trade; few labourers could aspire to such heights. Women gained their husband's legal settlement automatically on marriage and bastard children by reason solely of their place of birth.

Unless a newcomer could afford to rent a property worth at least £10 a year he could be thrown out within 40 days of his arrival by a magistrate's order following a complaint by a parish officer and then removed to the place where he last had a legal settlement. Parish records are replete with examinations as to settlement when, for whatever reason, a parish wished to rid itself of an 'incomer'. Thus, William Groves was examined before two of His Majesty's Justices at Bedford:

> "This Examinant, on his Oath, saith that he is 21 years of age, is married and his wife's name is Martha, that he was born at Wellingborough in the County of Northampton, his father being legally settled there, and that he served an apprenticeship with Joseph Mimms of Wellingborough aforsd

weaver, (John and William's second cousin) who was also a legal inhabitant there, and that he hath not done any act to gain a settlement in any other place."[13]

The Bedford magistrate's decision is not recorded but it seems most likely that he would have been returned to Wellingborough, and at the latter's expense.

The overseer or, to give him his proper title, the Overseer of the Poor, was an unpaid official (a large parish might have several) elected annually at the Easter vestry meeting. The vestry governed the village and its monthly meetings held in the vestry of the parish church or at a local inn, were attended by those who paid the parish rates. As the century progressed the business of the vestry became increasingly dominated by the raising of the Poor Rate and its disbursement by their appointed officer, the overseer. Those villagers likely to be on the receiving end of its favours did not always look kindly on their vestry. To John Clare, a Northamptonshire labourer's son, its members were endowed

'With learning just enough to sign a name
And skill sufficient parish rates to frame
And cunning deep enough the poor to cheat . . . '[14]

The vestry was answerable only to the local magistrates who, at least in theory, confirmed the appointments it made, approved the accounts of churchwardens and overseers, and could be appealed to by those who objected to the vestry's decisions.

The overseers at Eaton Socon in Bedfordshire were clearly uneasy about assuming responsibility for Jacob Newman, a mentally handicapped lad of twenty whose ' . . . incapacity is so great that he cannot give a reasonable answer.' Instead, his mother Ann was examined explaining that she had given birth to this illegitimate son about twenty years ago at Thornby in Northamptonshire and whose father was John Newman, now her legal husband. Jacob had left there at one month old and had always lived and worked with John Newman as a chimney sweep until 13 months ago, but since then had held down several jobs, all for less than a year.[15] No decision in his case is recorded, but one can imagine the legal arguments, not to mention the fees involved, had the case been appealed, as to whether Jacob, as a bastard child born at Thornby, fell to their charge or, as a child of Ann now properly married and legally settled with her husband, John, in Eaton Socon, was the latter's responsibility.

Many parishes spent enormous sums in legal costs to ensure the removal of 'undesirables' to another parish even when those costs would far have exceeded the actual charge to the parish of paying poor relief to those unfortunates they tried so hard to remove.

A parish would often employ devious means to rid itself of a pauper and land him in some other parish's lap. 'Pauper marriages were enforced by the overseers. Ann Hudson of Northill was seduced by William Onions of Bolnhurst, who fled to Barnet. He was fetched back by overseer and constable, put in the house of correction at Bedford while the banns were read, and forcibly married to Ann at St. Paul's church in Bedford; then a removal order was obtained, and the couple were despatched to Bolnhurst. The total outlay, including coach fares, payment to the Barnet constable for his help, a "yellow ring" at 3d. eating and drinking at the wedding, was nearly £5, but Northill was rid of a bastard.'[16]

The cost of these removals was not inconsiderable, especially where the officer was required to accompany the vagabond personally. A Bedfordshire overseer's claim for taking a man from Eaton Socon to Barton Bendige in Norfolk was, 'For maintenance of self and Heard & his wife in the journey into Norfolk & my comeing back again, £1.10s: for my horses charge & meat for them, 12s; for my horses journeys, £1: for my trouble 10s'[17]. That sum of £3.12s. would have provided more than three months' relief to Heard had he instead been paid, say, 5s. a week.

'Pregnant women and the sick were pushed about with particular haste for fear lest they either gave birth to a child which would then be a charge upon the parish or die in it and require burial. At Wymswold 'a Bygg belly woman' was given 2d to help speed her 'forth of the towne!'[18]

The main reason for effectively restricting freedom of movement, especially of the poor, was clearly stated in the Preamble to the 1662 Act of Settlement

> '. . . by reason of some defect in the law, poor people are not restrained from going from one parish to another, and therefore do endeavour to settle themselves in those parishes where there is the best stock, the largest commons or wastes to

> build cottages, and the most woods for them to burn and destroy; and when they have consumed it, then to another parish; and at last become rogues and vagabonds.'[19]

One effect of the settlement laws was 'to prevent workmen leaving their homes in order to find work elsewhere. A new kind of serfdom was imposed on the poor. They were compelled to remain in their place of settlement, not because they were forbidden to leave it, but because no other place would receive them'.[20]

The foremost economist of the period, Adam Smith, commented, 'To remove a man who has committed no misdemeanour, from a parish where he chuses to reside is an evident violation of natural liberty and justice . . . There is scarce a poor man in England of forty years of age, I will venture to say, who has not, in some part of his life, felt himself most cruelly oppressed by this ill-contrived law of settlements.'[21]

Another contemporary, Thomas Paine, a supporter of both the American and French revolutions, in putting forward some suggestions for social reform wrote, 'By the operation of this plan, . . . The dying poor will not be dragged from place to place to breathe their last, as a reprisal of parish upon parish'.[22]

Until 1795 'a labourer could only make his way to a new village if his own village would give him a certificate, or if the village invited him. His liberty was entirely controlled by the parish officers.'[23] The 'certificate', therefore, was often the key to mobility and one can readily understand how, once obtained by a labourer from his own parish officers, he treasured it beyond all imagining. The certificate of indemnity acknowledged that the person it named was, and remained, the responsibility of the home parish wherever he might wander in search of work and for the whole of his life unless he subseqently established a legal settlement elsewhere.

Certificates were not freely given however. Where demand for labour was high, in the expanding northern industrial towns for example, they were often refused. Sometimes they permitted a man to travel only within a limited distance from home for fear of the expense in bringing him back should he fall on hard times. This was, in all probability, the means which allowed John and William to move from Wellingborough to Bedfordshire. John, certainly, established a new settlement in Higham Gobion in

The dying poor . . . dragged from place to place to breathe their last . . .'

south-east Bedfordshire not far from the Hertfordshire town of Hitchin. When he had married and wished to move to the next parish of Shillington in 1768 he was granted a certificate which reads in part.

> 'We the Church Wardens and Overseers of the Poor . . . do hereby certify, own and acknowledge John Mimms and Elisabeth his Wife to be our Inhabitants legally settled in the said Parish of Higham Gobion.'

The overseers of Shillington, evidently cautious men, were not entirely satisfied with the strict legality of the certificate as they sent it back with a note appended. 'There shd be 2 witnesses to attest ye certificate, one of which must make Oath before 2 Justices of the Parish Officers signing and sealing ye same'[24] The addition of George Hawkins' name as a second witness must have satisfied them because John settled in Shillington, his children and grandchildren being born in the village until his male line became extinguished with the death of his young grandson, Thomas, aged 8 ' . . . kill'd by a cart of Mr. Fossey passing over his Body.'

In his turn, William settled in the parish of Eaton Socon in north Bedfordshire adjoining St. Neots, a Huntingdonshire market-town, but we shall return to William later.

Those who paid 'the Poor's Rate' were no different from any other tax-payers when demands upon them kept increasing at what seemed an alarming rate. A Wellingborough Vestry meeting passed a resolution ordering ' . . . all Persons who are not Inhabitants be removed immediately at the cheapest Expence.'[25] This order was probably not carried out very vigorously or for very long but it indicates the ratepayers' frustration at the mounting cost of maintaining those who would or could not maintain themselves.

Orphans were apprenticed as early as possible, often at the age of only seven or eight. Joseph Mims, a weaver, John's and William's second cousin, had died leaving a widow, Phebe, and her surviving son Thomas. Phebe herself died five years later and within three weeks of her burial the parish had apprenticed the ten year old orphan to Thomas Curtis, a mason, until ' . . . he shall accomplish his full Age of One and Twenty Years. 'there to be instructed . . . in the Art or Mystery of a Mason'. The indenture required Thomas Curtis to provide '. . . meet, competent, and sufficient Meat, Drink, and Apparel, Lodging, Washing, and all other Things necessary and fit for an Apprentice', and to ensure '. . . that he be not any way a Charge to the said Parish.'[26] The overseers' accounts show that the cost of relieving themselves of his continued upkeep amounted to £3.10s.[27] Curtis was a Wellingborough man but, whenever possible, apprentices were placed with masters settled in parishes elsewhere to avoid a legal settlement being gained when the apprentice had served his time. At Maulden in Bedfordshire, for example, 45 out of 66 parish apprenticeships were so arranged.[28]

There is, perhaps, no better summary of the methods used to reduce the burden of the poor rate than Dr. Richard Burn's ironical admonition to parish officers to

- keep a lookout to prevent persons coming to inhabit without certificates
- caution the inhabitants not to rent a newcomer a farm of £10 p.a. or more
- assist a poor man with a large family to help him take a farm in some neighbouring parish and pay the first year's rent
- keep him out of any parish office
- warn inhabitants to hire servants for less than a year; or, if for a year, then pick a quarrel with them before the year's end
- bind (apprentice) children to a master in another parish
- be generous in giving a portion (dowry) to a bastard child's mother to marry the reputed father, or to a poor widow (for why should she be deprived of the comforts of matrimony?) – always provided the husband is settled elsewhere[29]

A labourer, had he been able to read Dr. Burn's treatise, might not have appreciated his sardonic humour: it was too close to the truth.

Farm servants were commonly hired at special fairs held once or twice a year but more usually at Michaelmas (September 29th) or a little later when the harvest work was done at Martinmas (November 11th). Young men and girls anxious to be hired for the following year dressed in all their finery often wearing or carrying something to indicate their special skill to their prospective employers – a shovel, a billhook, a woolcomb: a waggoner would wear a piece of whipcord round his hat; a thatcher, a piece of plaited straw, or a dairymaid a pail and a strand of cow-hair tucked in her cleavage.

The hiring fairs were not solely a labour exchange but a rare opportunity for young people from the surrounding district to meet and enjoy a day out together. Not everyone approved of its occasional consequences:

> "Its effects are seen . . . before the end of the year' wrote one, 'for, when bastardy cases are being adjudicated, many a poor girl declares that her ruin was effected at the last Martinmas Hirings."[30]

The fairs were an opportunity for traders to set out their stalls, as John Gay, the poet and author of 'The Beggar's Opera', described them in 'The Shepherd's Week':

> ' . . . Pedlar Stalls with glitt'ring Toys are laid,
> The various Fairings of the Country Maid.
> Long silken Laces hang upon the Twine,
> And Rows of Pins and amber Bracelets shine;
> How the tight Lass, Knives, Combs and Scissars spys,
> And Looks on Thimbles with desiring Eyes;'[31]

The patent medicine men, quack doctors and those who promised painless tooth extraction – without anaesthetic of course – all took advantage of the crowds to peddle their infallible nostrums and cures for all human ills:

> 'The Mountebank now treads the Stage, and sells
> His Pills, his Balsoms, and his Ague spells.'

Young men vied for prizes at wrestling, cudgelling or at single-sticks. A French traveller described the difference:

> ' . . . the single-stick player having the left-hand tied down, and using only one stick to defend himself and strike his antagonist. The object of each gamester in this play, as in cudgelling, is to guard himself, and to fetch blood from the other's head . . .

> In cudgelling, as the name implies, the weapon is a stout cudgel; and the player defends himself with another having a large hemisphere of wicker-work upon it.'[32]

When George Parker was examined at Eaton Socon about his legal settlement he claimed that he had let himself to John Mayes, the younger, of Ravensden at Bedford Fair on October 11th 1794 for one year, although he was only employed for fifty one weeks.[33] James Jopham claimed that about twelve years previously he had been hired at St. Neots' Statue by Mr Joseph Eden of Eaton Socon and had no other legal settlement.[34] St. Neots had, and still has, one of the largest market squares in England. Its fairs and markets were famous and the hiring of labour at the statue was a regular occurrence.

Perhaps it was from there that William Mims was hired by a Bedfordshire farmer from Eaton Socon as Eaton was only a little over a mile from St. Neots across the bridge over the River Ouse. Even more likely is the possibility that he met his future wife, Mary Darrington, at one of the town's fairs, feasts or days of national celebration. Mary, aged 26, was the eldest daughter of a labourer from the neighbouring parish of Little Barford. They were later married in the beautiful late fifteenth-century parish church of Our Lady at St. Neots, 'the cathedral of Huntingdonshire,'[35] on October 30th 1764, both signing their names with a shaky cross.

William and Mary settled in Eaton Socon, just across the county boundary. After Luton and Leighton Buzzard, Eaton was the third largest parish in Bedfordshire and the most populous village in the county with about 1500 inhabitants at this time, but it was widely scattered with as many as thirteen separate hamlets spread amongst its 7602 acres, some as far as 3½ miles from the main village. They interconnected with a maze of side roads.[36] To the east the parish was bounded by the River Ouse, the county boundary with Huntingdonshire, and is traversed by the Great North Road, or, as it was locally known, the 'York Road'. The parish lies almost midway between Bedford and Huntingdon, some ten or eleven miles in each direction and fifty-five miles north of London. Its nearest market town, only a mile away across the Ouse, was St. Neots. The condition of Eaton's roads was notorious: in winter they were generally so deep in mud that, despite the iron pattens fitted to their shoes, people found it easier to skate to St. Neots whenever the Ouse was frozen over, than to trudge through the mud or the frost-bound rutted roads.[37]

Eaton was predominantly an agricultural area of rich loam with a gravel or clay subsoil, ideal for arable or mixed farming, and with a hundred acres of well-wooded land. It was then still an 'open' parish – one not controlled by one landowner squire – 'remarkable for being almost wholly in the hands of neither one large proprietor, nor numerous small people'[38]. It still retained a common-field system with a traditional three-crop rotation in which each large field grew wheat or barley, followed by beans and was then left fallow for a year to recuperate.[39] A deed recording the letting of a cottage to a St. Neots surgeon, William Halliley, described it as, 'A Cottage in Cow Turd Lane and ten acres of land *dispersed in open fields* in Eaton Socon.'[40]

This was where William and Mary's two sons were born and baptised: John almost exactly nine months after their marriage, and William two years later. Their marriage was to prove a very short one as Mary's husband died aged 33 only five months after the birth of his second child. The parish clerk, perhaps understandably, must have assumed that the burial referred to the infant, William, as the register shows the words, "son of William and Mary" crossed through. This was to prove prophetic, however, as young William himself was buried in the same churchyard in the following year aged only two. In less than eighteen months, Mary had lost both her husband and her second child, and was left a widow with a four year old son, John, – a desperate plight for a young woman of 29.

It was at such times of tragedy that the parish overseers could usually be relied upon to help a distressed widow but, as is often the case, the records no longer survive to tell us what happened to this small family. However unfeeling it might seem, a young widow would often have to find a new husband to support her as soon as possible but there is no evidence to show that Mary remarried. Perhaps her own parents in Little Barford sheltered her and young John but they too were a labouring family and would have had little to spare.

Eaton Socon had its own parish workhouse described as 'a convenient and proper House, in good Repair, with an Orchard well planted with Fruit, Trees, and a Piece of Ground contiguous to the same, proper for a Garden'[41]. It had eleven rooms, six on the ground floor and five on the first, described as a kitchen, a buttery and a little room adjoining it which contained thirteen 'jersey and linen wheels' (the inmates were expected to work to contribute to their keep), a hall, parlour, brewhouse and great chamber and four more rooms over the brewhouse. The parlour doubled as sleeping accommodation containing six bedsteads. The twenty-seven inmates (in 1736) - nine males and eighteen females including six children - shared fifteen bedsteads and fourteen bolsters sleeping on two feather beds, two straw beds and the less fortunate on flock mattresses[42].

This, in all probability, was where John and his mother spent at least some part of their life until John was old enough to work or to be apprenticed. It was the later nineteenth century workhouses, the Bastilles of the New Poor Law Unions with their punishing, prison-like conditions which became the feared and hated last resort of the old and the destitute but, even so, those who were obliged to seek sanctuary in the parish workhouses of the latter part of the eighteenth century found little comfort there as the clergyman-poet George Crabbe wrote

> 'Theirs is yon House that holds the parish-poor,
> Whose walls of mud scarce bear the broken door;
> . . . There children dwell who know no parents' care:
> Parents, who know no children's love, dwell there!
> Heart-broken matrons on their joyless bed.
> Forsaken wives, and mothers never wed;
> Dejected widows with unheeded tears,
> And crippled age with more than childhood fears;
> The lame, the blind, and, far the happiest they!
> The moping idiot, and the madman gay.'[43]

If young John Mimms was indentured by the Eaton Socon parochial overseers it was as an apprentice to a Gamblingay farmer, Thomas Hall. Half a dozen miles south of Eaton and just over the county boundary, Gamblingay was the largest village in west Cambridgeshire and another totally rural parish still set in open fields which were not to be enclosed until the middle of the nineteenth century.[44] The only surviving evidence that it was there that John spent his youth as a farm servant is that when, much later, he came to apply for a marriage licence, it was Thomas Hall who stood surety for him and witnessed his marriage. Who, one might ask, would have risked a large sum of money to guarantee that a poor labourer was legally free to marry except one who had known him for some years?

A parish apprenticeship could be from as early as seven or eight years of age and last until the age of twentyone. On reaching his majority we know that John bound himself to an Eynesbury farmer for two years and later, at the Michaelmas Hirings of 1787 he became a horsekeeper to Robert Wiles, a farmer in the hamlet of Wyboston in the parish of Eaton Socon and so finished up where he had started. It was at the Michaelmas Hiring Fair or during that year's harvest that he got Lydia Endersby pregnant. Thomas Hardy aptly describes what happened:

> 'Love matches that had populated the adjoining hamlet had been made up there between reaping and carrying. Under the hedge which divided the field from a distant plantation girls had given themselves to lovers who would not turn their heads to look at them by the next harvest; and in that ancient cornfield many a man had made love-promises to a woman at whose voice he had trembled by the next seedtime after fulfilling them in the church adjoining.'[45]

Little could John have imagined the trouble he brought on himself 'in that ancient cornfield' with young Lydia from St. Neots. Not that it was at all unusual for brides to be pregnant; more than a third of labourers' brides were. The clergy may have condemned such immorality but could do little about it – "He is very anxious to put to shame all brides who are not virgins," wrote a lady about one vicar, "I am afraid he will find this sort of reformation a difficult one to effect, and it is no new custom".[46] They could, however, make their disapproval felt in the parish registers as did a Northamptonshire vicar when he recorded the baptism of Joseph and Eleanor Mallard's first child, adding the reproving comment, '*born a few days after marriage*'.[47]

By February of 1788 Lydia Endersby's pregnancy must have been obvious and John would have been expected to fulfill his 'promises'. Why he applied for a special licence is unclear as there was still plenty of time for banns to be called, except that Easter was only four weeks away and Lenten marriages were strongly disapproved of by the clergy: Lent was for self-denial, not for self-indulgence. But once he had set matters in train on

Saturday 23rd February he was caught up in a whirl of legal formalities. First, he had to swear an oath before the Reverend Littlehales, acting as Surrogate for the Bishop of Lincoln – the same clergyman who, as vicar of St. Neots, had married his parents twenty-four years earlier. In this oath, or Allegation as it was called, he swore that he was '... of the Age of Twenty One Years and intends to marry with Lydia Endersby of the Parish of St. Neots ... Not knowing or believing any lawful Let or Impediment ... to hinder the said intended Marriage AND he prayed a Licence to solemnize the said Marriage in the Church of St. Neots aforesaid, in which said Parish the said Lydia Endersby hath had her usual Abode for the space of four Weeks last past.'

His word that he was free to marry was not enough. Additionally he had to bind himself and find one willing and substantial guarantor prepared to enter into a marriage bond which stated that

> 'John Mimms of the Parish of Eaton Socon, Labouring Man, & Thomas Hall of the Parish of Gamblingay, Farmer, are held and firmly bound to Richard Shepherd LL.B. in One Hundred Pounds of Lawful Money to be paid to the same Richard Shepherd'

That sum was to be forfeited if it was later discovered that John and Lydia were not free to marry or '... if either of them be of any other Parish or of better State or Degree than to the Judge at the granting of the Licence is suggested and by John Mimms sworn to.'[48]

Whether John understood much of this legal rigmarole is open to doubt. He could only acknowledge that it had been read to him by adding his cross to the document where the Revd. Littlehales pointed. One thing at least would have been mightily impressed on him. If he had lied he would have to find £100 – a sum so enormous that it would have swallowed up his total earnings for the next four years.

By this time he must have wished that he had asked for the banns to be posted instead of applying for a licence, but his trials were not yet over. He was about to marry a pregnant bride from another parish and bring her to Eaton Socon. That would have meant three more mouths to feed if John later found that he couldn't support his new family. The Eaton overseers naturally wanted proof that he was some other parish's responsibility, so he was sent off that same Saturday to appear before a nearby Bedfordshire magistrate, Sir Philip Monoux, who lived at Sandy. It is not difficult to visualise this uneducated farm worker, hat doffed and eyes cast down, standing self-consciously before the wealthy landowner, a knight of the shires, representing King George III, probably being made to feel ashamed at having got a girl into trouble, and mumbling his life story as the attendant clerk wrote:

> 'The examination of John Mimms touching his legal place of settlement taken upon oath before Me, Sir Philip Monoux Bart. one of his Majesty's Justices of the Peace in and for the County of Bedford the 23rd day of February 1788 - The examinant saith that he was born and brought up at Eaton Socon in this County, that he is now he believes upwards of 21 years of age and is in Service as horsekeeper with Mr. Robert Wiles of Wyboston in the said County being hired as Servant for a year from last Michaelmas to Michaelmas next, but that his legal settlement is in the Parish of Eynesbury in the County of Huntingdon which he acquired by being hired for a year as Servant in husbandry to Mr. Charles Vessey, Farmer and serving him 2 years pursuant to such hiring, the expiration of which said Service ended at Michaelmas last and which was Completed at Eynesbury aforesaid - since which he hath gained no legal settlement elsewhere.'[49]

Having established that he was the responsibility of the parish of Eynesbury, John was now free to marry Lydia and their marriage took place the very next day - Sunday 24th February, the third Sunday in Lent, at St. Neots parish church by John Bewsher, its curate. Less than three months later the first of their eleven children, George, was baptised at St. Mary the Virgin, Eynesbury, just a few hundred yards down the road across the Hen Brook which separated the market town of St. Neots from its adjacent rural parish where John and Lydia lived for the rest of their lives.

References

[1] Digby, 'Pauper Palaces', p.83

[2] Cole, 'Wellingborough', p.152
[3] Cambridge Chronicle and Journal, 9 MAY 1795
[4] Poster, 'George Crabbe, Selected Poetry', p.24
[5] Gentlemen's Magazine, vol. VI, 1736: quot. in Genealogical Magazine, vol. 23, no.5, p.366
[6] Smith, 'The Speckled Monster', pp.15/16
[7] Huntingdon Record office, 2519/116 (1753)
[8] Emmison, 'The Relief of the Poor at Eaton Socon', pp.80–82
[9] Malcolmson, 'Life and Labour in England', p.60
[10] Watts, I., 'Divine Songs for the Use of Children', (1715)
[11] Malcolmson, 'Life and Labour in England', p.70
[12] Hammond, J.L. and B. 'The Village Labourer', p.112.
[13] Bedfordshire Record office, P1/13/4/1 (1771)
[14] Robinson and Summerfield, p.20
[15] Bedfordshire Record Office P5/13/4/19 (1803)
[16] Godber, 'History of Bedfordshire', p.378
[17] Emmison, 'The Relief of the Poor at Eaton Socon', p.89.
[18] Hibbert, 'The English, A Social History, p.256
[19] Hammond, J.L. & B., 'The Village Labourer', p.112
[20] Southgate, 'English Economic History', p.280
[21] Himmelfarb, 'The Idea of Poverty', p.61
[22] Thompson, E.P., 'The Making of the English Working Class', p.102
[23] Hammond, J.L. and B., 'The Village Labourer' p.114
[24] Bedfordshire Record Office, P44/13/1 (1768)
[25] Northants. Record Office, 350p/163 (1771)
[26] ibid., 350p/537/5 (1783)
[27] ibid., 350p/163 (1783)
[28] Emmison, 'The Relief of the Poor at Eaton Socon' p.70
[29] Eden, 'The State of the Poor', Book 1. p.347.
[30] Malcolmson, 'Popular Recreations', p.78.
[31] ibid., p.20
[32] ibid., p.44
[33] Bedfordshire Record Office, P5/13/4/16 (1794)
[34] ibid., P5/13/4/1 (1778)
[35] Tebbutt, 'St. Neots', p.59
[36] Emmison, 'The Relief of the Poor at Eaton Socon', p.8.
[37] Wilson, F.M., 'Life in Eaton Socon, 1750 – 1850'.
[38] Emmison, 'The Relief of the Poor at Eaton Socon', p.8.
[39] Wilson, F.M., 'Life in Eaton Socon'.
[40] Bedfordshire Record Office, P5/28/7 (1755)
[41] Northampton Mercury, 27 MAR 1749.
[42] Emmison, 'The Relief of the Poor at Eaton Socon', p.30.
[43] Poster, George Crabbe, Selected Poetry', p.23.
[44] Brown, J., 'Gamblingay', p.205
[45] Hardy, T., 'Jude the Obscure'.
[46] Rule, J., 'The Labouring Classes', p.197.
[47] Northants. Record Office, Ecton Baptismal Register (1773)
[48] Bedfordshire Record Office ABM 42/1
[49] Cambridgeshire Record Office P76/13/7

CHAPTER THREE

TEN TERRIBLE YEARS

'This life is a city of crooked streets.
Death is the market-place where all men meet.
If life were merchandise that money could buy
The rich would live and the poor would die.'

Gravestone inscription (1798)[1]

'As a sportsman, I hate enclosures, and, as a citizen, I look on them as a greedy tyranny of the wealthy few to oppress the indigent many.'

John Byng (1781)[2]

'To two male beings – whose nakedness was not conceal'd by rags, (who held my mare) I gave my loose halfpence, and never had they possess'd before such treasure! Covering for head, and feet, they had never known! They seem'd to be about 12 or 14 years of age.'[3] That entry in John Byng's diary in the early summer of 1794 could stand as a symbol of the condition of the rural poor for the whole of the final decade of the eighteenth century.

Col. John Byng, a retired Grenadier Guards officer then employed in the Somerset House revenue office, was an inveterate traveller and diarist, noting his acerbic comments and his descriptions of the towns and countryside he passed in what became known as 'The Torrington Diaries'. He had met those two young boys on a ride from St. Neots when staying for a time at 'The Cock' at Eaton Socon. His description of that ride, on the Cambridge road ' . . . thro' a vile, dreary country with nothing to see, hear or to amuse,' continues,' . . . the few people, and the few cattle seem nearly starv'd; an old shepherd is sometimes to be seen: But will any man abide in this misery that can get 10 guineas from a recruiting sergeant?'[4]

Recruiting sergeants and navy press-gangs were, of course, very active at the time raising fighting men for the war against revolutionary France which had broken out the year before. – 'On Saturday morning last, the men raised to serve in the Navy for the County of Huntingdon, set off from that place in coaches and other carriages, and arrived at the rendezvous at (King's) Lynn the next day in a very orderly manner. They are a set of fine young fellows, and were uniformly clad in Blue Jackets trimmed with Gold, striped Trowsers, and a Gold laced Hat' wrote a Cambridge Chronicle reporter.[5]

Louis XVI and his Queen, Marie Antoinette, had been guillotined during Robespierre's Reign of Terror less than a year and a half before. English landowners and politicians (practically one and the same) feared a similar revolution on this side of the Channel. A few days before his meeting with the 'two male beings', Byng had visited the remnants of St. Neots Ascension Day Fair with its elephant and a waxwork show depicting 'the King of France guillotin'd (Is this not a *bad* exhibition for the lower people?', he asked.)[6]

But it was not only the war which made the 1790's such a terrible decade. By the end of the century the population of England and Wales exceeded nine million – half as many again as there had been mouths to feed only forty years before,[7] and for year after year the weather was so awful that the harvest failed repeatedly, food prices rose alarmingly and near starvation was frequently the lot of those who, at the best of times, were living at a bare subsistence anyway.

With such adverse weather it is scarcely surprising that shortages caused prices, especially of wheat, to rise: a quarter of wheat which cost 58 shillings at the beginning of the decade was selling for as much as 128 shillings by its end.[8] An agricultural reporter, Nathaniel Kent, writing half-way through this decade, claimed that in the past 40 or 50 years the price of provisions had gone up by 60 per cent but that wages had increased by only a quarter.[9] By the century's end another agriculturalist, Arthur Young, pointed out that 'the quantity of food which a labourer could have bought for 5 shillings would now cost him 26s. 6d.,

'. . . will any man abide in this misery that can get 10 guineas from a recruiting sergeant?'

supposing he had the money to pay for it.'[10]

It was against this background that a concerned country parson, David Davies, wrote 'The Case of Labourers in Husbandry Stated and Considered.' Davies was rector of Barkham, a small village near Wokingham in Berkshire. Living amongst his parishioners, unlike so many of his clergy colleagues who took the tithes, installed an ill-paid curate and lived elsewhere, Davies saw their poverty and tried to awaken the conscience of the wealthy by publishing details of their family incomes and outgoings.

'In visiting the labouring families of my parish, as my duty led me,' he wrote, 'I could not but observe with concern their mean and distressed condition. I found them in general but indifferently fed; badly clothed; some children without shoes and stockings; very few put to school; and most families in debt to little shopkeepers.'[11] His concern for the ill-educated children did not blind him from an understanding that, 'though the schooling of a child costs but two-pence or three-pence a week, yet this pittance is wanted for so many other purposes, that it would be missed in the family.'[12]

One of Davies' many critics pointed out that despite all their hardships, families still managed to 'live on'. This gentle man's untypically trenchant reply was – 'Yes, they *do* live on, to be sure, but *how* do they live? – by aids out of the poor rates; by Charity; by begging; by poaching; by pilfering; by wearing Rags instead of Clothes'.[13] Adding later, when he had published some of their household budgets, 'it is but little that in the present state of things the belly can spare for the back.'[14]

Apart from the costs of the French war, the appalling weather which drove up prices and the population explosion which had produced a superabundance of labourers, another factor contributing to their poverty was the cumulative effect of decades, even of centuries, of land enclosures. Davies himself was in no doubt about their adverse consequences, 'depriving the peasantry of all landed property has beggared multitudes' he wrote, condemning a practice which had reduced 'the generality of small farmers into day-labourers, and the great body of day-labourers into beggars, and has been multiplying and impoverishing even beggars themselves.'[15]

What we, today, regard as the 'typical English countryside' of a multi-coloured patchwork of small fields, hedged and ditched with an occasional copse or larger wooded hillside, is really only two or three hundred years old. It was the enclosure of the large open fields, common lands and 'wastes' (moor, scrub and fen) which gave us modern husbandry and 'the chess-board pattern of fenced fields which has ever since been the hallmark of the English landscape', as the social historian, G.M. Trevelyan described it.[16] The Board of Agriculture commissioned two surveys of Huntingdonshire at this time. The first in 1793 found that 130,000 acres, or more than half the county, were still in the form of 'commonable meadows, commons and common fields'. Only eighteen years later a second survey revealed that 'most of the best commons in the county are now enclosed.'[17]

Six million acres of England and Wales, a quarter of the cultivated acreage, became enclosed land as a result of 4000 private acts of parliament, three-quarters of which were passed in two waves of intense activity in the 1760's and 1770's and again during the French wars which spanned the turn of the century and 'left (their) mark on the nature of English farming and, indeed, on the very appearance of the countryside.'[18]

Enclosure was not a new phenomenon. It had been going on for centuries by agreement between owners of land who preferred to fence off what was theirs and to grow what crops they liked when they wanted, rather than what everyone else in the community decided should be the crop rotation. The dangers of disease spreading amongst sheep and cattle were lessened if animals were kept in a fenced field rather than being turned out on the common land with everyone else's and the time and effort wasted carting tools, seed and harvested crops between widely dispersed strips in the open fields was irksome to many. But obtaining everyone's agreement to combining separate holdings spread all over the village into discrete parcels of land which could conveniently be fenced off could not have been easy. The fertility or the accessibility of one area over another and their proximity to the village had to be evaluated. Some parts of the open fields would be more stony or hilly than others or with heavier soil making tilling difficult and time-consuming. The arguments must have been endless. How much easier, then, especially for the larger landowners, to petition Parliament for a private Act to enforce enclosure on everyone?

Each such Act named Commissioners who were empowered to make an Award, that is to distribute the fields, the common land, the meadows and even the 'waste' in proportion to the land previously held by all the owners and to map out the new village – And their decision was final. One of the Commissioners was normally the nominee of the largest landowner, another often represented the holder of the great tithes. None was specifically charged with the responsibility of acting independently to ensure that the final distribution was equitable as between competing parties and, certainly, none of them was required to consider the interests of those who might be adversely affected but had no rights which could actually be proved in a court of law.

'Most Enclosure Acts specified a date before which all claims had to be presented. It is obvious that very many small proprietors who had neither the courage nor the knowledge necessary to put and defend their case', often in writing and in due legal form. ' . . . if this was a difficult fence for the small proprietor, unaccustomed to legal forms and documents, or to forms and documents of any kind, what was the plight of the cottager? Let us imagine the cottager, unable to read or write, enjoying customary rights of common without any idea of their origin or history or legal basis; knowing only that as long as he can remember he had kept a cow, driven geese across the waste, pulled his fuel out of the neighbouring brushwood, and cut turf from the common, and that his father did all these things before him. The cottager learns that before a certain day he has to present to his landlord's bailiff, or to the parson, or to one of the magistrates into whose hands perhaps he has fallen before now over a little matter of a hare or a partridge, or to some solicitor from the country town, a clear and correct statement of his rights and his claim to a share in the award . . . Is a cottager to be trusted to face the ordeal, or to be in time with his statement, or to have that statement in proper legal form?' – The answer to those questions, posed by the Hammonds[19] was, of course, 'No', because such 'rights' were not generally recognised in law and, as a modern commentator has wryly observed, enclosure was 'played according to fair rules of property and law laid down by a parliament of property-owners and lawyers!'[20]

Enforcing enclosure by Act of Parliament may have been convenient, but it was far from cheap. The costs involved in obtaining the Act itself, of the subsequent Award and the Commissioners' expenses all had to be shared by those who had received an allotment. Once allotted, the land had to be fenced or hedged within a reasonable time. The Eaton Socon churchwardens had to pay Thomas Cell of Riseley £2.2s an acre for fencing but it could cost much more,[21] not that the large landowners always paid it themselves. At Wigston, near Leicester, the Duke of St. Albans was allotted 387 acres and the Vicar 88 but, 'as was customary in such cases, the allotments to the Duke and the vicar were to be mounded and fenced round by ditches and quickset hedges guarded or fenced with good posts and double rails, at the expense of the other proprietors. Not only this, but the Duke's land was to be subdivided into closes which were to be similarly fenced at the cost of others.'[22]

> 'Inclosure came and trampled on the grave
> Of labours rights and left the poor a slave,

wrote John Clare when his Northamptonshire village of Helpstone was enclosed. As the son of a labourer himself he knew what it would mean and this gentlest of rural poets expressed his hatred of the intrusive fences in sarcastic verse:

> 'Fence now meets fence in owners little bounds
> Of field and meadow large as garden grounds
> In little parcels little minds to please
> With men and flocks imprisoned ill at ease . . .
> 'Each little tyrant with his little sign
> Shows where man claims earth glows no more divine
> But paths to freedom and to childhood dear
> A board sticks up to notice 'no road here'
> And on the tree with ivy overhung
> The hated sign by vulgar taste is hung
> As tho the very birds should learn to know,
> When they go there they must no further go.'[23]

On the very heavy Midland clay soil enclosed land had often to be drained. In the open fields surplus water drained off the ridges and down the furrows between the strips but to work a large enclosed field efficiently the ridges and furrows had to be levelled (the ridge was sometimes five feet above the furrow) and a new drainage system installed.[24] In all, the costs of enclosure could be as much as £5 an acre and, inevitably, fell disproportionately upon those who had only received a small allotment.

Many could not afford to pay and were forced to sell up, adding even further to the already inflated number of labourers for hire. St. Neots was enclosed in the 1770's but sixteen years later a local gentleman complained that, 'the poor were ill-treated by having about half a rood given them in lieu of a *cow keep*, the inclosure of which land costing more than they could afford, they sold the lots at £5, the money was drank at the ale-house, and the men, spoiled by the habit, came, with their families, to the parish.'[25]

One reason for enclosure was the desire of many of the landed gentry, and those with pretensions to that status, to increase the size of their parklands: this, after all, was the age of Lancelot 'Capability' Brown and Humphry Repton and the height of the fashion for 'natural', if sculptured, landscapes with lakes and Gothic ruins when whole villages like Milton Abbas in Dorset were demolished and rebuilt elsewhere because they spoilt the view from the house. It must be added that in such cases the displaced families were generally re-housed in far better conditions than they had enjoyed previously. As Oliver Goldsmith wrote indignantly:

> 'The man of wealth and pride
> Takes up a space that many poor supplied;
> Space for his lake, his park's extended bounds,
> Space for his horses, equipage and hounds;
> The robe that wraps his limbs in silken sloth
> Has robb'd the neighbouring fields of half their growth
> His seat, where solitary sports are seen,
> Indignant spurns the cottage from the green;[26]

David Davies complained of the increasing number of 'gentleman-farmers, who are in general fond of grass-farms, as requiring least trouble.'[27] This creation of pasture from what had been arable land was especially prevalent in the Midlands, one of the most heavily enclosed areas of England[28] and had the effect of drastically reducing the demand for labour. 'Arable farming required much more labour than did permanent pasture: about two men for every 50 or 60 acres of arable compared with one man for the same area of grass.'[29] At Kibworth – Beauchamp in Leicestershire 3600 acres were enclosed and changed from arable into grazing land. Sir Frederic Eden wrote at the time that the poor of that village had had 'plenty of employment in weeding, reaping, threshing etc, and could collect a great deal of corn by gleaning, but that after enclosure a third or perhaps even one-quarter of the number of hands would have been sufficient to do all the farm work required.'[30]

Once the land had been enclosed many owners combined the several farms into a single large one. Engrossing, as it was called, resulted in surplus farm-houses and cottages, especially if, overall, less labour was then needed. These were either sub-let with little more than a small garden attached or, quite frequently, demolished. Demolition had the side-benefit of helping to keep down the burden of the local poor rate – if there were fewer houses for them to live in, there would be fewer paupers. Such irrefutable logic ignored the fact that they would go elsewhere, despite the settlement laws, but then that was some other parish's problem.

On one of his travels John Byng asked an old woman about the enclosure of Meriden common, "Ah, lackaday Sir, that was a sad job; and ruin'd all us poor volk; and those who then gave into it, now repent it." Asked to explain why, she added, "Because we had our garden, our bees, our share of a flock of sheep, the feeding of our geese; and could cut turf for our fuel. Now all that's gone! Our cottage, as good a one as this, we gave but 50 shillings a year for; and for this we are obliged to pay £9.10s; and without any ground . . . My cottage with many others is pull'd down; and the poor are sadly put to it to get a house to put their heads in!"[31]

For those who had no land at all, the loss of the common and the 'waste' was unquestionably a grievous blow. At no cost they had been able to gather fruit, nuts and berries, material for roof thatching, cut turf and collect wood and gorse for heating and cooking and keep a few geese, a pig or graze a cow. Gleaning after harvest in the open fields often enabled their wives and children to gather enough wheat to supply them with bread for a year and sufficient beans to keep a pig.[32] Gleaning did not cease entirely, of course, but it came to depend much more on the goodwill and caprice of those who now owned the land.

Even if there was no paid work, a cottager's family, though not entirely independent, could normally avoid total starvation by relying upon the produce of a small garden and what could be gained from exercising those rights of common. With these lost, or severely curtailed, their plight became desperate. David Davies claimed that, 'an amazing number of people have been reduced from a comfortable state of partial independence to the precarious condition of hirelings, who, when out of work, must immediately come to their parish.'[33]

Earlier this century J.L. and Barbara Hammond wrote, 'The effect on the cottager can best be described by saying that before enclosure the cottager was a labourer with land, after enclosure he was a labourer without land!'[34] More recent historians have supported that stark judgement in these words, 'There is indeed a good deal of truth in the Hammonds' brief summary for access to commons and waste may have played an important part in the economy of many cottagers. Such access might make it possible for them to keep pigs, a cow or some geese, to gather fruit and firewood, and, in the case of squatters to find a place for their dwelling, such as it was. The removal of this prop of the labourers' existence was undoubtedly a factor in the increasing poverty which characterised much of the countryside in the later eighteenth century and after.'[35] And Professor Thompson states that 'access to an extensive common could be critical to the livelihood of many villagers even if they had no common right, for they could rent upon it grazing for a cow, or parking and some fuel for that essential transport: i.e. grazing for a horse.'[36]

As the poor saw it the double standards which the law imposed on them well justified the contemporary jingle:

> They hang the man and flog the woman
> That steals the goose from off the common,
> But leave the greater criminal loose
> That steals the common from the goose![37]

Not every villager, however, had been entitled to exercise common rights. These generally went with land holdings in the open fields or belonged only to occupiers of certain cottages, but the enclosure of all or part of the common inevitably affected the economy of all the inhabitants. Enforcement of common rights in many villages was less rigid than in mediaeval times and those without rights were often able to take advantage of at least some of them. Those who kept a cow could sell their surplus milk to neighbours more cheaply than it could now be bought in local shops, especially as the now larger graziers sold their milk wholesale to supply the ever-growing towns. The value to a family of a cow kept on common land was estimated by Arthur Young at between 5 and 6 shillings a week, not far short of a labourer's weekly earnings.[38] Young had been an enthusiastic proponent of enclosure as a means of improving agricultural productivity, but even he acknowledged its darker side by quoting with apparent sympathy a comment made by one who had served as an Enclosure Commissioner: 'By nineteen out of twenty Inclosure Bills the poor are injured, and some grossly injured . . .The poor in these parishes may say, and with truth, "Parliament may be tender of property: all I know is that I had a cow and an Act of Parliament has taken it from me." '[39]

In telling the story of the Leicestershire village of Wigston, Professor Hoskins has said:

'Even Arthur Young confessed that in the five midland counties of Leicester, Warwick, Northampton, Huntingdon and Buckingham parliamentary enclosure had generally resulted in a decay of tillage and in rural depopulation.

> 'This great block of country, filling the entire middle of England, had long been the home of a numerous free peasantry. Scattered all over the four or five thousand square miles of the Midland Plain were hundreds of villages which, since the twelfth or thirteenth centuries, at least, had been largely composed of such a peasantry as we have described at Wigston in Leicestershire. To a large extent, therefore, what happened at Wigston is what happened in all those other villages up and down the Midlands, notably the wholesale conversion of arable to pasture, the engrossing of farms by large graziers at a much-enhanced rent, the displacement of the peasant farmer, and the final collapse in ruins of the peasant society which had prevailed for so long over so wide an area of England.'[40]

Moreover, Arthur Young had seen where the collapse of that peasant economy had led, 'Go to an ale-house kitchen of an old enclosed county,' he wrote, 'and there you will see the origin of poverty and poor-rates. For whom are they to be sober? For whom are they to save? For the parish? If I am diligent, shall I have leave to build a cottage? If I am sober, shall I have land for a cow? If I am frugal, shall I have half an acre for potatoes? You offer no motives; you have nothing but a parish officer and a workhouse! – Bring me another pot – .'[41]

Such resignation and surly acceptance of the seemingly inevitable was not, however, the only response. In Northamptonshire in the last year of the century a troop of yeomanry escorting wagons loaded with fencing had been stopped by a crowd of 300 people who had lit a bonfire in the road. The Riot Act had to be read and several arrests made before the wagons could pass.[42] In the same year this anonymous threat was addressed to Oliver Cromwell of Cheshunt Park:

> 'Whe right these lines to you who are the Combin'd of the Parish of Cheshunt in the Defence of our Parrish rights which you unlawfully are about to disinherit us of . . . if you proceede in the aforesaid bloudy act Whe like horse leaches will cry give, give until whe have spilt the bloud of every one that wishes to rob the Inosent unborn. It shall not be in your power to say I am safe from the hands of my Enemy for Whe like birds of pray will prively lie in wait to spil the bloud of the aforesaid Charicters whose names and places of abode are as prutrified sores in our Nostrils.'[43]

Village people's memories are long and the strength of impotent rage felt by those who believed they had been dispossessed by enclosure can be judged from an interview with an old labourer recorded by George Sturt and published in 1912 in his book, 'Change in the Village':

> 'Pointing to the woods which could be seen beyond the valley, he said spitefully, while his eyes blazed: "I can remember when all that was open common, and you could go where you mind to. Now 'tis all fenced in, and if you looks over the fence they'll lock ye up. And they en't got no more *right* to it, Mr. Bourne, than you and me have! I should *like* to see they woods all go up in flames!" '[44]

But what of John and Lydia Mimms during this terrible time? By the end of the decade they had had eight children all of whom surprisingly, had survived. Their situation, like that of any large family must have been dire. There is no question but that they would have been almost permanently in receipt of allowances from the overseers of the poor of Eynesbury. No overseers' accounts survive for the parish from that time, unfortunately, but we can build up a picture of how they fared from a series of extensive surveys of labouring families' budgets collected and published in the second half of the decade by Sir Frederic Morton Eden in his impressive three-volume work, 'The State of the Poor'. These show in great detail what each family earned in a year and exactly what they spent those earnings on. Eden gives examples of families of different sizes from a wide range of counties and so it is possible to show more or less precisely how a family like John and Lydia's lived.

The budgets themselves were collected exactly half-way through the decade at which time his family consisted of John himself, now 30 years of age, his wife, Lydia, 28, George, the first-born, aged 7, the twins, Mary and a second George, 6, Thomas, 4, Elizabeth, 3 and new-born Sarah - a family of seven if one discounts the babe-in-arms.

Of the budgets quoted by Eden, the nearest in terms of distance was a family of seven living at Buckden, Hunts, about six miles north of Eynesbury. In addition to the parents, there were three girls aged 11, 6 and 2½ and a boy of 9. Another, presumably older, son lived out as a farm-servant but 'costs more than he earns'. The man earned 7s 3d a week and his wife 1s 2d, probably from making lace at home. They spent 4s 10½d on bread, flour or oatmeal, 1s on tea and sugar, 6d, on potatoes, 3d. for yeast and salt and the same for candles, 2¾d. on soap and 1½d. on thread and worsted for mending clothes. Nothing could be afforded for bacon or meat, cheese, milk or beer. Eden comments that even allowing for heavily subsidised barley sold to them by the parish this family lived almost entirely upon barley and water and a few potatoes.' The rent for their cottage was £2.7s a year and the only other annual costs were £1.11.6d for shoes, £3.11s for clothes and furniture and an average annual expenditure of £1.1s for births, burials and sickness but nothing at all was spent on fuel - perhaps they could collect gorse or cut turf from the common.

This family's yearly earnings, therefore, amounted to £21.17.8d and its outgoings £27.6.5d, leaving an excess of expenditure over income of £5.8.9d. Harvest earnings would have halved that deficiency but, 'This family, notwithstanding their scanty fare, is getting into debt very fast. During the last year they received 1s a week from the parish: but never received a farthing before.'[45]

Nearly three-fifths of this family's weekly earnings went on bread, flour or oatmeal. Not only had the price of wheat almost doubled in the past ten years[46] but its distribution through middlemen added extra costs, as Davies explained:

> 'Formerly the labourer could have corn of different kinds mixed in any proportion, in exchange for his labour, even more readily than he could get money. His wife carried it to the mill, had it ground and dressed, and then brought it home, and baked it for the family. There was no intermediate person except the miller, between the farmer and the consumer, to receive a profit. But now . . . the great farmer deals in a wholesale way with the miller; the miller with the mealman; and the mealman with the shopkeeper; of which last the poor man buys his flour by the bushel. For neither the miller, nor the mealman, will sell the labourer a less quantity than a *sack* of flour *under* the retail price at shops: and the poor man's pocket will seldom allow of his buying a whole sack at once. Formerly then the wife saved the profits of the mealman and the shopkeeper, who now, without adding to the value of the manufacture, do each receive a profit out of the poor man's earnings.'[47]

Davies might have added that a lack of fuel for baking caused the poor man to buy bread and thus pay the baker's profit as well. In this same year an Eynesbury baker, Peter Wildman, a prominent Baptist, was reported to the justices by a private in the Essex Fencibles for supplying short-weight bread. At the Huntingdon Quarter Sessions he was found guilty of selling a quarter-peck loaf 8½oz. short and fined three shillings for each ounce by which it was deficient. He was lucky not to have been stoned through the village.[48].

A not infrequent complaint was that the poor displayed extravagance by eating good quality wheaten bread rather than the coarser, cheaper kind made with rye, barley or oats, but Davies had an answer for that – or, rather, an unanswerable question: 'Upon the whole, labouring people, having neither meat, nor cheese, nor milk, nor beer, in sufficient quantities, eat good bread where every body else eats it. You say, they cannot afford to do this: and you blame their extravagance. But can you, who blame them, give a reason, why they, whose hands have tilled the ground, and sown and reaped the grain, are not as well entitled to eat good bread, as manufacturers? or, as servants in gentlemen's families? or, as paupers in houses of industry and parochial work-houses? or, as the felons in your gaols?[49]

'Wheaten bread may be eaten alone with pleasure,' added Davies responding to another criticism that the poor should make even more use of potatoes, 'but potatoes require either meat or milk to make them go down:', he continued remorselessly, 'you cannot make many hearty meals of them with salt and water only. Poor people indeed give them to their children in the greasy water, in which they have boiled their greens and their morsel of bacon: and, blessed be God! children will thrive, if they have but enough of anything. As to meat, we know very well how little of that they are obliged to content themselves with.'[50]

Another family of seven living fourteen miles south of Eynesbury at Clophill in Bedfordshire, almost managed to make ends meet with the husband's harvest money, two shillings a week earned by their eleven year old son who drove a plough and what the mother and three daughters, aged 5 to 13, earned from lace making at home.[51]

It was a different story, however, at Hinksworth, in Hertfordshire, about the same distance south-east of Eynesbury. Here, the wife contributed 1s 6d. to the family's weekly income and the children, 6d., probably by picking stones or scaring crows. The four boys were aged 11, 7, 5 and 2 and, 'the eldest girl 14 tends the little ones and, therefore, cannot earn much.' This family lived a little better than those at Buckden and Clophill, buying 4½lbs of pork bacon a week (at 10p lb) about 2lbs of cheese – the dearest article a poor family can buy, according to Davies – and a little milk. This 'extravagance' brought their annual expenditure to the staggering sum of £39.15s, or £10 more than the total earnings of the whole family for a twelve month.[52]

David Davies, in one of *his* budgets, gave a figure of 6d, a week *on average* for a wife's earnings, adding: 'If anyone should think that the *woman's* earnings are stated too low in these accounts, he will be convinced they are not, on considering that these women commonly begin the world with an infant, and are mere nurses for ten or twelve years after marriage, being always either with child, or having a child at the breast; consequently incapable of doing much other work besides the necessary business of their families, such as baking, washing, and the like.'[53]

In the Hinksworth budget, Eden allowed £1.3.6d p.a. for births and burials, explaining that, 'it is computed a labouring woman has a child once every 2½ or 3 years. The lowest expence attending the birth of a child is £3. One-third of this, therefore, may be reckoned as the annual expence. The expence of a child's funeral is 10s. Of an adult about £1. Three shillings and 6d is reckoned as the annual expence of each family.' Put another way, a death in the family could be expected once every three years. He goes on to add, 'many families pay £2 and some as much as £3 or £4 a year for medicines and surgical assistance.'[54]

Davies' estimate of the costs of a birth to a labouring family is half that of Eden's but much more detailed and provides a fascinating insight into the customary way these matters were arranged two hundred years ago:

> 'Lying-in: the child's linen 3 or 4s.; the midwife's fee 5s.; a bottle of gin or brandy always had upon these occasions 2s.; attendance of a nurse for a few days, and her diet, at least 5s.; half a bushel of malt brewed, and hops, 3s.: to the minister for churching 1s; – call this sum £1 and suppose this to happen but once in two years: this per annum, 10s.'[55]

The gin or brandy undoubtedly served the dual purpose of anaesthesia for the mother and stimulant for the midwife and the brewing of malt and hops was to provide for a celebration of the birth.

Clothing a family would have been an enormous burden for the parents even with older children's hand-me-downs and gifts from neighbours and the church. As Davies explains:

> 'Even such persons as may have been provident enough, when single, to supply themselves with a small stock of clothes, are, after marriage, from inability to buy more, soon reduced to ragged garments. And then the women spend as much time in tacking their tatters together, as would serve for manufacturing new clothing, had they the skill to do it, and materials to do it with. One bad consequence of this meanness of dress is, that many of the poor are ashamed to appear among decent people at our churches; they either neglect the duty of public worship altogether, or they assemble at places where they are sure of meeting people as ill-clothed as themselves.'[56]

By this, of course, he meant the Dissenting chapels which were springing up everywhere amongst the rural and urban poor and where those with a mind to worship could feel more comfortable than in the parish church rubbing patched elbows with the local gentry.

If John Byng's experience was common then church worship was not always uplifting. On one of his visits to Eaton Socon he 'devoutly march'd into the church; which is large, and handsome; and has been adorn'd with much stain'd glass. The psalm singing, in a singing gallery, was tolerable, accompany'd by a flute and a hautboy (a sort of oboe): but such a reader, and preacher, as Mr. Littlehales I hope is not often heard; tho' I fear so! Nor can a gleam of instruction dart from such drawling explanations about St. Peter, and St. John.' He was clearly unimpressed with the clergyman who had licensed John and Lydia's marriage, adding this verse:

> 'By our pastor perplext,
> How shall we determine?
> Watch and pray, says the text,
> Go to sleep, says the sermon.'[57]

What, one might ask, amongst all this misery, were those who regularly ate meat and drank claret doing about the plight of the poor? They were, of course, writing homilies about it, castigating the poor for their improvidence, recommending dietary improvements and suggesting how the charitable might provide them with a cheap meal: 'Cut a very thick upper crust of bread,' wrote a Lady, 'and put it into the pot where salt beef is boiling and near ready; it will attract some of the fat, and when swelled out, will not be an unpalatable dish for those who rarely taste meat.'[58] Mrs Shore, of the Society for Bettering the Condition and Improving the Comforts of the Poor, suggested that with a stewed ox's head costing 2s 6d. added to 'the leavings of the family, a savoury mess for fifty-two persons could be prepared.'[59]

It was to such well-meaning philanthropists that George Crabbe directed the lines

> 'Oh! trifle not with wants you cannot feel,
> Nor mock the misery of a stinted meal;

> Homely, not wholesome, plain, not plenteous, such
> As you who praise would never deign to touch.'[60]

Four Bedfordshire magistrates meeting at the Falcon Inn at Bletsoe sent a resolution to the Bedford Quarter Sessions recommending that half the relief to each family be paid in kind rather than in cash. For every shilling so deducted they advised the overseers to buy 'a pound and a half of beef, two pounds of potatoes and a quarter of a pound of rice,' thoughtfully adding a recipe:

> 'the meat must be cut into small slips, the potatoes cut into slices and the rice added, to which put nearly one gallon of water and let it stew or bake which is preferred for two or three hours, it will make a meal for 5 or 6 persons, the expence to the parish only one shilling.'[61]

Perhaps it was from their having to eat such unimaginative, if well-intentioned, meals that led even Frederic Eden to comment on the ingratitude of the poor: 'I have known instances during the last winter,' he wrote, 'when the Poor were extremely distressed by the high price of provisions, of their rejecting soup which was served at a Gentleman's table. Their common outcry was: "this is washy stuff, that affords no nourishment: we will not be fed on meal, and chopped potatoes, like hogs!" '[62]

'Many poor families are said to subsist entirely on bread and tea', admitted Eden[63] and those who were too poor to buy it, 'begged once-used tea leaves from neighbours or even simulated its colour by pouring boiling water over a burnt crust.'[64]

But even boiling water and hasty pudding – just flour and hot water – called for a fire and coal was very expensive, having to be shipped in from the northern coalfields, up the Ouse to St. Neots. Kindling, too, was hard to come by and taking it from woods or hedges a punishable offence. Even when a fire was lit it often failed to warm the room, as Eden complained, '... their fireplaces are, in general, constructed upon the most wretched principles and, the fuel they consume in them, instead of heating their rooms, not unfrequently renders them really colder, and more uncomfortable, by causing strong currents of cold air to flow from all the doors and windows to the chimney.'[65] But the inventive 'ingineer' Richard Gosling, was equal to the problem of finding a substitute fuel. In his pamphlet, 'Artificiall Fire or Coale for Rich or Poore', he suggested 'cow dung mingled with saw-dust and smal-coale made up into bals, or in a square like a tile, not too thick, and dryed, make a very good fewell, but something noisome,' and, 'Horse-dung in balls, with saw-dust, or the dust of smal-coale, or charcoale dust, dryed, is a good fewell, but the smell is offensive.'[66] Another ingenious writer suggested that the poor should resort to the stables for warmth in winter, 'for cattle were so obliging as to dispense warmth from their persons for nothing.'[67]

John Byng was outraged when he compared the labourers' living conditions with those of the Duke of Bedford's foxhounds which were kennelled at Eaton Socon:

> 'Now as some people may be so ignorant as not to know what a fox-hound kennel is, I will explain to them that it consists of various well built buildings of brick with strong good doors and well tiled; that there is a kitchen, boilers, and coppers; with separate apartments for the female hounds during their accouchments; that coals and straw are laid in great abundance for these hounds – nor is the most regular attendance of any kind of physick wanting for such hounds as are sick: Milk is also supplied in great abundance. This grand building is built close to the churchyard; that they may be listen'd to during divine service.
>
> 'The dog kennels for these noble animals proudly overtops those miserable mud hovels erected for the sons of Adam; who, looking askance, with eyes of envy at the habitation of these happier hounds, regret their humanity and that they are not born fox hounds . . . but when the farmer is over rented and the pauper finds himself without the habitation, or assistance given to dogs – flesh and blood will rebel . . . the truth is that this would make the best cottage in the village: But whilst the unaided paupers of the country will look at a dog-kennell with envy . . . I will say '*Something is rotten in the State of Denmark*!'[68]

It might seem from the above that no one really cared enough actually to take some practical action, but that would be misleading. There was much genuinely charitable help given. On the Wrest Park Estate in Bedfordshire, Pawsey, the estate steward, wrote to his employer, Lady Lucas, that he had bought 'a Barrell of Scotts Herrings last week . . . and the Poor are very *thankfull* for them at *A Farthing Each* and I have had a 2d Barrell down last night by the Waggon and if they go off Readily, I will have one Every week, for three or four weeks to come; a Barrell contains 12 Hundred Herrings and Cost rather more than a Halfpenny Each.'[69]

Even in the worst years the Eaton Socon overseers, who were neither heartless nor unfeeling, – 'Gave to the workhouse people for Fair, 4s 3d.'[70]

The Huntingdonshire magistrates at a meeting chaired by the Earl of Sandwich recommended the overseers in the county to buy bread and flour and sell it cheaply, adding that they were to compile lists of such paupers as should receive it at the reduced price, and 'strictly take care that there be no collusion between the poor and bakers or mealmen.'[71]

One of David Davies' proposals to relieve the poor was to fix their wages relative to the fluctuating price of bread:

'As *bread* is the principal part of the food of labouring people, making full two-thirds of the whole in value wherever wheaten bread is in common use, *I think the price of bread might with great propriety be made to regulate the price of labour*.'[72] This is precisely what was done by the magistrates in Speenhamland, now part of Newbury in Berkshire, in May 1795.

The principle of a sliding scale of income subsidised from the poor rates and based on the price of bread spread rapidly throughout southern England and, in one form or another, was adopted in a very large proportion of parishes. Although it was intended as a temporary expedient only, it lasted for almost forty years. In time these payments from the parish overseers came to be regarded as a matter of right creating other problems, but where they were introduced the benefit was tangible and immediate.

Even so, such allowances were still a charitable hand-out, however welcome. Nor did they ever have the backing of the law. Samuel Whitbread, a member of the brewing family and member of Parliament for Bedford, saw the need for a more effective remedy. He introduced a bill six months after the Speenhamland magistrates had taken their action. This would have given legal powers to local magistrates to fix and enforce a statutory minimum wage and hours of work for agricultural labourers, the rate to be posted on the church doors. William

Pitt, the Prime Minister, opposed the bill arguing that it was a false remedy to allow the law to interfere and 'to establish by authority what would be much better accomplished by the unassisted operation of principles'.[73] The fact that those 'principles', i.e. market forces, had singularly failed to bring about any alleviation in the labourers' lot was ignored and the bill rejected.

The only action taken by Parliament, at a time of severe grain shortage, was to curtail the use of corn used in making hair powder. The wearing of wigs had practically died out by this time but people still powdered their natural hair, the men tying back their long hair with ribbon into a 'queue' or tail.[74] This momentous Act of Parliament imposed a penalty of £20 for wearing hair powder of any kind unless a duty of a guinea a year was paid for a licence. During the Committee stage of the bill a clause was approved 'exempting persons having more than two daughters for paying for more than two,'[75] and other exemptions included the Royal Family and their immediate servants, junior ranks in the armed forces and clergymen and Dissenting Preachers having an income of less than a hundred pounds a year.[76]

How seriously this crucial piece of legislation was viewed by the public may be judged by an 'Epigram' published in a Cambridgeshire newspaper:

> 'Since the Foes of the Powder-Tax grumble and rail,
> And each Son of Liberty cuts off his Tail,
> O! give us dear Billy, the Poll-tax instead,
> That every booby may cut off his HEAD'.[77]

But 'Billy' Pitt did nothing of the sort, introducing instead a resolution in the Privy Council urging those with servants to deny them pastry and restrict their diet to a quartern loaf a week each.[78]

Perhaps the last word on the Hair Powder Act should be given to the humourist responsible for the publication of this letter in a local newspaper:

'Though I am only a House-maid, I always dress my hair with powder, which I crib from my Lady, in the absence of her own woman; mixing it, that it may not be discovered, with flour, which I crib from the Cook. Thus I have comfortably managed matters ever since I came into this Family. But now, Sir, here is a dreadful tax, – and one cannot wear one's own things, honestly come by, without paying a guinea a year! I never heard of such a shameful thing; and they say it is all on account of the war. Now, I think the more soldiers are killed, the less powder will be wanted by the army . . .

Sir, your humble servant,
Mary Brush[79]

'Everyone but an idiot knew,' wrote Arthur Young, that 'the lower classes must be kept poor, or they would 'never be industrious'.[80] The pious Hannah More added: 'Scarcity has been permitted by an all WISE and gracious Providence . . . .to show the poor how immediately dependent they are upon the rich.'[81] The belief that those who laboured in the fields would only be goaded to work by threat of starvation and were, in any case, largely the architects of their own misfortune, was common at the time and echoed even by Frederic Eden, 'There seems to be just reason to conclude,' he wrote, 'that the miseries of the labouring Poor arise, less from the scantiness of their income . . . than from their own improvidence and unthriftiness.'[82] – and this from a man who had catalogued their meagre household budgets. David Davies strongly disagreed: 'This charge of mismanagement made against labouring people, seems to rest on no solid ground. For a long time past their condition has been going from bad to worse continually. Small indeed is the portion of wordly comforts now left them. Instead therefore of grudging them so small an enjoyment as a morsel of good bread with their miserable tea; instead of attempting to shew how it may yet be possible for them to live worse than they do; it well becomes the wisdom and humanity of the present age to devise means how they may be better accommodated. Give to some the ability to keep a cow; and then all will have milk. Give to all the ability to drink small beer at home; and then few will frequent alehouses. He that can procure for them these two benefits, nay, he that can procure for them one of these two, will receive the blessing of the grateful poor, and deserve the applause of all good men.'[83]

Others did not see the poor as trying to exist in adverse circumstances beyond their ability to control but as 'designing rogues, who under various pretences, attempt to cheat the parish

. . . their whole abilities are exerted in the execution of deceit, which may procure from the parish officers an allowance of money for idle and profligate purposes.'[84] The author of that description was by no means alone in deprecating the common practice of granting allowances from the poor rates in aid of wages which, at Eaton Socon, had increased the annual cost of poor relief in the last decade from £736 to £2633.[85] 'Nothing in nature can be more disgusting than a parish pay-table', thought the Revd. Joseph Townsend; he far preferred the exercise of private charitable giving which evoked a more grateful response from the recipients: ' . . . nor in nature can anything be more beautiful', he continued, ' . . . more pleasing (than) their sparkling eyes, their bursting tears, and their uplifted hands, the artless expressions of unfeigned gratitude for unexpected favours.'[86]

That view might well be contrasted with the words of another cleric, David Davies, who understood the unexpressed aspirations of even illiterate farmworkers:

> 'I cannot subscribe to this doctrine of *extreme necessity*, and keeping wages *as low as possible*. In my humble opinion Hope is a far better motive to impel men to work: – the hope of bettering their condition, if they are sober, industrious, and virtuous; a hope, which alas! very few labourers can now entertain.'[87]

References

[1] Ashby, 'Joseph Ashby of Tysoe', p.138
[2] Andrews, 'The Torrington Diaries', p.33.
[3] ibid. p.492
[4] ibid. p.491
[5] 'Cambridge Chronicle and Journal', 9 MAY 1795.
[6] Andrews, 'The Torrington Diaries', p.489.
[7] Hibbert, 'The English, A Social History', p.466
[8] Malcolmson, 'Life and Labour in England', pp. 145/6.
[9] Hammond, J.L and B., 'The Village Labourer', p.111.
[10] Chambers and Mingay, 'The Agricultural Revolution', p.119.
[11] Horn, 'A Georgian Parson', p.61.
[12] ibid. p.74.
[13] ibid. p.32.
[14] ibid. p.74.
[15] ibid. p.58.
[16] Trevelyan, 'Illustrated English Social History,' pp.143/4

[17] Peacock, 'Bread or Blood' pp.16/17.
[18] Hey, 'Family History and Local History in England', p.204, and Chambers and Mingay, 'The Agricultural Revolution', p.77.
[19] Hammond, J.L. and B., 'The Village Labourer', p.63.
[20] Thompson, E.P., 'The Making of the English Working Class', pp.237/8.
[21] Bedfordshire R.O. P5/5/1 (1797).
[22] Hoskins, 'The Midland Peasant', p.265.
[23] Robinson and Summerfield, pp.169/171.
[24] Trevelyan, 'Illustrated English Social History', p.152.
[25] 'Annals of Agriculture', vol. xvi p.482 (1791): quot. Hammond, J.L. and B. 'The Village Labourer' p.102.
[26] Goldsmith, 'The Deserted Village' p.30.
[27] Horn, 'A Georgian Parson', p.79.
[28] Chambers and Mingay, 'The Agricultural Revolution' pp 94 and 103.
[29] ibid. p.18.
[30] Eden, 'The State of the Poor', vol II, p.384.
[31] Andrews 'The Torrington Diaries', p.207
[32] Eden, 'The State of the Poor', vol. II p.547
[33] Horn, 'A Georgian Parson', p.80.
[34] Hammond, J.L. and B. 'The Village Labourer', p.100.
[35] Chambers and Mingay, 'The Agricultural Revolution', p.96/97.
[36] Thompson, E.P., 'Customs in Common' p.177.
[37] Briggs, 'A Social History of England', p.174.
[38] Snell, 'Annals of the Labouring Poor', p.177.
[39] Young, A., 'An Inquiry into the Propriety of Applying Wastes to the Better Maintenance and Support of the Poor', (1801): quot. Snell, 'Annals of the Labouring Poor', p.226.
[40] Hoskins, 'The Midland Peasant', p.267.
[41] Young, A., 'An Inquiry into . . . Wastes etc.': quot. Snell, 'Annals of the Labouring Poor' pp.213/214.
[42] Hibbert, 'The English, A Social History', p.490.
[43] Home Office papers, HO. 42. 46 (27 FEB 1799): quot. Thompson, E.P. 'The Making of the English Working Class', p.240.
[44] Sturt, 'Change in the Village', p.73.
[45] Eden, 'The State of the Poor', vol III App XII p.cccxli
[46] Stevenson, 'Popular Disturbances in England', p.92.
[47] Horn, 'A Georgian Parson', p.75.
[48] Huntingdon R.O. Quarter Sessions papers (1795).
[49] Horn, 'A Georgian Parson', p.76.
[50] ibid. pp 76/7.
[51] Eden, 'The State of the Poor', Vol III, App. XII p. cccxxxx.
[52] ibid., Vol III, App. XII p. cccxliii.
[53] Horn, 'A Georgian Parson', p.69.
[54] Eden, 'The State of the Poor', Vol III, App. XII p. cccxliii.
[55] Horn, 'A Georgian Parson', p.70.
[56] Horn, 'A Georgian Parson', p.74.
[57] Andrews, 'The Torrington Diaries', p.333
[58] Hobsbawm, 'Labouring Men', p.96.
[59] Reports of the Society for Bettering the Condition and Improving the

Comforts of the Poor', (1795 – 1808), Vol. I, p.60: quot. Hammond, J.L. and B., 'The Village Labourer', p.125.
[60] Poster, 'George Crabbe, Selected Poetry', p.21.
[61] Emmison, 'The Relief of the Poor at Eaton Socon', p.59.
[62] Eden, 'The State of the Poor', vol. I p.533.
[63] Eden, 'The State of the Poor', Vol III, App XII, p.cccxli
[64] Thompson, E.P., 'The Making of the English Working Class', p.351.
[65] Eden, 'The State of the Poor', vol I, p.548.
[66] ibid., vol I, p.550.
[67] 'Annals of Agriculture', vol iv, p.496: quot. Hammond, J.L. and B., 'The Village Labourer', p.131.
[68] Andrews, 'The Torrington Diaries', p.494.
[69] Horn, 'Life and Labour in Rural England, p.52 and Godber, 'History of Bedfordshire', p.415.
[70] Emmison, 'The Relief of the Poor at Eaton Socon', p.92.
[71] ibid. p.56.
[72] Horn, 'A Georgian Parson', p.87.
[73] Hammond, J.L. and B., 'The Village Labourer', p.141.
[74] Hibbert, 'The English, A Social History', p.340.
[75] Cambridge Intelligencer, 4 APR 1795.
[76] Cambridge Chronicle and Journal, 9 MAY 1795.
[77] ibid.
[78] Resolution of the Privy Council, 6 JUL 1795: quot. Hammond, J.L. and B., 'The Village Labourer', p.123 (Note).
[79] Cambridge Chronicle and Journal, 16 MAY 1795.
[80] Hibbert, 'The English, A Social History', p.470.
[81] ibid.
[82] Eden, 'The State of the Poor', vol I. p.495.
[83] Horn, 'A Georgian Parson', p.78.
[84] 'Commercial and Agricultural Magazine' (1800): quot. Thompson, E.P., 'The Making of the English Working Class', p.243.
[85] Emmison, 'The Relief of the Poor at Eaton Socon', pp.42–44
[86] Townsend, Revd J., 'A Dissertation on the Poor Laws', (1786). pp.23 and 69: quot. Snell, 'The Agricultural Revolution', p.123.
[87] Horn, 'A Georgian Parson', p.27.

CHAPTER FOUR

EYNESBURY

'A little, insignificant Man, not more than fifty inches high, with an half starved Army, that would faint at the sight of an English Bull, has dared to say he will

CONQUER FOUR MILLIONS OF ENGLISHMEN!!

... Can you indifferently allow yourselves to be accused of forgetting the enjoyments of your mild laws, which equally afford to every man protection to his property and person; of your fertile soil which rewards the labourer's toil with plenty?'

An 1803 Broadside[1]

As the threat of a French invasion loomed and war fever was drummed up by stories of the atrocities commited by Napoleon's armies Hannah More contributed to the hysteria:

I've a dear little wife,
Whom I love as my life,
To lose her I should not much like, Sir;
And t'would make me run wild,
To see my sweet child,
With its head on the point of a pike, Sir.'[2]

Those lines from 'The Ploughman's Ditty' she described as being an answer to the foolish question, 'What have the poor to loose?'

Whether or not the labouring poor actually had much to lose, they were certainly persuaded that they would be very much worse off under an occupying army as their resolve was stiffened against the French

> 'With their maws stuff'd with frogs, soup and jellies,
> Brave Nelson's sea thunder
> Shall strike them with wonder.
> And make the frogs leap in their bellies.'[3]

The best of today's xenophobic tabloids would have been proud of such sentiments, claiming credit for a prophecy which was to be fulfilled two years later at the Battle of Trafalgar.

The year after that great sea battle, John and Lydia's family was completed with the birth of their eleventh child, Mary. She was named after her elder sister, a twin, who had died aged fifteen a year earlier. These ten all survived into adulthood – a rare occurrence at a time when infant and childhood death was commonplace. Their eldest child, George, was 17; his namesake, the surviving twin, a year younger and both may well have left home to live in with the family of the farmers for whom they worked as farm servants. This practice, however, was beginning to die out as the farmer became richer and acquired social aspirations and no longer wanted live-in servants to share his table,

> 'Where master, son and serving man and clown
> Without distinction daily set them down,
> Where the bright rows of pewter by the wall
> Served all the pomp of kitchen or of hall –
> These all have vanished . . . .'[4]

wrote John Clare with sorrow.

The remaining family, four boys and four girls ranging in age from new-born to 14, would have been living with their parents. At best, then, ten people (or twelve if the two eldest boys had not left home) shared a labourer's cottage in Eynesbury.

The county of Huntingdon's fine churches were built of imported stone brought up the Ouse by barge, but farm-houses and, especially, labourers' cottages were made from the only indigenous materials. Known as 'stud and mud', or 'wattle and daub', a two-roomed cottage (one up and one down) consisted of a stout timber frame resting on boulders and pebbles or gravel –

damp courses were unheard of. When the frame was in position, the spaces betwen the studs (the upright timbers) were fitted with thin strips of split timber and interwoven with pliable hazel or willow. This open-work basketweave was then filled with wet clay mixed with chopped straw, cow hair and dung for strength and, when dry, given a lime wash for protection from rain.[5]. The floor was just trampled earth (boarded floors were a luxury) and the roof thatched but without a ceiling.

If maintained in good repair, such dwellings were adequate for a small family in a dry summer. At least they kept out the worst of the weather and, heated by an open fire, which was also the only means of cooking, they could be comfortable enough. New, sound thatch makes fine protection from the weather, but 'decaying thatch is neither wind – nor rain-proof and makes, besides, a first-rate harbour for vermin. Because the cottages had neither ceiling nor flooring, the droppings from the roofs fell directly upon the inhabitants and their bits of furnishings and added to the muddy filth underfoot.'[6]

The very first official report on the housing and sanitary conditions of the poor contains innumerable descriptions of what life was really like in picturesque rural cottages. This from Aylesbury, Bucks: 'The vegetable substances mixed with the mud to make it bind, rapidly decompose, leaving walls porous. The earth of the floor is full of vegetable matter, and from there being nothing to cut off its contact with the surrounding mould, it is peculiarly liable to damp. The floor is frequently charged with animal matter thrown upon it by the inmates, and this rapidly decomposes by the alternate action of heat and moisture. Thatch placed in contact with such walls speedily decays, yielding a gas of the most deleterious quality.'[7]

Or this, from Dorset: 'I have often seen the springs bursting through the *mud* floor of some cottages, and little channels cut from the centre under the doorways to carry off the water.'[8]

> 'Some of the cottages had two bedrooms, others only one, in which case it had to be divided by a screen or curtain to accommodate parents and children. Often the big boys of the family slept downstairs, or were put to sleep in the second bedroom of an elderly couple whose children were out in the world . . . Still it was often a tight fit, for children swarmed eight, ten or even more in some families, and although they

were seldom home all together, the eldest often being married before the youngest was born, beds and shake downs were often so closely packed that the inmates had to climb over one bed to get into another . . .'

'In nearly all the cottages there was but one room downstairs, and many of these were poor and bare, with only a table and a few chairs and stools for furniture and a superannuated potato-sack thrown down by way of hearthrug. Other rooms were bright and cosy, with dressers of crockery, cushioned chairs, pictures on the walls and brightly coloured hand-made rugs on the floor . . . .The interiors varied, according to the number of mouths to be fed and the thrift and skill of the housewife, or the lack of those qualities; but the income in all was precisely the same, for ten shillings a week was the standard wage of the farm labourer at that time in that district.'[9]

Flora Thompson's graphic picture of farm cottages in an Oxfordshire hamlet in the 1880's will serve well for Eynesbury in the earliest years of that same century – even the wages were the same.

As might be expected, sanitary arrangements were crude, 'consisting for the most part of a hole in the ground under a lean-to shed, emptied only when the garden plot needed manure.'[10]

In mid-century a reporter for a newspaper toured the counties around Huntingdonshire, observing

'The effluvia from the dung heap,the drain, or the adjoining privy,or the closeness of the room, appear to give them no concern; they will sit, together with their families, unmolested by a stench, which, in many cases has compelled me . . . to retreat to the door for fresh air. In one case I inquired whether the smell of a dung heap,the steam from which was reeking through the windows, was not offensive to them – the answer I obtained was, "Oh, no, we be used to it."[11]

There was no piped water supply in Eynesbury and St. Neots until the very end of the century,[12] but water was never a problem – or rather, it only became a problem when there was too much of it. Built on water-bearing gravel in the flood plain of the river Ouse, the whole area was regularly flooded[13]. The effect of flood water on the mud floors and walls of Eynesbury cottages calls for little imagination, especially when one adds that no form of sewage disposal existed, except for open ditches which only discharged into the river after a heavy rainfall. 'Both cess pits and drains were often quite close to the drinking water well and the ground between saturated with sewage.'[14] If a cottage had no well then water had to be fetched by pail from the sole village pump in Eynesbury's Montague Street next to the parish church. Clothing was washed either in the Hen Brook, the Washbank on the banks of the Ouse or the village pond, whichever was the nearest, and hung out to dry on the hedgerows.

Hippolyte Taine, a French traveller visiting villages 30 to 40 miles from London, noted that, 'Some of the cottages are very poor, built of wattle and daub with thatched roofs, the rooms too low and too small, the windows also too small, the interior walls too thin. Think of a large family crowded into two such rooms in winter, with clothes drying on them, baby linen hung up to air, and a roaring fire . . . Many of the mothers have haggard faces blotchily red, and a wasted exhausted look; they have too many children and are all overtired. The tenant of one of these cottages was a day-labourer, married, father of six children . . . His face was drawn, strained, sad and humble.'[15]

A modern historian has commented, 'Houses without floors or ceilings, with unlined walls, unsound foundations and no drainage cannot help but become slums. They provide only the most basic shelter from the worst of the weather. They were intended for what their builders felt was an inferior class of human being, and so the provision of warmth and comfort was not necessary.'[16] Some contemporary observers were even more scathing. Arthur Young called them 'mud-cabins', whilst William Cobbett contrasted the labourers' 'miserable sheds' with their near neighbours, the beautiful churches and impressive vicarages. 'Look at these hovels', he demanded, 'made of mud and of straw; bits of glass, or of old cast-off windows, without frames or hinges frequently, but merely stuck in the mud wall. Enter them, and look at the bits of chairs or stools; the wretched boards tacked together to serve for a table; the floor of pebble, broken brick or of the bare ground; look at the thing called a bed; and survey the rags on the backs of the wretched inhabitants; and then wonder if you can that the gaols and dungeons and treadmills increase . . . '[17]

Forty years after Cobbett wrote those lines a housing inspector reported that in Eynesbury a father, a son aged 16, and two daughters aged 14 and 20, were all sleeping in one room on beds of straw with a cover of ticking and no blankets. In another house five people were sleeping in a room eight feet by ten feet and only five and a half feet high.[18]

To the west, Eynesbury was bounded by the river on the other side of which was the rural Bedfordshire parish of Eaton Socon where John had been born forty years before. To the north a small tributary of the Ouse, called the Hen Brook, separated Eynesbury from the thriving market town of St. Neots, Lydia's home before she married John eighteen years earlier and in whose church their wedding had been solemnized after the groom had finally obtained a special licence. On one of his visits to The Cock at Eaton Socon, which he said must have been a gluttonous place from its name – 'Eat-on-Soak-on', John Byng described the area thus: 'From the hill above Eaton Socon there is a view of the large market town of St. Neots in the vale which join'd to Eynesbury village makes a great shew : St. Neots Church, and steeple, are much admir'd . . . The pleasantest walk around the place is that which leads from the mill across the staunches – and some foot-bridges – over the meadows, to the village of Eynesbury.'[19]

Whilst the village was almost an appendage to St. Neots, it was, nevertheless, totally independent of the market town inasmuch as it was governed by its own vestry, chaired by the Rector. The vestry comprised those who owned property in the parish and who annually appointed the two churchwardens, the constable, the surveyor of the highways, the parish clerk and the overseers of the poor. Property rated at up to £50 a year entitled the owner to one vote at vestry meetings. Additional votes were allowed for each £25 rateable value above that figure to a maximum of six votes.[20] Needless to add, of course, that those without property had no say in parish affairs.

At the beginning of the nineteenth century the village had a population of less than six hundred (although it was to increase by more than 50 per cent within twenty years); St. Neots was three times larger, but, even so, nothing more than a medium-sized village by modern standards.

From Eynesbury bridge, which linked the two parishes over the Hen Brook boundary, the High Street (or Bridge Street, now called St. Mary's Street) led south to the church where it forked. At this point stood the stocks and whipping post for minor village criminals[21]. At the fork the road continued south as Montague Street leading to the square and the only public pump. Off the square Mill Lane (now Washbank Road) ran down to the river and the Washbank. From the church the eastward fork became Front Street (now Berkeley Street) with houses on only one side all facing on to the green. The end of Front Street was the southernmost tip of the village where the washpond, called Townsend Pond was situated. Montague Street and Front Street formed two sides of a triangle enclosing the village green, its third side, running west to east was Luke Street where the parish workhouse stood. That was all there was of Eynesbury in 1800.

At the apex of the triangular green stood St. Mary's church – all the Mimms' children had been baptised, and their daughter Mary buried there. Next to the church was the second most important building, the fifteenth-century Nag's Head inn.[22]. But this was by no means the only inn, there were at least three others, the Chequers and the Golden Ball in Front Street and the Dog and Duck. This last stood practically on Eynesbury Bridge with a water frontage on to the Hen Brook and was so named as the place where local sportsmen enjoyed a contest in which dogs were set upon pinioned ducks in an area enclosed by netting – the winner being the dog which slaughtered the most birds.[23]

The green was the recreation centre of the village where the annual parish feast was celebrated for three days from the Sunday nearest to September 8th, the Nativity of St. Mary the Virgin, Eynesbury's patron saint. Harvest Festival frequently coincided with the parish feast and both would be celebrated together when all the farmers and their men assembled at the southern end of the village and marched together to St. Mary's church, afterwards retiring to the green to eat, drink, dance, watch or take part in wrestling, cudgels or single-stick contests and patronise the stalls and sideshows set up by travelling showmen.[24]

The green contained the pound for impounding straying animals and for whose release a fine was imposed. It was also the traditional place for the women and children to take their harvest gleanings which they beat with a small stick, winnowing away the chaff in the breeze before taking the remaining corn grains to be ground at the Duloe or Eaton Socon windmills: the miller's payment for this was to keep the bran[25].

There would seem to have been no formal school in the village until one was set up in the stables of the Rectory by the Revd. Palmer who was installed as Rector in 1808. It later moved to the building previously used as the parish workhouse when this became redundant after the St. Neots Union Workhouse was built at Eaton Socon in the 1840's. Certainly the older Mimms children could not write their names, signing the marriage register with a cross, but some of the younger ones could – the first generation to achieve a degree of literacy. Schooling cost money that a large family could ill afford but the Revd. Palmer's school was established specifically as 'a school for the poor of Eynesbury.'[26]

A farm labourer had no need of literacy. He learnt his catechism by rote at Sunday school, signed his name with a cross and, on the very rare occasions when he had need to write a letter, could pay someone a little better schooled than himself a penny to write it for him. The very first official survey in 1840 showed that in Huntingdonshire 46 per cent of men and 56 per cent of women were illiterate. That had to be a gross underestimate since the standard used to define 'literacy' was no more than the ability to sign one's own name in the marriage register, and that was as much as most labourers could, in fact, achieve. In Buckinghamshire it was reported that of all adult labourers and their wives no more than one in six could read and only one in ten write.[27]

For the children of the poor – at least until they were old enough to earn a shilling or so a week at the age of seven or eight – the most accessible schooling in terms of its availability and cost was the so-called 'dame school',

> ' . . . .where a deaf, poor, patient widow sits,
> And awes some thirty infants as she knits;
> Infants of humble, busy wives, who pay
> Some trifling price for freedom through the day.
>
> Her room is small, they cannot widely stray –
> Her threshold high, they cannot run away;
> Though deaf, she sees the rebel-hero shout:–
> Though lame, her white rod nimbly walks about;
> With band of yarn she keeps offenders in,

> And to her gown the sturdiest rogue can pin.
> Aided by these, and spells, and tell-tale birds,
> Her power they dread and reverence her words.'[28]

Such schools were sometimes run by disabled or even working men and women. They had few resources such as books. John Pounds, a crippled Portsmouth cobbler who ran a school for poor children for many years, replied to a visitor who remarked that he needed some new books:

> "Why so?"
> "Because those under that birdcage seem to be coming to pieces."
> "So much the better."
> "How can that be, Mr Pounds?"
> "Why, ye sees, Sir, when a book's new like, an' all tight together it sarves for only one at a time; but when it comes to pieces, every leaf sarves for one.
> Besides, I doesn't always larn 'em out o' books."

explaining, "I hears 'em read, an say their lessons; and it's no hindrance to my trade. My works a-going on all the same. Sometimes I lays down my tools a bit; and looks over their sums, an their writing, an sets 'em fresh lessons, to be larning; and then I goes on mending my shoe again."[29]

Probably more effective as educators were the Sunday Schools. 'Today "Sunday School" conjures up the image of an hour or two of religious instruction; in the early nineteenth century the school occupied the better part of the Sabbath, four to six hours, and included reading from the Bible and other texts . . . as well as writing and some arithmetic. The average length of attendance was four years, sometimes supplemented by intermittent spells at day school; more often the Sunday school was the only education available to a considerable number of children.' From the beginning to the middle of the century the number of children attending them multiplied tenfold until they were helping to give a basic education in the 'three R's' to some two million children.[30] In a return demanding to know the educational facilities in Eynesbury in 1839, the Revd. Palmer claimed 150 scholars at his Sunday school and a further 100 (many would, of course, have been the same pupils) at his day school. He also estimated 'the supposed population of persons who could not read or write' in his parish to be twenty in a hundred.[31]

Presumably if they could just write their name they would have been counted amongst the remaining 80 per cent, otherwise his figure would have been wildly optimistic by any national standard of literacy at that time.

A school primer published in 1813 gives some feel for the nature of the teaching children enjoyed. An arithmetic question asked:

'At the marriage in Cana in Galilee there were six water pots of stone, holding two or three firkins a-piece. If they had two firkins, how much water would it take to fill them? And how much if they held three each?'

and a teaching alphabet began:

> 'A – is an Angel who praises the Lord
> B – is for Bible, God's most holy word
> C – is for Church where the righteous resort
> D – is for the Devil who wishes us hurt'[32]

an alternative version promoted by subversive radicals who wished 'to instil into the minds of our children a deep and rooted hatred of our corrupt and tyrannical rulers' was the 'Bad Alphabet for the use of the Children of Female Reformers', which cleverly employed the device of association and included:

> 'B is for Bible, Bishop and Bigotry
> K is for King, King's evil, Knave and Kidnapper
> W is for Whig, Weakness, Wavering and Wicked'[33]

Such a book would never have found its way into the Revd. Palmer's School.

As to whether the children of the lower classes should be taught at all, there had been a continuing and furious debate for many years. Bernard Mandeville had written a century earlier: 'Going to school in comparison to working is idleness, and the longer boys continue in this easy sort of life, the more unfit they'll be when grown up for downright labour, both as to strength and inclination. Men who are to remain and end their days in a labourious, tiresome and painful station of life, the sooner they are put upon it at first, the more patiently they'll submit to it for ever after.'[34]

Nearly a century later during a Commons debate on Samuel Whitbread's bill to establish parochial schools, Davies Giddy objected in much the same terms, 'giving education to the labouring classes of the poor,' he asserted, 'would, in effect, be found to be prejudicial to their morals and happiness; it would lead them to despise their lot in life, instead of making them good servants in agriculture and other labourious employments to which their rank in society had destined them.' A somewhat more liberal Member in the same debate had no doubt that the poor ought to be taught to read, but as to writing he expressed some doubt, 'because those who had learnt to write well were not willing to abide at the plough, but looked to a situation in some counting house.'[35] Even the Bishop of London in 1803 thought it advisable 'to let the lower classes remain in that state of ignorance in which nature has originally placed them'.[36]

Not until a third of the way through that century did a government make the very first grant towards school building, not by direct involvement but by a payment to the religious charities which were already working in that field. The sum involved, £20,000, was niggardly in the extreme, even by the standards of the time and would have been won or lost in a night at Crockfords without much remark by any well-breeched blade. It was, nevertheless, the first step in what, much later, was to become a national system of elementary education.

If a mother could afford the few pence for tuition she would send her daughters to learn lace-making from a local woman who taught groups of young children in her own cottage – a variant of the 'dame school'. St. Neots was on the eastern edge of the Midlands lace-making area and many of its women had earned a living from it, especially at the height of the 'lace-mania' when, 'those who could afford it were christened, married and buried in lace. It was used to edge countless items such as bed-linen, napery, cushions and pin-holders, handkerchiefs, fans, sleeve-ends, stocking fronts, jabots, collars, capes, night attire (and night-caps), over-gowns, aprons, mobcaps, babies' cradles, bed-hangings, shawls, christening robes, dress-flounces, gloves, even shoes had lace 'uppers'.'[37]

By the end of the eighteenth century the trade had begun to

decline but, for those who had mastered this intricate and demanding skill, it still provided a useful supplement to the family income. It had always been a cottage industry with lace merchants travelling around, giving out thread and, sometimes, parchment patterns and collecting the completed work. This made it ideal as a means of earning in the time a busy woman could spare from her many other domestic duties and must have been a familiar sight to her younger children as it was to Flora Thompson: 'They loved to see the bobbins tossed hither and thither, at random it seemed to them, every bobbin weighted with its bunch of bright beads and every bunch with its own story, which they had heard so many times that they knew it by heart, how this bunch had been part of a blue bead necklace worn by her little sister who had died at five years old, and this other one had belonged to her mother, and that black one had been found, after she was dead, in a work-box belonging to a woman who was reputed to have been a witch.'[38]

Children, most especially girls, but not exclusively so, would begin to learn the craft at five or six years old, serving an 'apprenticeship' of as long as nine to thirteen years, so demanding was the dexterity required and the dozens of different designs to be mastered. Their hair had to be plaited to ensure that no stray hair fell on to the pillow and became entwined in the lace. The canvas pillow on which they worked rested on a wood-framed pillow-horse and they threw their lace-bobbins illuminated by a candle set in a glass globe to intensify the light with up to eight children crouched around each candle stool, so that bent posture and eyesight problems were commonplace in later life.

Discipline at such schools was, and perhaps had to be, strict. At a Spratton, Northants, lace school girls were expected to 'stick' 600 pins an hour and if, at the end of a long day, she was even five pins short, she was required to work an extra hour. Once they became sufficiently adept, their lace could be sold and they might earn a shilling or so a week after their tuition fees had been deducted from the proceeds.[39]

At least one of John's daughters, young Lydia named after her mother, earned her lifetime's living as a lace-maker in Eynesbury. She never married and died at the age of 65 in the St. Neots Union Workhouse at Eaton Socon.

A labourer's wife who had not learned to make lace earned

what she could at seasonal work in the fields in this predominantly arable area. Until around the middle of the eighteenth century women commonly worked alongside men, leading the plough-horses, beating manure and spreading the dung, shearing sheep, mowing the hay and, at the corn harvest, reaping, loading, threshing, winnowing and even thatching. For this hard manual labour they were paid half the rate of male labourers. But even this was denied them as the rural population grew and men were in over-plentiful supply. Whether this brought about a social change or whether it would have happened anyway we cannot know for sure, but, in general, the field-work available to women after the wars against the French was more or less restricted to picking and carting stones, planting peas and potatoes, hoeing, weeding and thinning turnip seedlings, helping at haytime and harvest in the less skilled jobs of binding, carrying and loading, turnip pulling and 'tatering' (potato picking). Merely listing the jobs makes one realise its back-breaking drudgery. In wet weather on the heavy Midland clay soil it was far from a rustic idyll. In a report on the employment of women and children in agriculture, Alfred Austin wrote; 'The upper parts of the underclothes of women at work, even their stays, quickly became wet through with perspiration, whilst the lower parts cannot escape getting equally wet in nearly every kind of weather. It not unfrequently happens that a woman, on returning home from work, is obliged to go to bed for an hour or two to allow her clothes to be dried. It is also by no means uncommon for her, if she does not do this, to put them on again the next morning nearly as wet as when she took them off.'[40]

Facing another day of mind-numbing drudgery and unable to afford even a change of clothing it can hardly be wondered at that the language and manner of the women was not the behaviour of the drawing room as Charles Kingsley observed: 'It's the field-work, sir, – the field-work that does it all. They get accustomed there from their childhood to hear words whose very meanings they shouldn't know; and the elder teach the younger ones, and the married ones are worst of all. It wears them out in body, sir, that field-work, and makes them brutes in soul and in manners . . . they get to like the gossip, and scandal, and the coarse fun of it, while their children are left at home to play in the roads, or fall into the fire, as plenty do every year . . .

it is very little of a father's care, or a mother's love, that a labourer's child knows in these days.'[41]

'I do not remember a time when I did not earn my living,' wrote William Cobbett of his childhood, 'My first occupation was driving the small birds from the turnip seed, and the rooks from the peas . . . My next employment was weeding wheat, and leading a single horse at harrowing barley. Hoeing peas followed, and hence I arrived at the honour of joining the reapers in harvest, driving the team and holding the plough.'[42] In the time which could be spared from stone-picking and bird-scaring the younger boys could indulge their destructive natures and earn a few pence by birds-nesting and trapping. The Eynesbury vestry encouraged this form of pest control by agreeing, 'that two pence a dozen is to be given for Sparrows and a penny a dozen for Sparrow Eggs.'[43]

At Eaton Socon a dead hedgehog was worth 2d. and the older, more venturesome and, perhaps, more cunning boys could earn 4d. for catching a polecat which must have been a particular pest as a single page of the churchwarden's accounts lists not less than eleven payments for the creatures. In the following year fifteen polecats and sixteen hedgehogs were accounted for in eighteen out of the twenty-six entries for the year. The scale of reward rose in proportion to the damage a pest could cause, so that a dog fox or otter was worth 1s 8d to the community but a bitch fox fetched twice that amount – almost half as much as a man could earn in a week.[44]

An occasional source of income for small boys and a major commercial event for all who lived within travelling distance of the town was market day. A twelfth century charter entitled St Neots to hold a market every Thursday in the Square and the surrounding streets. 'St Neots Market Square is, without doubt, the principal feature that gives the town its character and the one that is most remembered by passing strangers. Its large size, about 7,500 square yards, makes it one of the biggest in the country.'[45] Immediately to the west of the Square, the bridge over the Ouse to Eaton Socon encouraged farmers from north Bedfordshire to drive their carts to market and put up at one of the many inns in and around the Square where people knew where to find them. Running east from the Square was a very wide High Street constructed as an extension to the Square itself and previously know as 'Sheep Street' where sheep sales were held.[46]

'It wears them out in body, sir, that field-work, and makes them brutes in soul and in manners . . .'

Whilst all kinds of farm produce and livestock were bought and sold here, its main commodity was corn as St. Neots was geographically part of the great grain growing Midland Plain and, until the railway came in 1850 and cheap imported corn from America in the third quarter of the century, up to half the total area of the Square was covered with enormous heaps of corn in bulk, sacked or just pitched from the carts.[47] Much of this was purchased for export and carried by 40 foot long lighters in gangs of five or six down the Ouse to King's Lynn on the Wash from where it was shipped to Scotland, Norway and the Netherlands[48].

The south and west sides of this great square were occupied by merchants' houses and yards backing on to the river and the Hen Brook where grain was stored in outhouses and any odd place which could be found until it was shipped out. The north side of the Square, 'Shop row', contained mostly retail shops with stalls set outside on market days. There were maltsters, brewers, bakers, fell-mongers, grocers, linseed cake makers, saddlers, curriers, chemists, perfumiers, millers, ironmongers and braziers, coopers and bootmakers; the sounds and, even more distinctive, the smells must have been memorable especially on the day following the market when the butchers brought their waste to Samuel Bedell's tallow-chandlers manufactory where it was rendered down to make rush-lights and 'farthing dips' – the only form of domestic lighting a labourer could afford.[49]

Market Square, which 150 years earlier had been the site of the Battle of St. Neots where the Parliamentary forces defeated the King's army, boasted at least a dozen inns. The Cross Keys, just east of the bridge on the north side of the Square, like many inns of the period, served the coach trade, supplying refreshment to the coachman and travellers and fresh horses for the coach. The Old Boston Coach changed horses at the Cross Keys and a local inhabitant described the scene as it set off over St. Neots bridge for the Great North Road around, 1827; 'Carrying a breakdown load of three tons of Christmas fare; turkeys, geese, and game: piled to a great height and suspended from temporary rails so that no portion of the coach was visible except the wheels. Six horses brought it to the Keys with a like number of postillions, and it could not mount the bridge until Arnold the landlord had received the assistance of (three) porters . . . '[50]

On the north side of St. Neots Market Square, William Ward

'. . . the sounds and, even more distinctive, the smells must have been memorable . . .'

Abbott with his brother (or cousin) James carried on a practice as auctioneers, architects and surveyors. William lived in the big house at Eynesbury and, for reasons which are now obscure, was heartily detested throughout the whole district. He owned a foundry and a great deal of property, taking advantage of the growing demand for workmen's cottages as St Neots expanded. Amongst these was a long terrace of small houses on the north side of Russell Row (now Russell Street) built on low ground below the level of the town's drainage and sewers and described as 'typical of workmen's slum-type dwellings of that period'.[51] By the time William Ward Abbott was 30 years old he was already a wealthy man and had bought Berkeley House in Eynesbury's Front Street which was later re-named after the house itself.

He was clearly an aggressive and litigious character who both brought actions against others and stood accused of violence himself before the Huntingdonshire Quarter Sessions on many occasions. In 1824 he accused his partner, James, of threatening his life, 'using most opprobious language towards him,' and of chasing him home through the streets of St. Neots to Eynesbury accompanied by 'a great assemblage of the common people.' The two men's partnership was clearly not a harmonious one as only a year later he accused James of threatening and abusing him. In his turn, William was brought before the court in that same year for assaulting Thomas Kay.[52].

The job of Overseer of the Poor was not one to which many parishioners aspired. It carried a heavy responsibility at this period of severe unemployment and great want and one demanding a degree of detached fairness, an equable temperament and enormous compassion from its office-holders. How the Eynesbury vestry came to elect William Ward Abbott to this arduous, unpaid post for the first time at its Easter Vestry meeting on Ladyday 1828 given his disputatious record is a profound mystery: perhaps he and his colleague, John Chapman, were the only ones who could be persuaded to accept it.[53]

Whether the events which followed were caused directly by some action of his in that capacity we cannot know, but he was never re-elected to that position. Whatever its immediate cause, the detail of the allegations he made give the impression of strong, pent-up emotions on the part of the populace suddenly released against him as over 100 men from as far as Eaton Socon, unlawfully and tumultuously 'assembled near Berkeley House carying a wooden gibbet from which they hanged 'a certain figure of a Man . . . as the effigy of the said William Ward Abbott', and made 'a great noise and disturbance for a long time to wit for the space of one hour.'[54]

Popular outrage expressed in this fashion was a form of rough justice directed at anyone who, in the eyes of a village community, had offended against their standards of acceptable behaviour. An oppresive overseer, a wife beater or a flagrant adulterer would be singled out for a public shaming. The 'Skimmington', or 'charivari' as it was known, most usually took the form of a procession of villagers to the offender's house where they kept up a cacophony of 'rough music', banging kettles and pots or blowing whistles: the proceedings often culminating in burning an effigy of the culprit. Overseers whose behaviour was thought to be excessively harsh might be paraded through the village in the parish cart and unceremoniously dumped over the parish border.

Ousley (or Owsley) Rowley was accorded a 'rough music' send off from Huntingdon when he eventually left the town to found a family seat at Priory Hill, St. Neots, where he and his successors as squires dominated the market town for a century. On leaving Huntingdon his neighbours 'tin kettled and hooted him out of the town', they were so overjoyed to see the back of him. Quite why he was so disliked there is not known but it is, perhaps, illustrative of him that when a violent thunderstorm broke over his fields at St. Neots, the squire's haymakers ran for shelter as he galloped his horse furiously round the field in a rage trying with every insult and obscenity to force them back to work. As the local historian, C. F. Tebbutt, has written, 'No surviving records depict Ousley Rowley as a likeable or popular figure', adding, 'Of the first four generations that lived at Priory Hill few were loved and most feared but respected. They were all wealthy and accumulated more wealth by marriage and shrewd investment. They were not, however, notably generous, except to the church. None were spendthrifts, and indeed a mean and miserly streak was a family characteristic.' Ousley's wife, and co-founder of the dynasty, bearing in all nine children, was herself the daughter of a 'miserly and eccentric' St. Neots attorney, William King. Ann King was described by her contemporaries as dwarfish and even slightly deformed and even with her 'weight of gold' as a dowry was a long time in finding a suitable husband.

It was even said that one had been advertised for and the locals believed that it was the prospect of her £30,000 inheritance from her father which was the reason for Ousley's marriage to Ann and his founding of the family seat in St. Neots where in time they purchased all the land to the east of the town and sold none, thus effectively preventing its expansion in the only direction it could have grown.[55].

As the squire he automatically became a magistrate, was Chairman of the Huntingdonshire Quarter Sessions for 25 years and conducted the local Petty Sessions with the only other Justice of the Peace in the area – the Revd. Palmer, Rector of Eynesbury, where each Thursday they held court at the house of their clerk, John Wells, at Church House, Eynesbury.[56]

A present-day descendant of Ousley has condemned Tebbutt's 'acrimonious attack on the Rowley family', and specifically refuted the allegation that Anne was 'dwarfish' by quoting her grandson's memory of her as '. . . of middle size, of fine complexion, had dark hair and good teeth, was an heiress and very good looking and consequently with many candidates for her hand.' Ousley, like his father, was Receiver General or chief tax collector for the county and as such was responsible for all bills and accounts connected with the militia – a conscript civilian defence force raised against the possibility of a French invasion. Perhaps it was these activities which led to his apparent unpopularity. Not only did he act as attorney for the 4th and 5th Earls of Sandwich, but in 1808 became one of the most powerful figures in Huntingdonshire when his other patron, the Duke of Manchester, was appointed Governor of Jamaica and left Ousley as his local representative rewarding him with a profitable legal sinecure connected with the Jamaican judiciary which he was able to fulfill without ever having to leave England. Whatever the truth of Anne's physique and Ousley's character he clearly demonstrated a singular ability to acquire a more than adequate fortune to finance the dynasty he had created at Priory Hill, St. Neots.[57]

If Ann King was dwarfish in stature, then another, contemporaneous, inhabitant was a giant. At a time when an agricultural labourer over 5'6" was considered exceptional,[58] James Toller reached a height of 8'6". He was born and died in Eynesbury and would have been well known to John and Lydia's family whose middle child, John, was of an age with the Eynesbury Giant as he was internationally known. Such prodigies and curiosities were of great public interest and, as such, were exploited by showmen as 'exhibits' in Raree Shows all over Europe. Toller was toured around the country, featuring in London's Piccadilly in 1815 as a double-bill with Simon Paap, a 28 inch dwarf, and where he was presented to the King of Prussia and the Russian Czar.

> 'To see him hundreds day by day did throng,
> As he from place to place did pass along.
> His 'bode uncertain for to think 'tis vain
> One place so tall a wonder to contain.
> His whole proportion was upright and straight
> 'Twas eight foot fully and a half in height . . . '

wrote one versifier of him. Perhaps growing weary of being gawped at as a freak, he enlisted in the Life Guards but his health began to fail. He left the army and returned to Eynesbury to live with his mother in Rectory Lane where the Revd. Palmer allowed him to stroll in the Rectory grounds out of sight of curious and insensitive onlookers until he died, aged 20, in 1818, a local newspaper describing him as 'the celebrated Huntingdonshire Gigantic Youth'. At a time when anatomists and curiosity collectors prized such specimens, it was feared that bodysnatchers would resurrect his corpse for its commercial value, so the Rector once again displayed his compassion by allowing his body to be interred in the middle aisle of Eynesbury church where it could lie undisturbed.[59]

St. Neots had a paper mill which had been converted from a mediaeval flour mill in 1804.[60] That apart, the only other large-scale manufacturing in the whole of Huntingdonshire were two sacking factories at Stanground in the north of the county and a lace factory at Kimbolton in the west.[61] Virtually the only employment for unskilled men, therefore, was farmwork. As there was no outside competition for labour, farmers could offer the lowest possible wages or, as John Clare bitterly expressed the choice a master offered his labourers, "work for the little I chuse to alow you and go to the parish for the rest – or starve."[62] In these circumstances men were known to walk to neighbouring counties for better-paid work throughout the summer months leaving the local farmers with a labour shortage and at the mercy of the 'peregrinating Irish', as they condescendingly described the gangs of Irish labourers who travelled from farm to farm looking for seasonal work.[63]

A Board of Agriculture report stated that in 1811 wages paid in Eynesbury were 10s for 11 months of the year and 11s for the other month (the corn harvest) and the hours of work as from light till dark in winter and at harvest and at other times from 6 till 6.[64] Those who looked after the farm horses, however, had to start two hours earlier in order to feed and muck out the animals. Until 1808 an early morning bell was rung from St. Neots' church steeple at 4 am to wake the early risers.[65] When he was examined as to his legal place of settlement, John was 'in service as a horsekeeper' and so his day would have started at that hour in summer or two hours before dawn in winter.

Another Eynesbury labourer, John Irons, recalled a typical day of his life. His experiences in the middle of the century would not have been significantly different from those of John Mimms in the early 1800's. Irons would arrive at the farm where he worked in the 1860's by 6 am when he ate his breakfast of bread with milk supplied by his employer. Sometimes it was 'toad in the hole' – a piece of lard put into a hole cut in a lump of bread. At 9 am he took a short break for 'lunch' which was just bread alone. When the horses had finished work for the day at 2 pm he ate his dinner which, almost invariably, consisted of a dumpling made of flour, lard and onions, and a small piece of fat pork, boiled in a bag and brought from home ready cooked. In the winter he recalled throwing his frozen dumplings against the barn wall to soften them, but sometimes the farmer's wife would heat them up for the men and dish up hot soup – just water in which meat or vegetables had been boiled. When meat was dear that same piece of fat pork was taken home to be used again to flavour tomorrow's dumpling. Supper was eaten at home with all his family. On most days it was just bread and lard with vegetables and perhaps one red herring to be shared between two or three people.[66]

Potatoes had, by this time, become a generally accepted staple vegetable, but turnips were a symbol of dire poverty, the lowest form of human food. 'In times of real hardship, when prices soared beyond reach or when sickness or unemployment reduced a household to a truly desperate condition, then this root, thought of as more appropriate for livestock, was the food of last resort: often begged or stolen from the fields. To be so reduced was to reach the depths of dietary deprivation.'[67]. Such must have been the condition of a distant cousin of John, another John Mimms aged 39 of Kempston, who was imprisoned for two months in the Bedfordshire House of Correction in October 1818 for having stolen 'a Quantity of Turnips' from Joseph Warth. Sharing the prison was 34 year old William Hart for having 'pulled up, injured, and destroyed growing turnips', and James Skip, 18, for stealing potatoes from a field. Three other men were also awaiting trial in Bedford Gaol charged with intending to poach at night from a private parkland in Eaton Socon being armed with bludgeons and hare snares and accompanied by a dog. They were facing seven years' transportation under the Night Poaching Act passed two years previously to punish those armed with a net or stick and intending to take game, or even rabbits.[68]

Of the 300 or so working days in the year a labourer was fortunate if he worked for as many as 250. In winter especially, when the weather was too wet or the ground too frozen he was laid off without pay; but even when the land was workable, regular or casual employment was not always readily available. A report to the Board of Agriculture by a Bedfordshire farmer explained that, 'The increase of population has caused a deficiency of employment , which is so remarkable in some seasons that a great proportion of the labourers 'go the rounds'. This 'roundsman' system became more prevalent in Eaton Socon after Napoleon's defeat but had existed elsewhere for many years. The same report explained how it operated. 'When a labourer can obtain no employment he applies to the acting overseer, from whom he passes on to different farmers all round the parish, being employed by each of them after a rate of one day for every £20 rent. The allowance to a labourer on the rounds is commonly 2d a day below the pay of other labourers which is found to be a necessary check upon those who love liberty better than labour'.[69] The farmer had no choice but to find some work for these roundsmen to do, but half the wages he paid were reimbursed from the poor rate. Whatever the labourers might have thought of the system it was not popular with farmers and landowners. In 1819 the Duke of Bedford proposed a resolution which was carried unanimously at the Bedfordshire Quarter Sessions and circulated to the press that the roundsman system was 'destructive of the moral energies of the labourer and injurious to the interests of the farmer'.[70] Its publication probably prompted the Eynesbury vestry in April of that year to declare; 'That to pay the labourer a part of his wages earned in the service of any private individual out of the parish poor rate is illegal' and the overseers were instructed 'to discontinue the practice in future.'[71] Such declarations, however, were futile when parish officers were faced with a choice between paying a subsidy 'in aid of wages', a straightforward dole based on the fluctuating price of bread or the slow death by starvation of half the families in the village.

As if the wages they earned or the parish relief they could apply for were not small enough, the taxes imposed by the government at the end of the Napoleonic Wars took half a labourer's income. To pay the enormous costs of the war William Pitt imposed taxes on servants, racehorses, carriages, hats, paper, gold and silver plate among other things. These the poor escaped altogether. Nor were they required to pay the window tax as cottages were exempt. Income tax at 2d. in the £ affected them not at all since its graduated scale applied only to incomes greater than £60 per annum.[72]

A tax on income was an intrusive novelty and widely detested. So great was the outcry that the government was forced to withdraw it in 1816 and, instead, resorted to indirect taxation on food and ordinary domestic items. These, of course, applied to rich and poor alike but bore most heavily on those with low incomes. In fact it was calculated that a labourer who was fully employed for fifty weeks of the year and earning on average 9s a week would pay for food, clothing, housing, sugar, malt, tea, coffee and sugar 4s.4½d, or almost half his total earnings, in taxes alone.[73]

A living wage was unobtainable. The authorities had long ago opted instead for a regular dole paid out of the poor rates, the burden of which grew heavier and was increasingly resented. The labourer had come to regard the parish dole as his by right so that 'the traditional social order degenerated into a universal pauperism of demoralised men who could not fall below the relief scale whatever they did, who could not rise above it, who had not even the nominal guarantee of a living income since the 'scale' could be – and with the increasing expense of the rates was – reduced to as little as the village rich thought fit for a labourer'.

For their part, labourers 'were encouraged to do as little work as they possibly could, since nothing would get them more than the official minimum of subsistence. If they worked at all, it was only because their fathers had done so before them, and because a man's self-respect required him to.'[74]

References

[1] Klingberg and Hustvedt, pp. 175/176.
[2] ibid., pp 188/9
[3] ibid., pp 196/7
[4] Tibble, 'John Clare, Selected Poems' p.140
[5] Green, 'Village Life in the Eighteenth Century', pp.68/9,Hoskins, 'Local History in England', p.196 , McCann, 'Clay and Cob Buildings'
[6] Gauldie, 'Cruel Habitations', p.22
[7] Flinn, 'The Sanitary Condition of the Labouring Population', p.329.
[8] ibid., pp.82/3
[9] Thompson, 'Larkrise', pp. 18/19.
[10] Gauldie, 'Cruel Habitations', p.57
[11] Morning Chronicle, 28 Oct 1850
[12] Tebbutt, 'St. Neots, p.42.
[13] ibid., p.91
[14] ibid., p.46
[15] Hyams, 'Notes on England', pp 128/9
[16] Gauldie, 'Cruel Habitations' p.26.
[17] Cobbett, William, 'Rural Rides', p.266
[18] Tebbutt, 'St. Neots', p.47.
[19] Andrews, 'The Torrington Diaries' pp.483, 493 and 503
[20] Tebbutt, St. Neots', p.313
[21] ibid., p.44
[22] ibid., p.327
[23] ibid., p.326
[24] ibid., pp.110/1
[25] ibid., p.349
[26] ibid., pp.55 and 322
[27] Hobsbawm, and Rude, 'Captain Swing', p.42
[28] Crabbe, 'The Borough', Letter XXIV.
[29] Harrison, 'The Common People' pp.290/1.
[30] Himmelfarb, 'The Idea of Poverty', p.373.
[31] Huntingdon R.O., 2603/3/18.
[32] Poole, J. 'The Village School Improved' (1813): quot. Tonge, and Quincey, p.71.
[33] Thompson, E.P., 'The Making of the English Working Class', p.788.
[34] Mandeville, B., 'The Fable of the Bees' (1714): quot. Eden, 'The State of the Poor', Vol I. p.286.
[35] Hansard, 13 JUL 1807: quot. Tonge and Quincey, pp.67/8.
[36] Hibbert, 'The English, A Social History, p.450.
[37] Palmer, J and M, 'Wellingborough', p.176.

[38] Thompson, 'Larkrise', p.83.
[39] Palmer, J and M.,'Wellingborough', pp.177/180.
[40] Austin, A. 'Report of the Special Assistant Poor Law Commissioners on the Employment of Women and Children in Agriculture'. Parliamentary Papers (1843), Vol XII, p.22: quot. Horn, 'Life and Labour in Rural England.' p.77
[41] Kingsley, C. 'Yeast' (1848), pp.243/244: quot. Horn, 'Life and Labour in Rural England', p.78.
[42] Reitzel, W (ed.), 'The Autobiography of William Cobbett', Faber edn., 1967 p.11: quot. Rule, J. 'The Labouring Classes', p.110.
[43] Huntingdon R.O., Eynesbury Vestry Minute Book (1822) 2603/8/2
[44] Bedfordshire R.O., Eaton Socon Churchwarden's Accounts (1765/6), P5/5/1
[45] Tebbutt, 'St. Neots', p.103.
[46] ibid., p.232
[47] ibid., p.107
[48] ibid., p.87.
[49] ibid., pp.186-231.
[50] ibid., p.211
[51] Tebbutt, 'St. Neots', pp.302/3.
[52] Huntingdon R.O., Quarter Sessions Papers (1824/5)
[53] Huntingdon R.O., Eynesbury Vestry Minute Book (1828) 2603/8/2
[54] Huntingdon R.O., Quarter Sessions Papers (1828), Tebbutt, 'St. Neots', pp.335/7.
[55] Tebbutt, 'St. Neots', pp.151/153.
[56] ibid., pp.43 and 334.
[57] Rowley, P., 'English Life in the 18th and 19th centuries: The Chronicles of the Rowleys', unpublished typescript, Huntingdon, R.O.
[58] Snell, 'Annals of the Labouring Poor', p.330.
[59] Tebbutt, 'St. Neots', pp.321/2.
[60] ibid., p.130.
[61] Peacock, 'Bread or Blood', p.27.
[62] Snell, 'Annals of the Labouring Poor', p.67.
[63] Peacock, 'Bread or Blood', p.24.
[64] Parkinson, R., 'General View of the Agriculture of the County of Huntingdon', (1811) p.270: quot. Peacock, 'Bread or Blood' p.22.
[65] Tebbutt, 'St. Neots', p.63.
[66] Tebbutt, 'Hunts. Folklore', pp.8/9.
[67] Rule, J., 'The Labouring Classes', p.54.
[68] Bedfordshire R.O., QSCI (1818),Hopkins, 'The Long Affray', p.306.
[69] Batchelor, 'A General Review of the Agriculture of Bedfordshire', (1808): quot. Emmison, 'The Relief of the Poor at Eaton Socon,, p.50.
[70] Godber, 'History of Bedfordshire', p.416.
[71] Huntingdon R.O., 'Eynesbury Vestry Minute Book (1819), 2603/8/2.
[72] Southgate, 'English Economic History', pp. 238/9.
[73] Thompson, E.P., 'The Making of the English Working Class', p.336.
[74] Hobsbawm and Rude, 'Captain Swing', p.31.

CHAPTER FIVE

CAPTAIN SWING IN HUNTINGDONSHIRE

'There is one farmer, in the North of Hampshire, who has nearly eight thousand acres of land in his hands; who grows fourteen hundred acres of wheat and two thousand acres of barley! He occupies what was formerly 40 farms! Is it any wonder that *paupers increase*?'

William Cobbett (1821)[1]

'What is that defective being with calfless legs and stooping shoulders, weak in body and mind, inert, pusillanimous and stupid, whose premature wrinkles and furtive glance tell of misery and degradation? That is an English peasant or pauper; for the two words are synonymous.'

Gibbon Wakefield (1831)[2]

By the time John Mimms's youngest children had reached their twenties conditions for labouring families had deteriorated even further if that were possible. The population of England and Wales had continued to grow at an accelerating rate from nine million at the beginning of the new century to fourteen million thirty years later. At Eynesbury there were 70% more baptisms in the ten year period centred on 1830 than there had been at the turn of the century. At next-door St. Neots the number of births had almost doubled in that same generation.[3]

A severe agricultural depression followed the end of the war as food prices fell and a quarter of a million soldiers and sailors returned to the land when the armies were demobilised after the defeat of Napoleon. Employment, precarious at the best of times, became even more scarce as an increasing number of men competed for less and less work. A man was frequently unemployed for the whole winter from the end of harvest until the beginning of March and wages, when in work, had fallen by between a quarter and a third.[4]

In the year when Napoleon was exiled to the island of Elba the number of able-bodied unemployed in Eaton Socon was forty-five. Three years after the battle of Waterloo, which effectively ended the Napoleonic Wars, that number had doubled, and by 1830 the figure stood at 135 or almost 45 per cent of the available workforce.

F.G. Emmison made a particular study of this parish[5] and calculated the number of its dependent inhabitants. Two-thirds of the unemployed, he said, supported families of an average size of four-and-a-half persons and there were some fifty regular pensioners – the old, the sick and the workhouse inmates. Based on the 135 men unemployed in December 1830 we can calculate:

90 unemployed family men x 4½	405
45 unemployed single men	45
pensioners and workhouse inmates	50
a total of	500 persons

supported by the parish. And this out of a total village population of just under 2,500. Approximately 200 inhabitants had sufficient property to be called upon to contribute to the poor rate and were thus supporting more than twice their own number of paupers. In some rural areas the situation was even worse. At Kettering, which had twice Eaton's population, half the inhabitants had been in receipt of parish relief.

The overseers' records for the parish of Ampthill, some seven miles south of Bedford, have fortunately been preserved and record the extent to which the unemployed labourer relied on relief. So prevalent was the unemployment problem that the overseers maintained a special account book entitled "Surplus Labourers"[6] in which they recorded the name of each labourer applying for assistance, the number of days he had not worked each week and the amount of relief he had received. A married man's allowance was 1s 8d for each day he could find no work – or 10s for a six day working week. During the first two months of 1830 thirty-one names are listed of men wholly or partly unemployed, more than half of them for six out of the eight weeks. Quite separate from these payments to 'surplus labourers' was another list of what we should describe as family allowances called "Weekly Relief on Account of Large Families".[7] Payments ranged from 1s to 4s a week depending on the number of children. Six of the men recorded as 'surplus labour' also appear on this large families list. The 1831 census records Ampthill as having 140 labourers employed in agriculture so that at least one-fifth of the able-bodied men were almost permanently without work.

Although they may not have been separately recorded as such, every parish made similar payments and the burden on those who paid the poor rate became heavier as unemployment worsened and, increasingly, the labourer came to depend more and more upon parish relief to keep his family from starving. 'The Poor Law was no longer something to fall back on in times when a man could not earn his living, it became the general framework of the labourer's life. The distinction between worker and pauper vanished.'[8]

Farmers had lived well during the boom years of the war. 'Landowners and farmers after 1815 measured their prosperity not against the remote pre-war years, but against the abnormal boom profits of 1795 - 1815, when the golden sovreigns had rolled in, when credit had been easy, when marginal land had been leased at inflationary rents, money borrowed in the confidence that prices would stay up and luxury articles accumulated in the parlours of farmers who saw themselves as potential gentlemen, and on the backs of their wives and daughters who saw themselves even more passionately as ladies.'[9]

The farmers' social pretensions were, not unnaturally, resented by the poor, who had not benefitted from the boom times, as this popular street ballad "The Times Have Altered"[10] shows:

> 'Some years ago the farmer's sons were learnt to plough and sow,
> And when the summer-time did come, likewise to reap and mow:
> But now they dress like Squire's sons, their pride it knows no bounds,

They mount upon a fine blood horse to follow up the hounds.

For lofty heads and paltry pride,
I'm sure it's all the go,
For to distress poor servants
and keep their wages low.'

ridicule extended also to their fashion-conscious sisters:

'In a decent black silk bonnet to church they used to go,
Black shoes, and handsome cotton gown, stockings as white as snow,
But now silk gowns and coloured shoes they must be bought for them,
Besides they are frizzed and furbelowed just like a friezland hen.'

William Cobbett castigated the farmer for his attempts at gentrification which led to his increasing isolation from his workmen. No longer would he board them in the farmhouse or sit down to share his meals with them as had been common a generation or so before. Instead, Cobbett wrote scathingly:

' . . . the labourers retreated to hovels, called cottages; and instead of board and lodging, they got money; so little of it as to enable the employer to drink wine; but, then, that he might not reduce them to quite starvation they were enabled to come to him, in the *king's name* and demand food *as paupers*.'[11]

'Going the rounds' was still as common a practice for the able-bodied unemployed as it had been for their fathers. The farmers found work for men where they could and paid them less than the usual daily wage which the parish poor rate then supplemented. But, increasingly, as the smaller farmer was forced by the depression to mortgage his land and eventually to sell up, less and less work could be found. The overseers then had to put them to work on the roads which the men were well aware was merely a way of trying to dispose of them. 'On the other hand, some in regular work were feeble and ineffective, and humane employers hesitated to discharge old men: thus in 1830, "Saunders is almost blind; when he comes to get his money, he can't see 2s 6d if placed a foot away from him, and a sixpence has to be put into his hand"; in 1831, "Old Stopp carries a broom about the park to show what his work ought to be if he would (could) do it".'[12]

At Eynesbury the farmers drew lots at a vestry meeting to decide which of them should find work for the twenty-six unemployed at rates of pay ticketed for each man. If, because of the size of his family, he was also receiving a supplement from the parish then the farmer had to agree to pay that as well and claim it back later from the overseer.[13] Elsewhere a pauper auction, not utterly dissimilar, it would seem, from a slave market, was operated. A Poor Law Report from Northamptonshire describes how it worked. 'In many places the roundsman system is effected by means of an auction. Mr. Richardson states that in Sulgrave the old and infirm are sold at the monthly (vestry) meeting to the best bidder, at prices varying according to the time of the year from 1s 6d a week to 3s.; that at Yardley Hastings, all the unemployed men are put up to sale weekly and that the clergyman of the parish told him that he had seen ten men the last week knocked down to one of the farmers for 5s., and that there were at that time about seventy men let out in this manner out of a body of 170.'[14]

Such insensitive and degrading measures can have left men with very little pride and self-respect. The Chartist leader, Ernest Jones, probably summed up their feelings in his ironic "Song of the Lower Classes":

> "We plough and sow – we're so very, very low,
> That we delve in the dirty clay,
> Till we bless the plain – with the golden grain,
> And the vale with the fragrant hay,
> Our place we know, – we're so very low,
> 'Tis down at the landlord's feet:
> We're not too low – the bread to grow,
> But too low the bread to eat."[15]

Those who were not totally cowed resorted to petty crime and poaching despite the keepers' man-traps and spring-guns or the law's draconian punishments.

A past Member of Parliament for Bedford, T. Potter Maqueen, displayed more sympathy than most after visiting the county gaol:–

> 'In January 1829, there were ninety-six prisoners for trial in Bedford Gaol, of whom seventy-six were able-bodied men, in the prime of life, and chiefly of general good character who were driven to crime by sheer want, and who would have been valuable subjects had they been placed in a situation, where, by the exercise of their health and strength they could have earned a subsistence. There were in this number eighteen poachers, awaiting trial for the capital offence of using arms in self-defence when attacked by gamekeepers; of these eighteen men, only one was not a parish pauper, and he was the agent of the London poulterers, who, passing under the apparent vocation of a rat-catcher, paid these poor creatures more in one night than they could obtain from the overseer for a week's labour. I conversed with each of these men singly, and made minutes of their mode of life. Two first I will mention are the two brothers, the Lilleys, (of Kempston, near Bedford) in custody under a charge of firing on and wounding a keeper, who endeavoured to apprehend them whilst poaching. They were two remarkably fine young men, and very respectably connected. The elder, twenty-eight years of age, married with two small children. When I enquired how he could lend himself to such a wretched course of life, the poor fellow replied: "Sir, I had a pregnant wife, with one infant at her knee, and another at her breast: I was anxious to obtain work. I offered myself in all directions, but without success: if I went to a distance I was told to go back to my parish, and when I did so, I was allowed . . . What? Why, for myself, my babes, and my wife, in a condition requiring more than common support, and unable to labour (herself), I was allowed 7s a week for all; for which I was expected to work on the roads from light to dark, and to pay three guineas a year for the hovel which sheltered us". The other brother, aged twenty-two, unmarried, received 6d a day. These men were hanged at the spring assizes.'[16]

Of the convicted prisoners in Bedford gaol in January 1830, exactly a year after Macqueen's report, whose crimes are specified in the Calendar of Prisoners no fewer than forty-seven out of the eighty-two were convicted of offences against the Game Laws or for cutting trees, hedges or brushwood.

It was against this background of misery and repression that the labourers of southern England, the Midlands and East Anglia rebelled in the autumn and winter of 1830 in what were to become known as the 'Swing Riots', described by its two greatest authorities as '... the most impressive episode in the English farm-labourers' long and doomed struggle against poverty and degradation.'[17]

The harvest of 1828 had been poor and that of the following year even worse and had not been gathered until snow was on the ground in early October. The 1830 harvest promised no better. Threshing the corn by hand with the flail was the main winter work for farm labourers lasting from November to at least January and amounting to a quarter of the entire labour requirement of the farm. Primitive horse- or water-powered threshing machines had been introduced during the labour shortages of the war years, but their continued use at a time of high unemployment was for the labourers '... an unqualified tragedy, for it left them, or threatened to leave them, totally dependent on relief for the hardest part of the year. The threshing machine thus became the symbol of their misery.'[18]

William Cobbett had watched seventeen unemployed men working on the roads 'though the harvest was not quite in, and though, of course, it had all to be threshed out; but, at Monckton, they had *four threshing machines*'.[19]

Although the revolt took many forms – wage demands, attacks on workhouses, abuse of overseers, cattle maiming, threatening letters and arson – it was the destruction of machinery, and especially of threshing machines, which particularly characterised it as 'the greatest machine-breaking episode in English history.'[20]

The Hammonds, those two early twentieth century socialist historians, expressed their personal indignation eighty years afterwards in that thundering and impassioned polemic 'The Village Labourer'. After describing the dreadful conditions of this world – almost an 'underworld' – of thc rural labourer they preface a re-telling of the events of that winter in these words:

> 'This world has no member of Parliament, no press, it does not make literature or write history; no diary or memoirs have kept alive for us the thoughts and cares of the passing day.
> It is for this reason that the events of the winter of 1830 have

> so profound an interest, for in the scenes now to be described we have the mind of this class, hidden from us through all this period of pain, bursting the silence by the only power at its command.'[21]

That 'power' was first demonstrated at Lower Hardres, a village near Canterbury in East Kent, on the night of Saturday, August 28th, when the first threshing machine was destroyed. By the end of September there had been twenty incendiary fires in the neighbourhood of Bromley, Sevenoaks and Orpington. By the third week in October something like a hundred machines had been destroyed mostly in East Kent.[22]

At first the riots spread slowly from village to village and it was two months before they crossed the county border into the Sussex Weald. There they continued for a further fortnight before extending into West Sussex which they crossed in three days as the momentum increased. By November 18th rioting had spread to Surrey, Hampshire and Berkshire. The next day the first illegal act was reported from Wiltshire and two days after that in Oxfordshire.[23]

'Inevitably some actions of the Swing rioters, such as arson, were best conducted in secret, with blackened faces and at night. But the meetings with farmers about wages and the attacks on justices and overseers were in daylight with the rioters sometimes in their Sunday best carrying banners and emblems'[24] and collecting donations much as they were used to doing at waits or Plough Monday festivals, but occasionally by the use of threats or intimidation.

At Brede, near Battle in East Sussex, the men made an agreement with local farmers on November 5th at the Red Lion Hotel that they would in future pay every able-bodied labourer with a wife and two children 2s 3d a day (13s 6d a week) throughout the winter and 2s 6d a day (15s a week) from March to the end of September plus 1s 3d a week for each additional child. This was virtually the same wage demand which had been made by the men of Maidstone a week previously.[25] In fact, throughout the disturbances the men's demands were never exorbitant and, if met, would have provided little more than an acceptable subsistence, exemplified by Wiltshire labourers who were reported in The Times as claiming, "We don't want to do any mischief, but we want that poor children when they go to bed

'. . . some actions of the Swing rioters, such as arson, were best conducted in secret, with blackened faces and at night.'

should have a belly full of tatoes instead of crying with half a belly full."[26]

The men of Brede, however, had another complaint. This was against an unpopular assistant overseer, one Mr. Abel, who had demeaned the poor by conveying them around the village in the parish cart. The previous evening fifty of the paupers had decided to take action against him and at the meeting at the Red Lion the next day it was agreed to take Mr. Abel ' . . . to any adjoining parish and to use him with civility.'[27] 'The villagers brought the cart to Abel's door, siezed him and placed him in it with a rope round his neck, to which a large stone was tied. Without scarcely an exception, the whole of the inhabitants accompanied the labourers, who thus drew him out of the parish attended by 'rough music'.' This was only one of ten Sussex villages in which Poor Law officials or tithe holders were either expelled or threatened.[28]

Some overseers certainly acted thoughtlessly or with deliberate cruelty. In Kent an unemployed shepherd living near Margate with his wife and five children was made to walk to and from Ash, a total distance of twenty-six miles, every day to collect an allowance of 1s 9d from the overseer. He did this for nine weeks before his strength gave out. At Fawley in Hampshire, the labourers had combined to raise their wages and to get rid of their detested overseer who had introduced a parish cart with which he had humiliated the poor by yoking women and boys to it and, on one occasion, had harnessed an idiot women, Jane Stevens. They were only dissuaded from breaking up the cart by a local farmer's promise to provide a horse for it.[29]

The movement became known as the 'Swing Riots' after several threatening letters signed "Swing" or "Captain Swing" had been received by magistrates and landowners. Some of these letters were more literate than others but they all carried much the same message. One to Joseph Biddle of Wycombe in Buckinghamshire read:

> "This is to acquaint you that if your thrashing machines are not destroyed by you directly, we shall commence our labours. Signed on behalf of the whole - SWING!"

Another, somewhat more menancing,:

> "Sir
> Your name is down amongst the Black hearts in the Black Book and this is to advise you and the like of you, who are Parson Justasses, to make your Wills.
> Ye have been the Blackguard Enemies of the People on all occasions, Ye have not yet done as ye ought.
> Swing."[30]

This mythical character was never identified and is thought never to have existed but 'he' exercised great influence and induced considerable fear amongst the landowning classes. He was 'seen' everywhere. Reports of his description varied greatly and rumours concerning him spread alarm throughout the countryside. John Clare, satirised this rumour-mongering, albeit anonymously:

> 'For some said his clothing was light, lack-a-day,
> And some said his clothing was black,
> Some saw him as two in a gig that was green;
> Some as one on a horse that was black;
> Today he sold matches and begged for a crust,
> To keep a poor beggar alive,
> Tomorrow he scares all the dogs in the town,
> Driving hard as the devil can drive,
> While a day or two's wonder goes buzzing about,
> Like a swarm of bees leaving a hive.'[31]

The first report of 'Swing' disturbances in Huntingdonshire appeared in the weekly Herts, Huntingdon, Bedford, Cambridge and Isle of Ely Mercury under the headline, "Capture of Forty-seven Machine Breakers".

The first intimation of trouble had occurred on the evening of Wednesday, November 24th, 'a party of from 40 to 50 men assembled in the village of Sawtry . . . . and proceeded to demolish two thrashing-machines without molestation.'

Mr. Newton, a Sawtry farmer, gave evidence at the later trial that he had been using a threshing machine belonging to Mr. Hatfield, a farmer from the same village when, at about 9pm, he saw some 25 men on his farm, a number which quickly grew to a mob of 100 amongst whom he recognised John Simon Clark, William Hughes, William Colley, John Buck and Thomas

Stapleton. When asked what they were doing they replied, "We are going to break Mr. Hatfield's machine, for machines have pined us and we are determined to destroy them". Hughes was armed with an axe, Colley, a stone-hammer, and Buck, a hatchet.

The next evening a much larger party, estimated at 200 – 300 strong, all labourers from the nearby villages of Upton, Alconbury and Stukeley, set about destroying threshing machines at Monkwood House, Upton (Mr. William Wright), Alconbury-hill (Mr. Sturton) and Stukeley Lodge (Mr. Dann) amongst others. From a bedroom window Mr. Fuller watched as the men broke open his barn at Stukeley and destroyed his machine. They then came to the door and demanded beer. He claimed to have none, so they threatened to pull his house down unless he gave them money instead, saying that Mr. Dann of Stukeley Lodge had given them a sovreign. Fuller eventually gave them some money which the men later spent in ale-houses at Alconbury and Old Weston.

The crowd then turned west to the village of Buckworth. By the time they had destroyed two threshing-machines belonging to Messrs Gray and Bowker it was 3 o'clock on the Friday morning. They had by now also destroyed John and Christmas Bullen's machine which was their sole means of livelihood when it was hired out to local farmers. As the men passed from village to village they tried to persuade every labourer to join them; many did but, where some showed reluctance, the men attacked their cottages, smashing in doors and breaking windows.

At the Buckworth clergyman's house they demanded, and were given, food and drink and at this point they split up into several parties. One turned north-west to Old Weston. At Hamerton the vicar, the Rev. Nash, 'earnestly exhorted them to desist from their illegal purposes; but to no avail, as they quickly destroyed the only threshing-machine in the parish' – as the Mercury reporter pithily described the episode. At Old Weston, a village on the western edge of the county bordering Northamptonshire, Thomas Briggs, the blacksmith, said that his machine had been at work and he was bringing it home when he heard the mob approaching. He started to dismantle it himself and had taken the iron-work apart when the men arrived and helped him to break up the rest of it.

A second party, intending to make for Godmanchester through the county capital, turned south but the mayor of

Huntingdon roused the citizens and arrested these, by now tired and jaded, labourers led by William Horner and John Foster.

A third group of some 60 men headed by William Hughes, John Clark, William Colley and Thomas Stapleton, all of whom had been involved at Sawtry on Wednesday night, had, by the early hours of Saturday morning, November 27th, reached the northernmost part of Huntingdonshire where, in Morborne village between 4 am and 6 am they demolished a machine belonging to Thomas Cox of Folksworth where it stood in Mr. Simpson's barn and another owned by a Morborne farmer, Robert Wright Laxton. In the neighbouring village of Elton, a millwright, James Hayes's machine worth £90 loaned to a local farmer, Edmund Jones, was also broken up.[32]

Later that morning John Traylin, an Alwalton farmer, heard that the men were making for his farm in the next parish of Chesterton. He saw 50 or 60 of them break up a plough, damage farmbuildings and move on to Alwalton where they destroyed his threshing-machine. He claimed that Stapleton said they should go on to Haddon, then Yaxley, stop at Norman Cross to refresh themselves, break another machine at Holme and " . . . that will finish the week's work. We should rest on Sunday, then on Monday another party will knock down butchers' and bakers' shops". But there is no evidence that this plan was ever carried out.

Hughes, Clark, Colley, Stapleton and the others from this northern party had travelled as far south as Stilton when they were met by a force of gentlemen farmers assembled by the Duke of Bedford and the Earl of Westmoreland and headed by the Rev. Gordon and local landowners, Charles Berkeley and Tycho Wing. A 'severe skirmish' followed in which the only injury throughout the whole episode occurred. John Clark, it was said, 'used great violence with a bludgeon loaded with lead' and one of the labourers, 20 year old William Wyles, in an attack on Richard Perceval with a felling axe had his own arm broken by a bystander (Mr. Boor). The fight continued to the next village of Glatton where the rioters were finally overcome and eighteen of the ringleaders led off to Huntingdon gaol.

Special constables had been sworn in at Huntingdon on the Friday evening and had kept watch all night. At about 5 am on Saturday they set out accompanied by the Undersheriff for the villages where trouble had occurred and where some of the labourers involved were known to live. Some were arrested in their beds, others were rounded up at Alconbury with only token resistance.

The so-called 'Swing Riots' in Huntingdon were confined to the north and west of the county, lasted less than four days and involved, at most, 300 labourers but they created alarm and fear throughout the county that a general uprising might be imminent.

It was widely believed that the riots had been, if not incited, then at least, encouraged and supported, by revolutionaries as can be seen from the following resolution passed by the Cambridge magistrates on the 3rd December:

> 'That in order to allay the irritation which appears to exist in the minds of many of the Labouring Classes, and which has been encreased and fomented by the representations of evil-disposed persons, the Magistrates of the County of Cambridge will immediately make particular ENQUIRY into the actual STATE and CONDITION of the POOR in every parish in the County.
>
> And, whilst on the one hand they will ascertain, and endeavour to remedy, by the best means in their power, any Grievances which may be found to exist, they are determined, on the other, to use the utmost power which the law has put into their hands to SUPPRESS OUTRAGE and PROTECT PROPERTY, and they will in no case yield to demands made in a tumultuous and disorderly manner.'

As well as threats, exhortation, sympathy and promises also had their place. Someone described as 'a very respectable and liberal minded gentleman' wrote:

> 'My Fellow Countrymen – No one can deplore more deeply than I do the present distressed condition of the labouring poor, or deprecate more strongly the introduction of that machinery which has deprived them of their employment; but I must tell them that *all attempts* to obtain an increase of wages or to better themselves in *any way* by *violent* methods, will *entirely* defeat their object.
>
> Besides, according to the nature of the crime, *imprisonment, transportation* and *death* will be inflicted on those who may be

discovered in taking part in such outrages – and the consequences of the sin in the sight of God will be *awful indeed*!

Have patience, and your grievances will be redressed . . . Let me then, as a friend to your *best interests*, *beseech* you to be *quiet*, and to place *full* confidence in his Majesty's Ministers, who are, I am *sure*, *fully* aware of the wants of the people, and will hasten to satisfy them.'

A rather more practical response came from Godmanchester where Messrs. Sweeting, Martin and 'several other landed proprietors and tenantry have entered into a subscription to find employment for those labourers who cannot obtain work: and they are widening and raising a bank on the side of the river (Ouse) to prevent its overflow upon the meadows.' The editor followed this report with the comment – 'This subscription, at this moment, is highly praiseworthy; but something more permanent must be done in order to prevent a recurrence of the present want of regular employment for the labourer – the *interests of all classes* demand it.'

The inhabitants of the little village of Hartford, just east of Huntingdon, voted at a vestry meeting on the Thursday after the riots to subscribe to a collection 'for the purpose of giving a small acknowledgement to each labourer, as a gratuity for his prompt, spirited and Englishman-like conduct, in forming a nightly watch for the protection of agricultural and other property.'

Some of the farmers in Ramsey, on the north-eastern border with Cambridgeshire discontinued the use of threshing machines and set men to thresh their corn with the flail and on Sunday, November 28th, 'Mrs. Fellows distributed gratuitously 30 pairs of blankets and 90 yards of flannel among the poor of Ramsey.' But perhaps the most remarkable response on the night of most of the arrests, was that of a 'great landholder near Ramsey last Saturday night' (November 27th) who ' . . . raised his labourers' wages from 9s to 12s 6d (almost 40%) per week and offered 2d per quarter more to his men to thrash his corn with the flail than they demanded. Instead of a tumult this generous act caused rejoicing among the poor of the village.'

There was, perhaps, less rejoicing amongst the labouring population on Wednesday, March 9th, in the following year when the two High Court judges, Alderson and Gazelee, opened the

Huntingdon Lent Assizes. Mr. Justice Alderson had come from Bedford where he had presided over trials of the rioters in that county. He was escorted into the town by the sheriff's 'very elegant cortege. The javelin-men were attired in white kerseymere frock-coats, with waterloo blue trousers and waistcoats.'

The prisoners themselves might well have been less than comforted had they been allowed to hear the sermon given by the High Sheriff's chaplain, Rev. W. Metcalfe, at divine service which preceded the Assize sessions, the text of which was verse 4 of the 9th chapter of the Book of the Prophet Ezekiel:

> 'The Lord said unto him, Go through the midst of the city, through the midst of Jerusalem, and set a mark upon the foreheads of the men that sigh and that cry for all the abominations that be done in the midst thereof'.

In his address to the twenty-two peers and gentry of the Grand Jury, Mr. Justice Gazelee complimented the magistrates and sheriff's officers for the promptitude and energy they had displayed in suppressing the recent disorders mentioning the state of distress amongst the lower classes of the community and regretted 'that designing men had for their own wicked purposes taken occasion to exasperate the passions of the poor, and to represent the rich as their oppressors; and that the use of machinery was destructive to their interests. Now, nothing could be more easy than to show', he continued . . .' that the use of machinery was not detrimental to the labourer, and in proof of this it was only necessary to refer to our great manufacturing towns, all of which had increased in property in proportion to the increased use of machinery.'

He then outlined the penalties which the law laid down for the type of offences on the calendar before him: for the destruction of any building in the course of a riot and for demanding food or money with menances – death as a felon: causing damage to any machinery or for sending any letter anonymously or with a fictitious signature threatening to burn houses, stacks or other property – transportation.

The learned judge concluded these remarks by exhorting the influential gentlemen of the county to exert themselves to removing the causes which led to these outrages 'by giving a proper education to the poor – not merely by teaching them to read and write, but by early instructing them in their duty to society.'

During the next three days fifty-three men were arraigned on the same charge of 'feloniously destroying a Threshing Machine'. Eighteen of them were acquitted, thirty received sentences of imprisonment with hard labour for periods ranging from three to eighteen months, including William Wyles, whose arm was broken in the axe attack on Richard Perceval in the final battle at Glatton, and who received a twelve-month sentence. The most severe punishment was reserved for the five ringleaders; John Simon Clarke, aged 20, and Thomas Stapleton, 39, who were present when the riots began at Sawtry on Wednesday November 24th and were also in the group which roamed north to Morborne and Alwalton on the 27th. They were sentenced to be transported for fourteen years. William Horner, one of the ringleaders of the southern group which was broken up near Huntingdon, was transported for seven years as were William Hughes, aged 23, and 26 years old William Colley. All five later sailed together to Van Dieman's Land to serve their time.

At an earlier trial in Wiltshire, Mr. Justice Alderson, one of the two Huntingdonshire judges, had commented when passing a sentence of seven years' transportation on three men for machine breaking:

> "I hope that your fate will be a warning to others. You will leave the country, all of you: you will see your friends and relations no more: for though you will be transported for seven years only, it is not likely that at the expiration of that term you will find yourselves in a situation to return. You will be in a distant land at the expiration of your sentence. The land which you have disgraced will see you no more: the friends with whom you are connected will be parted from you for ever in this world."[33]

These chilling words, spoken with apparent relish, demonstrate not only the essential cruelty of the punishment but also the callous vindictiveness of those who had felt threatened by the labourers' abortive uprising.

Throughout the 34 counties affected by the riots nearly 2,000 were charged, although many more had taken part. A Dorset magistrate wrote to the Home Office, "had we committed for participating in and aiding the burning of machinery, we might have committed two-thirds of the labouring population of the district." In all more than 600 were imprisoned, 500 transported and 252 sentenced to death, only 19 of whom were actually executed,[34] the rest having their sentences commuted mainly to transportation to the Australian colonies.

On the very day the Huntingdon Gazette published the main details of the Assize trials Richard Newby, a Cambridge bookseller, placed the following advertisement at the head of column one of the relevant page of the newspaper:

'HERTFORDSHIRE
Cambridgeshire and General Country
FIRE OFFICE

RICHARD NEWBY, Bookseller, Trinity Street,
AGENT to the above Establishment
respectfully informs the public that he is authorized
to receive Orders for INSURANCES on FARMING
STOCK at the rate affixed on that species of property
prior to the disturbances and firings which recently
raged throughout the country, and without any
additional charge for the use or keep of THRASHING
MACHINES.'

References

NOTE: Reports of the riots and the subsequent trials are taken from 'The Herts., Huntingdon, Bedford, Cambridge and Isle of Ely Mercury', 4 DEC 1830 and 'The Huntingdon, Bedford and Peterborough Gazette', 4 DEC 1830, 12 and 19 MAR 1831, and the verdicts from PRO, Criminal Registers, Huntingdon, 1831 (HO27/41)

[1] Cobbett, 'Rural Rides', p.29
[2] Wakefield, 'Swing Unmasked'
[3] Huntingdon R.O., Parish registers
[4] Hoskins, 'The Midland Peasant', p.266
[5] Emmison, 'The Relief of the Poor at Eaton Socon', pp. 54/5
[6] Bedfordshire R.O. P.30/12/12
[7] ibid., 30/12/14
[8] Hobsbawm and Rude, 'Captain Swing', p.27.
[9] ibid., p.10
[10] Pinto and Rodway, 'The Common Muse', p.180.
[11] Cobbett, 'Rural Rides', p.267
[12] Godber, 'History of Bedfordshire', p. 472.
[13] Huntingdonshire R.O., 2306/8/2 (21 DEC 1831)

[14] Horn, 'Life and Labour in Rural England,' p. 91
[15] Pinto and Rodway, 'The Common Muse', p. 187.
[16] Hammond, J L. and B., 'The Village Labourer, p. 278
[17] Hobsbawm and Rude, 'Captain Swing', Intro. xxi
[18] ibid., p.51
[19] Cobbett, 'Rural Rides, p.248
[20] Hobsbawm and Rude, 'Captain Swing', Intro. xxiii
[21] Hammond, J.L. and B., 'The Village Labourer', p.243
[22] Hobsbawm and Rude, 'Captain Swing', pp.71-73
[23] ibid., pp.86/7
[24] Harrison, 'The Common People', p.251
[25] Hobsbawm and Rude, 'Captain Swing', pp.76-78
[26] ibid., p.94
[27] ibid., p.78
[28] Rule, J. 'The Labouring Classes', p.359
[29] Hammond, J.L. and B., 'The Village Labourer', pp.183and 278
[30] Hobsbawm and Rude, 'Captain Swing', pp.113 and 177
[31] Horn, 'Life and Labour in Rural England', p.84
[32] Huntingdon R.O., Quarter Sessions Papers, DEC 1830.
[33] Hammond, J.L. and B., 'The Village Labourer' p.295
[34] Hobsbawm and Rude, 'Captain Swing' pp. 100 and 224

CHAPTER SIX

THE RESURRECTION MEN[1]

'When you're in bed you'll hear my tread, the middle of the night time;
I does my work in dark and murk – for me that's just the right time.
I digs the nice new corpses up from their graves so dark and narrer;
I lugs 'em out and wraps 'em up and bungs 'em in my barrer.
The stiff 'uns never worry me when I'm upon my mettle;
You take my word, the new-interred they don't have time to settle.'
Anon: early music hall song

In the same week in which the destruction of threshing machines had started at Sawtry in mid-Huntingdonshire, an outrage of a different kind occurred just ten miles due north on the county boundary with Northamptonshire.

On Monday 22nd November William Weston, who had lodgings in the New Town area of Peterborough, crossed the River Nene to visit his wife who lived in the nearby Huntingdonshire village of Woodstone. As he was returning to Peterborough he noticed a sack lying in a hovel near Thorpe Lane belonging to a Mr Johnson. The door of this lean-to shed had been left open and, as something about it had clearly aroused his suspicion, he went in, felt the sack, and became convinced that it contained a corpse. He returned to his lodging at three in the afternoon but, being frightened, he told no-one about it until six hours later when, presumably fortified by drink, he confided in John

Spriggs, the landlord of a local New Town beerhouse. Spriggs called his lodger and the three of them went to the hovel and agreed that the sack's contents certainly felt like a dead body. Between them they carried it about twelve yards away and hid it behind a hedge. Not being sure what to do, Spriggs then left to seek advice and was told to put the sack and its contents back where they had been found.

In the meantime, William Weston had obviously repeated his secret to others so that when Spriggs returned an hour later a crowd of curious onlookers had gathered at the hovel. He waited another hour for them to disperse, but as it was now half-past eleven at night, he decided to take the sack to a safe place in case someone should steal it and he be blamed for making the story up. So Spriggs, his lodger and two other men took the sack from behind the hedge and set off towards Spriggs' beer house. On the way they met Samuel Ladds, a Peterborough whitesmith, a Mr Grimmer and another man making their way to Mr Johnson's hovel. Ladds later said that Grimmer and his companion had come to his yard at 11pm, told him that a body had been discovered and asked him to help them with it. The two parties then joined forces and together they carried the sack and put it in John Spriggs' brewhouse where, for the first time, the sack was opened. By this time Grimmer had disappeared but he will feature prominently later.

When the sack was opened up it revealed what the men had all along suspected. It was a woman's body with one of her top front teeth missing which Samuel Ladds thought was that of Mrs Elizabeth Billings, a Peterborough woman who had been recently buried in St. John the Baptist's churchyard. The brewhouse door was then locked and the men all went home in the early hours of Tuesday.

At eight-o-clock that same morning the widower, William Billings, and several others came to identify the corpse. After he had looked at the face and hair Billings said he thought it was his wife but that, "she has altered a good deal". He left and came back at ten with a coffin and the startling news that his wife's body had gone from the churchyard. Once again he confirmed that he was sure the corpse was hers. At this the men left the brewhouse to Spriggs' wife and three other women who prepared the corpse and laid it in the coffin. Spriggs then replaced the lid, locked the door and left the coffined corpse there until the next day.

William Billings returned at 7am on the Wednesday with Samuel Ladds; both still believing the corpse to be that of Billings' wife. Whilst they and Spriggs looked on, the coffin was screwed down and Ladds, with five other men who had come by, accompanied by Billings and his mother-in-law, carried it to the same grave in Peterborough churchyard from which it had been taken. The coffin was lowered into the grave and half covered with earth when Samuel Ladds left.

All the participants clearly suspected that what had happened was a bungled body snatching, and they were right but it was not, as they had thought, an attempt by the 'sack-'em-up men' to steal Mrs Billings' body, but that of another woman from a quite different churchyard.

Body snatching was big business in the first thirty years of the nineteenth century. For more than fifty years there had been a growing demand for corpses by the anatomy departments of the large London and provincial hospitals and the many private anatomy schools. They were needed by surgeons for dissection in order to learn more about the human body, to train their successors and to improve their own surgical skills. That these needed improvement is evident when it is recalled that no form of anaesthesia, except alcohol, was known and 'surgery was accomplished on the conscious, screaming patient, by surgeons with dirty overalls, dirty instruments and dirty hands. The operating table was a slab of wood, channelled to allow the blood to drip down into buckets of sawdust'.[2] If a patient did not die from the trauma of the operation itself, then there was every chance that septicaemia would succeed where the knife had failed. 'Wounds were dressed using methods known almost from the beginning of recorded history, with no regard for cleanliness'.[3]

But bodies were in extremely short supply. The only corpses which could legally be used for dissection were those of hanged murderers so that demand exceeded supply and the most eminent of surgeons connived at, and even encouraged, the activities of the body-snatchers or 'Resurrection Men' as they were also irreverently known.

This callous exhumation of the newly dead understandably induced a sense of horror. Those who could afford them purchased impregnable triple coffins or protected their graves with iron cages. The poor would keep a watch all night over the burial places of their loved ones until the corpse had decomposed sufficiently to be of little, or no, commercial value. That fear of desecration is echoed in the epitaph inscribed over the body of Mary Gidney who died at Great Yarmouth where there had been a spate of grave robberies:

> 'May spotless spirits of the just
> Watch o'er her Tomb and Guard her Dust;
> Preserve it safe in soft repose,
> Till the Arch Angel's Trumpet blows,
> And then immortal may it rise
> And mount in glory to the skies!'[4]

The outraged sensibilities of the bereaved were compounded by that popular half-belief in the physical resurrection of the body when 'the trumpet shall sound and the dead shall be raised incorruptible'.[5] Without the remains of the earthly body, it was thought, what would the soul inhabit on the day of judgement? Or, as a prosecuting lawyer expressed it:

'every decent man would expect, that when he had followed the body of his wife or daughter to the silent tomb, "where the wicked cease from troubling, and the weary are at rest," their cold clay should there remain till the last trump shall sound, and the graves give up their dead.'[6]

In the 'Pathetic Ballad of Mary's Ghost', Thomas Hood described how the bereaved William was woken in the middle of the night by the ghost of his recently deceased wife with the words:

> 'The body-snatchers they have come,
>   And made a snatch at me;
> It's very hard them kind of men,
>   Won't let a body be!'
>
> 'That arm that used to take your arm
>   Is took to Dr Vyse;
> And both my legs are gone to walk
>   The hospital at Guy's'[7]

As this ghoulish verse makes clear, it was not only whole bodies which were needed by the anatomists or their pupils, but any spare limbs or organs were useful for cutting up for practice or study. One of the most valuable items was teeth which were in great demand for making dentures. In fact, many body-snatchers extracted the teeth as soon as the corpse was 'lifted' because, as one explained, 'if the body be lost, the teeth are saved.'[8] One enterprising man, named Murphy, managed to gain entry to the burial vault attached to a Nonconformist chapel and in a few hours extracted enough teeth to earn himself £60.[9] The so-called 'Waterloo teeth', taken from the corpses of dead soldiers on Continental battlefields were shipped over in their thousands after the end of the Napoleonic Wars for this same purpose. Even a good set of teeth from a decomposed corpse could fetch up to £30.[10]

Tom Butler, a porter in the dissecting room at St. Thomas' Hospital procured bodies for the surgeon, Sir Astley Cooper, and was suspected of digging them up himself. When he had to leave his hospital job, Cooper sent him with a letter of recommendation to his nephew, Bransby, who was gaining experience as an assistant surgeon with the Royal Artillery, then serving in Spain under Wellington. When Bransby Cooper asked Butler the purpose of his visit, Butler replied, "Teeth" adding, "Oh, sir, only let there be a battle and there'll be no want of teeth. I'll draw them as fast as the men are knocked down". When he returned to England he sold the teeth he had pulled from the dead and dying for £300 and used the money to set up as a dentist in Liverpool.[11]

This trade in teeth was notorious and openly discussed. A Professor of Anatomy at Trinity College, Dublin, objected to a charitable offer to pay for a watch to be kept on the hospital burial ground, which held a large concentration of pauper graves, including those buried from the hospital, on the grounds that it would damage the interests of the medical school which brought business to the value of £70,000 to the city. He argued:

'I do not think the upper and middle classes have understood the effects of their own conduct when they take part in impeding the process of dissection . . . very many of the upper ranks carry in their mouths teeth which have been buried in the hospital fields.'[12]

This lucrative trade attracted those with even fewer scruples than were displayed by the 'legitimate professionals' of the bodysnatching fraternity. Two years before Elizabeth Billings' body was discovered at Peterborough Burke and Hare had committed at least sixteen murders, selling the bodies for between £5 and £10 each to an Edinburgh anatomy school.[13] Almost three years after Hare had turned King's evidence and, in so doing, convicting his accomplice to hanging and public dissection, two London men, Bishop and Williams were executed for what by then had become popularly known as the crime of 'burking'. They had murdered Carlo Ferrari, a poor Italian boy from Bethnal Green, who made his living by showing white mice.[14] Like their other victims he had been doped with rum laced with laudanum and, when insensible, suspended upside down in the well in Bishop's garden. This ingenious method left no marks or other evidence of violent death. It was only the freshness of the body, still in rigor mortis, and the fact that it had not been prepared for burial, which aroused the suspicions of an anatomy demonstrator at King's College Hospital and eventually betrayed them. On the eve of his execution it was rumoured that Williams confessed that he and Bishop had together murdered about sixty people for sale to the anatomists.[15]

Before offering the body at King's College, May, a confederate of Bishop and Williams, removed all its teeth leaving blood in the mouth – another most suspicious circumstance: "It was the blood that sold us," complained Bishop to May. The latter was sentenced to be transported but the two murderers were hanged. After their execution it was said that a finely polished set of teeth was displayed in the window of a Southwark dentist with a label attached which read, 'The teeth of Carlo Ferrier (sic) the murdered Italian Boy'. His teeth had been sold for only 12s.6d.[16]

Mrs Billings had lost only one tooth from her upper jaw, very probably during her lifetime. She had not been cruelly disfigured by her adbuctors. After her body had been safely re-interred at Peterborough on Wednesday, November 24th, the matter might have rested there – an unpleasant but by no means uncommon fact of life (or death) in early nineteenth century England – had it not been for a wedding at the parish church of Yaxley, a Huntingdonshire village four miles south of Peterborough, on the morning of Thursday, November 25th.

Near the grave of Jane Mason, who had been buried a week earlier, the wedding party found a flannel cap and near it some lace which had been in her coffin. Closer inspection showed that the grave had been disturbed and they quickly informed Thomas Gilbert a Yaxley labourer and the son-in-law of Jane Mason.

When Gilbert had buried his wife's mother the previous Friday he had been warned by his friend, Abraham Rist, that there were bodysnatchers in the area and the two of them had kept watch over the grave that night until the early hours of Saturday morning. Again, the next night, he repeated the watch with Abraham's brother, John, until two or three on Sunday morning. Once more, at midnight on the Sunday, he went to Yaxley churchyard and twice shot off a gun to frighten off any would-be resurrectionists.

On being told that his mother-in-law's grave had been disturbed, Gilbert set off for Yaxley churchyard with Abraham Rist, opened the grave finding three screws missing from the coffin-lid and the body gone, but the burial linen had been left behind in the earth and underneath the coffin they found hair torn from the back of the head. They also noticed marks made by a sharp instrument on the underside of the coffin as though a hook had been used to pull it out of the grave. Rist immediately told Gilbert that he suspected a certain William Patrick to be the culprit.

Rist had good reason to suspect Patrick – a labourer who lived opposite the Plough beer house in the small village of Farcet which lay half-way between Yaxley and Peterborough – as a result of a Saturday evening spent with him four weeks earlier. On that Saturday Rist had gone to a dance at the Plough and got into conversation with Patrick. He told him of his concern that his brother, John Rist, was about to be arrested for poaching. Patrick replied, "I think I can trust you." Rist said that he thought he could (assuming that Patrick was referring to a poaching exploit) but was surprised when Patrick then asked, "Can you tell me whether any body has been buried lately about here?" When Rist said that he thought not, Patrick continued, "I have lost a good deal of money by not having a constant partner. If I had a constant partner he would have the same money as I get; but if I only get one for a bye night I always give him a sovreign." By this time Rist realised that Patrick was talking about body-stealing and asked, "How can you have the heart to do such things?" Patrick answered, "The first time I went I was drunk or else I could not have done it, but after you have once done it, it is nothing", and went on to explain that he tipped the paid grave watchers with 'a bit of silver' to turn a blind eye to his activities and that he could get rid of the bodies in Peterborough and was never short of money. He was not afraid of being shot on his night time excursions, he claimed, because, "I always carry a blunderbuss and a brace of pistols with me." Rist refused to have anything to do with the business and later warned Gilbert of the threat of local body-snatchers when the latter's mother died three weeks after Patrick's grisly proposition.

Taking the flannel cap discovered by the wedding party near Jane Mason's grave, Gilbert, accompanied by Abraham Rist, went to the Plough at Farcet. There they showed the cap to a local man pretending that they had found it in a field. He immediately recognised it as belonging to Patrick. In his anxiety over the body, Gilbert offered the man a gallon of ale if he would swear to it. At this the man panicked and retracted his statement with the words, "I don't think it is his cap". Being thus baulked of their only witness and having no idea where the corpse might be – by this time it might well have been lying on a London hospital's anatomy slab – they could do no more and returned to Yaxley.

Thomas Gilbert having, presumably, given up all hope of ever finding his mother-in-law's body again, must have been surprised when he heard a rumour that she might have been buried at Peterborough. The next day he set off to obtain the incumbent's permission to re-open the Peterborough grave.

Once more Samuel Ladds, the Peterborough whitesmith, was called out. This time it was to help Thomas Gilbert open up the same grave in which exactly one week earlier Ladds had seen the corpse he had identified as Mrs Billings re-interred (as he had thought at the time). William Billings, the grieving widower, accompanied the exhumation party. Ladds opened the grave and, as soon as he had unscrewed the coffin lid, Gilbert recognised the body of his mother-in-law, Jane Mason. Samuel Ladds later testified that he did not hear Billings say a word. Poor Billings must have been dumbstruck as he had earlier identified his wife's corpse, although, "she had altered a good deal", and moreover, had gone to Peterborough churchyard and returned saying that his wife's body had disappeared. As Thomas Gilbert immediately recognised the corpse as that of Jane Mason it could not have been badly decomposed, leaving us with the thought that Billings must either have been a peculiarly unobservant husband or more than usually stupid, more especially as he had been married less than a year and his wife at 23 had been only half Jane Mason's age. Whether or not Elizabeth Billings' body had been 'lifted' we shall never know but, at least, Jane Mason's was once more put to rest in her original coffin in Yaxley churchyard by her son-in-law.

Abraham Rist's suspicions of William Patrick combined with the earlier identification of Patrick's cap were strengthened by another witness who had met two men he believed to be Patrick and a young Farcet labourer called William Whaley late on the evening of Sunday November 21st near Farcet church: the night when it was believed Jane Mason's corpse had disappeared.

Taken together, these facts were enough to persuade Thomas Gilbert to lay charges against both men. They were immediately arrested and, after a week in Huntingdon gaol, young William Whaley confessed the whole story. In it he described how he was lured into this gruesome trade, of how he and Patrick actually went about 'resurrecting' Jane Mason's corpse and of its subsequent intermittent four-mile journey from Yaxley churchyard to Peterborough.

Whaley claimed that since last Michaelmas Patrick had tried several times to persuade him to go along with him to steal corpses until about five weeks earlier when he had finally agreed to accompany Patrick to Peterborough. When they reached the burial ground Patrick opened up the grave, looked at the corpse and complained, "It will not do, the man who has put me into this business has marked the wrong grave." This one abortive attempt must have frightened Whaley. As they left the graveyard he allegedly said, "I will never be concerned in this business again; thank God I've got out of it."

One Sunday, three weeks later however, Whaley was drinking in the Plough beer house at Farcet and had already drunk three or four pints when Patrick sat down beside him saying, "I know of a corpse at Yaxley", and, holding out a half-sovreign, asked, "Do you know what this means, will you go with me? I'll give you this if we have luck tonight." Whaley refused and they sat drinking until ten o'clock when the landlady turned them out. As they left to go to Patrick's house across the road, Patrick stole a shovel belonging to the Plough landlord. By this time Whaley had been drinking for over four hours and put up no resistance when he was given the shovel, a plank hook and a potato sack which was later identified by John Spriggs, the New Town beerhouse keeper, as the one in which he had found what he thought to be Elizabeth Billings' corpse.

The two of them set off on the two-mile walk to Yaxley which they reached a little before midnight. Patrick pointed out a new grave between the causeway and the churchyard wall and Whaley started to dig whilst Patrick kept a lookout. They continued digging in turns until the coffin lid was cleared when a gun-shot rang out. After waiting at the graveside for a short while there was a second shot so close that Whaley saw the powder flash. These were the shots fired by Thomas Gilbert to scare off any would-be bodysnatchers from his mother-in-law's grave where she had been buried only two days before. "For God's sake we shall be taken", cried Whaley, but nothing more was heard and Patrick set to work with a knife to remove the screws from the head and shoulders of the coffin lid. Then, using the plank hook, he tried to prise open the lid but could not get it to spring off. He said to Whaley, "You try to pull the corpse out while I hold the lid up", but this gruesome task did not appeal to young Whaley and they changed places. Patrick dragged out Jane Mason's corpse, cut off the burial linen and threw it back in the grave, sacked up the body 'neck and heels' and together they re-filled the hole.

Patrick lifted the corpse on to Whaley's back whilst he carried the tools and they set off along the lane leading towards Peterborough. After a short distance the body's dead weight became too much for Whaley. "For God's sake take this away from me for I can't carry it no farther", he complained and so they exchanged burdens until they reached a little close where they put the corpse in a ditch by the side of a hedge and, carrying the tools, they retraced their steps northwards to Farcet. On their way home young Whaley asked how the body was to be taken away, but his companion only replied, "You have no occasion to see any fear so long as you get your money", adding, "the Gentleman that takes these bodies off me gets so much of the money that I hope another year I shall have a letter from London directing me where to send them to, so that I may have the whole myself." Then he swore, "I've lost my cap. My gloves are in my hat but my cap's gone." But despite this they carried on to Patrick's house where Whaley was given a half-sovreign with the words, "Here old boy, this is easier than going to work a whole week for it." Whaley eventually got home betwen two and

'You try to pull the corpse out while I hold the lid up.'

three in the morning of Monday, November 22nd. Much later that morning on his way to work rather later than usual he met Patrick again and learned part of the answer to his question of the previous night as Patrick told him, "As soon as I got in bed a man with a cart and horse came to my door and called me up and I went with him and put the corpse in a cart and I came about my business and he went about his." It must have been this unknown man who carted the body of Jane Mason to Peterborough leaving it in Mr Johnson's hovel for someone else to collect, box up and, in all probability, convey by carrier cart to London for dissection. Unfortunately for them it was first discovered by William Weston returning from visiting his wife in Woodstone.

When William Patrick was examined by a Huntingdonshire magistrate, he declined to say anything about the Yaxley affair but did confess to previous exploits and the involvement of a certain Mr Grimmer – an appropriate name for one engaged in so grisly a business. He claimed that this Grimmer had at first asked him how he managed with a sick wife and young children. Patrick admitted, "Very badly: I have a nurse to find and a wife, three children and myself to keep and it takes all I can earn. I'm forced to run in debt at times." To which Grimmer replied, "I think I can put you in a way to get a little money if you do as I tell you, that is if you'll raise me a body or two." Patrick protested, "Sir, I don't know how to do it – I don't know what tools they have neither." "Damn it, man alive," said Grimmer, "Spring has got a set of tools and I'll see if I can get them off him."

When Patrick next met him on his way to Peterborough fair, Grimmer explained that he had seen the man called Spring but that the only tool he had left was a hook which he then described to Patrick who recognised it, saying, "If that's all, I can get such a one made, it's only a plank hook" and he later had a strong hook attached to a length of rope made up locally. When asked how he was to get rid of any bodies he dug up Grimmer explained, "That you'll have nothing to do with – I'll take it all upon myself to convey them away. When there's any interred I'll let you know".

A few days later Grimmer informed him that one was to be buried at Peterborough. Patrick persuaded William Whaley to go with him but they 'got disappointed'. Grimmer had obviously marked the wrong grave and, on his first outing, Whaley had got cold feet. Patrick claimed one success when Grimmer told him of the burial of a man and a child and that night he did that job alone, packing the bodies in a hamper and taking them to Farcet from where they were sent on to Peterborough. From there to be collected by Grimmer, one supposes.

Grimmer was undoubtedly a middle-man with contacts in London to whom he sold the bodies dug up by men like Patrick who were paid a few pounds. The going rate for an adult corpse at this time was around eight guineas, double what it had been fifteen years earlier and, such was the demand, especially in the London hospitals and anatomy schools, that it had risen about four-fold since the 1790's when an adult body fetched two guineas and a crown (£2.7s), whilst those of children sold for 'six shillings for the first foot, and nine (pence) per inch for all it measures more in length'[17] – or £1.8.6d for a child three feet six inches tall – such were the macabre financial calculations.

Patrick had told Abraham Rist that he paid a casual partner a sovreign (although he only gave poor William Whaley half that sum), but that he would pay a regular helper the same as he received. If, therefore, he were to pay both himself and his regular partner double what a casual was worth it would have amounted to four pounds, leaving the middle-man, Grimmer, with at least four pounds profit less the cost of transporting the corpse to London. Such a sum, equivalent to two months' wages for a labouring man, was quite enough to tempt Grimmer to try to recover the body from Mr Johnson's hovel.

Jane Mason's corpse had been dumped there in the early hours of Monday morning, November 22nd, by the mysterious man with the horse and cart who had collected it from a Yaxley ditch where Patrick and Whaley had left it. By mid-afternoon that same day William Weston had found it but only told John Spriggs, the New Town beer-house keeper, at 9 o-clock that evening. At 11 pm Grimmer came to Samuel Ladds' whitesmith yard and persuaded Ladds to help him take it away. But they had been beaten to it by John Spriggs and his party whom they met coming away from the hovel carrying the sacked-up corpse. At this point Grimmer disappears from all the witnesses' evidence and one presumes that he then decided to cut his losses having already paid William Patrick earlier in the day when the latter went to Peterborough to collect his money.

Grimmer was never identified. Young William Whaley was

induced to turn King's evidence and went free, whilst William Patrick pleaded 'guilty' and received a twelve-month prison sentence on January 4th 1831[18] at the Epiphany Quarter Sessions and was committed to Huntingdon gaol from where he escaped four months later.[19]

In an age when to steal the body of a dead sheep was a capital offence and even to receive it, knowing it to have been stolen, was punishable by transportation to Botany Bay or Van Dieman's Land, it seems strange that William Patrick, for an action which appears to us to be far more reprehensible, received so light a sentence. The answer lies in an anomaly of English law which did not recognise any property rights in a dead human body: it could not be owned and, therefore, it could not be stolen.[20] A body-snatcher could be found guilty of theft of the coffin itself or of the grave clothes, but Patrick had carefully cut these off and left them behind in the earth with the coffin. He was originally charged with '. . . breaking open the grave in which one Jane Mason had been there lately interred and with taking and carrying away the body . . . ' The minute of his trial records that he was convicted, 'For a Misdemeanour in breaking open a Grave at Yaxley and thereout taking of dead Body of Jane Mason'. There was, however, no such crime in English law, but, equally, everyone thought that there should have been, especially when it was known that a stolen corpse was to be 'anatomised'.

It was for flagrantly flouting community morality – not for breaking the criminal code, that William Patrick was gaoled by the Huntingdon Grand Jury, but we should be wrong to say that it was a miscarriage of common justice when Jane Mason's relations had been outraged and distressed by the callous desecration of her grave. A prosecutor in another case summed up what most people felt about grave robbery when he indicted the accused with these words:

'. . . for the sake of wicked lucre and gain (the accused) did take and carry away the said body, and did sell and dispose of the same for the purpose of being dissected, cut in pieces, mangled and destroyed, to the great scandal and disgrace of religion, decency and morality."[21]

It is pleasing to note that this sinister trade in dead bodies practically ceased two years later, but, perhaps, less so when one realises that the means whereby it was ended was an Act of Parliament which empowered workhouse masters to send the mortal remains of the destitute to the dissecting rooms instead.

References

[1] The chapter is largely based on the evidence of William Patrick, William Whaley (or Whayley), Thomas Pindard, William Weston, Thomas Gilbert, Abraham Rist, Samuel Ladds and John Spriggs - Quarter Sessions Papers, 1830 - Huntingdon R.O.
[2] Richardson, 'Death, Dissection and the Destitute', p.41.
[3] ibid.
[4] ibid., p.85
[5] I. Corinthians, ch.15, v. 52.
[6] Richardson, 'Death, Dissection and the Destitute', p.77.
[7] Jerrold, 'Thomas Hood', p.77
[8] Richardson, 'Death, Dissection and the Destitute', p.67
[9] ibid.
[10] Hibbert, 'The English, A Social History', p.444
[11] Low, 'Thieves' Kitchen', pp.88/9
[12] Richardson, 'Death, Dissection and the Destitute', p.106
[13] ibid., p.337
[14] Low, 'Thieves' Kitchen', p.103
[15] Richardson, 'Death, Dissection and the Destitute', p.196/7
[16] ibid., p.352
[17] ibid., p.57
[18] Huntingdon R.O., Quarter Sessions Minute Book, 1829-35, and PRO., HO27/41.
[19] Huntingdon R.O., Quarter Sessions Papers, 28 May 1831.
[20] Richardson, 'Death, Dissection and the Destitute, p.59.
[21] ibid., p.27

CHAPTER SEVEN

THE POVERTY PRISON

> 'As an invariable rule, the agricultural labourer commences his career as a weekly labourer; and, whatever may be his talents and industry, he must inevitably end his days as a labourer, or, when unfitted through old age to continue his work, die as a pauper.'
>
> – The Morning Chronicle (1849)[1]

> 'Nearly all the agricultural labourers of England may be said to be paupers, either actual, or past, or prospective. In many counties there is scarcely a labourer who does not contemplate the possibility of having to apply for relief for his family or for himself in sickness, and who does not reckon upon the certainty of coming to his parish in his old age.'
>
> – The Times (1849)[2]

' . . . the bodies of those who during life have been maintained at the public charge, and who die in workhouses, hospitals, and other charitable institutions, should, if not claimed by next of kin within a certain time after death, be given up . . . to the Anatomist.'[3] These were the words which effectively destroyed the grave-robbers' trade in exhumed bodies. They formed the main recommendation of the Select Committee on Anatomy which reported to Parliament in July 1828. The Committee took evidence from medical men on the vital need for anatomical specimens for dissection in order to improve knowledge and surgical skills, on the great difficulty in obtaining an adequate supply, and their affected distaste in having to deal with the criminals who provided the bodies – although in law the doctors were as guilty as their suppliers, but no-one raised that awkward point.

If a legal source of bodies were needed for the purposes of medical science then they had to come from somewhere. Such was the horror at the thought of one's mortal remains being dismembered that virtually no-one was sufficiently public-spirited to volunteer their own for this worthy cause, but the recipients of public charity would, some thought, be only too pleased to have the opportunity to repay the kindnesses they had received in this corporeal form. Ralph Leycester, a member of the Select Committee, claimed that "it would, indeed, be a melancholy satisfaction to those whose last moments received consolation from the public charities, to know that they would be able after death . . . to repay the debt they owed to those who administered comfort to them during the last stage of their existence."[4] What Leycester and his fellow legislators conveniently ignored was that for 80 years the only legal source of dissection material had been the corpses of executed criminals.

Until the middle of the eighteenth century the law prescribed only one of method disposing of an executed body – hanging in chains. The hangman cut the rope, covered the body with tar and enclosed it in an iron cage which was left to hang on a creaking gibbet in a public place or at the scene of the crime as a terrible warning to others until the flesh had rotted or the birds had picked its skeleton clean. In 1752 an Act was passed which allowed the judge the discretion of ordering instead what was thought to be an even more terrifying punishment, hanging followed by dissection, which was described as 'a further Terror and peculiar Mark of Infamy'.[5]

Dr Thomas Southwood Smith, a proponent of dissection as a means of enhancing medical knowledge, nevertheless had some understanding of the abhorrence with which ordinary people regarded the practice when he wrote that the poor imagine '. . . that they live only for the rich; this detestable practice leads them to suppose that they must still serve their masters even after death has set them free from toil, and that when the early dawn can no longer rouse them from the pallet of straw to work, they must be dragged from what should be their last bed, to show in common with the murderer, how the knife of the surgeon may best avoid the rich man's artery, and least affect the rich man's nerve.'[6]

Of course, if the body was claimed by the next of kin it would not suffer the indignity of dissection. The Select Committee recommended that the anatomists should only have those bodies 'who have either no known relatives whose feelings would be outraged, or such only as, by not claiming the body, would evince indifference on the subject of dissection.' One might have thought, therefore, that if the deceased's relatives turned up at the parish workhouse to attend the funeral the corpse would then be buried in the normal way. But the authorities interpreted the somewhat ambiguous provisions of the Act differently. Everything hinged on the word 'claimed'. Parish officers considered that if the body was claimed by the next of kin then it was no longer their responsibility. Instead, the relatives were expected to remove the body and arrange and pay for the funeral. If they could not afford the cost then they were considered to have given up any right to decide how it should be disposed of. Thus it was that many a grieving family had to witness a perfunctory funeral and watch as the parish cart trundled the body off to be dismembered.[7]

During the first one hundred years of the operation of the Act 'almost 57,000 bodies were dissected in the London anatomy schools alone, less than *half a percent* came from anywhere other than institutions which housed the poor.'[8] – and those institutions were about to be transformed by a Parliament which had recently 'reformed' itself but remained as grossly unrepresentative as ever.

Those who paid the poor rate increasingly complained of its heavy and growing burden: it had risen from £1.5m to £7m in fifty years.[9] As the farmers saw it, the practice of paying labourers an allowance from the rates to supplement their inadequate wages had made them so dependent on the parish that they had come to regard the weekly dole as their right and not as relief paid at the discretion of the overseer. The men were not grateful, but insolent and surly, they worked reluctantly and needed constant supervision, confident that their parish allowance would be paid whether they worked conscientiously, lazily or not at all.

The government responded to this rising tide of complaint by appointing a Royal Commission to investigate the Poor Laws and implemented their recommendations in 1834 under the innocuous-sounding 'Poor Law Amendment Act.' Only in the sense that it changed the system of aiding the destitute could it be described as an 'amendment'. In truth it swept away the existing system and, in its place, imposed something entirely new. Out went the old parish workhouses administered by the Vestry and its unpaid, elected overseers in favour of a Union workhouse serving twenty or thirty parishes run by a Board of Guardians of the Poor who acted under the direct control of a centralised bureaucracy, the Poor Law Commissioners, based in London. All over the country new 'Bastiles', as the people unflatteringly dubbed them, were built at some central point covering an approximate radius of ten miles, in a forbidding architectural style, almost as though they were intended as an ever-present reminder to the local population of what was in store for them if they failed to maintain themselves. One of the Assistant Commissioners later admitted, 'at present their prison-like appearance, and the notion that they are intended to torment the poor, inspires a salutary dread of them.'[10]

At the heart of the New Poor Law lay the principle that an able-bodied man who relied on the Guardians for relief should not find himself to be better off than the poorest labourer capable of maintaining himself and his family by his own efforts – miserable though his existence might be, or, as the Poor Law Report put it, his situation 'shall not be made really or apparently so eligible (i.e. agreeable) as the situation of the independent labourer of the lowest class.'[11]

In practice this so-called 'less-eligibility' rule could never have been effected by providing workhouse inmates with food, clothing and shelter of a lesser quality than that of a labourer in work earning around ten shillings a week and living in a hovel on little more than bread, potatoes and tea – the result would have been the total starvation of the pauper population. Instead, the 'less-eligibility' standard recommended by the Report was achieved by imposing a strict discipline, a denial of comforts or individuality, an ugly uniform, adequate but monotonous meals eaten in complete silence and degrading work with every minute of the day regulated by the workhouse clock. Conditions were deliberately designed to deter all but the most desperate from applying for help. George Crabbe's description of the old parish workhouses could well have been written about the new, improved Bastiles:

> 'That giant-building, that high-bounding wall,
> Those bare-worn walks, that lofty thund'ring hall!
> That large loud clock, which tells each dreaded hour,
> Those gates and locks and all those signs of power;
> It is a prison with a milder name,
> Which few inhabit without dread or shame.'[12]

"Our intention is to make the workhouses as like prisons as possible", said one Assistant Commissioner; another admitted that their object was 'to establish therein a discipline so severe and repulsive as to make them a terror to the poor and prevent them from entering.'[13] Thus, the 'workhouse test' acted as a self-justifying and self-regulating mechanism: if an offer of 'the House' was refused by an applicant, it demonstrated that he was not in real need, if it was accepted then that proved his destitution.

There was to be no 'out-relief' for an able-bodied male applicant. If he fell on hard times his choice was 'the House' or nothing and if he accepted the Guardians' offer he presented himself and his family at the door of the workhouse at the appointed time, since, if a man applied for relief then all his family were required to enter the house with him. A Parliamentary Committee later explained that ' . . . rather than simply taking into the workhouse some of the children of large families, it is recommended that the whole family be taken in earlier, and split up there.' This, the Guardians believed, 'afforded a larger amount of protection to the labourer having a large family.'[14] In other words, it effectively prevented further breeding.

Once in the receiving ward they were examined by the medical officer, their clothes were taken away for fumigation, to be returned on release, and any small private possessions confiscated. Their hair was cropped, they were bathed, disinfected and given the shapeless workhouse uniform,[15] and, finally, the family was broken up by being sent to different wards depending upon their classification by sex, age and fitness.

The women were put to work in the laundry, the kitchen, or as nurses to the elderly and infirm, the men pounded stones for road-mending or crushed bones for sale as fertiliser. Oakum-picking was done by both sexes and all ages; old tarred and matted rope, if unravelled and torn apart, could be sold to the navy for caulking ships. Often no tools were provided, not even a nail, which made the task painful as well as irksome and humiliating.[16]

Children, although separated from them, had to remain in the house as long as their parents were there, although orphans could be apprenticed to a master when they reached the age of nine. They were given a basic education in elementary literacy and Bible study, sometimes supplemented by history and geography, but not all Guardians approved of teaching paupers' off-spring anything which would not be immediately useful to them as adult farm labourers or domestic servants. One East Anglian farmer was quoted as being totally opposed to all the 'new-fangled education that they were giving to the paupers', "I am", he said, "one of the guardians of our union; and I just happened to go into the school-room, and there if the master wasn't telling the boys to point out with a stick, on some big maps that were hanging up, where South Amerikey was, and France, and a lot of other places; and they did it too. Well, when I went home, I told my son of it, and asked him if he could tell me where them places was; and he couldn't. Now, is it right that these here pauper children should know more than the person who will have to employ them?"[17]

Each Union had discretion over the food it provided but most adopted one of the recommended model diets. They had calculated that the average independent labourer ate 122 ounces of solid food a week, but the model diets provided up to half as much again, so the rule of 'less-eligibility' required that workhouse meals should be 'as dull, predictable and tasteless as ingenuity and poor cooking could make them.' Gruel features prominently in fiction and was a virtually universal breakfast dish. It was just 'a thin oatmeal porridge made with water and unflavoured with milk or sugar.' In the early years no cutlery was provided, 'so that bread and cheese had to be broken in the fingers, meat and vegetables were scooped up by hand and gruel was drunk from the bowl.[18]

The whole purpose of the New Poor Law had been to discourage able-bodied men from applying for relief and force them, instead, to support themselves and their families. It had not been the intention of the reformers to punish those who could never be independent. For this reason each inmate was assigned to one of seven categories. The infirm, from whatever cause, the able-bodied aged 15 or over, boys and girls aged 7 – 15 were each strictly separated by category and, of course, by sex. All children under seven formed a single class but rarely, if ever, were allowed to see their parents if, indeed, they had any. In practice, each category was treated in a similar fashion so that the aged, the sick, the feeble-minded and the infant suffered equally under the same severe regimen originally intended to apply only to shiftless, work-shy males. 'Its restrictions', wrote one anonymous supporter of the system, 'are intolerable to the undisciplined mind and vicious habits which generally characterize paupers.'[19] One Assistant Commissioner went so far as to admit that in the minds of some bureaucrats at least, all paupers, whatever their condition, needed to be drilled in the virtues of thrift and independence; 'Neither widows with families, nor the aged and the infirm, nor the sick,' he declaimed, 'should be spared these workhouse humiliations, for fear of sustaining improvidence and imposture, and of sapping the motives to industry . . . '[20]

'The Lay of the Labourer,' written by Thomas Hood only ten years after the New Poor Law was enacted, expresses the bitter hatred of the workhouse engendered in the mind of those its existence was intended to deter:

> 'Wherever Nature needs
> Wherever Nature calls,
> No job I'll shirk of the hardest work,
> To shun the workhouse walls;
> Where savage laws begrudge
> The pauper babe its breath,
> And doom a wife to a widow's life,
> Before her partner's death.'[21]

If there is one thing about the workhouse system which became indelibly imprinted on the national consciousness, apart from the gruel, it was the forcible separation of married couples, especially of those who were nearing the end of their days. "They won't give us anything, except we goes into the house," complained an elderly man to a reporter from the Morning

Chronicle, "and as long as I can arne a sixpence anyhows, they sharn't part me from my wife."[22] Well into the twentieth century old couples still feared the workhouse even though conditions had, by then, improved considerably. Laurie Lee told of Joseph and Hannah Brown, grown too frail even to stand, who were to be moved to the workhouse for their own good in the 1920's:

> 'The old couple were shocked and terrified, and lay clutching each other's hands. 'The Workhouse' – always a word of shame, grey shadow falling on the close of life, most feared by the old (even when called The Infirmary); abhorred more than debt, or prison, or beggary, or even the stain of madness.'
>
> They pleaded in vain to be left alone but 'that same afternoon, white and speechless, they were taken away to the Workhouse, Hannah Brown was put to bed in the Women's Wing, and Joseph lay in the Men's. It was the first time, in all their fifty years, that they had ever been separated. They did not see each other again, for in a week they both were dead.'[23]

In the same year in which Thomas Hood composed his defiant poem, 'The Lay of the Labourer', William Howitt, a Quaker reformer, wrote of the New Poor Laws that 'every poor man's family is liable, on the occurrence of some chance stroke of destitution, to have to their misfortune, bitter enough in itself, added the tenfold aggravation of being torn asunder, and immured in the separate wards of a POVERTY PRISON.'[24] The feeling that it had now become not simply a misfortune, but a crime, to be poor was not confined to a soft-hearted Quaker; many shared the same thought and, like this political broadsheet, asked the question

> 'Why should the Whigs raise up their Prisons high
> With gloomy fronts, and walls that reach the sky;
> Are such dark Dungeons to immure a band
> Of Rogues and Swindlers that infest the land?
> 'No!' some cry – 'They are for one crime more
> The crime of being old, infirm and poor!'[25]

The nineteenth century workhouse was all of these:

> an asylum for the insane, the feeble-minded and the socially inadequate;
> a hostel for the vagrant and the derelict;
> an orphanage for the fatherless;
> a hospital for the sick;
> a refuge for the widowed, the deserted wife, the aged, the senile, the handicapped and the incurable, but above all it was a penal institution for the underpaid and unemployed - the only difference being that prison food was better but a workhouse inmate could discharge himself at will.

The old parish workhouse system had had its cruel abuses, its ill-treatment and deprivations, but these were largely as a result of incompetence, the meanness of parish ratepayers or the callousness of individual overseers or workhouse masters. The New Poor Law, on the other hand, was a systematic and brutal attack on the 'lower orders' deliberately designed to cow them into a state of fear of becoming destitute. Its success was judged solely in terms of how many it deterred from accepting the 'hospitality of the House' - and in those terms it was successful far beyond the hopes of its creators.

As the Leeds Mercury reported after the first two years of the new regime's operation 'The workhouse, with continued toil and a bare subsistence, was offered to every able-bodied applicant. *The effect was miraculous.* Idle, profligate, sponging, insolent paupers fled the workhouse, and became steady labourers . . . It has not merely diminished the rates, in whole counties by *one-half*, but it has had an effect absolutely inconceivable before it was produced, in *absorbing* an immense *surplus population*, or apparently surplus population; so that - as it were by magic - where there were before *hundreds* of labourers *unemployed*, there are now absolutely *none*; and - what renders it yet more amazing - this is under a system which makes the labourers *far more industrious*.'[26]

The miraculously beneficial effects of the new laws extended beyond an unbelievably eager willingness to work to what seemed to amount to a revolution in manners and attitude amongst the labourers. 'An improved state of feeling has been brought about between the employer and the employed,' reported the Morning Chronicle, 'men no longer come before the Board (of Guardians) in the rudest possible manner, with their hats on and pipes in their mouths, and insolently demand their scale allowances.'[27] Instead, they showed a proper deference as one of the Guardians of the Ampthill Union in Bedfordshire witnessed, " . . . people now touch their hats to you as they pass; before they were always sulky . . . now they are civil and polite."[28] The Poor Law Amendment Act must be the only piece of legislation in the history of mankind to have achieved so radical an improvement in the behaviour of a whole sector of society.

The imposition of the New Poor Laws did not, however, pass without some expression of popular anger. At Ampthill in mid-Bedfordshire some fifteen miles from St Neots it was the Guardians' insistence on paying an allowance in the form of bread rather than money which sparked a riot.

Mr Osborne, the newly appointed Relieving Officer of the Ampthill Union, rode over to the village of Lidlington on Monday May 11th, 1835 to discuss with the overseer what was to be done about what he described as 'the surplus labourers'. He was met at the overseer's gate by a group of men and women who alledgedly told him, "We don't want you here, we'll have money or blood, and before you leave this place we'll have the money out of your pocket or the blood out of your veins." To make his escape Osborne handed over all the money he had on him. The following day he visited the next parish of Millbrook where he was assaulted by a mob of about 200 and had to take shelter with the local magistrate and remained in hiding until nightfall.

News of these incidents quickly reached Ampthill and on the Wednesday half a dozen constables were sent to Lidlington and arrested two women but were forced to release them when a body of men armed with sticks and hoes threatened them with 'instant annihilation'.

Thursday was the usual day for the Board of Guardians to meet at the Ampthill House of Industry (workhouse). They had not long been in session when people 'came flocking in from the surrounding villages in great numbers' – some claimed as many as five hundred – armed with sticks and bludgeons. They told the Guardians that they wanted to work and to be paid for it in money, but would not take relief in bread. When told that this was not allowed 'the whole body commenced a most furious attack upon the windows with stones, brickbats etc., and when at a loss for those missiles, they tore up a large bed of cabbages and dashed the stalks at the windows, the whole of which were shattered.' The Chairman of the Board, H.M. Musgrave, who was also a magistrate, twice read the Riot Act which had little immediate effect, so in the late afternoon D.G. Adey, the Assistant Poor Law Commissioner who was present at the meeting, was sent to London by express coach to seek help. It arrived next morning in the form of twenty two Metropolitan Police officers who, with the help of some special constables, were sent to arrest the ringleaders. They were examined that same day by four magistrates, three of whom were local clergy. During this week of rioting a large number of special constables were sworn in from the parishes which made up the Ampthill Union, but there is an interesting sidelight in that upwards of one hundred pounds was paid in fines from those who neglected or refused to undertake the office of constable – whether through fear of the mob or in sympathy with them we shall never know.[29]

After the trials at Quarter Sessions and Assize five men were sentenced to death, although the sentence was subsequently commuted and altogether twenty two served terms of imprisonment ranging from three months to two years.[30] Twelve months later Mr Musgrave, the Chairman of the Ampthill Board, was pleased to be able to report to a Parliamentary committee that "the men are more willing to work; the farmers have not anything like the same trouble in looking after them: we are getting, generally speaking, more money than we did before: the master can now leave home with greater comfort than he could before, and when he has returned he has not to find the same fault: there is nicer feeling between master and man; that is increasing very fast indeed."[31]

That 'nicer feeling between master and man' was a self-delusion. The men may have touched their caps in a deferential fashion as they acknowledged the farmer or the squire, but their servile manner cloaked a murderous resentment at having been cowed – Even so, a spark of sturdy independence occasionally surfaced as Alexander Somerville, himself the son of a field-labourer, found when he reported a conversation with a Dorset road-mender breaking flints for eight shillings a week, soon to be reduced to seven shillings. He accused his wealthy-seeming interviewer in these defiant words:

> "You be either a farmer or somebody else that lives on somebody else . . . One thing I see, you ben't one of them as

> works fourteen hours a day, to feed lords, and squires, and parsons, and farmers . . . I dare say you be one of them as has your daughter . . . playing the piano on a Saturday night to drown the noise of them brutes of labouring men what come to get their wages through a hole in the wall; what cannot be allowed to set foot within a farmer's house now-a-days; what must be paid through an opening in the partition, lest they defile the house of a master what gets rich as they get poor; a master what must get his daughter to play music lest the voice of a hard-working man be heard through the hole in the wall!"[32] "

Although the Ampthill riot was one of the most violent of the many protests at the new regulations, the St Neots Union did not escape unscathed. So concerned were the St Neots' Guardians at the activities of a local agitator that they wrote to the Home Secretary: 'On Thursday 4th Instant (AUG. 1836) Mr Maberly came into St Neots accompanied by a large Body of Men with Bludgeons, and Band of Music and Flags, and the language he used was most violent and tending to inflame the minds of the Poor, and to make them dissatisfied with the proceedings of the Guardians.' After describing an attack on one of their officers, their letter continued, 'The Relieving Officers state that the Conduct of the Poor when receiving their Relief since the Meeting is much worse than before and that they are now exceedingly dissatisfied with the Relief as ordered by our Board', and further, 'if some Measures are not adopted to prevent Mr Maberly calling another Meetg. it will be quite impossible to carry on the business of the Union during the Winter in a manner satisfactory either to the Govemt. themselves or the Poor.'[33] This 'Mr Maberly' loomed large in the demonology of those who administered the New Poor Law in the eastern counties. The Revd. F.H. Maberley was the incumbent of a Suffolk parish but lived in the Cambridgeshire village of Bourn only a dozen miles east of St. Neots. His continuing crusade against the new regulations frequently took the form of addressing large assemblies of labouring men which, following his inflammatory rhetoric, sometimes got out of hand and led to violence. His expressed opinion of the New Poor Law was that it was, 'tyrranical, unconstitutional, anti-scriptural, anti-christian, illegal, unnatural, cruel, and impolitic in the extreme. Also, that it is a system of robbery and degradation towards the poor.'[34]

To many farmers the new workhouses were a boon. The 'roundsman' system had required them to find work for the unemployed of the parish, albeit paying them only half the usual wages. Now, with a clear conscience, they could direct them to the care of the Guardians. One spoke of his labourers in terms of 'pitting' or 'clamping' potatoes. He did not keep all the potatoes out for use every day: 'he did not, like some farmers, try to find work for the men all the year round. When he did not need them he put them in the workhouse until they were needed.'[35]

It was the usual custom in parts of East Anglia 'for the farmers to send their teams in order to convey their labourers with their families to the union workhouse for the winter months, and as many as 70 persons have been seen thus to pass through Trimmingham on their way to the union workhouse.'[36] An Essex farmer explained to a London reporter how well cared for his labourers really were: "A man with a family of five children will be nearly able with 6 shillings a week to buy bread enough, if he buys the coarsest flour; his rent he generally pays out of his harvest money; his clothes he gets by some means or other – people sometimes give them to him – and then, when he is unoccupied why we keep him in the workhouse. So you see, sir, he is amply provided for, even with wages at 6s. a week."[37]

The labourers themselves didn't see their situation in quite the same light, as this Suffolk man told the same reporter:' "There's some weeks", said the poor fellow to me, "that we only get four shillings – sometimes less than that – and in very wet weather we gets nothing at all." "How then," said I, "do you manage to subsist, and pay one shilling and sixpence a week for that cottage of yours?" "We can't do it on our wages, you may be sure," he said, "the truth is, master, that we're often driven to do a many things those times that we wouldn't do if we could help it. It is very hard for us to starve; and we sometimes pull some turnips, or p'raps potatoes, out of some of the fields, unbeknown to the farmers . . . "[38]

Given these attitudes and practices, it can scarcely be wondered at that violent and non-violent protests continued. But despite all opposition the new laws were quickly put into effect, at least in the southern counties. The three Poor Law Commissioners together with their indefatigable Secretary,

Edwin Chadwick, held their first meeting on August 23rd 1834. Only thirteen months later the Board of Guardians of the St Neots Union met for the first time at the Cross Keys Inn in St Neots Market Square. Within a very few years the Commissioners' small staff had re-cast the administrative map of England and Wales and, in place of 15,000 parishes, had created 647 poor law unions which ignored traditional county boundaries.[39] They had issued a never-ending stream of regulations, recommendations and exhortations covering everything from detailed account books and admission registers to suggested designs for workhouse construction and model diets for their inmates.

The Huntingdonshire Union of St Neots comprised twenty-eight parishes covering an area eighteen miles long by ten miles wide. Seven Bedfordshire parishes, including Eaton Socon, and one (Graveley) in Cambridgeshire were included in the Union which was responsible for a total population of just over 16,000. The Guardians' first act was to instruct their Clerk to write to the overseers and churchwardens of each parish demanding a list of all paupers relieved by them during the previous week, to be returned within a fortnight.

Two months later, when they knew the extent of the problem facing them, they divided their area into two Districts of roughly equal size and appointed a Relieving Officer to each at a salary of £100 p.a. which was to be paid 'only for the time he acts; the Salary to include all their Services, travelling Expenses, Horse and Horsekeep.' As there was no existing work-house in a central location large enough to be used or adapted for use, they resolved to advertise for land within half a mile of St. Neots for the erection of one to house up to 200 paupers at a cost not exceeding £3,500.[40] In the meantime the three parish workhouses in Eaton Socon, Eynesbury and St Neots were to be rented for that purpose.

Within six months the Guardians, under the guidance of their Assistant Commissioner, Mr Adey, who, it will be remembered, had been involved in the Ampthill riots, had laid down the rules governing the granting of relief. Weekly allowances to the widowed, the orphaned and the old could be continued except that in the case of the aged and infirm the maximum allowance was to be 3s 6d a week. Until Ladyday out-relief could continue to be given to able-bodied men but half had to be in the form of bread. After that date only the workhouse was to be offered to those aged between 30 and 60, whilst men under 30 should get nothing at all. If an applicant had relatives then they were expected to contribute half the cost of support. The Relieving Officer was instructed to report such cases 'to the Board at their next Meeting and order the Pauper to attend.'[41]. Three weeks later the Guardians added a further proviso to cater for instances where an applicant undertook work for the parish, such as road-mending or scavenging, by ruling, 'That the relief given to able-bodied Men in return for Parish work shall be less than the ordinary rate of wages for Labourers in the parish, and shall not exceed ¾ of such Average except in the case of Sickness.'[42]

Mr Gibson, a retired Guards sergeant, was appointed Keeper of the workhouse, his wife Sarah acted as matron and together they were expected to cover all three parish workhouses until a purpose-built house could be constructed. In deciding upon his salary they again consulted Mr Adey who recommended £80 p.a. 'with an allowance of 3 pauper rations daily – house and the necessary Coals and Candles.'[43]

Samuel Bedells, grocer, tea-dealer and tallow chandler of St Neots High Street had tendered for the supply of foodstuffs. The Guardians accepted his prices which included

'Tea for the Master of the Workhouse	5s per lb
Do. for Paupers	4s per lb
Pale Soap	50s per cwt
Oatmeal	12s per bushel'

They also agreed to his additional suggestion that he supply cheese at 72s a cwt. for the Master and 40s a cwt. for the paupers. This discrepancy in quality proved to be a false economy as a month later the Minutes record that 'the cheese from Mr Bedells not being good enough, the Board agreed to contract for cheese at 62s per cwt. from him.'[44] Meat, it would seem, was a rarity in the workhouse diet and justified a special resolution in the Minutes. It was proposed by the Revd. Ridley, 'that the Poor Inmates of the Workhouse have provided them a Dinner of Meat on Christmas Day.'[45]

Local tradesmen were doing quite well out of the New Poor Law as the Guardians accepted a tender from John Brown of St Neots to supply the Union 'with good Wheat Straw, to have the same back after used (sic) for Beds and other purposes – with the Cinder Dust and other Soil being at no Expence for getting it out of the different Vaults.'[46] John Brown, the farmer, clearly knew a good deal when he saw one: he sold his straw to the Union to be stuffed into paupers' mattresses, there to be crushed and pulverised until it had to be replaced when he collected it together with the workhouse's night-soil, dust and ashes which, mixed together, he could use as a fertiliser on his fields to nourish next year's wheat crop, from which the straw could be sold to the Guardians . . . .

The ratepayers of every parish in the Union were entitled to elect one, or in the case of a large parish, two, Guardians to represent their interests. To be eligible one had to occupy property worth at least £25 a year,[47] equivalent to a labourer's annual wage. This effectively precluded any of their number from standing, that is assuming that one might have had the temerity to contest an election against a local farmer or tradesman. In addition, nine 'ex officio' Guardians were entitled to attend and these included the Revd. William Palmer, the rector of Eynesbury and a local magistrate. Altogether, therefore, the Board comprised over forty members but, perhaps fortunately, very few attended the weekly meetings regularly; in fact their Clerk had to record many meetings which were abandoned as none of the Guardians had appeared at the appointed time. Their first Chairman was Henry Peter Standly, a landowner of Paxton Park to the north of St Neots. Eynesbury was represented by Edward Peck, a substantial farmer who had married well and, through his wife, had inherited Shirdley House in Eynesbury's Front Street facing the Green.[48] St Neots was entitled to two representatives, G.A. Peppercorn, brother of Lord Sandwich's agent, owned Manor Farm in St Neots[49]. The second Guardian was Edward Toogood the owner of St. Neots Paper Mill, the only substantial manufacturing plant in the town.[50] These four men were not untypical of Guardians in the rural areas who tended to represent landowning, farming and small business interests. In fact, of the Eynesbury and St Neots Guardians elected during the first five years of the Union, there were four farmers, one manufacturer and William Islip, 'a linen and woollen draper and dealer in broad cloth'.[51] They were all men of standing and some education and probably not, for the most part, as ignorant as an East Anglian Guardian who was reported to have argued against giving a man an honorarium on the grounds that, "If he had one he couldn't play on it. I am for giving him hard cash."[52] Nor, in all probability, as crass as Mr Blackwood who considered it an excessive expense to spend £6 'to keep the kitchen, serving room and dining hall of the Paddington Union free of beetles and cockroaches', he could kill them for next to nothing, he claimed, adding, "You should get a hedgehog and a tortoise."[53]

The Guardians' initial enthusiasm for building a new workhouse quickly waned. After advertising for land and agreeing to offer a prize of £15 to the winner of a competition to design the building, they seem to have had second thoughts. Within a year they were asking permission of the London Commissioners instead to take out a long lease on the three old parish workhouses and had even considered asking the Bedford Union if they would take the St Neots paupers for a fee. This Board of Guardians exasperated their Assistant Commissioner who wrote to his superiors in London asking for a simple workhouse plan with comparative costings in an effort 'to disarm those who have been hitherto frightened by the expense and too architectural appearance of some of the New Houses', adding that 'this is a most difficult Union to manage.'[54]

The Guardians' infirmity of purpose was ended, however, by the election of William Ward Abbott, the unpopular surveyor and auctioneer who had earlier been hanged in effigy outside his own home. William Ward Abbott lived in Eynesbury, had his offices in St Neots but eventually managed to get himself elected as Guardian for Midloe which was not a parish at all but still entitled to one representative. At only his second meeting he gave notice of his intention to propose a resolution that a workhouse should be built. His motion was eventually carried by a majority of one at a meeting attended by nineteen Guardians.[55] Still nothing happened for a further eighteen months when Abbott tried again by proposing a building to house 300 paupers at a cost not to exceed £5,000. This was deferred for four weeks. The minutes record no further action for another twelve months except for a vain attempt by Abbott to have the new Clerk's salary reduced from £90 to £60 per annum which was lost by 26 votes to 7.[56] That topic, at least, brought the Guardians out in force. Finally, on Boxing Day 1839, after more than four years of the Union's existence, the Board approved plans proposed by the

Commissioners and accepted William Ward Abbott's offer 'to make out the working drawings and specification gratuitously for the purpose of submitting them to public competition.'[57] A plot of land in Eaton Socon, half a mile from St Neots Market Square, was purchased from William Peppercorn, the brother of one of St Neots' original Guardians, and tenders sought for building materials including '400,000 hard burnt white mingled Bricks.'[58]

At last, in late October, Abbott was appointed Surveyor and Architect to the Board – a position, we might be forgiven for suspecting, he had been angling for ever since his election three and a half years earlier. At its next meeting the Board, quite properly, accepted Abbott's resignation as the member for Midloe, but a week later, in Abbott's absence, his appointment was rescinded. His friends must have rallied round quickly as his appointment was re-confirmed within a week.[59] The contract to build the workhouse at a cost of £5,000 was finally signed on January 28th 1841 with William Ward Abbott in charge.

Abbott's turbulent relationship with the St. Neots Board of Guardians was not quite over. When he submitted his bill for services it was found that he had charged on the basis of five per cent of the contract price, precisely double what had been agreed with the architects of two neighbouring Unions. A nominal ten guineas was deducted and Abbott was paid £140:11:6d. for his work.[60] The workhouse still stands today – less forbidding than most because of the scale of its cruciform construction and the creamy-white brick of which it is built, but the workhouse clock still dominates the male and female yards on each side of the central block which housed the paupers' receiving ward, a new applicant's first introduction to 'the House.'

Unfortunately the workhouse admission registers have not survived, but we know that at least one member of John Mimms' family was a guest of the Guardians on at least two occasions. One of John's younger daughters, Lydia, was a lace-maker but as she never married her only income was what she could earn by the skill in her fingers. The trade, which had once been profitable was, by the 1840's, in sad decline. As part of its series, 'Labour and the Poor', the Morning Chronicle commissioned an article on pillow lace-making in the East Midlands and reported: 'The trade in this article was once very considerable, but the introduction of machinery, and the extensive manufactures of Nottingham and other places, have reduced it so low that it has ceased, almost as if by common consent, to be considered as a means of subsistence . . . .I visited several of the poor persons who were employed in lace-making. None of those whom I saw, however, were dependent upon lace for their support, nor could I find any person who was solely dependent for existence upon it. Indeed, it would be a difficult matter to see how it would be possible for any human beings to exist upon the amount which can be earned at lace-making.' The reporter interviewed a Bedford woman who told him, "I gets 2d. a yard for it from the lace-buyers, and it takes me, if I stick close to it, six hours and a half to make a yard of it." Years ago she was paid up to three times as much and continued, "Now I can't make more than six yards in the week, do all I can; and that is a shilling – that's just what it is."

A fancy lace-maker of Wootton, in Bedfordshire, said that the neck-tie she was making would take her 10-12 days' hard work and she had been promised five shillings for it. She was clearly very skilled and her pride in the quality of her work was evident as she told her story: "I made a veil-piece, and I dare say it were sold for four or five guineas. I don't know what the rich folks give for such things, but it was a regular beauty. They told me it was for a weddin' of some lady in London, Lor' bless me, I was at work for two months at it, I do think." She expected to be well paid and had decided how she would spend her small fortune, "I know one thing I was goin' to do was to take my old man home a new flannel jacket, and I did mean to have a warm gown for myself; but I couldn't do neither. I bought a few little things for the young 'uns and I paid off a little score at the shop, and it was all gone. They guv' me a sovrun' for my veil." That buyer had paid her about two shillings and sixpence a week for two months' work. Moreover, the lace-buyers insisted on selling their own thread for which they charged the makers up to 15% of the value of the lace they bought. One maker complained, "they made me take sixpennorth of thread, that I could have bought for a penny anywhere else." It was a buyer's market and the lace-buyers took advantage of it. "There's one man," explained a Bedfordshire woman, "he'll buy as much as you like to take him, and give you a ha'penny a yard more than t'others. He keeps a grocer's shop, but then he won't give you no money; he makes you take it all out at his shop." The same woman expressed it as her firm conviction that, "There isn't nobody that works at the lace as hasn't got a husband to bring 'em home something as they can(not) live upon what they arnes. The girls as isn't married, and works at the lace, are obliged all of 'em to have something from the parish to keep 'em from starving – or else they're not virtuous, and goes in the streets."[61]

Lydia was not herself married and we don't know if she was virtuous but we can be certain that at times she must have applied to Leonard Addington the Relieving Officer for her district, for an allowance from the Guardians. At the time of the 1841 Census she had actually been admitted to St Neots workhouse. This was the old parish workhouse on the east side of Church Street, a little distance north of the present-day nineteenth century vicarage,[62] as the new workhouse in Eaton Socon had not yet been built. When Col. Wade, the Assistant Commissioner, had inspected it two years before Lydia's admission he described it as 'without exception the most wretched and very worst Old Parish House I have ever visited.'[63] It included both a hospital and an almshouse and it may have been that Lydia, then aged 37, had become too ill to work. The staff consisted of the Master and his wife acting as matron, a schoolmistress and a 65 year old nurse. Between them they were responsible for 93 pauper inmates.

The 1850's saw a brief revival in demand for Midlands lace, partly stimulated by the success of the showy Maltese lace on display at the Great Exhibition of 1851. This may have improved Lydia's situation. At all events, in that year she and her father were living in the cottage of a family of lace-makers, William and Mary Moore and their two children in Eynesbury High Street.

Lace-makers were prone to illness as a direct consequence of long hours crouched over their pillows which constricted the chest. The Medical Officer to the Privy Council reported that in the lace-making districts more than twice as many women as men died from lung disease.[64]. That was not to be Lydia's fate, she died of 'Exhaustion from Chronic Disease of brain & Epilepsy' at the age of 65 having spent her last days in the care of the St Neots' Guardians in their new workhouse at Eaton Socon. She had no close relatives living locally and her burial in Eynesbury parish churchyard would, in all probability, have been paid for by the Union.

'Rattle his bones, over the stones;
He's only a pauper, whom nobody owns!'

'There's a grim one-horse hearse in a jolly round trot:
To the church-yard a pauper is going, I wot;
The road it is rough, and the hearse has no springs,
And hark to the dirge that the sad driver sings –
"Rattle his bones, over the stones;
He's only a pauper, whom nobody owns!"[65]

At about the time of Lydia's last admission to the workhouse, John Bundy, an 87 year old Eaton Socon man, whom she may well have known, expressed his resignation at the fate which awaited him and his contemporaries in a long doggerel poem of which these lines summarise his sense of hopelessness;

'A poor old man when he reaches fourscore,
And has done all he can, can do no more;
To ask for relief it makes him afraid.
Since they have took up with this body-snatching way
He must go and die in the Union.'[66]

When Lydia was an inmate of the St Neots parish workhouse in June 1841, her father, John, then aged 75, was living with his youngest daughter, Mary, and her husband, Joseph Chamberlain. Joseph, an agricultural labourer like his father-in-law, had been a widower with a young son when he married Mary. She was almost thirty at the time and with an illegitimate daughter of her own. With two sons of their marriage, Joseph and Mary's household consisted of eight people living in a cottage facing the Green in Front Street (now Berkeley Street), Eynesbury. Five houses down from them at the southern end of the village was Waterloo Cottage, built by Lt. Col. William Humbley after he had been invalided out of Wellington's army in 1815. Col. Humbley had been severely wounded by a ball in each shoulder at the battle of Waterloo and retired to the peace of Eynesbury with his wife, his only son, William Wellington Waterloo Humbley, born in the year of the great battle, and his manservant Francis Cave.[67] At the other end of Front Street opposite the parish church lived William Ward Abbott who, seven months earlier had been appointed Architect and Surveyor to the St Neots Board of Guardians. The wealthy and the poor at this time still lived cheek by jowl, the tradesman and the shopkeeper still lived over their workplace. The heads of households in Front Street included two carpenters, two farmers, a grazier, a mealman, a matmaker, two bricklayers, four ladies of independent means and fourteen labourers. One of John's near neighbours was Edward Peck, the first Guardian of the Poor elected to represent Eynesbury.

Although the census returns describe his occupation as 'Ag. Lab.', it is doubtful whether John was still capable of earning an independent living at the age of 75 and there is evidence that, in addition to any out-relief he might have been granted by the Guardians, he was an object of local charity.

The Huntington Record Office preserves a pocket-book belonging to the Revd. William Palmer, rector of Eynesbury, in which he recorded, in immense detail, gifts of money, clothing, fuel and even luxuries which he gave over a period of ten years to the poor of his parish.[68] These gifts came both from his own pocket and from 'sacramental money', or collections taken at Holy Communion which, traditionally, were intended for the poor. John Mimms features prominently amongst the recipients of William Palmer's considerate charity:

'9 Jan 1837	Mrs Chamberlayne ½ pint of Hollands (gin), John Mimms do.
12 July 1837	Old Mims pr. of old shoes . . . Waistcoat and neck hank. to Mrs Wall's nephew . . . a pair of buckskin gloves for Jos. Groome . . . a blk. hank. and pr. gloves for old Pearson.
13 March 1838	Old Pearson, Sacl. Money 1.0s Old Mims, do. 1.0s
February 1840	½ cwt of coals to John Mimms (and eleven others)
4 January 1841	Old Knight pint of Brandy John Mimms do. '

The girls at his village school were not forgotten when twentythree of them were given lengths of cloth at fivepence a yard, probably for making underclothes. One who received eight yards was John's illegitimate grand-daughter, Sarah. Nor did the rector allow himself to forget those who had offended him and stood to be struck off his list of the deserving as this side-lined note testifies:

'Memo: Not to forget that Wells opposite my Cottage was

> playing country dances while my Cottage door was open on Good Friday.'

John's daughter Mary Chamberlain with whom he had been living, had died at the age of 41 after which he and Lydia lodged with the lace-making family of William and Mary Moore and it was here that John died in his 86th year. He was buried in Eynesbury churchyard where his wife, Lydia, had been laid to rest thirty years earlier. The same Morning Chronicle contributor who interviewed the Midland lace-makers had earlier written this description of a farm labourer's life in the middle of the nineteenth century: 'His whole life appears to be constantly wavering between toil and charity. The parish doctor attends at (in all probability) his illegitimate birth; he is swathed in linen provided for him by the hands of some charitable individual, or benevolent association. A charity school doles out to him his scanty education in the irregular intervals of his youthful labour; as he advances in years the subscriptions of the more affluent are necessary to provide him with clothing; when unemployed, or unable through age or infirmity to do a fair day's work, the workhouse is his refuge; in sickness the parish doctor attends him, and his club supports him . . . in death . . . four of his neighbours, perhaps poorer than himself, sacrifice their half-day's wages to bear him gratuitously to the spot which the guardians of the poor have appointed as the pauper's final resting-place, and in which his ancestors and some of his offspring were perhaps laid before him. The clergyman waives his burial fees, or the Union chaplain consigns him to the ground which for half a century, in seed time and in harvest he had moistened with his sweat and enriched by his toil.'[69]

Although not a strictly accurate account of John Mimms' life in its every detail, those words could, nevertheless, have almost have been written about him. His had been a long and hard life. He had brought up a young family during the last desperate decade of the eighteenth century and throughout the French and Napoleonic Wars which gave prosperity to the farmer but nothing to his men. His children began to leave home as post-war depression led to unemployment and the 'last labourers' revolt', as the Hammonds described the 'Swing Riots' of 1830. He had survived the 'Hungry '40's' and died in the year of Prince Albert's Great Exhibition. In all probability his only family mourner would have been Lydia, the lace-maker, his other surviving children were by then widely dispersed.

John and Lydia's eldest daughter, Elizabeth, was 28 before she married - quite an advanced age for a girl in 1820. The wedding on Michaelmas Day was not celebrated in Eynesbury but in the more impressive parish church of St Neots. Her bridegroom was John Wright Davidson, a publican from North Repps a village on the Norfolk coast near Cromer, who could sign his name with a fluent flourish. It might be thought that he was a considerable catch for a labourer's daughter not in the first flush of youth, but was this so? The marriage was by licence rather than banns and John Davidson had to supply a guarantor in the sum of two hundred pounds, twice the figure required of Elizabeth's father thirty-two years earlier. The bond was provided by William Thornton, the landlord of the Old Falcon, a posting house on the west side of St Neots Market Square backing on to the river.[70] It would seem more likely that Thornton was John Davidson's employer and that John was perhaps a pot-boy rather than the more grandiose 'publican' he chose to be described as when he made his allegation that he was of age and free to marry. The wedding took place in St Neots church because Elizabeth must have been living in that parish and possibly employed in the same hostelry. On her wedding day she would have entered by the south door of the church, the north, or 'Devil's door', being considered unlucky,[71] and passing under this sobering seventeenth century inscription cut into a buttress just west of the south porch:

> 'Stay mortal stay, depart not from this tombe
> untill thou hast pondered well thy day of doome.
> My boew stands bent if yt thou canst but see
> aimeing to shoote and it may lighte on thee.
> Prepare to walk in duste take home this line
> the grave that is opened next it may be thine.'[72]

There may have been a quiet celebration at the Old Falcon or a family reunion at her parents' cottage a few hundred yards from the church as weddings were one of the few occasions when a large family would go to the trouble and expense of returning to the family home to be together for a day to drink and dance; Elizabeth's sisters, dressed in their best finery trimmed with lace they had made themselves and the boys standing awkwardly around who 'seldom lost their typical gait . . . as though they have a heavy weight tied to each leg, so that it can only be moved by a heave of the whole body in the opposite direction'.[73] George Eliot described such a village wedding celebration, 'kept between four brown walls, where an awkward bridegroom opens the dance with a high-shouldered, broad-faced bride, while elderly and middle-aged friends look on, with very irregular noses and lips, and probably with quart-pots in their hands, but with an unmistakable contentment and goodwill, "Foh!" says my idealistic friend, "What vulgar details! What good is there in taking all these pains to give an exact likeness of old women and clowns? What clumsy, ugly people!" '[74]

Elizabeth's older brothers, George and Thomas, were both about thirty years old when she married. They had come of age in the later years of the French Wars but probably left home to become live-in farm servants in their early 'teens. Their subsequent lives as farm labourers in Cambridgeshire and Bedfordshire respectively would not have been markedly different from that of their father. Both married, brought up families and died in the middle years of the century.

Her two younger brothers were more adventurous. John headed towards London, but met and married a Hendon girl, Sarah Peacock, and fathered seven children on what he could earn hawking fish around the old and select village of Hampstead where he spent his whole life until, in his late sixties, he died at a house in Flask Walk. James, the youngest son, actually reached the capital and it is his and his successors' fortunes in 'the greatest city in the world' which we now follow.

References

[1] Morning Chronicle, 26 DEC. 1849
[2] The Times, 14 NOV. 1849
[3] Richardson, 'Death, Dissection and the Destitute', p.121.
[4] ibid., p.146
[5] ibid., pp.36/37
[6] ibid., pp. 160/161
[7] ibid., pp.123/124
[8] ibid., p.271
[9] Longmate, 'The Workhouse', p.42
[10] Crowther, 'The Workhouse System', p.41
[11] Poor Law Report, 1834, p.228
[12] Crabbe, 'The Borough', Letter XVIII, lines 113–118

[13] Thompson, E.P. 'The Making of the English Working Class', p.295
[14] Select Committee on the Poor Law Amendment Act, XVIII (1837-8) Pt.1,pp481/2: quot. Snell, 'Annals of the Labouring Poor', p.352 (Note)
[15] Crowther, 'The Workhouse System', pp.194/195
[16] ibid. p.198
[17] Morning Chronicle, 29 DEC 1849
[18] Longmate,'The Workhouse', p.94
[19] Snell, 'Annals of the Labouring Poor', p.121
[20] Thompson, E.P., 'The Making of the English Working Class', p.296
[21] Jerrold, 'Thomas Hood,' p.651
[22] Morning Chronicle, 22 JAN. 1850
[23] Lee, 'Cider with Rosie', p.110
[24] Howitt, 'The Rural Life of England', p.406
[25] Digby, 'Pauper Palaces', p.126
[26] Leeds Mercury quoted in the Huntingdon, Bedford and Peterborough Gazette and Cambridge Independent Press, 27 AUG. 1836
[27] Morning Chronicle 26 DEC. 1849
[28] Select Committee on the Poor Law Amendment Act XVIII (1837 - 38) Pt. II p.69: quot in Snell, 'Annals of the Labouring Poor', p.115
[29] Huntingdon, Bedford & Peterborough Gazette, Cambridge and Hertford Independent Press, 23 MAY 1835
[30] Godber, 'History of Bedfordshire', p.474
[31] Select Committee on the Poor Law Amendment Act XVIII (1837-38) Pt.III p.208: quot. in Snell,'Annals of the Labouring Poor', pp.114/115
[32] Snell, 'Annals of the Labouring Poor', p.385
[33] Minute Book of the St Neots' Guardians, 12 AUG. 1836. Huntingdon R.O.
[34] Digby, 'Pauper Palaces', p.211
[35] Somerville, A 'The Whistler at the Plough', Manchester (1852) quot in Snell, 'Annals of the Labouring Poor', p.121
[36] Morning Chronicle, 22 DEC. 1849
[37] ibid., 29 DEC. 1849
[38] ibid., 8 DEC. 1849
[39] Williams, K., 'From Pauperism to Poverty', p.77
[40] Minute Book of the St Neots Guardians, 4 DEC 1835, Huntingdon R.O.
[41] ibid. , 4 MAR. 1836
[42] ibid. , 25 MAR. 1836
[43] ibid. , 11 MAR. and 24 JUN 1836
[44] ibid. , 23 APR. 29 APR and 27 MAY 1836
[45] ibid. , 14 DEC. 1837
[46] ibid. , 20 MAY 1836
[47] Longmate, 'The Workhouse', p.65
[48] Tebbutt, 'St Neots', p.333
[49] ibid. , pp. 33 and 270
[50] ibid. , p.131
[51] ibid. , p.221
[52] Longmate, 'The Workhouse', p.265
[53] The Indicator, Westminster, 13 OCT. 1899
[54] Public Record Office, MH12/4764, 9 JULY 1839

[55] Minute Book of the St Neots Guardians, 7 and 21 APR 1837, Huntingdon R.O.
[56] ibid. , 9 SEP. 1839
[57] ibid. , 26 DEC. 1839
[58] ibid. , 5 MAR. and 9 JUL. 1840
[59] ibid. , 5, 12 and 19 NOV. 1840
[60] ibid., 24 NOV and 29 DEC 1842
[61] Morning Chronicle, 5 APR 1850
[62] Tebbutt, 'St. Neots', p.164
[63] Public Record Office, MH12/4764 (1 NOV 1838)
[64] Hole, 'The Homes of the Working Classes', p.47
[65] Noel, T. 'The Pauper's Drive'; Mulgan, 'Poems of Freedom',p.116
[66] Godber, 'History of Bedfordshire', p.530
[67] Tebbutt, 'St. Neots', pp. 280 and 331
[68] 2603/3/18 'Account and Memorandum Book of the Rev. Palmer, 1835–45', Huntingdon R.O.
[69] Morning Chronicle, 2 JAN 1850
[70] Tebbutt, 'St. Neots' p.200
[71] Tebbutt, 'Hunts. Folklore', p.12
[72] Tebbutt, 'St. Neots' p.62
[73] Kerr, 'Bound to the Soil'
[74] Eliot, G. 'Adam Bede' Book II ch. XVII, Collins Library Classics edn., p.212

PART TWO

City Life, 1830 - 1940

CHAPTER EIGHT

TO LONDON

'If to the city sped – What waits him there?
To see profusion that he must not share;
To see ten thousand baleful arts combin'd
To pamper luxury, and thin mankind:
To see those joys the sons of pleasure know
Extorted from his fellow creature's woe.'

Oliver Goldsmith[1]

People fled to the towns for work, for somewhere to live and for what they must have believed would be a better life than they could possibly have enjoyed in the depressed rural areas. For those living in the southern counties, the capital city proved to be a great attraction: every child knew the tale of Richard Whittington. During the first half of the nineteenth century London's population grew at twice the national rate. At the beginning of the century the capital housed just under a million people, only thirty years later there were half as many again. In the third decade of the century alone its population increased by 20% and one of those quarter of a million extra people was James, the youngest son of John Mimms of Eynesbury. Born in 1801 he would probably have left home in his mid-to late twenties.

James's route to London had been mapped for him by the Romans. Half a mile across the river Ouse at Eaton Socon ran the Great North road and London was less than sixty miles due south through Biggleswade, Stevenage, Hatfield and Barnet. He would doubtless have walked or, occasionally, been given a ride on a passing carrier's cart and slept in a hedgerow. This was the height of the coaching era when one hundred and fifty stage coaches travelled that road every day, mingling with great herds of livestock being driven southwards to Smithfield market to feed the people of the capital. At the top of Highgate Hill London would have opened out before him, dominated by the dome of Wren's great cathedral. At that point the traveller could have chosen the gradual slope of the Archway Road, but why pay a toll on a new road running through a deep cutting when the steep gradient of Highgate Hill down to the Whittington Stone was more exhilirating and offered a better view of one's destination? As it was, it seems more likely and natural that James would have turned south-westwards across the heath to visit his brother John, busy hawking fish around Hampstead, whom he had probably not seen for five or more years.

The dramatic changes which were affecting the towns in the early part of that century had almost completely bypassed Hampstead. Practically nothing new had been built in what was still little more than a large rural village of some 8000 people. It was not on a main route out of London and its land was owned by a few landlords who showed no particular desire to cover their fields with bricks and mortar, so that outside the old town itself it was still almost wholly agricultural.[2] Perhaps James stayed with his brother and sister-in-law, Sarah, for a few refreshing days before plunging into the sights and slums of London.

From Hampstead to Regent's Park was mainly meadowland. The road ran between hedges with, here and there, a tavern and roadside cottages with occasional hamlets like Camden Town which had only started to become industrialised after 1820 when the Regent's Canal brought barges up from the Thames at Limehouse to join up with the Grand Junction Canal at Paddington. The canal ran along the north edge of what was then built-up London.[3] South of Camden High Street, the Hampstead Road at the point where it becomes Tottenham Court Road, was crossed by a wide drovers' road (now Marylebone and Euston Roads). This New Road, as it was then called, had been built seventy years earlier for the sole purpose of driving the herds of cattle which came from the west country towards Smithfield, avoiding the congestion of Oxford Street and Holborn.

Although now nearing the centre of town, Tottenham Court

and Tottenham Fields were still quite rural and a popular place for Londoners to seek refreshment and diversion:

> 'When the sweet-breathing spring unfolds the buds,
> Love flies the dusty town for shady woods.
> Then Tottenham-fields with roving beauty swarm,
> And Hampstead balls the City virgins warm;
> Then Chelsea's maids o'erhear perfidious vows,
> And the press'd grass defrauds the grazing cows.'[4]

John Gay had penned those lines a century earlier but even as late as 1840 Tottenham Court Road was still sufficiently rural that when Heal's took over Miller's Stables, belonging to Capper's Farm, for their house furnishing business the lease provided for 'the proper accommodation of 40 cows at least.' Those cow-sheds remained there for another thirtyseven years.[5]

The southern end of Tottenham Court Road, however, was another country altogether. Westwards ran Oxford Street, a broad, well-lit fashionable shopping district; but south - and eastwards lay St Giles, one of London's worst slums, or 'rookeries' as they were then known. Charles Dickens described the area for his 'Evening Chronicle' readers after making for Drury Lane 'through the narrow streets and dirty courts which divide it from Oxford Street, and that classical spot adjoining the brewery at the bottom of Tottenham Court Road':

'Wretched houses with broken windows patched with rags and paper: every room let out to a different family, and in many instances to two or even three - fruit and 'sweet-stuff' manufacturers in the cellars, barbers and red-herring vendors in the front parlours, cobblers in the back; a bird-fancier on the first floor, three families on the second, starvation in the attics, Irishmen in the passage, a 'musician' in the front kitchen, and a char-woman and five hungry children in the back one - filth everywhere - a gutter before the houses and a drain behind - clothes drying and slops emptying, from the windows; girls of fourteen or fifteen, with matted hair, walking about barefoot, and in white greatcoats, almost their only covering; boys of all ages, in coats of all sizes and no coats at all; men and women, in every variety of scanty and dirty apparel, lounging, scolding, drinking, smoking, squabbling, fighting and swearing.'

'You turn the corner. What a change! All is light and brilliancy.

'Wretched houses with broken windows patched with rags and paper.'

The hum of many voices issues from that splendid gin-shop which forms the commencement of the two streets opposite.' Dickens goes on to describe this gaudy palace with its plateglass, its gas lights in richly gilt burners, the green and gold painted casks and the elegantly carved, French-polished mahogany bar attended by 'two showily dressed damsels with large necklaces.' Seated on a bench are two old washerwomen drinking their half-quartern of gin and peppermint (a treble gin today). A flashily dressed young gentleman enters with a female companion in faded feathers who orders a glass of port wine 'with a bit of sugar', adding, "this gentleman pays". A group of Irish labourers at the end of the room, 'who have been alternately shaking hands with, and threatening the life of each other for the last hour', finally erupt into a fight – 'half the Irishmen get shut out, and the other half get shut in; the potboy is knocked among the tubs in no time; the landlord hits everybody, and everybody hits the landlord; the barmaids scream; the police come in; the rest is a confused mixture of arms, legs, staves, torn coats, shouting, and struggling.'

'We have sketched this subject very slightly,' admits Dickens, because 'Well-disposed gentlemen, and charitable ladies, would alike turn with coldness and disgust from a description of the drunken besotted men, and wretched broken-down miserable women, who form no inconsiderable portion of the frequenters of these haunts; forgetting, in the pleasant consciousness of their own rectitude, the poverty of the one, and the temptation of the other. Gin-drinking is a great vice in England, but wretchedness and dirt are a greater . . . If Temperance Societies would suggest an antidote against hunger, filth, and foul air,' then, 'gin-palaces would be numbered among the things that were.' As it is, 'gin-shops will increase in number and splendour'.[6]

Dickens had displayed considerable courage by wandering into St Giles where he might so easily have got lost, even though he knew London's byways well. 'All those streets twisted and turned, and broke into little alleys, which again curled into each other in not one but a series of labyrinths. Strangers seldom ventured into them. Without knowledge, one could not find a way out, and to ask a direction was only to be sent farther in, and perhaps in some locked courtyard to be seized by a group of hags or harridans and robbed.'[7]

By the middle of the century most of the St Giles' district had been demolished as New Oxford Street was driven through it. All that remained were 95 wretched dwellings housing 2850 people on an acre of ground – or less than two square yards each.[8] It was into this area that Charles Dickens once again ventured, but this time led and protected by Inspector Field and Sergeant Rogers of the Metropolitan Police. Writing for his own publication, 'Household Words' in June 1851, only four years after New Oxford Street had opened to traffic, he described his visit to an Irish tramps' lodging house:

> 'St Giles's clock, striking eleven, hums through our hand from the dilapidated door of a dark outhouse as we open it, and are stricken back by the pestilent breath that issues from within. Rogers to the front with the light, and let us look!
>
> 'Ten, twenty, thirty – who can count them! Men, women, children, for the most part naked, heaped upon the floor like maggots in a cheese! . . . Who is the landlord here? – I am, Mr Field! says a bundle of ribs and parchment against the wall, scratching itself. – Will you spend this money fairly, in the morning, to buy coffee for 'em all? Yes, sir I will! – Oh, he'll do it, sir, he'll do it fair. He's honest! cry the spectres. And with thanks and Good Night sink into their graves again!

'Thus, we make our New Oxford Streets, and our other new streets', commented Dickens, 'never heeding, never asking, where the wretches whom we clear out, crowd.'[9] But the London Statistical Society *did* ask. It made a study of Church Lane, St Giles, which revealed that this short street of 27 houses, averaging five rooms each, had housed 655 people in 1841, but six years later 1095 people were crowded into it – an increase in density from 24 to just over 40 persons per house, or eight bodies for every available room.[10]

Southwards from St Giles a visitor could not possibly miss the great fruit, flower and vegetable market of Covent Garden which is 'all bustle and activity, but the buyers and sellers stream to and from it in all directions, filling every street in the vicinity. From Long Acre to the Strand on the one side, and from Bow-street to Bedford-street on the other, the ground has been seized upon by the market-goers . . . the road is blocked up with mountains of cabbages and turnips; men and women push past with their arms bowed out by the cauliflowers under them, or the red tips of carrots pointing from their crammed aprons, or else their faces are red with the weight of the loaded head-basket . . . At every turn there is a fresh odour to sniff at; either the bitter aromatic perfume of the herbalists' shops breaks upon you, or the scent of oranges, then of apples, and then of onions is caught for an instant as you move along. The brocoli tied up in square packets . . . the sieves of crimson love-apples, polished like china, – the bundles of white glossy leeks, their roots dangling like fringe, – the celery, with its pinky stalks and bright green tops, – the dark purple pickling-cabbages, – the scarlet carrots, – the white knobs of turnips, – the bright yellow balls of oranges, and the rich brown coats of the chestnuts – attract the eye on every side.[11]

That vivid description is Henry Mayhew's, who recorded London and its poor in the middle of the century. Dickens also wrote of the boys who lived on what they could cadge or steal from the market stalls, – 'One of the worst night sights I know in London is to be found in the children who prowl about this place; who sleep in the baskets, fight for the offal, dart at any object they think they can lay their thieving hands on, dive under carts and barrows, dodge the constables, and are perpetually making a blunt pattering on the pavement of the Piazza with the rain of their naked feet.' Dickens points up the painful comparison one is forced to make between 'the so much improved and cared-for fruits of the earth,' and, 'these all-uncared-for (except inasmuch as ever-hunted) savages.'[12]

Some of the girls offered flowers as an aid to prostitution, one consequence of which Charles Dickens witnessed only a few yards away from the market outside Bow Street police station and regaled his 'Evening Chronicle' readers with this pathetic little sketch:

> 'After a few minutes' delay, the door again opened, and the two first prisoners appeared. They were a couple of girls, of whom the elder could not be more than sixteen, and the younger of whom had certainly not attained her fourteenth year. That they were sisters was evident from the resemblance which still subsisted between them, though two additional years of depravity had fixed their brand upon the elder girl's features, as legibly as if a red-hot iron had seared them. They were both gaudily dressed, the younger one especially; and,

> although there was a strong similarity between them . . . it is impossible to conceive a greater contrast than the demeanour of the two presented. The younger girl was weeping bitterly – not for display, or in the hope of producing effect, but for very shame; her face was buried in her handkerchief . . . "How long are you for, Emily?" screamed a red-faced woman in the crowd, "Six weeks and labour," replied the elder girl with a flaunting laugh . . . " and here's Bella a-going too for the first time. Hold up your head, you chicken," she continued, boisterously tearing the other girl's handkerchief away. "Hold up your head, and show 'em your face." . . . These two girls had been thrown upon London streets, their vices and debauchery, by a sordid and rapacious mother. What the younger girl was then, the elder had been once; and what the elder then was, the younger must soon become.'[13]

From Bow Street it was only a short step to the Strand, said by Disraeli to be 'perhaps the finest street in Europe', and the main thoroughfare linking Westminster, the home of the Court and Parliament, with the City, London's mercantile and financial centre. The Strand's wide, cobbled, gas-lit street with pavements on each side, its many narrow-fronted and bay-windowed shops, and its arcades and bazaars would have amazed a country visitor with the variety of goods they offered for sale.

The Strand from Charing Cross, only recently widened and improved and where, nearby, Trafalgar Square would soon be laid out, ran for three-quarters of a mile eastwards as far as Temple Bar. At that point the cities of Westminster and London met, as, of course, they do today. The Royal Courts of Justice were not to be built for another fifty years and that area was another notorious slum. Holywell Street ran off the Strand, 'a narrow dirty lane extending parallel to the Strand from St. Clement Danes to St Mary-Le-Strand occupied chiefly by old clothesmen and the vendors of low publications.'[14] Among the 'low publications' were numbered the bawdy songs and smutty ditties – 'The Drummer's Stick', 'Sally's Thatched Cottage', and 'O What a Queer Sensation' – cheaply printed in sheet and song-book form and performed in the 'song and supper' rooms around the Strand and Covent Garden area. These, the precursors of the late Victorian music halls, had an exclusively male clientele. In 'Pendennis', set in the 1830's, Thackeray describes the Back Kitchen of the Fielding's Head in the Covent Garden area, where the clientele, attracted by the jolly singing and suppers, included country tradesmen and farmers in London on business, apprentices, medical students and professional men who ate dishes of sausage and mash, Welsh rabbit, poached eggs and kidneys or devilled turkey and drank stout, punch, brandy, whisky, sherry and water, gin twist and champagne cup. Thackeray descibes a rendering of 'The Body Snatcher' by a noted bass who, as the curtain opened upon him dressed as the Snatcher, was found seated on a coffin with a flask of gin before him, a spade and a candle stuck in a skull. 'The singer's voice went down so low, that its grumbles rumbled into the hearer's awe-stricken soul; and in the chorus he clamped with his spade and gave a demoniac, "Ha! ha!" which caused the very glasses to quiver on the table, as with terror."[15]

In the Strand, and anywhere else a crowd could be gathered, were the street performers, clowns, sword swallowers, acrobats, fire-eaters, conjurors and stilt-dancers. The Punch and Judy shows and the Fantoccini street theatres with their dancing marionettes set up to collect an audience. Passers-by were entertained by the hurdy-gurdy players with their portable, hand-cranked organs, the reciters and the ballad-singers. Proprietors set up their booths offering waxworks, dwarfs, giants and physical deformities, and the peepshows with their moving mechanical depictions of the 'Death of Nelson' or the execution of an infamous murderer set up wherever a promising site appeared to offer an opportunity to make a shilling or two.

Slap-up Peter was a ballad singer but had started his long street-performing career as an acrobat until he injured his wrist in a fall and had turned instead to swallowing hot iron bars, pokers and red-hot coals. Later he took up knife swallowing which worked well providing he stayed sober. His wife suggested he should try snakes and, when he objected, asked him: "Wot difference does it make, Peter, whether you swallow red-hot coals or snakes? The snakes has their stings taken out, and it's nothing more than swallowin' a sausage or pork saveloy." He explained that he took a fifteen – or eighteen-inch long snake by the head, placed it in his mouth and, if it didn't slide down his throat, he pinched its tail: "You see he doesn't go hall the way down. He is afraid, is the snake, and if you cough he'll come up and draw himself up and coil in a bunch in your mouth. But the duffers who pay their money think that the snake is in your stomach . . . Well, when I began snake-swallowing it was rather new, and I had it all my own way for a long time, but finally, lots of men began to swallow snakes, and coal-swallowing was not as good as it used to be; so I took to ballad singing . . . "[16]

Slap-up Peter's story was told to an American journalist who also described the street acrobats he had seen performing in alleys off the Strand where, 'a curious crowd will collect around a man and boy or boys, who will in the most business like fashion proceed to divest themselves of their rather shabby outward clothing, and in a few moments will appear in all the glory of flesh-colored tights. Their foreheads are glorious with silver tinsel or silk ribbon fillets, their loins girt with strips of velvet . . . and for half-an-hour will amaze and delight the grown children, larking street boys, and nursery maids of the neighborhood, and having collected perhaps ten-pence or a shilling, (will) . . . don their sober, shabby garments, and find another quarter to do their trapeze, pyramid, and dancing feats.'[17]

Henry Mayhew interviewed a man who had performed as a street acrobat for sixteen years: 'He was a melancholy-looking man, with the sunken eyes and other characteristics of semi-starvation, while his face was scored with lines and wrinkles, telling of pain and premature age.'

'I saw him performing in the streets with a school of acrobats soon after I had been questioning him, and the readiness and business-like way with which he resumed his professional buffoonery was not a little remarkable. His story was more pathetic than comic, and proved that the life of a street clown is, perhaps, the most wretched of all existence. Jest as he may in the street, his life is literally no joke at home.' His costume consisted of red striped cotton stockings, padded trunks and tight-fitting bodice dotted in red and black with full sleeves and frills and a horse-hair wig sewn on to a white cap. He painted his face with white lead after greasing it (the safer flake-white was too expensive), "after that," he added, "I colour my cheeks and mouth with vermilion. I never dress at home; we all dress at public-houses. In the street where I lodge, only a very few know what I do for a living. I and my wife both strive to keep the business a secret from our neighbours." On average he earned enough to take six shillings a week home to his family. "Most of the street clowns die in the workhouse", he told Mayhew, "In their old age they are generally very wretched and poverty-stricken. I can't say what I think will be the end of me. I daren't think of it, sir."[18]

From the Strand eastwards ran Fleet Street downhill to the Fleet river, by this time largely running underground beneath Farringdon Street; then up Ludgate Hill in the sober shadow of St. Paul's cathedral, set on a hill overlooking all London. Beyond St. Paul's, Cheapside was still a thriving shopping street, rivalling the West End itself, and as it merged into Poultry the three imposing symbols of the City's power surrounded the visitor – the Mansion House and the Bank of England on either side and the Royal Exchange ahead. From there it was a short walk up Cornhill, past the front of the Exchange and down Gracechurch Street and Fish Street Hill to the tallest isolated stone column in the world – the Monument, the City's memorial to the great fire.

South from the Monument and straight ahead lay London Bridge, Southwark and the Surrey countryside.

References

[1] Goldsmith, 'The Deserted Village', p.31
[2] Thompson, F.M.L. 'Hampstead', p.75.
[3] Bell, 'London in the Age of Dickens', p.57.
[4] Cunningham, P., 'Handbook of London', p.499.
[5] Weinreb, and Hibbert, 'The London Encyclopaedia',pp 372 and 869.
[6] Vallance, 'Dickens' London', pp 73 – 76
[7] Burke, 'The Streets of London', p.101
[8] Cunningham, P., 'Handbook of London', p.369.
[9] Vallance, 'Dickens' London', pp.138/139
[10] Flinn, 'The Sanitary Condition of the Labouring Population', p.5
[11] Canning, 'The Illustrated Mayhew's London', pp. 55 – 59
[12] Vallance, 'Dickens' London', p.237
[13] ibid., pp 85/6
[14] Cunningham, P.,'Handbook of London' p.232
[15] Speaight, G., 'Bawdy Songs of the Early Music Hall', p.6
[16] Kirwan, 'Palace and Hovel', pp. 32/34
[17] ibid., pp. 125/126
[18] Canning, 'The Illustrated Mayhew's London', pp.249/252.

CHAPTER NINE

SOUTHWARK

'Some of the principal streets even in the metropolis almost justify the description of being 'streams of mud and filth in winter,' and 'seas of dust in summer'
The Sanitary Report (1842),[1]

'Even if the house did possess a privy, it might have nowhere to deposit the contents. There were houses whose yards were completely covered with human ordure six inches deep, across which inhabitants stepped on bricks.'
The Sanitary Report (1842),[2]

'When the ground rose out of the great Lambeth and Bermondsey Marsh', wrote Walter Besant, 'it opened out into one wild heath after another – Clapham, Wandsworth, Putney, Wimbledon, Barnes, Tooting, Streatham, Richmond, Thornton and so south as far as Banstead Downs. The country was not flat: it rose at Wimbledon to a high plateau; it rose at Norwood to a chain of hills; between the Heaths stretched gardens and orchards; between the orchards were pasture lands; on the hill sides were hanging woods . . . the loveliness of South London lay almost at the very doors of London: one could walk into it; the heaths were within an easy walk, and the loveliness of Surrey lay upon all.'[3] That is not a description of London south of the Thames we should recognise today, but perhaps it was that rural vista which tempted James to cross London Bridge after the sights and smells of the capital city north of the river – an experience which must have been bewildering, even frightening, to a country lad to whom a large, bustling town meant St Neots on market day.

Immediately south of the river, which had no embankments to contain it, the land was marshy. Battersea Fields were 'low, damp, and, I believe, treeless; they were crossed, like Hackney Marsh, by paths raised above the level.'[4] 'Only on the river bank was the area at all densely populated – the only portion that was laid out in streets and houses and might be considered "town" was the portion comprised within the curve of the river, and bounded by a line drawn from Lambeth Palace by Newington, and ending at Bermondsey. Outside this "pale", as we might call it, all lay open'[5] Dulwich, Peckham and Stockwell were mere villages, Rotherhithe was little more than a single street fronting the river off which which ran small lanes and courts with tiny houses. As Besant described it – 'this street with its little lanes was the whole of Rotherhithe. Inland – or in-marsh – ponds and ditches and creeping streams lay about.'[6] Even neighbouring Bermondsey had far more open land in the form of pasture, market gardens and paddock than it had houses – 'I see a small town, or collection of small towns, occupying the district called the Borough Proper, Lambeth, Newington, Walworth and Bermondsey. In some parts this area is densely populated, filled with narrow courts and lanes; in other parts there are broad fields, open spaces, unoccupied pieces of ground,' continued Besant, 'in Bermondsey there are also open spaces, some of them gardens, or recreation grounds, without any buildings.'[7]

When James crossed the Thames for the first time two bridges stood almost side by side. The old London Bridge with its nineteen arches was over six hundred years old and about to be demolished and replaced by Sir John Rennie's five-arch bridge opened in August 1831 by William IV. This new bridge lasted only 140 years until it was sold in 1972 to Lake Havasu City in Arizona[8]. The tale that the purchasers believed that they were buying the more visually impressive Tower Bridge is probably apocryphal.

On the south side of London Bridge was the ancient borough of Southwark. Until a bridge-building boom ten to fifteen years earlier, when Vauxhall, Waterloo and Southwark bridges were constructed, London Bridge had been one of only three Thames bridges serving London. It was the gateway to the south. No railway yet served any part of London so travellers to the continent had little choice but to use the horse-drawn coaches across London Bridge, through the Borough High Street, along the recently constructed Great Dover Street to the Old Kent Road and thence to the Channel ports.

The Borough High Street was lined with coaching inns, many, like the Tabard Inn, had originally been built to serve the pilgrims making their way to Canterbury. As Chaucer's Miller began his tale he prefaced his story with the excuse

> 'if the words get muddled in my tale,
> Just put it down to too much Southwark ale'[9]

Their narrow frontages, little wider than was necessary to allow a coach to enter, opened out into a long yard with stabling on either side and above the stables and store rooms on the ground floor rose two or three tiers of open, balustraded landings overlooking the yard, unprotected from the weather, which led to the guests' bedrooms. In Pickwick Papers, Charles Dickens described them as, 'Great, rambling, queer, old places they are, with galleries, and passages, and staircases, wide enough and antiquated enough to furnish material for a hundred ghost stories.'[10]

Southwark was the only ward of the City of London south of the Thames and was no more than one-and-a-half miles wide by one-and-a-quarter miles deep, apart from a narrow strip stretching south to Camberwell along the old coach road to Kent, on either side of which lay Newington on the west and Bermondsey to the east.

Along the Thames river-front, Southwark ran downstream from Paris Garden Stairs (roughly Blackfriars Bridge) eastwards to St Saviour's Dock (a few hundred yards east of where Tower Bridge now stands). At that point the riverside area of Bermondsey began. Within Southwark were five separate parishes, each governed by its own vestry. As one crossed London Bridge, St. Saviour's lay to the right and St. Olave's to the left, and beyond St. Olave's, St. John Horsleydown adjoined Bermondsey. The southernmost, and largest, parish, St. George the Martyr, stretched south – and westwards as far as St. George's Fields and Bedlam (The Bethlehem Hospital for Lunatics; now the Imperial War Museum). The fifth, was a parish within a parish: St. Thomas's fell almost entirely within the boundaries of St. Olave's and served only the hospital after which it was named, its sister hospital, Guy's, and a few nearby properties.[11]

It was in this small parish of St. Thomas that James eventually settled for twenty years – just a short walk from London Bridge in the area traditionally known as 'The Borough' – that part of Southwark which had no defined boundary but comprised the district immediately surrounding the Borough High Street. In fact, for the next hundred years his family, although they later moved frequently, never lived further than a mile and a half from London Bridge.

From the bridge and down the Borough High Street he would have passed thirty or forty small houses, shops and inn-yards, then, just after the imposing, but still narrow, forecourt entrance of St. Thomas's Hospital, turned left into St. Thomas's Street which ran along the south side of that great hospital. Within a few yards the street widened as it passed the parish church. The church was itself part of the hospital and the old herb room at the top of its tower had been converted into the female operating theatre (it is still there today).[12]. Immediately past the church and guarded by a porter's lodge a small arch led into one of the hospital's four squares: this was the entrance used by those applying for admission. Past the arch a row of buildings housed the hospital's officers, the Treasurer, the Receiver who collected the rents from hospital-owned properties, the Minister and the Apothecary: then the stables, the bath houses and, finally, at the end of the street, the Foul Block, built as far as possible from the other wards to house those suffering from 'the foul disease' – the pox. On the right-hand side of St. Thomas's Street for the second half of its length stood south London's other great hospital, Guy's, founded by Thomas Guy, a governor of St. Thomas's, to house those patients the older foundation could not help – mainly the incurables.

At this point Joiner's Street led left to the rear entrance of St. Thomas's and its Back Yard, the only place in the hospital where male patients were allowed to smoke.[13] Opposite the back gate and eastwards again ran St. Thomas's Broad Way which ended in a narrow alley of some twenty small houses called New Way. The other end of New Way was the Maze, a road leading north to Tooley Street and thus back to London Bridge. New Way had been 'new' at some time, but it is clearly shown with a similar outline of houses when John Roque mapped London almost a century earlier.

Within Southwark's confined space more than a hundred thousand people lived and worked in tiny unpaved or cobbled streets, courts and alleys with such bizarre names as Dog and Bear Yard, Frying Pan Alley, St. Thomas's Rents, Naked Boy Alley and Great Maze Court. The courts and yards were crammed with houses, often on all four sides, their only entrance a gap perhaps two feet wide in one corner, or a narrow arched passage running under the upper storey of one of the houses. Many of these were 'wooden houses and houses in which the so-called ground floor was several feet below the level of the street. In some of the areas the courtways were only four feet wide and the walls of either side of the court between houses could be touched by either elbow when walking through.'[14] Space was scarce as more and more families moved to London from the rural areas, so every available scrap of land was used to run up housing. 'Corner sites and the open-ends of quadrangle courts were built in first. Then building took place within the courts themselves so that only pedestrian ways were left between warrens of houses crammed together, windows looking into high walls.'[15]

Most of the houses themselves were tiny. A typical labourer's tenement was such that a lecturer in forensic medicine at Charing Cross Hospital, who conducted a house-to-house survey, calculated that if all its doors and windows were shut tight, the maximum time a man could live before all the available oxygen was used up was just seven hours.[16] Such a house, moreover, would frequently be shared by two or more families.

About three-quarters of a mile from New Way, just on Southwark's eastern boundary where Tooley Street ends and Jamaica Road begins at Dockhead, stood one of London's most notorious rookeries, a haunt of criminals and those at the very bottom of London's heap of the desperately poor, Jacob's Island. 'Near to that part of the Thames on which the Church at Rotherhithe abuts, where the buildings on the banks are dirtiest, and the vessels on the river blackest with the dust of colliers and the smoke of close-built low-roofed houses, there exists . . . the filthiest, the strangest, the most extraordinary of the many localities that are hidden in London, wholly unknown, even by name, to the great mass of its inhabitants.' So, in 1838 did Charles Dickens define the location of the chase which ended in Bill Sikes' death.

'... more than a hundred thousand people lived and worked in tiny unpaved or cobbled streets, courts and alleys...'

'To reach this place,' he continued, vividly describing sights which would have been familiar to James, 'the visitor has to penetrate through a maze of close, narrow and muddy streets, thronged by the roughest and poorest of waterside people . . . The cheapest and least delicate provisions are heaped in the shops; the coarsest and commonest of wearing apparel dangle at the salesman's door and stream from the house parapet and windows. Jostling with unemployed labourers of the lowest class, ballast-heavers, coal-whippers, brazen women, ragged children and the very raff and refuse of the river . . . assailed by offensive sights and smells from the narrow alleys which branch off on the right and left, and deafened by the clash of ponderous waggons that bear great piles of merchandise from the stocks of warehouses that rise from every corner. Arriving, at length, in streets remoter and less frequented than those which he had passed (Sikes) walks beneath tottering house-fronts projecting over the pavement, dismantled walls that seem to totter as he passes, chimneys half crushed, half hesitating to fall, windows guarded by rusty iron bars that time and dirt have almost eaten away, and every imaginable sign of desolation and neglect.

'In such a neighbourhood beyond Dockhead, in the Borough of Southwark, stands Jacob's Island, surrounded by a muddy ditch, six or eight feet deep, and fifteen or twenty wide when the tide is in, once called Mill Pond, but known these days as Folly Ditch. It is a creek or inlet from the Thames, and can always be filled at high water by opening the sluices at the lead mills from which it took its old name. At such times a stranger, looking from one of the wooden bridges thrown across it at Mill Lane, will see the inhabitants of the houses on either side lowering, from their back doors and windows, buckets, pails, domestic utensils of all kinds, in which to haul the water up; and when his eye is turned from these operations to the houses themselves, his utmost astonishment will be excited by the scene before him. Crazy wooden galleries common to the backs of half-a-dozen houses, with holes from which to look upon the slime beneath, – windows broken and patched with poles thrust out on which to dry the linen that is never there; rooms so small, so filthy, so confined that the air would seem too tainted even for the dirt and squalor which they shelter; wooden chambers thrusting themselves out above the mud and threatening to fall into it, as some have done; dirt-besmired walls and decaying foundations;

every repulsive lineament of poverty, every loathsome indication of filth, rot and garbage – all these ornament the banks of Folly Ditch.

'In Jacob's Island the warehouses are roofless and empty; the walls are crumbling down; the windows are windows no more; the doors are falling into the streets; the chimneys are blackened, but they yield no smoke . . . The houses have no owners, they are broken open and entered upon by those who have the courage; and there they live, and there they die. They must have powerful motives for a secret residence, or be reduced to a destitute condition indeed, who seek refuge in Jacob's Island.'[17] – As George Orwell truly wrote, 'When Dickens has once described something, you see it for the rest of your life.'[18]

Jacob's Island may have been an extreme example of London's living conditions in the early decades of the nineteenth century, but only in the matter of degree, not of essence. London's major problem was that no-one was responsible for it, or, rather, too many people had a hand in its government. One way of thinking about London at this time is to imagine three hundred separate villages all compressed into a parcel of land measuring less than five miles by three – or one decent-sized provincial town. Each of these 'villages' was a distinct parish governed by its own vestry of rate-paying parishioners. But the vestries were not responsible for everything within their parish boundaries; nuisance abatement was the duty of the Poor Law Guardians; the responsibilty for paving and lighting was split up between the vestries and numerous trusts and commissions; sewerage and main drainage were administered by eight separate Commissioners of Sewers appointed by the Crown, and the supply of water was in the hands of eight private companies. Each of these bodies was constituted differently with different and, sometimes, overlapping powers. Even single streets were divided, often along their length, and paved and cleansed at different times and under different jurisdictions. These bodies acted under the authority of two hundred and fifty separate Acts of Parliament, competing and conflicting, but rarely co-operating with each other.[19] Householders were bemused and indignant as separate rates were levied for the poor, the highways, sewers, paving and lighting, watchmen etc., each independently valued, separately assessed and collected individually by the various bodies at odd times.[20]

London's government, if such it can be called, was little more than a barely controlled anarchy. The great sanitary reformer, Edwin Chadwick, vented his frustration at this farcical state of affairs in a letter to his friend Lord Morpeth when he wrote: 'Cesspools may be emptied: but stinking dust heaps are left, because the scavenger removes them when it suits his convenience. The cesspools may be cleansed and the dust removed but heaps of old dung are left which it is neither the business of the dust contractor nor the sewer men to remove. By a fortunate concurrence the night soil, the coal ashes and the dung may be removed and the court would smell sweet but for some dead cats, or a dead dog, or fish garbage which the dustmen and the sewer men under some contracts declare it is not "their place" to remove. The Inspector of Nuisances is sent for and he says it is not his place to do it, he has no allowance to pay anybody to take it away: the overseer wont allow it and overseer says he would not mind but the Poor Law Commissioners wont allow it. The Inspector of Nuisances says his place is to prosecute the parties who left the animals there – if he could only find them!'[21]

"The filth of their dwellings is excessive, so is their personal filth. When they attend my surgery, I am always obliged to have the door open. When I am coming down stairs from the parlour, I know at the distance of a flight of stairs whether there are any poor patients in the surgery." This was part of the reply by John Liddle, the medical officer of the Whitechapel Union in London's East End, and given to one of the first enquiries into the health of the poor. Written by Edwin Chadwick and presented to the House of Lords in 1842 it was the result of three years' work of investigation. The 'Report on the Sanitary Condition of the Labouring Population of Great Britain' disclosed for the first time the insanitary state of the whole nation but, because of the size of its population, especially of London itself. When John Liddle was asked how the inhabitants of Whitechapel got their water he replied, "They get it for the most part from a plug in the courts," adding, "When I have occasion to visit their rooms, I find they have only a scanty supply of water in their tubs. When they are washing, the smell of the dirt mixed with the soap is the most offensive of all the smells I have to encounter. They merely pass dirty linen through very dirty water." On being asked, "are the courts in which the labouring classes reside, in your district, paved or cleansed?"

Liddle answered, "They are not flagged, they have a sort of pebbles; they are always wet and dirty. The people, having no convenience in their houses for getting rid of waste water, they throw it down at the doors . . . I do not think that one house for the working classes will be found in which there is such a thing as a sink for getting rid of the water."[22]

From this one witness alone the Commission learned three important facts: that the only supply of water was from a shared stand-pipe, with no means of disposing of it apart from throwing it out on to an unpaved court and, unsurprisingly, that the people stank. Nor was this all. Half a century later that energetic campaigner, Lord Shaftesbury, described how things were at this time: 'In the old times the water was supplied sometimes only once a week, and at other times twice a week. In particular courts there was a stand-pipe put up and the water came up at a certain time and lasted for twenty or twenty-five minutes. All the vessels were arranged in a single file on each side to catch the water, and an old woman was placed in an upper window to shout and give notice when the water supply was coming on. The people rushed to get the water as they could before the supply ceased.'[23]

Joseph Quick, the engineer of the Southwark Water Company, told a Parliamentary enquiry that they supplied about 18,000 tenants of whom only 4,000 had an exclusive supply, a further 11,000 shared a water tap with two or three other families and 2,000 more depended upon one of 250 common standpipes, but that about 5,000 tenements containing 30,000 people had no water supply whatsoever, adding "They depend for their supplies on pumps or such rainwater as they catch."[24] The Southwark Water Company's engineer listed some of his company's larger consumers which, in itself, paints a graphically gruesome picture of the industries polluting Southwark's residents at this time – 'manufactories, tanners, fellmongers, hair washers, glue-makers, curriers, dyers, hatters, brewers, distillers, steam-engines, railway stations, hospitals etc.'[25] In describing the activity he had witnessed at the common standpipes he said' "I have seen as many as from 20 to 50 persons with pails waiting round one or two standpipes. Then there is quarrelling for the turn; the strongest pushing forward, and the pails, after they are filled being upset".[26]

To those of us who take a constant supply of fresh water for granted and even object to having to pay more than a nominal sum for what is, after all, 'supplied naturally', it seems almost inconceivable that most of the population should have regarded it as a scarce, infrequent and valuable commodity. Charles Dickens' brother-in-law gave evidence to another enquiry two years after Chadwick's 'Sanitary Report': "On the principal cleaning day, Sunday," he explained, "water is on for about five minutes and it is also on three days a week for half an hour, and so great is the rush to obtain a modicum before it is turned off that perpetual quarrelling and disturbance is the result and water-day is but another name for dissension."[27]

Apart from its unpredictability, London's water was unpurified and, therefore, unhygenic, not to say downright dangerous. Most of the capital's supplies and every drop piped to the southern side of the Thames came straight out of the river, and the river was the receptacle for more than two hundred sewer outfalls.[28]

John Hollingshead interviewed an old workman with fifty years' experience of south London sewers: "Some of the shores (sewers) was made o' wood, spesh'ly about Roderide (Rotherhithe): an' at S'uth'ark the people used to dip their pails in 'em for water." He explained, "They made holes in 'em, so's to get at the water when the tide was up."[29]

The sewers had been built to drain off surface rainwater and had never been intended for the purposes of sanitation. In fact, it was an offence to discharge human waste into them, a law often ignored by those who could afford to connect their privy to a common sewer which passed their property. A more usual method was to connect the privy to a cesspool under the house. 'In poor districts these would often overflow through the floorboards into the rooms above.'[30] Chadwick reported that cesspools 'were allowed to accumulate and fill up with the disgusting liquid. At the best, they were cleaned out two or three times a year, more usually once every two years. On these rare occasions men with two-horse carts would shovel the sickening mess into buckets until the carts were full, and then drive away with it to fling it in the river.

When Mr Quick, the water engineer, was asked if the poorer areas of Southwark were drained, he explained that it was the lack of any drainage which was the greatest obstacle to providing a water supply to many of the houses. When approached with the suggestion that water pipes should be laid on, the landlords' answer was generally, "But we have no drains to carry off the waste. If we have more water brought into the premises, we shall have more damp, and rot the floors, and make the houses more untenantable."[31] As to the conduct of the inhabitants, the engineer reported that in the Mint area, the oldest part of Southwark, "the people in many houses throw everything out of the windows into the 'back yards'."[32] The infant death rate at that time was horrendous as Edwin Chadwick's 'Sanitary Report' had demonstrated two years earlier. One in five children of the gentry and the professional classes died before they were five years old, but half the children of labouring families were dead by that age.[33]

The 1841 census counted 270,000 houses in London, most of which had a cesspit underneath. In an attempt to deal with this growing problem the Metropolitan Commission of Sewers was formed to amalgamate the eight separate bodies nominally responsible for London's drainage. 'It decreed that all cesspits must be abolished and so some 200,000 cesspits suddenly went out of use. The effect was disastrous, for now all the main sewers and underground streams discharged their new contents into the Thames which was compelled to accept the ordure of three million human beings. The river became a huge open sewer.'[34]

Just three years after this action had been taken, at the midpoint of the century, the Edinburgh Review reported derisively: 'The refuse and the dirt from 2m. of individuals, – the enormous accumulation of waste and dead animal and vegetable matter, – the blood and offal of slaughter houses, the outpourings from gas-works, dye-works, breweries, distilleries, glue-works, bone-works, tanneries, chemical and other works, and a thousand nameless pollutions, – all find their way into the Thames. The mixture is next washed backwards and forwards by the tide; and having been thoroughly stirred up and finely commuted by the unceasing splash of 298 steamboats, is then pumped up for the use of the wealthiest city in the world!'[35]

In that same year Arthur Hassals made a 'Microscopic Examination of the Water supplied to the Inhabitants of London', which revealed that, 'the waters supplied by those Metropolitan Companies whose source is the Thames, are in a high degree impure and, therefore, unfit for use, and detrimental to health: in this condemnation the waters of the Companies which supply the Surrey side of London, viz. the Vauxhall, Southwark and Lambeth, ought to stand first . . . ' Of the Southwark and Vauxhall Company, Hassals wrote that its water was 'in the worst condition in which it is possible to conceive any water to be, as regards its animalcular contents,' and 'that a gauze bag tied to the tap of the water cistern is found at the end of a few days to contain a mass sufficient to fill an eggshell, consisting principally of the hairs of mammalian animals.' His forthright summary could not have been bettered by the crusading journalists of the Morning Chronicle or the satirists of Punch: 'It is beyond dispute', he concluded, 'that, according to the present system of London Water Supply, a portion of the inhabitants of the metropolis are made to consume, in some form or other, a portion of their own excrement, and moreover, to pay for the privilege.'[36] As Edwin Chadwick's biographer has said, 'It was fortunate for the working classes that they possessed such a preference for beer.'[37]

These conditions, of course, bred disease. Outbreaks of typhoid fever were frequent and typhus, known as 'the fever' and acknowledged to be 'the poor man's disease'[38] was endemic. But in 1830 something new was awaited with horror. In September cholera had reached Moscow along the trade routes from India and it could not be long before it arrived in Britain. Throughout the following year it spread across northern Europe and by October it was raging in Hamburg, only a few hours' sailing time across the North Sea.[39] The first reaction amongst the radical writers and the working population seems to have been that these warnings were 'humbug', a scare story put about by 'half-starved doctors, apothecaries' clerks and jobbers in the parish funds' for the purpose of lining their own pockets.[40]

But the fear was not long delayed. The first reported victim was William Sproat, a Sunderland keelman, who died on Wednesday, October 26th 1831.[41] From there it spread rapidly throughout the country reaching London early in the new year. London's first victims were three Rotherhithe labourers living in or near Jacob's Island – an unemployed seaman, a coal-dredger and a ship-scraper who had been working on a collier from Newcastle[42]. This was probably the initial cause of the outbreak, but even if that voyage had not been undertaken, there would have been plenty of other infected travellers to bring the disease to the capital. From February to the end of the year, when winter finally killed it off, the cholera infected 11,000 Londoners, killing almost half of them. Throughout the rest of the country over 25,000 victims died.[43]

Death from Asiatic cholera was often swift, sometimes a matter of hours only, but it was certainly not merciful. From feeling vaguely unwell, the victim was quickly overtaken by violent sickness and diarrhoea causing dehydration and loss of body salts which brought on agonising muscular cramps, severe thirst and fever.[44] An Edinburgh surgeon with cholera experience in India described a patient in the last stages of the illness: 'The eyes surrounded by a dark circle are completely sunk in the sockets, the whole countenance is collapsed, the skin is livid . . . The surface (of the skin) is now generally covered with cold sweat, the nails are blue, the skin of the hands and feet are corrugated as if they had been long steeped in water . . . the voice is hollow and unnatural. If the case be accompanied by spasms, the suffering of the patient is much aggravated, and is sometimes excruciating.'[45] The damage these symptoms caused to the circulatory system and the internal organs led to collapse and the death of half those who caught the disease.

The age pattern of deaths from cholera was distinctly different from that normally expected. The regular death rate of the under-fives was horrendously high, but they seem to have been largely spared, as were those in their teens and twenties. The heaviest toll occurred amongst the over thirties – those with dependent families, whose members would then fall to the care of the parish workhouse.[46]

The tiny parish of St Thomas contributed thirteen cholera deaths to the London total between March and September of 1832. Three of those lived in New Way, that narrow alley where James and Ann lived after their marriage. They were Thomas Rowland a 49 year old labourer, a charwoman named Mary Casnell and Frances Hopkins a 53 year old nurse at St Thomas's Hospital. In fact, at least four of the thirteen victims were known to have been employed at the hospital including a nursing sister, a cupper and a porter. Eight of the thirteen died within 24 hours of the initial seizure and one lingered for as long as eight days. Of the twelve whose ages are known or can be assumed only two were children and the ten adults ranged in age from 30 to 63.[47]

The better-off citizens generally considered themselves to be at little risk, although later studies show this complacent attitude not to be entirely justified.[48] However, their belief that 'the more respectable and prosperous sections of society' would probably be safe was undoubtedly a comfort, bolstered by reports that the incidence of cholera was confined to the 'poor, the distressed, the badly fed, the badly clothed, the filthy and the intemperate.'[49]

'O how has this sweeping scourge cut down the ungodly!' wrote the Wesleyan Methodist Magazine, 'Some pious souls may have been removed by it, and have spent their last moments in peace; but the dissipated, dissolute, profane, and intemperate, are the general victims of the disease,' it concluded.[50] Some of the more fervent evangelicals saw apocalyptic visions in the advent of one of the most feared of the Four Horsemen. Spencer Perceval, son of the assassinated Prime Minister, told Parliament, "I tell you this land will soon be desolate; a little time and ye shall howl one and all in the streets. I tell ye that pestilence which God is now holding in, will be let loose among ye and that the sword will follow."[51]

If that was rather too extreme for some churchmen, most considered it to be a visitation of the Almighty calling for repentance, a return to religious observance and clean living. Consequently, Parliament declared March 21st 1832 a day of 'fasting, prayer and humiliation', provoking the radical press to ask how the poor should observe a fast when this was their natural lot for a good part of their lives.[52]

To ascribe the epidemic to an Act of God, however, was no less illogical than most of the reasons adduced. Electrical fluid, lightning strikes, volcanic eruptions, clouds of minute insects too small for the eye to see, waterspouts and whirlwinds were all proposed as possible causes.[53] The belief that the sickness was contagious led to a quarantine ban on all incoming ships until commercial pressures caused it to be lifted. But the theory which came to dominate medical thought was that the cholera was generated in clouds of poisonous vapour given off by decaying organic matter which lay, to a greater or lesser extent, over inhabited areas. This 'miasma' theory, simply and crudely put, meant that 'smells generated disease.'[54] This 'insidious miasma of sewer gas'[55] over London was later described by the registrar-general who wrote that if it could be made visible it 'would be found to lie dimly over Eltham, Dulwich, Norwood, Clapham, Battersea, Hampstead and Hackney; growing thicker round Newington, Lambeth, Marylebone, Pancras, Stepney; dark over Westminster, Rotherhithe, Bermondsey, Southwark; and black over Whitechapel and the City of London.'[56]

There were certainly enough smells around to give superficial credence to this belief, and the burial practices only added to them as Chadwick explained: 'In the Metropolis on spaces of ground which do not exceed 203 acres, closely surrounded by the abodes of the living, layer upon layer, each consisting of a population numerically equivalent to a large army of 20,000 adults, and nearly 30,000 youths and children, is every year imperfectly interred.' Describing a burial ground in Rotherhithe: '. . . the interments were so numerous that the half-decomposed organic matter was often thrown up to make way for fresh graves, exposing sights disgusting, and emitting foul effluvia.'[57]

In comparing these living conditions with our present-day sensitivities, Enid Gauldie points up the most significant factor a modern time traveller would immediately notice with these words: 'The smell alone must have been nearly intolerable. To a generation which spends thousands of pounds on scents and deodorants to ensure that we are never aware of the odours of other bodies, it is astonishing that the smell of the 1830's could have been (even temporarily) endured. Yet thousands of families lived with years' old accumulations of filth permanently accosting their nostrils.'[58]

John James Bezer was the author of one of the very few autobiographies written by a London working man at this time. After listing the advantages of his new job as a grocer's assistant in the pure country air of Camberwell, he adds in the ironical vein of a true radical:

> 'The change was like emigrating to another country - another world. I had lived previously for a long time in Whitecross Place, near Barbican.
>
> It is said, God made everything. I don't believe it; He never made Whitecross Place, the entrance to which was the narrow way that leadeth unto stinks. A gutter passed through the middle of the court - a pretty looking gutter, from which the effluvia rose up, without ceasing, into our elegant second floor front; a room, or rather a cell (we paid 2s.3d. rent weekly, for the blessed privelege of breathing in the accumulated filth below); a hole in which bugs held a monster public meeting every night, determined to show what a co-operative movement could do. I say, God never made Whitecross Place.

> He is not the author of filthy lanes and death-breeding alleys. Landlords and profit-mongers make them, and then proclaim national fasts to stay the progress of the cholera.'[59]

Cholera, of course, is a water-borne disease, caused by swallowing water infected with the excreta of a cholera sufferer, but more than half a century was to pass before Robert Koch identified the microbe, by which time three further outbreaks had killed 30,000 people in London alone.[60] By then the disease had been finally conquered by adequate sanitation and a clean water supply, although it was not until the very last year of the nineteenth century that London's supply was a constant, rather than an intermittent, one.[61]

Ignorance of the medical causation of the epidemic did not mean that the authorities took no action. On the contrary, for the first time ever a government took energetic steps to prevent the spread of a fatal disease. Unfortunately, those steps frequently provoked resentment, leading to riot, amongst that part of the population who were worst affected – the poor. Burial regulations laid it down that victims 'should be buried as soon as possible wrapped in cotton or linen cloth saturated with pitch, or coal tar, and be carried to the grave by the fewest possible number of persons.' If possible the bodies were to be interred in ground adjoining the cholera hospital.[62] Such rules contravened traditional burial customs whereby the body was laid out for several days so that relatives and friends could pay their last respects before attending the burial service in the parish church on their only free day, Sunday, a rite which proved impossible if burial had to take place within twentyfour hours of death, unless the mourners took an unpaid day off work. Some of the local Boards of Health which were set up for the emergency designated special burial areas for the victims, not always in consecrated ground; quicklime was often used to promote rapid decomposition, but this practice was associated in the public mind with executed criminals. The victim's clothes, bedding and even furniture were burned as a precaution, but compensation was not always paid to the families whose sole possessions they may have been.

Whenever possible the sick were removed to hospitals (where they had even less chance of surviving than if they had stayed at home). 'Some were temporary buildings, others damp and chill warehouses, schoolrooms, tents and one was a steam-laundry in the Isle of Dogs.'[63] The City of London Board of Health asked the governors of St. Thomas's Hospital how many patients they could admit. They replied that they could accommodate 50-100 by putting up huts in the forecourt, 'since the physicians advised that it would not be desirable to admit cholera patients into the wards.'[64] But the sick and their families had no wish to enter the isolation hospitals anyway in case they were used as anatomical specimens for dissection. At the height of the epidemic the Anatomy Bill was being debated in Parliament to provide a legal supply of corpses from amongst unclaimed workhouse and hospital inmates; the Burke and Hare murders were a recent memory, and the occurrence of 'burking' in London had been confirmed only in the month following the first reported cholera death.[65] In such a highly charged atmosphere it is scarcely surprising that a crowd, said to number six thousand, seized an old man from a surgeon and his assistant as he was being taken in a chair to St Marylebone hospital and carried him naked through the night back to his own house, 'saved from being "burked" '. The doctors tried to retrieve the patient but the crowd broke up the chair and pelted them with the pieces. The police eventually restored order at the cost of one casualty – a constable felled with a warming pan.[66]

Linked to this dread of dissection, whether preceded by medical murder or not, was the surpassing fear of being buried alive. The muscular cramps or spasms, which frequently accompanied the latter stages of the disease, often relaxed only after death had occurred, 'causing sudden convulsions which could be mistaken for signs of life. Signs of death could be equally deceptive, as in many cases the body was blue ('as if dip't in a solution of indigo'), stiff from muscular spasm, 'cold as marble', and with heart and breathing rates so low as to be imperceptible. Cases were reported of people who survived a medical diagnosis of death, and when we consider that the medical test for death was merely the holding of a mirror near the mouth to seek signs of breath, we need not disbelieve such reports, nor discredit as unreasonable the widespread fear of premature burial or of dissection taking place before life was extinct.'[67] That, at least was a genuine and understandable dread – the stuff of nightmares.

When the cholera returned after sixteen years, Henry Mayhew observed that, 'so well known are the localities of fever and disease, that London would almost admit of being mapped out pathologically, and divided into its morbid districts and deadly cantons. We might lay our fingers on the Ordnance map, and say here is the typhoid parish, and there the ward of cholera; for truly as the West-end rejoices in the title of Belgravia, might the southern shores of the Thames be christened Pestilentia.'[68]

James Mimms, from the quiet little Huntingdonshire village of Eynesbury, might well have wondered what strange land this was in which he had chosen to live.

References

[1] Flinn, 'The Sanitary Condition of the Labouring Population', pp.130/131
[2] Finer, 'Edwin Chadwick', p.219
[3] Besant, 'South London', pp.307/308
[4] ibid., p.303
[5] Fitzgerald, 'Victoria's London', p.3.
[6] Besant, 'South London', p.306
[7] ibid., pp.301/302
[8] Weinreb, and Hibbert, 'The London Encyclopaedia', pp.468/9
[9] Davies, A., 'The Map of London ', p.78
[10] Prettejohns, 'Charles Dickens and Southwark', p.9
[11] Cunningham, P. 'Handbook of London', p.462
[12] Boast, 'The Story of the Borough', p.13
[13] Parsons, 'St. Thomas's Hospital', pp.11–28.
[14] Wohl, 'The Eternal Slum', p.135.
[15] Gauldie, 'Cruel Habitations', p.83.
[16] Wohl, 'The Eternal Slum', p.3
[17] Prettejohns, 'Charles Dickens and Southwark', p.21/22
[18] Orwell, 'Decline of the English Murder' p.118.
[19] Finer,'Edwin Chadwick', pp.306/307
[20] Flinn, 'The Sanitary Condition of the Labouring Population', pp.391/392.
[21] Finer,'Edwin Chadwick', p.337
[22] Flinn, 'The Sanitary Condition of the Labouring Population', pp.135/136
[23] Gauldie,'Cruel Habitations', p.77
[24] House of Lords R.O., 'First Report on the State of Large Towns and Populous Districts', (1844), XXIV, p.393, paras. 5874–6
[25] ibid., para. 5874
[26] ibid., p.397, para. 5898
[27] Gauldie,'Cruel Habitations', p.76
[28] Finer,'Edwin Chadwick', p.392
[29] Hollingshead, 'Underground London', p.77
[30] Weinreb and Hibbert, 'The London Encyclopaedia', p.237 and Flinn, 'The Sanitary Condition of the Labouring Population', p.369
[31] House of Lords R.O., 'First Report on the State of Large Towns and Populous Districts', (1844), XXIV, p.393, para. 5881
[32] ibid., para. 5882
[33] Flinn, 'The Sanitary Condition of the Labouring Population', p.233
[34] Weinreb and Hibbert, 'The London Encyclopaedia', p.237

[35] 'Edinburgh Review', (1850), vol. xci, p.381: quot. in Finer, 'Edwin Chadwick', p.392
[36] Weinreb and Hibbert,'The London Encyclopaedia', pp.804 and 931.
[37] Finer, 'Edwin Chadwick', p.220
[38] Millar, R., 'Clinical Lectures on the Contagious Typhus', Glasgow, (1833) p.11: Flinn, 'The Sanitary Condition of the Labouring Population', p.10
[39] Morris, 'Cholera 1832', p.23
[40] ibid., p.97
[41] Morris, 'Cholera 1832', pp.11 and 42.
[42] ibid., p.70, and Himmelfarb, 'The Idea of Poverty', p.314
[43] Morris, 'Cholera 1832', p.75
[44] ibid., pp 15/16 and Hibbert, C., 'The English, A Social History', p.439
[45] Bell, G.H., 'Treatis on the Cholera Asphyxia,' Edinburgh, (1831): quot. in Morris, 'Cholera 1832', p.16
[46] Morris, 'Cholera 1832', pp.82/83
[47] P71/TMS/512, Greater London R.O.
[48] Morris, 'Cholera 1832', pp.85 - 93.
[49] ibid., p.84
[50] 'Wesleyan Methodist Magazine', vol. 11, 3rd series, (1832) p.205: quot. in Morris 'Cholera 1832', p.135
[51] Hansard, 3rd series, vol.11, 20 March 1832: quot. in Morris, 'Cholera 1832', p.151.
[52] Morris, 'Cholera 1832', pp.147-149
[53] ibid., pp.170/171
[54] Flinn, 'The Sanitary Condition of the Labouring Population', p.62
[55] Wohl, 'The Eternal Slum', p.16
[56] 'Journal of the Statistical Society of London', vol.X (September 1847), p.277: quot. in Wohl, 'The Eternal Slum', p.16
[57] Finer, 'Edwin Chadwick', p.230
[58] Gauldie, 'Cruel Habitations', p.73
[59] Vincent, 'Testaments of Radicalism', pp.173/4
[60] Weinreb and Hibbert, 'The London Encyclopaedia', p.155
[61] Finer, 'Edwin Chadwick', p.503
[62] Morris, 'Cholera 1832', pp.104/105
[63] ibid., p.104
[64] Parsons, 'St. Thomas's Hospital', p.69
[65] Richardson, 'Death, Dissection and the Destitute', p.193.
[66] Morris, 'Cholera 1832', p.108
[67] Richardson, 'Death, Dissection and the Destitute', p.227
[68] 'Morning Chronicle', 24 SEP. 1849

CHAPTER TEN

MARKETS, DOCKS AND RAILWAYS

> 'The wonder to me is, not that so many of the labouring classes crowd to the gin shops, but that so many are to be found struggling to make their wretched abode a home for their family.'
>
> –Witness to the Royal Commission on the State of Large Towns (1844)[1]

> '. . . each day's investigation brings me incidentally into contact with a means of living utterly unknown among the well-fed portion of society.'
>
> – Henry Mayhew (1849)[2]

The responsibility for policing the tiny parish of St Thomas in Southwark was shared between the Beadle, the Constable and the Watchman. At its Easter Tuesday meeting in 1829 the Vestry noted that 'Frequent complaints having been made to the Vestry by several of the Inhabitants That very great nuisances, Noise & other Disorders existed in the Streets of this Parish,' they ordered, 'That the Beadle do go Daily, or as frequently as occasion may require, around the Parish, to suppress all Nuisances, Noise and Disturbances.' A copy of that resolution was to be delivered to Mr Weare, the parish Beadle and, for good measure, they appended a note reminding him of his duties, which read:

> 'The Duty of the Beadle
> Your business is to give notice to the Parishioners when and

> where a Vestry is appointed to be held by the Churchwardens, to attend such Vestries when met and to execute its orders.
>
> He is also to assist the Churchwardens, Overseers and Constables, in the discharge of their respective duties and generally, to do and execute all the Orders and business of the Vestry and of the Parish.'[3]

Richard Weare's response to what he clearly interpreted as an additional burden of responsibilities was to petition the Vestry that October for a salary rise. He had served as Beadle for six years and now complained that his increased duties 'do not allow him to obtain other employment', which he found necessary having a wife and three children to support, 'one of whom is unfortunately an Idiot.'[4] The Vestry must have been sympathetic to his request as they granted him an increased salary of £40 p.a. at their next annual meeting. At the same time they agreed to pay Fanny Hayes 8 guineas for her work as sextoness and a further 12 guineas 'for washing Surplices, Church Covering, Cleaning the Church, Church Porch Gateway and Vestry Room.' Perhaps she considered £21 a year an insufficient recompense for all that work as eighteen months later it was reported that she 'had left the parish and her house keys and church keys with the Beadle.'[5]

If Richard Weare was considered a valuable employee, the same could not be said of Thomas Couchman, the Watchman. He was repeatedly accused of neglecting his duties. The Vestry gave him a final warning at their meeting in the February of 1829 that if any more complaints were made against him he would be discharged. By the August he faced another complaint and the Vestry resolved, 'That the Watchman be discharged to Remain a fortnight on Duty till a Man can be found.'[6] Within that fortnight they had found Edward Ashley of Long Walk, Bermondsey and appointed him to act as Watchman for the nine night-time hours from 9pm to 6am in winter and for two hours less in the summer months.[7] But the Vestry had not heard the last of Thomas Couchman. Immediately after his dismissal he applied to his erstwhile employers for relief. This was granted, one assumes with some reluctance, at a rate of five shillings a week 'untill he can get employ or be employ'd.'[8] The Vestry itself tried to find employment for him to relieve the ratepayers of the parish by writing to William Peel Esquire at the Home Office recommending 'Thomas Couchman our present Parochial

Watchman whom we trust they will find to be a fit and able bodied Man, well qualified to be placed upon the Metropolitan Police Establishment.'[9] The Vestry Clerk was not being strictly truthful as Thomas Couchman had been dismissed for incompetence five months earlier, but then, relations between the parish and the Home Office were under some strain at the time as the Home Secretary, Robert Peel, was engaged in imposing his new police upon the reluctant parish ratepayers. The St Thomas Vestry never did relieve themselves of the burden of supporting Thomas Couchman; he pestered them for financial help, for bread and for 'Cloathing for his Son', until, at last, they added him to their annual 'Pension List' and continued to pay him an average of five shillings a week until, under the New Poor Law, he became the responsibility of the Poor Law Guardians of the St Olave's Union four years later.

In their letter to the Home Office recommending Thomas Couchman, the Vestry Clerk, William Barber, explained how the parish was so well protected already that they had no need of the Home Secretary's new 'Peelers':

'. . . the two Hospitals of St Thomas and Guy occupy the greater part of our Parish and employ their own Watchmen, Maze Pond forming the Eastern part of the Parish is watched jointly by this and St Olave's Parish under the management of the Commissioners of Sewers for the Eastern division. The remaining portion of the Parish is protected by our Parochial Watchman who has hitherto been found amply competent and Sufficient for that purpose.'

Needless to add that this plea had no effect and the ratepayers had to accept Robert Peel's constables with their blue tail coats, tophats, white trousers and short wooden batons and the heavy police rate of four shillings in the £ which accompanied them.

It was not long before the Vestry found occasion to complain of 'the gross neglect of the New Police', recording in their minutes, 'On Sunday evening last there were assembled in New Street (on the eastern border of Guy's Hospital) thirty or forty persons of the basest stamp who continued there from six o'clock until eight – fighting – using the vilest language – and otherwise conducting themselves in the most riotous and disorderly manner: during the whole of which period not one police officer came nigh the place.'[10] They complained, too, of its cost and ineffectiveness,

> '. . . the introduction of that system has burdened the Rate payers with three times the Annual expence of the nightly Watch and with the additional inconvenience of the parish having always to pay the Police Rate half a year in advance, that it further appears to this meeting that there is no Police Station within the parish nor any particular part of the parish where a policeman can with certainty be found if wanted but that they merely pass to and fro thro' the parish and that on several occasions when they have been wanted in the night none could be found for a considerable time and the Inhabitants have been much more annoyed by nightly disturbances in the Streets since the introduction of the new System.'

This meeting of the Vestry in October 1830 evidently had a great head of steam behind it as its members went on to resolve, 'That the new Police Act as far as it relates to this parish is found to be oppressive in its taxation, imperfect in its operation, inefficient in the security it was intended to give, and every way inferior to a well regulated nightly watch. And that it ought to be repealed and done away.' Not being satisfied with merely noting these expressions of disfavour in its minutes, the meeting went as far as it felt it could go, short of declaring secession from the kingdom, by resolving 'That a firm but respectful petition grounded on the preceding resolutions be prepared by this parish to his Majesty and both Houses of Parliament praying for the immediate repeal of the new Police Act and the total abolition of that system' and they appointed five of their number to form a committee to draw up the petition.[11] They could have saved themselves the trouble and expense and, instead, concentrated on matters over which they could exercise some influence such as dealing with a request from Richard Hill for 'two or three pounds to enable him to get into the Muffin and Crumpet business and thus relievc the parish from the burden of maintaining himself, his wife, and 3 children.'[12]

* * *

In the early 1830's, James Mimms met and married a Southwark girl, Ann Wingfield. Ann came from that part of Southwark to the west of the Borough High Street. Her parish church was St Saviour's which stood immediately next to the new London Bridge and has since become Southwark Cathedral. At the time of their marriage St Saviour's was in a sorry state. The church tower, choir and Lady Chapel had recently been restored but the wooden roof of the nave had become so dangerous that it was taken down in 1831 and remained roofless for nine years. Their wedding ceremony in May 1833 was therefore conducted in a church which was permanently open to the heavens.[13]

A year later their first child, Francis, was baptised at St Saviour's and this is the first record we have of how James earned a living since he had arrived in London. In the baptismal register his 'Quality, Trade or Profession' is described simply as 'Hosier'. This term usually meant one who was engaged in the hosiery trade, making and selling cravats, shirts and pantaloons as well as stockings,[14] but was applied more to the owners of small workshops or middle men who put the work out than to the framework-knitters or stockingers as the weavers themselves were called. Mostly these men were self-employed outworkers who hired their frames, bought their yarn from 'putters-out' and sold the finished article to the merchants.[15] But framework-knitting was a dying industry and had virtually disappeared from London altogether. Moreover, James had no experience of this trade and, although stockingers also manufactured lace, the county from which he came had no tradition of weaving lace – pillow-lace was their cottage industry. It seems much more likely, therefore, that James was a street vendor, hawking stockings, socks, neckerchiefs and suchlike articles in the streets, courts and alleys of Southwark and Bermondsey.

Only those who were comfortably off patronised what we should recognise as a shop, nor did shopkeepers encourage the less well-off whose presence would only drive away the respectable trade. Instead, most Londoners bought everything from street markets and the regular daily round of itinerant street sellers:

> 'The first hawker was the cats-meat man. Then came a young girl in a pink-ribboned bonnet, carrying a large basket of flowers made by herself out of tissue-paper . . . for decorating the empty fireplaces of summer. Next came the cane-chair mender, who collected damaged chairs, and sat on the kerb

> and repaired them, at ninepence a chair. Then the hawker with pot-flowers – "All a-blowing and a-growing!" . . . Then the journeyman glazier, looking about for broken panes. Then the clothes-line and clothes-prop woman. Then in quick succession, the journeyman tinker, the umbrella-mender, the "chamois-leather woman" (going from door to door cleaning plated articles) and the man collecting rabbit-skins and hare-skins . . . In the afternoon came the "watercreases" man. Then the lucifer-man. At five o'clock, the muffin-man with bell. The last arrival came at seven – the beer-boy ("Beer-ho!"), carrying long double-deck trays fitted with cans of beer.'[16]

Hawkers had only their voices to advertise their wares and services: "Knives, scissors and razors to grind!", "Long thread laces, long and strong!", "Any umbrellastermend?", "Six bunches a penny, sweet blooming Lavendar!", "Fine warnuts, penny for ten, all cracked!", "Any corns to pick?" " 'Ere's yer toys for girls and boys!". "Dust O!", "Sw-e-e-p!", and the yodelling milkman and maids, bearing their milk pails on a wooden yoke across the shoulders, were all common sights and cries at this time. Some hawkers deliberately distorted their cry to make a dishonest sale: a seller of song-books yelled, "Three un-derd an' fifty songs for a penny!", but meant, "Three under fifty songs for a penny!" Others did so from ignorance or for comic effect – "Ripe Speregas (asparagus)!", "En endy shoo-awn frer penny (a handy shoe-horn for a penny)!", or "Lice, lice, penny a pair boot-lice!"[17]

Coleridge was so annoyed by an old Jewish trader's repeated cry of " Ogh clo', Ogh clo'!", that he asked him why he so distorted his call. "Sir", replied the Jew, "I can say "old clothes" as well as you can, but if you had to say so ten times a minute for an hour together, you would say "Ogh clo' " as I do now." The poet rewarded him with a shilling.[18]

Doctors were an expensive luxury, so that most minor ailments were treated by pills and potions concocted and hawked by 'herbalists'. Andrew Tuer, who collected many of these London traders' cries, was offered dandelion tea by one of these as a better remedy for liverishness than the physicians' blue mineral pills with this explanation: "You've noticed the 'oles in a sheep's liver after it's cut up 'aven't you?", he asked, "Well, them 'oles is caused by slugs, and 'uman bein's is infested just the same . . . I calls out-of-sorts-ishness 'slugs in the liver', and pizens 'em with three penn'rth of dandelion tea, for which I charges thrippence. *They* calls it 'sluggishness of the liver', and pizens 'em with a penn'rth of blue pill, for which they charges a guinea, and as often as not they pizens the patient too."[19]

'"Dogs-meat! cats-meat! nice tripe! neats' feet! Come buy my trotters!", and other such cries were heard even more stridently on a Saturday night and a Sunday morning in London's many street markets. Between 8 and 10 o'clock on a November Saturday evening, Henry Mayhew counted nearly three hundred itinerant salesmen packing the half-mile length of Lambeth's New Cut and offering fruit, vegetables, fish, boots and shoes, cakes, pies, hot eels, baked potatoes, boiled whelks, nightcaps, lace, ladies' collars, artificial flowers, silk and straw bonnets, saucepans, tea-kettles, glass, crockery, brooms and brushes, books, songs and almanacs, baskets, toys, flowers, jewellery, sheep's trotters and peepshows. 'The class of customers at these places', he wrote in his Morning Chronicle column, 'are mostly the wives of mechanics and labourers. Here, and in the shops immediately adjoining, the working-casses mostly purchase their Sunday's dinner.'[20]

When he subsequently re-wrote and published his experiences under the title 'London Labour and the London Poor', Mayhew offered his book reading public this description of the New Cut on that evening:

> 'The scene in these parts has more the character of a fair than a market. There are hundreds of stalls, and every stall has its one or two lights; either it is illuminated by the intense white light of the new self-generating gas-lamp or else it is brightened up by the red smokey flame of the old-fashioned grease lamp. One man shows off his yellow haddock with a candle stuck in a bundle of firewood; his neighbour makes a candlestick of a huge turnip, and the tallow gutters over its sides; while the boy shouting 'Eight a penny, stunning pears!' has rolled his dip in a thick coat of brown paper, that flares away with the candle. Some stalls are crimson with the fire shining through the holes beneath the baked chestnut stove; others have handsome octohedral lamps, while a few have a candle shining through a sieve: these, with the sparkling ground-glass globes of the tea-dealers' shops, and the butchers' gaslights streaming and fluttering in the wind, like flags of

'Here, and in the shops immediately adjoining, the working-casses mostly purchase their Sunday's dinner.'

> flame, pour forth such a flood of light, that at a distance the atmosphere immediately above the spot is as lurid as if the street were on fire . . . A bootmaker, to 'ensure custom', has illuminated his shop-front with a line of gas and in its full glare stands a blind beggar, his eyes turned up so as to show only 'the whites', and mumbling some begging rhymes, that are drowned in the shrill notes of the bamboo-flute-player next to him . . . Then the sights as you elbow your way through the crowd, are equally multifarious. Here is a stall glittering with new tin saucepans; there another, bright with its blue and yellow crockery, and sparkling with white glass. Now you come to a row of old shoes arranged along the pavement; now to a stand of gaudy tea-trays; then to a shop with red handkerchiefs and blue checked shirts, fluttering backwards and forwards, and a counter built up outside on the kerb, behind which are boys beseeching custom . . .
>
> 'Go to whatever corner of the metropolis you please, either on a Saturday night or a Sunday morning', Mayhew concluded, 'and there is the same shouting and the same struggling to get the penny profit out of the poor man's Sunday dinner.'[21]

It would have been in such markets that James, the hosier, with his tray strung around his neck, would have had to compete for custom by peddling his "Stockings, stockings, twopence a pair!"

Behind the bustle and the colour and the garish lights, the harsh reality of that market was not lost on Daniel Kirwan, an American who made a similar visit to the New Cut a decade after Henry Mayhew: 'I bought a hot potato and a sprat', he wrote, 'and passed through the crowded streets, past butchers standing at their doors in dirty aprons, sharpening their knives in a business like manner; past water-cress and match girls, who seemed to spring out of the gutters, so thick were they; past drunken, noisy women, staggering home to their miasmic dens, with bunches of vegetables or chunks of meat in their arms, wrapped in coarse brown papers, dirty children following their footsteps, gaunt and shadow-like; past reeking, greasy coffee-shops, the very sign-boards of which were redolent of eel-pies, kidney stews, and all the abominations which are devoured in this neighbourhood daily and nightly, by the poor people who are forced to eat this food, the refuse of the slaughter-houses of mighty, populous London.'[22]

One of the products of London's slaughterhouses provided the raw material for a major industry centred on Southwark and Bermondsey – that of leather-processing. Different areas of the capital traditionally specialised in particular trades. Printing, bookbinding, jewellery and watch-making were concentrated in Holborn and Clerkenwell; Shoreditch and Bethnal Green produced toys, furniture and silk, whilst metalwork and cheap clothing were manufactured in Mile End and Whitechapel. Southwark and Bermondsey were the almost exclusive home of the hatters, the brushmakers, tanners and leather-dressers.[23] Tanyards abounded in Bermondsey and animal skins were used in both the leather and hatmaking industries, whilst their bones were rendered down in the nearby glue factories where, as The Times complained, 'great mounds of scutch (lay) putrefying in the Bermondsey glue yards.'[24] In the 1840's Henry Mayhew counted some thirty tanyards employing up to five hundred men engaged in scraping the hides, curing, tanning and, finally, dressing the leather. The purification process called for a small army of independent suppliers – Mayhew estimated two to three hundred who scoured London's streets for 'pure'. As he explained: 'The pure-finders meet with a ready market for all the dogs'-dung they are able to collect, at the numerous tanyards in Bermondsey, where they sell it by the stable-bucket full, and get from 8d, to 10d. per bucket, and sometimes 1s. and 1s. 2d. for it, according to its quality. The 'dry limy-looking sort' fetches the highest price at some yards, as it is found to possess more of the alkaline, or purifying properties; but others are found to prefer the dark moist quality.' 'Pure' was especially prized for dressing the thinner and finer leather products such as calf, kid and morocco used by bookbinders, glovers and high quality shoemakers. A 'pure-finder' could expect to collect a pail-ful a day and Mayhew had been assured that a few years earlier 'when they got from 3s. to 4s. per pail (18s – 28s a week), many of them would not exchange their position with that of the best paid mechanic in London.'[25] In that part of modern Southwark where the trade was particularly concentrated, Leathermarket Street, Morocco Street and Tanner Street still exist today, although the tanyards are long gone.

Hatmaking was practically confined to the south, or Surrey,

side of the Thames and concentrated in that part of Southwark which lay between Blackfriars Road to Tooley Street.[26] This highly skilled trade, however, depended on outworkers who collected rabbit skins from the workshops and prepared them at home for the furriers and hatters. George Sims, a crusading journalist of the late nineteenth century, described a visit he had made to the home of one of these 'fur-pullers':

> 'When we open the door we start back half choked. The air is full of floating fluff, and some of it gets into our mouths and half chokes us. When we've coughed and wheezed a little we look about us and gradually take in the situation.
> 'The room is about eight feet square. Seated on the floor is a white fairy – a dark-eyed girl who looks as though she had stepped straight off a twelfth cake. Her hair is powdered all over *a la Pompadour*, and the effect is *bizarre*. Seated beside her is an older woman, and she is white and twelfth-cakey too . . . They are simply pulling rabbit-skins – that is to say they are pulling away all the loose fluff and down and preparing the skins for the furriers . . . .Floors, walls, ceiling, every inch of the one room these people live and sleep in, is covered with fluff and hair. How they breathe in it is a mystery to me. I tried and failed, and sought refuge on the doorstep.'[27]

It is hardly surprising that many landlords, even of near-slum properties, refused to rent them to families engaged in fur-pulling. Unpleasant and unhealthy the work may have been, but it was one of the very few employments (sack and paper-bag making were the only others) available to the housebound wives of South London's casual labourers.[28]

After the birth of their first child, Francis, in 1834 another four and a half years elapsed before Ann had a second child, named James after his father, which survived. In all probability she suffered a still-birth or a series of miscarriages during this long period between her first and second children as there is no record of a baptism and burial in any of the local parish registers, which would have been recorded had a child survived even for as short a time as a few minutes. In July 1837 the government set up a national system to register births, marriages and deaths and, although it was not a compulsory requirement for many years thereafter, James and Ann faithfully registered each birth of their subsequent eight children – one every two or three years, and each one born at number 8 New Way, the little alley in St Thomas's parish close to the great hospital. The children's birth certificates issued by the Registrar General are valuable in that they show the father's occupation, making it clear that for a period of at least fourteen years James was a dock or riverside porter and later, as his age advanced, a 'warehouseman', 'light porter' or 'labourer'.

James's formative years had been spent as a farm labourer and he had few skills, apart from muscular strength, to offer an urban employer – unless milking cows in St James's Park could be so considered. One is tempted to believe that he found hawking stockings to be both irksome and unrewarding in competition with the sharp-witted and, as we should now say, 'streetwise', Townies brought up from infancy in the cunning skills of parting a hesitant buyer from his money.

Whatever the reason for his change of employment, the rest of James's life was spent in Southwark and Bermondsey's third major industry – the wharfs, warehouses and docks of South London's riverside.

'Dockwork is precisely the office that every man is fitted to perform,' wrote Henry Mayhew, 'and there we find every kind of man performing it. Those who are unable to live by the occupation to which they have been educated can obtain a living there without any previous training. Hence we find men of every calling labouring at the docks. There are decayed and bankrupt master butchers, master bakers, publicans, grocers, old soldiers, old sailors, Polish refugees, broken-down gentlemen, discharged lawyers' clerks, suspended Government clerks, almsmen, pensioners, servants, thieves – indeed every one who wants a loaf and is willing to work for it.'[29] Dockside labour demanded little more than human muscle power, unless it was a sharp instinct for self-preservation in avoiding serious injury. It consisted of lifting and then moving heavy cargo. The lifting was done by winches or by wheel. The wheel was like a large treadmill some sixteen feet in diameter and eight to nine feet wide. Six or eight men worked inside this wooden cylinder, walking on battens and so turning the whole contraption around themselves, lifting anything up to a ton in weight twentyseven feet into the air forty times every hour. Moving the cargo, porters' work, consisted of pushing a truck an average of thirty miles a day and it was said that for two-thirds of the time a porter 'is moving 1½ cwt at 6½ miles an hour.' Mayhew described dock labourers as 'a striking instance of mere brute force with brute appetites. This class of labourer is as unskilled as the power of a hurricane. Mere muscle is all that is needed: hence every human "locomotive" is capable of working there. All that is wanted is the power to move heavy bodies from one place to another.'[30]

London was the busiest port in the world. In 1842 nearly three thousand sailing ships and two hundred and thirty steamers were registered in London with a total burden of 650,000 tons. In that same year almost 6500 British and foreign vessels with a capacity of 1¼m tons entered the Port of London, with cargoes from all over the world which realised £12m. in customs duty alone.[31] Southwark and Bermondsey's riverside ran for three and a half miles along the Thames taking its share of this lucrative trade on to its jetties and wharfs and into its great warehouses.

As his ship came up-river towards the Pool of London, a French visitor described the sight: 'To the west of us a forest of masts and rigging grows out of the river: ships coming, going, waiting, in groups, in long files, then in one continuous mass, at moorings, in among the chimneys of houses and the cranes of warehouses – a vast apparatus of unceasing, regular and gigantic labour.'[32] 'The cellars and warehouses are collossal,' he wrote, 'beneath vaults equal in span to a mighty bridge, the crowded, busy, dimness fades distantly into deep shadow: Rembrandt would have found pictures ready-made in these mysterious perspectives, in the shifting darkness of these crammed and peopled cellars, in this infinity of store-rooms swarming with workers, like an ant-hill. They roll great bales and barrels calmly and without confusion. You hear the voices of clerks calling over numbers. In the middle of each cellar a 'foreman' sits at a small table, watching and making entries in a ledger. The masters, sober men in black hats walk about, supervise, say nothing.'[33]

'In the warehouses are stored goods that are, as it were, ingots of untold gold', wrote Henry Mayhew, 'Above and below ground you see piles upon piles of treasure that the eye cannot compass. The wealth appears as boundless as the very sea it has traversed. The brain aches in an attempt to comprehend the amount of riches before, above, and beneath it. There are acres and acres of treasure – more than enough, one would fancy, to stay the cravings of the whole world; and yet you have but to visit the hovels grouped round about all this amazing excess of riches, to witness the same amazing excess of poverty . . . Pass from the quay and warehouse to the courts and alleys that surround them, and the mind is as bewildered with the destitution of the one place, as it is with the superabundance of the other.'[34]

Henry Mayhew has been described as a 'one-man Royal Commission'[35] and 'incomparably the greatest social investigator' in the middle part of the nineteenth century.[36]. He shocked his complacent middle-class readers with a series of articles for the Morning Chronicle under the headline 'Labour and the Poor' based on interviews conducted amongst the mass of London's poorer citizens. In one of his reports he quoted a porter at the Surrey docks who described how the contractor who employed him paid his wages: "he pays the publican, where we gets our beer, all that's owing to us deal porters, and the publican pays us every Saturday night. I can't say that we are compelled to take beer – certainly not when at our work in the dock; but we're 'expected' to take it when we're waiting.

Payment of wages in public houses was common around the docks. The men who unloaded the coaling ships by climbing long ladders out of the holds with a sack of coal on their backs could only get employment from the innkeepers who controlled the gangs and who would only employ men if they spent up to half their wages in the public house.[37] An Act of Parliament outlawed the practice, but it was difficult to eradicate because the men were often grateful for any work on any terms at all. They were rarely employed on a regular basis, only for a day or an hour at a time and only then if they were at the dock gate when work was available and they were lucky or ruthless enough to catch the foreman's eye. Mayhew described a hiring scene at about 7.30 in the morning: 'Presently you know by the stream pouring through the gates, and the rush towards particular spots, that the "calling foremen" have made their appearance. Then begins the scuffling and scrambling, and stretching forth of countless hands high in the air, to catch the eye of him whose voice may give them work. As the foreman calls from a book the names, some men jump upon the backs of the others, so as to lift themselves high above the rest, and attract the notice of him who hires them. All are shouting. Some cry aloud his surname, some his christian name; others call out their own names to remind him that they are there . . . Indeed, it is a sight to sadden the most callous to see *thousands* of men struggling for only one day's hire, the scuffle being made the fiercer by the knowledge that hundreds out of the number there assembled must be left to idle the day out in want. To look in the faces of that hungry crowd is to see a sight that must be ever remembered.' Henry Mayhew had seen many memorable sights during his investigations which gives added force to his comment, 'Until I saw with my own eyes this scene of greedy despair, I could not have believed that there was so mad an eagerness to work, and so biting a want of it among so vast a body of men.'[38]

That mad scramble was for work which paid 2s. 6d. a day, or fourpence an hour. A full week's work for any continuous period was rare. The peak season for the Surrey Dock's timber trade with Scandinavia was from July to December, followed by little or no work during the three hardest winter months[39] but even when trade was not slack, bad weather affected the work on the Thames. A thick fog lasting for days at a time made manoeuvring in a crowded river dangerous; 'a sharp and prolonged frost . . . could bring all riverside work to a halt'[40] and, as Mayhew discovered, sailing ships found it difficult to come up the Thames in an easterly wind which could prevail for two or three weeks and deprive the port of all work, but, almost as catastrophic was the glut of vessels which needed to be unloaded as soon as the wind changed. This provided an over-abundance of work for a few weeks during which time thousands of unemployed men were drawn to the docks from all over London, many of whom stayed on after all the ships had been cleared, thus swelling the labour force far above its normal over-supply and so intensifying the competition for work.[41]

Mayhew reckoned that twelve thousand men depended on dock work 'whose daily bread is as fickle as the winds itself (sic)', and of these two-thirds might be out of work at any one time and whose average weekly earnings over a twelve month amounted to only five shillings.[42]

To those of his readers who accused the dock labourer of extravagance when work was plentiful, or lack of thrift when income occasionally soared, and of intemperance all the time, Mayhew commented: 'Were the income of the casual labourer at the docks five shillings per week from one year's end to another, the workman would know exactly how much he had to subsist upon, and might therefore be expected to display some little providence and temperance in the expenditure of his wages. But where the means of subsistence occasionally rise to fifteen shillings a week, and occasionally sink to nothing, it is absurd to look for prudence, economy, or moderation. Regularity of habits are incompatible with irregularity of income . . . It is a moral impossibility that the class of labourers who are only occasionally employed should be either industrious or temperate.' – and for good measure, Mayhew added this little homily for the benefit of those of his readers whose sanctimoniousness so clearly irked him: 'If the very winds could whistle away the food and firing of wife and children, I doubt much whether, after a few weeks' or a month's privation, we should many of us be able to prevent ourselves from falling into the very same excesses. It is consoling to moralize in our easy chairs, after a good dinner, and to assure ourselves that we should do different. Self-denial is not very difficult when our stomachs are full and our backs are warm; but let us live a month of hunger and cold, and assuredly we should be as self-indulgent as they.'[43]

But Mayhew was nothing if not inconsistent, and on another, later occasion offerred the opinion that London's labourers were 'nine times as dishonest, five times as drunken, and nine times as savage as the rest of the community.'[44]

* * *

Within a fortnight of James' and Ann's marriage the King had signed the Royal Assent to a private bill which authorised the construction of London's very first railway. In this respect the capital was well behind the northern towns – Liverpool and Manchester, for example, had been linked by a steam railroad for some years. The proposed service was not an ambitious one. It was to be only 3¾ miles long linking London Bridge and Greenwich via Deptford but in one respect, at least, it was unique in that it was to run on a twenty-two feet high viaduct for the whole of its length. The first mile eastwards from London Bridge was the densely populated area of Southwark and Bermondsey and the construction of an elevated railroad meant that the company would not need to buy up as many properties as if the line were to be built at ground level. The remaining distance to Greenwich lay below the Thames high-water mark and was naturally marshy so that a viaduct on raised piers became a practical necessity.[45] Each pier was twentyeight feet wide and they stood approximately eighteen feet apart forming almost nine hundred arches[46] carrying just an up and a down line.

The work of buying up houses and land and digging deep pits in which to construct a base for each pier proceeded very quickly, so that by the time James and Ann's first child was born a year after their marriage the first of the viaduct's sixty million grey bricks had already been laid. On its completion the viaduct must have been a most impressive sight, running in a straight line eastwards for almost the whole of its length. During the summer of 1835 hundreds of people climbed the still rural Nunhead Hill to view it, prompting a writer to say of the Greenwich Railway arches: 'The country which they overlook is very rich, and is almost wholly laid out in vegetable gardens. These will probably disappear ere long before the encroachments of brick and mortar. ' His prophecy was soon fulfilled as within only four years it was reported that 'the intermediate space (between Bermondsey and Deptford) is almost covered with houses.'[47]

James and Ann could not but be aware of the progress of the work since the viaduct was being built through Southwark only some seventy yards north of their home in New Way and the hundreds of labourers who had been imported to carry out the construction were lodged all around them. So serious was the fighting which frequently broke out between the Irish and English labourers at weekends that they had to be segregated: an area off Tooley Street between Battle Bridge Lane and Morgan's Lane is still known as 'English Grounds', and the 'Irish Grounds' were a short distance away.[48]

The London and Greenwich Railway Company built its offices at the London Bridge end of the line from which a wide ramp led down to the southern end of the bridge itself, but the station was little more than an elevated and enclosed yard. It had no roof, buffers or platforms, 'only the three iron gates which separated it from the approach road (and) a small ticket-office . . . .distinguished it from any other part of the line', except that at this point the viaduct was sixty feet wide and had three tracks instead of two.[49] The central two and a half mile stretch of the railway from Deptford to Spa Road, Bermondsey opened in February 1836 and the line extended to London Bridge by the end of that year when the formal opening ceremony was performed by the Lord Mayor of London, but it was to be another two years before the line reached Greenwich across the Ravensbourne River. Not surprisingly in view of the cost of property and land at its western end and the feat of engineering involved in constructing nearly four miles of viaduct, the cost of building the London and Greenwich Railway was considerable. It has been estimated at £267,000 per mile or five times that of the 112 mile London to Birmingham line[50] which reached its Euston terminus a year later.

Within a very few years London had five main-line stations but the author of the Handbook of London, published in 1850, wrote enthusiastically: 'The traveller, on reaching London Bridge, obtains an admirable and almost instantaneous view of the Thames, with its busy shipping and noble bridges – the bustle of streets crowded with carriages, carts and foot-passengers – the noble dome of St Paul's Cathedral, the massive grandeur of the Tower of London, the well-proportioned Monument . . . A drive of less than five minutes will take him across one of the noblest bridges in Europe, and throw him at once into the heart of the richest, largest, best lighted and best drained, city in the world. This is the only station affording a favourable view of London at first sight. The others are very bad.'[51]

As soon as the engines started running on the viaduct complaints reached the company of red-hot cinders being thrown down causing small fires, and the fire insurance premiums on properties along the line were increased. Passengers also complained of the sparks, but they received little sympathy from the local press; one paper suggested ' . . . that the driver should play upon the passengers occasionally with a hose, or that a man in asbestos breeches should sit on the funnel to keep the sparks in.'[52] The second and third class passengers would probably not have noticed if they had been hosed down by the driver as their carriages generally had no roof anyway nor, for that matter, any sides or seats. As one of them complained to The Times: 'The Directors stick up large placards about town 'Go by the Greenwich Train, fare 6d.' . . . they have got one carriage or van stuck up in the middle of the train, without any covering to it, sometimes (in wet weather) 2 inches deep in water, having two or three short rough seats resembling huge salt boxes.' This van, he complained, 'may be more fitly described as a large, square, filthy dogs-meat cart.'[53] Within a few years the Directors acknowledged that their passengers should not be made to 'stand like cattle in open trucks to be gazed upon as they travelled along the viaduct', but did little about it apart from suggesting that, 'if it was quite impossible to provide seats in the open carriages, they should at least be fitted with iron rails to which the passengers could cling for support.'[54]

It is scarcely to be wondered at that 'there were fifteen times as many fatal accidents in England as there were in Germany, many of them the fault of the passengers who were constantly attempting to board moving trains, jumping off to pick up their hats, sitting on the tops of the carriages and falling over the sides of the open, seatless trucks.'[55] But it was not only passengers who fell off trains. Thirty-six years old George Mims, a distant relative of James was a coach guard for the Northern and Eastern Railway. When his 5.30pm train left Bishop's Stortford on Tuesday, September 19th 1843, he was stood on top of the Norwich Magnet coach strapping on the luggage. He must have forgotten that a short way up the line the train passed under South Mill Bridge. In the words of the reporter who covered the inquest held at the Crown Inn, Hockerill two days later, 'after passing the bridge a few rods he was seen by the guard of the Holbeach mail to fall off the coach and pitch upon his head. Endeavours were made to stop the train but without success until it reached Broxbourne station when an engine and carriage were immediately despatched to the assistance of the deceased, who was found lying quite insensible across the rail with his head so severely injured that no hope was entertained of his recovery and about 3 o' clock the following morning he expired.'[56]

Such was the frequency of railway accidents in the early years that a new insurance company, 'The Railway Passengers Assurance Company', was formed in 1849 specifically to arrange death and injury cover for those intrepid travellers who were prepared to trust their lives and limbs to this new and dangerous form of public transport. The premiums charged to 2nd and 3rd class passengers were higher than for those travelling 1st class, reflecting the increased risk to passengers in roofless, seatless and sideless carriages. Turning from their material to their spiritual needs, one of the many hundreds of religious tracts published at this time and aimed at such lower class readers as servants, drunkards, prostitutes and theatre-goers was one written especially for railway workers and passengers and engagingly entitled, 'The Importance of Constant Preparation for Death. A Railway Tract.'[57]

The London and Greenwich trains could manage only 15 – 20 mph on the down line and up to 30mph when London-bound, but the thought of being dragged at such incredible speeds behind an animated steam-pressure vessel was too much for some. When it had been suggested a few years earlier that a proposed railway from Woolwich would carry passengers at 18 – 20 mph, a writer in the Quarterly Review protested: 'We should as soon expect the people of Woolwich to suffer themselves to be fired off upon one of Congreve's ricochet rockets, as to trust themselves to the mercy of such a machine going at such a rate.'[58] Others complained of the speeds achieved but for quite different reasons. Betty Cringle, writing from 'Greenige, Ospittel', complained:

> 'The Greenige Homtribusses and Stagis will giv you a ryde for half an nour or three quatters, for six pense, but thes ralerode peopl dont give you no more than ten minnits of it – You jist git into there carridges and wiz gos the steme and their you are at Deptfurd in 10 minnites.'[59]

'Betty Cringle' may have been a joker's pen-name but she/he was clearly a Shillibeer supporter. George Shillibeer, a former midshipman, had trained as a coach-builder in London and then set up a small business in Paris until he decided to introduce his 'new carriages on the Parisian mode' to London by opening a regular service between Paddington and the City in July 1829 employing a three-horse van with windows at the side and a windowed door at the back.[60] Soon he had twelve horse-drawn 'omnibuses' running in various parts of the capital.[61] In January 1834, however, he abandoned all his former routes and concentrated his, by now twenty, vehicles on a single service from London to Greenwich and Woolwich in direct competition with the London and Greenwich Railway which was then under construction. It was popularly believed that his action would probably force the railway company to abandon their scheme. A contemporary popular song entitled, 'Shillibeer's Original Omnibus versus the Greenwich Railroad,' said of his 'buses:

> 'These pleasure and comfort with safety combine,
> They will neither blow up nor explode like a mine;
> Those who ride on the railroad might half die with fear,
> You can come to no harm in the safe Shillibeer.'[62]

but, like so many who set their faces against the march of 'progress' and back their prejudices with hard cash, George Shillibeer's omnibuses went out of business not long after the railway line opened.

The London and Greenwich Railway itself did not long survive as an independent entity. From its earliest days it had permitted other railway companies which served Kent and the South Coast to use its viaduct into London Bridge Station on payment of a toll. It was one of these, the South Eastern Railway, which took over the Greenwich line in December 1844[63]. The increasing traffic into London put such pressure on the station that it had to be widened at that time bringing the viaduct to within fifteen yards of James and Ann's house in New Way, but this narrow alley survived for another twenty years until it was finally absorbed and where its remains today lie under the southernmost platforms of one of the busiest commuter terminals in the world.

References

[1] P.P.XVII (1844) – First Report of the Commissioners for Inquiring into the State of Large Towns, p.340: quot. Wohl, 'The Eternal Slum', p.15.
[2] 'The Morning Chronicle', 26 OCT 1849
[3] P71/TMS/221 'St Thomas Parish Vestry Minutes, Easter Tuesday, 1829, Greater London R.O.
[4] ibid., 14 OCT 1829
[5] ibid., 14 SEP 1831
[6] ibid., 19 AUG 1829
[7] ibid., 2 SEP 1829
[8] ibid., 16 and 30 SEP 1829
[9] ibid., 19 JAN 1830
[10] P71/TMS/914, St Thomas Parish Vestry Minutes, JUL 1830, Greater London R.O.
[11] ibid., 27 OCT 1830
[12] ibid., 15 SEP 1830
[13] Cunningham, P., 'Handbook of London', p.439; Weinreb and Hibbert, 'The London Encyclopaedia' p.805, and Freeman, 'London for Everyman', p.214
[14] Hibbert,'The English, A Social History', p.482
[15] Harrison, 'The Common People', p.224

[16] Burke, 'The Streets of London', p.117
[17] Tuer, 'Old London Cries', passim.
[18] Weinreb and Hibbert, 'The London Encyclopaedia', p.836
[19] Tuer, 'Old London Cries', p.33
[20] Morning Chronicle, 27 NOV 1849.
[21] Canning, 'The Illustrated Mayhew's London', pp.15 – 19
[22] Kirwan, 'Palace and Hovel', p.45
[23] Stedman-Jones, 'Outcast London', p.142
[24] 'The Times', 26 SEP 1849
[25] Canning, 'The Illustrated Mayhew's London', pp.191–5
[26] Morning Chronicle, 7 NOV 1850
[27] 'The Pictorial World', 9 JUN 1883
[28] Stedman-Jones, 'Outcast London', p.86
[29] Morning Chronicle, 26 OCT 1849
[30] ibid.
[31] ibid., 30 OCT 1849
[32] Hyams, 'Notes on England', p.8.
[33] ibid., pp 27/28
[34] Morning Chronicle, 30 OCT 1849
[35] Himmelfarb, 'The Idea of Poverty', p.312
[36] Thompson, E.P., 'The Making of the English Working Class', p.276
[37] Thompson, E.P. 'The Making of the English Working Class', p.270
[38] Morning Chronicle, 26 OCT 1849.
[39] Stedman-Jones, 'Outcast London', p.377, Table 11 No.4 and p.36
[40] ibid., p.44
[41] Morning Chronicle, 30 OCT 1849
[42] Morning Chronicle, 30 OCT 1849
[43] ibid
[44] ibid., 1 FEB 1850
[45] Thomas, 'London's First Railway', p.16
[46] ibid., p.44
[47] ibid., pp.48 and 82
[48] ibid., p.31
[49] ibid., p.147
[50] ibid., p.124
[51] Cunningham, P., 'Handbook of London', p.XIX
[52] Thomas, 'London's First Railway', p.55
[53] ibid., p.80
[54] ibid., pp.207/208
[55] Hibbert, 'The English, A Social History', p.651
[56] The County Press for Herts, Beds etc., 30 SEP 1843
[57] James, 'Fiction for the Working Man, p.141
[58] Thomas, 'London's First Railway', p.13
[59] ibid. p.57
[60] Burke, 'The Streets of London', p.110
[61] Hibbert, 'The English, A Social History', pp.652/3
[62] Thomas, 'London's First Railway', pp.19/20
[63] ibid., p.111

CHAPTER ELEVEN

LADY MACBETH OF BERMONDSEY

'I believe that a sight so inconceivably awful as the wickedness and levity of the immense crowd collected at that execution this morning could be imagined by no man, and could be presented in no heathen land under the sun. The horrors of the gibbet and of the crime which brought the wretched murderers to it, faded in my mind before the atrocious bearing, looks and language, of the assembled spectators.'

– Charles Dickens (1849)[1]

One of London's most notorious murders occurred just a few streets away from James and Ann's home in New Way, Southwark. Their two eldest sons, Francis and James, were 15 and 11 years old at the time and, in the manner of all young boys, they would have taken a morbidly gleeful interest in all its gruesome details and especially, of course, in the public spectacle of the murderers' execution where they could join in the chilling bloodlust of a vast crowd eager to watch the double drop of two sordid criminals, one of whom was not only a woman, but a foreigner into the bargain:

'Maria Manning came from Sweden,
Brought up respectably we hear,
And Frederick Manning came from Taunton,
In the county of Somersetshire.
Maria lived with noble ladies,
In ease and splendour and delight,
But on one sad and fatal morning,
She was made Frederick Manning's wife'[2]

Maria Roux actually came from Switzerland, but either that did not scan so well (although the ballad-monger was none too skilful with rhyme or scansion) or he did not much care whether she was a Swiss or a Swede – the fact that she was not of British blood was enough in itself to add spice to his doggerel verse.

The Bermondsey Murder, as it was known, became such a *cause celebre* that the hawkers of that anonymous street ballad, 'The Life of the Mannings', were said to have sold two and a half million copies.[3]

Maria may have 'lived with noble ladies', but scarcely 'in ease and splendour and delight'. She had been in service with Lady Blantyre, the daughter of the Duchess of Sutherland when, at the age of twenty-six she had met and married a Great Western Railway guard, Frederick Manning, and together they set up as innkeepers in Taunton. Two years after the marriage they moved to London renting a six-roomed terraced house, number 3 Minver-place, New Weston-street in Bermondsey about half a mile from London Bridge – later described by The Times as 'a little street in the lowest of our suburbs' – and less than a quarter of a mile from James and Ann Mimms in New Way.

For some years prior to her marriage Maria had been courted by Patrick O'Connor, a customs official at the London Docks, and said to be worth £20,000, but she had rejected him in favour of twenty-eight years old Frederick Manning.

> 'Maria, dear, how could you leave me?
> Wretched you have made my life,
> Tell me why you did deceive me,
> For to be Fred Manning's wife.'

O'Connor did write to Maria but not quite in those terms. After expressing his sadness at her infidelity, he pressed upon her the fond hope that they would 'always entertain the same kindly feelings towards each other that is due to old friends . . . .When shall I have the pleasure of seeing you here? Bring your husband and any others you like. I will be able to show them the docks and the vaults . . . '

> 'At length they all were reconciled,
> And met together night and day,

Maria, by O'Connor's riches,
Dressed in splendour fine and gay.
Though married, yet they corresponded,
With O'Connor all was right,
And oft he went to see Maria,
Frederick Manning's lawful wife.'

Not only did O'Connor visit Maria and her husband at Minver-place, Bermondsey, but she was frequently alone with him in his rented rooms three miles away across the river in Stepney's Mile End. As Maria's defence counsel delicately phrased it, "Mr O'Connor seemed to have formed a connexion with Mrs Manning, of the nature of which no one could entertain any doubt." Adding that, " . . . O'Connor was past the middle age, and it was almost proverbial that at that time of life men were weak enough to yield anything to the women with whom they were connected."

Maria claimed that Frederick maltreated her and had once chased her with a knife and threatened to cut off her head: she sought comfort from an older man who was not only fond of her but wealthy enough to indulge her generously. With all this in mind, the most expected outcome would have been a plot by O'Connor and his mistress to get rid of the husband so that Maria could live in some luxury with her lover and eventually inherit his not inconsiderable fortune. Instead, it was Frederick and Maria who found themselves in the Old Bailey dock and Patrick O'Connor in a threefoot hole in the Mannings' back kitchen.

Two of O'Connor's colleagues from the Customs office in the London Docks had last seen him on London Bridge walking south towards Bermondsey on the afternoon of Thursday August 9th, 1849. By the following Sunday they had become concerned about him and called on Maria Manning at Minver-place who claimed that she had not seen O'Connor since the previous Wednesday. Mr Flynn, another Customs officer, also went to Minver-place on that same Sunday but could get no answer. His suspicions must have been sufficiently aroused to call there again the next day accompanied by a plain-clothes police officer. This time he did see Maria who seemed 'flurried and indisposed', and, without prompting from either visitor, exclaimed, "Poor Mr O'Connor; he was the best friend I had in London," and again denied that she had seen him since Wednesday, August 8th.

The day after Mr Flynn had spoken to Maria, both the Mannings had disappeared, but it was another three days before the police took any action. Two police constables went to Minver-place and, in the words of P.C. Henry Barnes, "In the back kitchen I observed a damp mark between the edges of two of the flag-stones, and this arrested my attention." They borrowed a crow bar from some labourers and lifted the two heavy flag-stones which covered an area five feet by two feet of mortar laid on earth. "When we had got about twelve inches down," continued Barnes, "we came upon the toe of a man, and when about six inches further we came upon the loins of a man. The body was lying on the belly and the legs were drawn back and tied to the haunches with a strong cord. The body was quite naked . . . (and) completely imbedded in slaked lime."

The police surgeon who examined the body found a bullet above the right eye and extensive fractures to the back of the head from which he extracted sixteen pieces of bone. Those fractures, he thought, could have been caused by a crowbar or chisel.

Before the end of August both suspects had been arrested but at opposite ends of the country, Maria in Edinburgh and Frederick in Jersey. Maria had fled within hours of being interviewed by Mr Flynn and the plain-clothes officer. She packed several boxes and other luggage, called a cab which took her to the South Eastern Railway Station at London Bridge where she left some of the boxes marked 'Mrs Smith, passenger to Paris', and drove on to Euston station from where she went to Newcastle and thence to Edinburgh, taking lodgings in Leith-walk under the name of Smith. Nine days after leaving London Maria was interviewed by Superintendent Richard Moxhay of the Edinburgh constabulary who had been alerted by a man whom Maria had approached in an attempt to sell some railway shares. Still claiming to be Mrs Smith, she did not object to a search of her luggage, but the first thing Superintendent Moxhay found was a tavern billhead which read 'F.G. Manning, Taunton', followed by dozens of foreign railway share certificates and about £180 in notes and coin. She explained that she had left London on the Monday afternoon whilst her husband was out: she did not know where he was: she had not seen O'Connor since Wednesday August 8th, and, although she had invited him to dine on the Thursday, he had not turned up. Asked about O'Connor's death she exclaimed, "Murder O'Connor! Certainly not; he was the kindest friend I ever had in the world; he acted the part of a father to me."

Frederick Manning's departure had been more leisurely. On the Monday of Maria's flight to Newcastle he was engaged in selling all the furniture in 3 Minver-place to a Mr Bainbridge, a furniture broker, for £13, insisting that it should all be removed at 5am the next morning. At the same time he arranged to lodge with the Bainbridges in Bermondsey-square for a fortnight. When Mrs Bainbridge asked him why he did not sleep in his own house that night as the furniture was not to be removed until the next day, Frederick replied that he would not sleep there for twenty pounds. On returning to Minver-place Frederick found that Maria had left with her luggage an hour earlier.

Perhaps Maria's surprise departure caused Frederick to panic, because he stayed at the Bainbridge's for only two nights instead of the two weeks he had contracted for, taking a hackney-cab from Bermondsey-square to the Southampton railway at Waterloo station which had opened only a year before. From Southampton he took the packet-boat to Jersey where he was arrested at Prospect-house by Sergeant Edward Langley who had followed him to Jersey twelve days later.

The Mannings' arrest had been hastened by modern technology of which the British press was inordinately proud – 'the guilty wretch, flying on the wings of steam thirty miles an hour, is tracked by a swifter messenger – and that the lightning itself, by the wondrous agency of the electric telegraph.' So wrote The Illustrated London News a few days after Frederick's arrest.[4] At various times on the return journey to London Manning laid the whole blame for O'Connor's death on his wife. "She shot him; the cloth was laid on the table, and she asked him to go downstairs and wash his hands. At the bottom of the stairs she put one hand on his shoulder, and with the other shot him in the back of the head." He claimed that she was a very violent woman and would think no more of killing a man than of killing a cat and that he had frequently been afraid for his own life – she had once chased him with a drawn knife. At no time, however, did Manning explain how the dreadful injuries to O'Connor's head had been caused. He did say, "She had a grave dug for him," but did not say by whom. The only motive he offered for the killing was that O'Connor had induced them to take Minver-place on the promise that he would lodge with them, and presumably contribute to the rent, but he had failed to do so, leaving them to find the £30 it had cost to furnish it, and that as a result Maria was determined to be avenged for his broken promise.

The trial, which opened at the Central Criminal Court on October 25th, had aroused intense interest. The well of the court was filled with notables or, as The Times described the scene, 'crowded with "beauty and fashion"; there are more ambassadors than judges on the bench, and the counsel or attorney who attempts to take a note is cramped and jostled by a privy councillor or a peer', and 'every portion of the court which could be made available for the purpose was appropriated to the accommodation of spectators'. Some 'gentlemen and one or two ladies' were even provided with seats in the dock. The only part of the court which was not packed out was the public gallery owing to the imposition by the Sheriffs of a high admission fee.

Frederick Manning, in a black suit and black neckerchief, took his place at the right-hand end of the dock. When Maria was put up she went to the other extreme corner without looking at her husband and was not seen even to glance in his direction all day. She wore a dark dress fitted closely up to the throat, a gaudy coloured shawl and primrose gloves, but no bonnet; instead, her head was covered with 'a very handsome white lace veil', and she seemed subdued in contrast to 'the cheerful bouyancy of spirits – amounting almost to levity' which had characterised her appearance at the earlier committal hearing.

The male prisoner was charged both with shooting O'Connor and 'striking, cutting, and wounding him on the back part of the head with a crowbar.' Maria was indicted for 'having been present, aiding and abetting' the commission of the crime. Each pleaded 'not guilty', but both would hang if the counts against them were proved.

The evidence against them was all circumstantial, but none the less highly damaging. The Mannings had taken a yearly tenancy on 3 Minver-place on Ladyday. A month later they took a lodger, William Massey, a medical student, who stayed with them for fourteen weeks until pressed to find other lodgings because, the Mannings said, they were leaving for the country. He eventually left at the end of July, eleven days before

O'Connor's disappearance. During the time he had lived with them Frederick asked his opinion on a variety of medical and metaphysical matters: What was the most vital part of the human body? – the jugular vein: Where was the seat of the brain? – Massey showed him: Where on the head would a blow be most likely to cause death? – behind the ear: Did an air gun make a noise when discharged? Would chloroform or laudanum act so as to stupefy O'Connor to such a degree that he could be persuaded to sign a note for £500 in his (Manning's) favour? Massey answered that no doubt such drugs had been used for such purposes: Would a murderer go to Heaven? – No.

Other witnesses testified that Frederick had ordered a bushel of lime – 'the kind that burned quickest' – for killing slugs in his garden. When the builder's boy delivered it on July 25th Maria told him to tip it into a basket in the kitchen. Frederick also ordered a long crowbar from an ironmonger in the City which Maria paid for when it was delivered on the 28th, and on the day before O'Connor's disappearance she bought a short-handled shovel from a Tooley-street ironmonger.

That same day, Wednesday August 8th, she wrote to O'Connor: 'Dear O'Connor, – We shall be happy to see you dine with us today, at half past 5. – Yours affectionately, MARIA MANNING.' The letter was not posted until 3 o-clock in the afternoon and could not have reached him until the following morning and so it seems strange that when O'Connor turned up at Minver-place at about a quarter to ten on Wednesday evening with a friend, Pierce Walsh, Maria berated him for not having come in time for dinner. Whether she repeated the invitation for the following evening is not clear, but there was more than sufficient evidence to show that O'Connor was making his way to Minver-place in time to dine at 5.30pm on the Thursday, and that was the last anyone saw of him until P.C. Barnes dug up the Mannings' back kitchen flag-stones. On that same Thursday evening at about the time O'Connor should have reached Minver-place in time to dine, Maria left home ostensibly to search for him, going across the river to O'Connor's lodgings three miles away in Mile End, Stepney, where she arrived at 6.15 pm and stayed for an hour alone in his room.

The day following O'Connor's last sighting, a Friday, a twelve years old girl, Hannah Firmin, was selling matches and shoelaces in Minver-place and asked Maria, whom she identified in court, if she wanted her steps cleaned. Maria, instead, asked her if she could do anything else and they agreed she should do some housework the next day for five pence. Hannah gave her evidence clearly and simply: "I offered to clean the back kitchen, but she told me she had done that herself, and she then wanted me to wash a basket with marks of lime on it. I told her I could not do so because my hand was bad." Maria then attempted to wash the basket herself until she had used up all the water stored in the house. Hannah did some work in the coal cellar. "They gave me 6d. for my work, but I was not scolded into the bargain" she said, as if she always expected to be abused by an employer. The favourable and sympathetic impression given by this poor little matchgirl was somewhat marred when, under cross-examination, she reluctantly admitted to having stolen an egg, a razor, a purse and a pair of stockings when she left the house. Frederick's counsel later commented that her admission of the thefts should be only "to excite the sympathies of those who heard it to endeavour to snatch her from sin and ruin" – by which, of course, he meant a life of prostitution to which she was almost certainly condemned.

On the Friday evening, Maria again went to O'Connor's lodgings at about the same time and stayed there for an hour. O'Connor's landlady, who kept a shop on the ground floor, said that as Maria was leaving she bought some articles, "I thought there was something singular about her appearance. She trembled very much. I noticed that she gave the money with her left hand . . . (and) seemed to have a parcel in her right." It was assumed by everyone that the parcel contained O'Connor's share certificates. Even Maria's counsel agreed with that except that he added the gloss that the shares had been purchased by O'Connor on her behalf or that she had assumed that to be so. When opened on the following Sunday the deceased's cash box held only I.O.Us but no cash or share certificates.

On the Saturday, two days after O'Connor's disappearance, Frederick Manning, using the name O'Connor, sold some shares registered in that name to a stock-broker for £110. Part of the purchase price was a £100 note which Frederick then had changed at the Bank of England into fifty sovereigns and five ten-pound notes. These notes were later identified by their numbers and found to be part of the money discovered in Maria's possession by the Edinburgh police.

Neither of the defendants called any witnesses, each relying on the forensic skill of their advocates to secure an acquittal. Maria's counsel, Mr Ballantine, argued that if she had wanted O'Connor's money she could have had that without killing him and it was, in any case, most unlikely that a woman could bring herself to commit an act of such 'cold-blooded and atrocious violence.' Those comments apart, he based her whole defence on the fact that Maria could not have been at Minver-place at the time when it was assumed that the crime took place; but learned counsel played fast and loose with the evidence – perhaps it was the only weapon he had.

Patrick O'Connor was last seen alive between 4.45 and 5.15 on the afternoon of Thursday, August 9th. At a quarter to five two of his friends stopped to chat with him on the Surrey side of London Bridge as he was walking towards Bermondsey. At ten minutes past five another friend saw him in Weston-street walking in the direction of Minver-place which was only 150 yards distant. A slight confusion was introduced by another witness who claimed to have seen him five minutes later but back on London Bridge walking slowly away from Bermondsey and apparently undecided as to which direction to take. This witness only saw O'Connor from the top of an omnibus and could have been mistaken, but even if he had been right O'Connor could still quite easily have reached Minver-place by 5.30pm as it was only a ten minute walk from London Bridge. His most likely arrival time was between a quarter and half-past five o'clock.

Ballantine argued that as O'Connor had not arrived at the expected time Maria had set out to walk the three miles to his lodgings in Mile End to find him and this would have taken her about three-quarters of an hour. An independent witness had already testified that the walk took him 43 minutes or only 25 minutes by cab. There was no argument about that, but Ballantine then went on to assert that Maria had been seen by O'Connor's landlady to go up to his room at 5.45. Had that been the case she would have had to have left Minver-place at or very shortly after 5pm at which time O'Connor was unquestionably on or near London Bridge, whether or not we discount the evidence of the man on the top of the Bermondsey omnibus.

The only evidence as to the time of Maria's arrival at O'Connor's lodgings was given by his Mile End landlady, Ann Armes, who stated with certainty "I saw Mrs Manning go up-stairs to Mr O'Connor's room at a quarter past 6 o'clock on the evening of the 9th of August." Mr Ballantine had tried to mislead the jury by bringing that time forward by half an hour. To arrive at Mile End at 6.15 Maria need not have left home before 5.30 (or 5.50 if she had taken a cab). Given that timescale it was perfectly possible for Maria to have been present when O'Connor arrived and to have been there with him for at least a quarter of an hour. According to Frederick Manning's admission to the police the murder was committed as O'Connor was walking downstairs to the kitchen to wash his hands before dinner which was generally at 5.30 – not 5 o'clock as Mr Ballantine had asserted in another attempt to confuse the jury.

In Frederick's defence his counsel, Mr Sergeant Wilkins, dismissed the purchase of the lime and the crowbar as ordinary domestic items which any householder would have bought for quite innocent purposes. He repeated Frederick's accusation that Maria was the murderer, adding that if his client had been involved at all it was only as her dupe in helping to conceal the evidence of a crime to the commission of which he had been an innocent witness. He certainly gained nothing financially by O'Connor's death, all the cash and shares had been found on his wife. The only other motive ascribed to Manning, his counsel argued, was sexual jealousy of O'Connor, but all the evidence showed that his relationship with the deceased had been entirely cordial, and he had throughout acted the part of a complaisant husband.

In his reply the Attorney General dismissed the arguments of defending counsel that the crime had been committed by only one person. He did not think that one person alone could possibly have "raised the stones in the kitchen, dug the grave, covered it over, and, above all, could have thrust the body into the grave in the manner which had been described." That, perhaps, was a doubtful proposition: Maria may not have been strong enough, but there is no reason to suppose that Frederick was not capable of doing it alone. However, the Attorney General added a further point, arguing that had Frederick been solely responsible, how would he have got hold of the murdered man's property from his lodgings without arousing suspicion? – and there was ample evidence that Maria had made two visits there, both on the evening of O'Connor's disappearance and on the following day. He made little of the time element – not even correcting Mr Ballantine's misrepresentations. There was no evidence as to the precise time of death and the victim could just as well have been murdered after Maria's return from O'Connor's lodgings sometime after 7.45pm.

The Lord Chief Baron, Sir Frederick Pollock the senior of the three judges, gave an exemplary summing up in his charge to the jury although his comment, "The crime in question was perhaps one of the most unexampled ever recorded in the history of this country." – was, perhaps, a bit strong., Possibly he was influenced by the enormous public interest in the case aroused by the pre-trial news reports and speculation and wanted the jury to give the evidence the highest possible degree of sober and considered judgement before he dismissed them to the jury room at exactly six o'clock.

> 'At length the jury them convicted,
> And doomed them for to leave this life,
> The judge pronounced the awful sentence,
> On Frederick Manning, and his wife.
> Return, he said, to whence they brought you,
> From thence unto the fatal tree,
> And there together be suspended,
> Where multitudes your fate may see.'

The jury stayed out for only forty-five minutes. The Mannings were brought back into the court after the dock had been cleared of spectators to hear the jury foreman pronounce a 'guilty' verdict on them both. When asked if either prisoner had anything to say why the death sentence should not be passed on them, Maria Manning burst into a vehement denunciation of English justice, her defence counsel and her husband: "I am not treated like a Christian, but like a wild beast of the forest, and the judges and jury will have it upon their consciences for giving a verdict against me. I am not guilty of the murder of Mr O'Connor. If I had wished to commit murder I would not have attempted the life of the only friend I had in the world – a man who would have made me his wife in a week if I had been a widow . . . " When Maria, with a strong foreign accent but a surprising fluency, concluded with the words, "I wish I could have expressed myself better in the English language" – the judge put on the black cap and added his own comments to the jury's verdict, " . . . the present murder was one of the most cold-blooded and deliberately calculated I ever remember to have heard or read of . . . that unhappy man was hurried into eternity. The law, more merciful, allows to you a space of time for preparation . . . ", concluding with that fearsome formula which accompanied every death sentence- " . . . it remains for me only to pronounce the dread sentence of the law, which is that you be taken hence to Her Majesty's gaol for the county of Surrey, and thence to the place of execution, and there to be severally hanged by the neck until you be dead; and that afterwards your dead bodies be buried within the precincts of the gaol in which you shall be confined after this sentence; and may the Lord have mercy on your souls!"

The jury had clearly been in no doubt that the Mannings had planned and carried out the murder together and were equally guilty before the law. Two weeks before O'Connor's death they had arranged to buy the lime and the crowbar. A week later they had got rid of their medical student lodger. Maria had bought the shovel only the day before the murder and had written inviting O'Connor to dine that evening. He failed to appear at the appointed time and when he did arrive much later he brought a friend which may have thwarted their plans for that Wednesday evening. The most likely sequence of events of the following day seems to be that O'Connor reached Minver-place around 5.15pm, was persuaded to go down to the kitchen to wash his hands where Maria shot him and Frederick finished him off with the crowbar. Immediately after the murder Maria left the house to go to O'Connor's lodgings in Mile End to plunder his cash box leaving Frederick to bury the body. The prime mover in all this would seem to have been Maria Manning – 'The Lady Macbeth of the Bermondsey stage,' as The Times leader dubbed her – desperate to get hold of O'Connor's railway shares before they depreciated too far in a falling market. Frederick – the 'weaker vessel', said the Times – seems to have been swept along by the force of his wife's strong and volatile personality, but equally as involved in the commission of the crime.

'See what numbers are approaching,
To Horse Monger's fatal tree,
Full of blooming health and vigour,
What a dreadful sight to see.

> Old and young pray take a warning,
> Females, lead a virtuous life,
> Think upon that fatal morning,
> Frederick Manning and his wife.'

The Surrey County Gaol to which the Mannings were committed and where they were to be executed was more commonly known as Horsemonger-lane Gaol and stood on what is now Newington Gardens Recreation Ground in Southwark's Harper Road, about three-quarters of a mile south of London Bridge. The prison walls enclosed an area of some three and a half acres and could accommodate over four hundred prisoners.[5] The Mannings were to be executed on Tuesday November 13th, 1849, two and a half weeks after their conviction. 'The enormity of the crime for which they suffered,' thundered The Times, 'and the remarkable circumstances attending its perpetration, detection, and punishment, all contributed to swell to an unusual extent the perverted curiosity which executions never fail to excite . . . On the level roof of the gaol, and to the left of the entrance, the dismal-looking gallows had been erected, a huge gaunt piece of framework, which, rising from the summit of the gaol, imparted to the whole building a more than usually ominous and repulsive appearance. Below thousands of the tatterdemalions of London were collected' – amongst which crowd, doubtless, at least two of James and Ann's sons could have been counted. But it was not only the poor and the depraved 'residuum of society' who gathered to enjoy the spectacle, the windows and house-tops of surrounding houses 'were filled with people belonging to the more respectable classes of society, who were made to pay exorbitantly for the gratification of witnessing the execution undisturbed by the invasions of the rabble.'

The crowds had started to collect the day before. Barriers were erected at every entrance to Horsemonger-lane to lessen the crush and four hundred police constables were on duty to keep the peace, but fights broke out in the crowd, the pick-pockets were busy and the air was full of whistles, cat-calls and what The Times reporter described as 'the usual disgusting levity observable on similar occasions.' Not to be outdone in its condemnation of the crowd which had gathered overnight, 'The Daily News' wrote of 'an immense assemblage, composed for the most part, as we anticipated, of the filth and scum, "the cankers of a long peace and hard times," with which the population of this vast metropolis is infested.'

'When I came upon the scene at midnight,' wrote Charles Dickens in a famous letter to the Times, from which the quotation at the head of this chapter is also taken, 'the *shrillness* of the cries and howls that were raised from time to time, denoting that they came from a concourse of boys and girls already assembled in the best places, made my blood run cold. As the night went on, screeching and laughing, and yelling in strong chorus of parodies on Negro melodies, with substitutions of "Mrs Manning" for "Susannah", and the like were added to these. When the day dawned, thieves, low prostitutes, ruffians and vagabonds of every kind, flocked on to the ground, with every variety of offensive and foul behaviour. Fightings, faintings, whistlings, imitations of Punch, brutal jokes, tumultuous demonstrations of indecent delight when swooning women were dragged out of the crowd by the police with their dresses disordered, gave a new zest to the general entertainment. When the sun rose brightly – as it did – it gilded thousands upon thousands of upturned faces, so inexpressibly odious in their brutal mirth, or callousness, that a man had cause to feel ashamed of the shape he wore'

> 'See the scaffold it is mounted,
> And the doomed ones do appear,
> Seemingly borne wan with sorrow,
> Grief and anguish, pain and care.
> They cried, the moment is approaching,
> When we, together, must leave this life,
> And no-one has the least compassion
> On Frederick Manning and his wife.'

As the clock struck nine a small procession came out on to the prison roof and stood bareheaded as the condemned couple passed them. Frederick supported by two warders and accompanied by the prison chaplain, came first. Calcraft, the hangman, placed a white nightcap over his head and adjusted the rope. Frederick was followed by Maria's stout figure, dressed in black satin and with a black veil over her face and head. The couple shook hands and exchanged a few words before turning their faces towards the crowd below, 'the drop fell, and justice

'. . . the pick-pockets were busy and the air was full of whistles, cat-calls and . . . the usual disgusting levity . . .'

had its due. Husband and wife were, in an instant, and almost without a struggle, launched into eternity, 'reported The Times. Their bodies were left hanging for an hour before being taken down to be buried in the corridor leading from the prison yard to the chapel in coffins 'partially filled with lime in order to insure an early decay of the remains' – exactly the fate they had prepared for Patrick O'Connor.

On the day after the execution The Times' first leader commented: 'It is not thirty years since one might walk out any Monday morning before breakfast and see half a dozen poor wretches dying the death of dogs for petty thefts committed in hunger, or trifling injuries done in a drunken affray. Capital punishment is no longer the normal award for a legal crime, not even for ordinary murder . . . ' True, the number of crimes for which the death penalty was prescribed had been dramatically reduced since the 1820's, but men and women were still held in the dreadful hulks moored in the Thames before being transported, effectively for life, to the other side of the world and executions were still allowed to continue as a popular public spectacle.

In a further letter to The Times, Charles Dickens described the effect of the heightened emotions generated by all that accompanied the Mannings' execution. One 'ferocious woman' in the crowd had a knife with which she threatened another that she would 'have her heart's blood, and be hanged on the same gibbet with her namesake, Mrs Manning, whose death she had come to see.' Just as she had had her evil passions aroused by the scene, wrote Dickens, 'so had all the crowd. I believe this was the whole and sole effect of what they had come to see, and I hold that no human being, not being the better for such a sight, could go away without being the worse for it.' Dickens was not arguing for the abolition of capital punishment itself, only for the cessation of public executions, but another twenty years were to pass before rich and poor alike were to be deprived of the entertaining spectacle of a fellow human being swinging from a gibbet accompanied, as Dickens complained, by the hangman's 'jokes, his oaths and his brandy.'

References

[1] Dickens, C., 'The Times', 14 NOV 1849 Note: unless otherwise stated the references in this chapter to the crime and the trial are taken from 'The

Times' reports of October 26, 27 and 29 and November 13, 14 and 19, 1849, and 'The Daily News'of November 12 and 14.

[2] All the verses quoted are from the street ballad, 'Life of the Mannings', published in Ashton, 'Modern Street Ballads'.

[3] Pinto and Rodway, 'The Common Muse', p.17.

[4] Illustrated London News, 1 SEP. 1849.

[5] Prettejohns, 'Charles Dickens and Southwark,' p.15.

CHAPTER TWELVE

DAY TRIPS AND CRUSHED HATS

> 'They only ask to be employed. They tramp through miles of mud – they stand for hours in work-room passages – they bear rain, and cold, and hunger without murmuring and they clear their little households of every saleable article rather than beg. When they have got their little strip of cloth, or leather, to stitch or cut into shape, they clasp it like some precious treasure, and hurry home to begin their ill-paid task'.
>
> – John Hollingshead (1861)[1]

> 'the poor wretches who lodge in the miserable dens of St Giles, pay rents averaging £6 per thousand cubic feet – as much as is paid for the most aristocratic mansions in London.
>
> – James Hole (1866)[2]

'The road to Greenwich during the whole of Easter Monday is in a state of perpetual bustle and noise. Cabs, hackney-coaches, 'shay-carts', coal-wagons, stages, omnibuses, sociables, gigs, donkey-chaises – all crammed with people (for the question never is, what the horse can draw, but what the vehicle will hold), roll along at their utmost speed; the dust flies in clouds, the ginger-beer corks go off in volleys, the balcony of every public house is crowded with people . . . .'

Greenwich Fair, for that was where they were all bound, reached the height of its popularity during the first half of the nineteenth century. For three days at Easter and at Whitsun, Londoners in their hundreds of thousands, rich and poor alike, make their way to Greenwich Park by road, by rail, and by river.

Charles Dickens visited the fair many times and has left us one of the best descriptions of this popular outing, admitting that he had once made the journey 'in a spring-van, accompanied by thirteen gentlemen, fourteen ladies, an unlimited number of children and a barrel of beer; and we have a vague recollection of having, in later days, found ourself the eighth outside, on the top of a hackney-coach, at something past four o'clock in the morning, with a rather confused idea of our own name, or place of residence.'[3]

The opening of the London and Greenwich Railway provided another means of reaching the Park and the fair, and the Greenwich line carried an enormous number of passengers throughout the summer, but, during the fair weeks, the crowds were so dense and unruly that extra police were normally on duty at the London Bridge and Greenwich stations.[4] Once on the train, however, the view from the viaduct of the road and river traffic all, seemingly, making for the fair would have been spectacular. A German visitor travelling by rail described the experience: 'Most odd is the atmosphere on such days, in the company of several thousand above the housetops, with the merrymaking of the Cockney 'day out' below . . . a railway carriage full of busker musicians immediately behind the tender at the beginning of the very long train . . . the incomprehensible roar, the product of a hundred various craft above the shouting of skippers, the hoisting of sails, the creaking of cables, the sound of cars, the groaning of cranes, the rattle of machinery, and lushing of waves through the ruddergear, the hammering noises on board and on the quays, makes a wonderful accompaniment to the music, and to the hissing and snorting of the iron horse.'[5]

James and Ann Mimms had only recently married when the Evening Chronicle first published Dickens' description of the fair and it is scarcely fanciful to suppose that they would have visited it together in their courting days and after their marriage, at least until their growing family began to make increasing demands upon their meagre and uncertain earnings. An excursion steamer would have carried them downriver from London Bridge or Cherry Garden pier and once on the landing-stage a young couple and their friends would make for one of Greenwich's many taverns 'to settle the stomach' and then spend much of the day in the Park 'in which the principal amusement

'. . . the London and Greenwich Railway provided another means of reaching the Park and the fair'

is to drag young ladies up the steep hill which leads to the Observatory, and then drag them down again, at the very top of their speed, greatly to the derangement of their curls and bonnet-caps, and much to the edification of lookers-on from below . . . Love-sick swains, under the influence of gin-and-water, and the tender passion, became violently affectionate: and the fair objects of their regard enhance the value of stolen kisses by a vast deal of struggling.'[6]

As night fell the lights of the fair-ground itself would become irresistible. A five-minute walk to the entrance and a dense crowd swallows you up and

> 'swings you to and fro, and in and out, and every way but the right one: add to this the screams of women, the shouts of boys, the clanging of gongs, the firing of pistols, the ringing of bells, the bellowings of speaking-trumpets, the squeaking of penny dittoes, the noise of a dozen bands, with three drums in each, all playing different tunes at the same time, the hallooing of showmen, and an occasional roar from the wild-beast shows; and you are the very centre and heart of the fair.'[7]

The smaller sideshows offered dwarfs, a giantess, a living skeleton, a wild Indian, 'a young lady of singular beauty, with perfectly white hair and pink eyes', and 'Wombwell's menagerie of dusty lions and tired-looking elephants, a man monkey, and Toby the learned pig, who could "spell, read, cast accounts, tell the points of the sun's rising and setting and the age of any party." '[8] If you could believe the barker's promises. On every side stalls and hawkers were selling gilt gingerbread, pen'orths of pickled salmon in little white saucers, peanuts and oranges, – the withered ones boiled up to look fresh, oysters with shells as large as cheese-plates, and whelks 'floating in a somewhat bilious looking green fluid.' One of the most popular ways of rounding off the day was an hour or two's dancing in The Crown and Anchor, a tented ballroom, several hundred feet long with a raised orchestra and a boarded floor:

> 'The dust is blinding, the heat insupportable, the company somewhat noisy, and in the highest spirits possible: the ladies, in the height of their innocent animation, dancing in the gentlemen's hats, and the gentlemen promenading . . . in the

> ladies' bonnets or with the more expensive ornaments of false noses, and low crowned, tinder-box-looking hats; playing children's drums, and accompanied by ladies on the penny trumpet . . . the ladies bounce up and down the middle, . . . the gentlemen, they stamp their feet against the ground . . . go down the middle and up again, with cigars in their mouths, and silk handkerchiefs in their hands, and whirl their partners round, nothing loath, scrambling and falling, and embracing, and knocking up against the other couples, until they are fairly tired out, and can move no longer.'[9]

A few miles further down-river from Greenwich was Gravesend, the nearest seaside resort to London and the Cockneys' Mecca on a summer Sunday. By the 1820's 300,000 passengers landed and embarked at Gravesend. Within a decade that number had doubled and by 1840 the steampackets and sailing vessels carried more than a million day-trippers to the town, and accounted for over sixty per cent of steamer passenger traffic out of London. £30,000 was spent on a new pier, but mostly the visitors seemed only to want to enjoy the fresh air. The agent of the Gravesend Steamboat company giving evidence before a Parliamentary Select Committee on the Observance of the Sabbath Day explained that, "you generally find that they disembark at Gravesend, walk up to the Windmill, and you generally find them spreading their little cloths and taking their refreshments on the grass."[10]

Gravesend, and its great rival Margate, had benefitted enormously from the new steamboats, but had attracted a lower class of visitor, mostly artisan day-trippers. With the coming of the railways Brighton was determined to avoid that mistake. The railway directors set their fares quite deliberately high to deter the poorer day-visitor and to encourage what they described as 'very superior traffic'. In consequence the line lost money until a new chairman, Rowland Hill of Post Office fame, reversed the policy encouraging cheap fares and excursion trains every Sunday, on the main public holidays and for the race meetings. Brighton's very first excursion train in 1844 'started from London Bridge at half-past eight in the morning with forty-five carriages and four engines, went on to New Cross where six more carriages and a fifth engine had to be added, and at Croydon took on another six carriages and yet another engine. By one o'clock this fantastic steam caterpillar had not reached Brighton and a director of the railway company went up the line in a pilot engine to look for it; but the passengers, who numbered close on two thousand, were delighted with their journey and half the townsfolk of Brighton turned out to welcome them.'[11]

Before the era of the railways the stage coaches had carried 50,000 travellers a year to Brighton, but within ten years of its opening the railway was bringing over 70,000 excursionists every week.[12] As they poured from the trains they crowded out the pubs before descending on to Brighton's stony beach where there were 'donkeys, ponies and dogs; little boys with spades and shrimping nets; young ladies with novels and young gentlemen with dandified canes; mamas with their babies, their sewing and their sunshades, and papas with *The Times* and their telescopes, their tall hats and their tobacco. Bottles of tea, of beer and ginger pop, hampers of buns, meat-pies and pasties were strewn around them, and the noise was continuous from the shouting, giggling, squalling multitude and the bright brass instruments of the German bands.'[13]

Greenwich Fair was by no means the only place offering cheap entertainment. London had dozens, perhaps as many as a hundred, 'Penny Gaffs' where for one penny, or 'twopence at the front', melodrama, dancing and comic songs, all of the crudest variety, could be enjoyed by audiences of both sexes but, in the main, comprising young people aged from 8 years to 20. The 'Penny Gaff' was often a converted shop the front of which had been completely removed to make a gaudily illuminated open foyer, invitingly decorated with rude pictures of the promised performers. The canvas back to the shop led to what had been the storeroom but now converted into a rough auditorium with planking for seats. The shop stairs led up to the gallery, which had been the first floor of the house, but with most of its floorboards removed so that the audience could look down through the whitewashed beams into the auditorium and on to the tiny eight-feet square stage. The orchestra was often little more than a tinny piano and a scratchy violin but the performers made up in volume and energy for what they may have lacked in skill. In the course of his investigations into London's low life Henry Mayhew visited such a theatre and came away disgusted with what he had seen and heard both as regards the entertainment itself and the enthusiastic audience's reaction.

'The most obscene thoughts, the most disgusting scenes were coolly described,' he wrote of the comic singer, 'making a poor child near me wipe away the tears that rolled down her eyes with the enjoyment of the poison . . . it was absolutely awful to behold the relish with which the young ones jumped to the hideous meaning of the verses.' Even worse was the ballet which followed, 'between a man dressed up as a woman, and a country clown. The most disgusting attitudes were struck, the most immoral acts represented, without one dissenting voice.' The whole experience had clearly shocked Mayhew into concluding that, 'if we would really lift them out of the moral mire in which they are wallowing, the first step must be to provide them with wholesome amusements.'[14]

Mayhew knew that there were few 'wholesome amusements' available – very few public parks or museums, no public libraries and an earnest and 'improving' lecture at a Mechanics' Institute was hardly likely to appeal to an uneducated coster or an unskilled labourer. Far more attractive and certainly more accessible and lively were the gin palaces and taverns which offered light, warmth, cheerful company and, in some cases, a back room or cellar with a cock-fight laid on, or an opportunity to gamble on the outcome of a ratting contest.'

That indefatigable Quaker author, William Howitt had watched cock-fights and described how 'the feathers are clipped off their stomachs; their heads cut clean of their wattles; their wings and tails cut short and square; that they are, in fact, metamorphosed from the most gallant-looking of birds into the most bare, comical, quaint and strutting objects in nature . . . and are, lastly, armed with steel or silver spurs of an inch long, sharp as needles. With these they kick and pierce each other, "lacerating their bodies, and bruising each other in every tender part;" fighting till their heads are all one mass of gore; till they are often stark blind, and go staggering about like drunken men, till one has the luck to strike the other clean through the head with his artificial spur.'[15]

Such contests between a matched pair of birds were the commonest form of the sport, but occasionally a match-play involving thirty-two birds would be held of which only a single bird survived.[16] The sport was banned by the first Cruelty to Animals Act of 1835, together with all blood sports which involved animal-baiting, but it could never be entirely suppressed.

More common in urban areas was the ratting 'fancy' where men pitted their dogs against sewer rats. Daniel Kirwan, a visiting American, was taken to a Thames-side tavern to watch one contest. The tavern-keeper led him down some stone steps into a cellar fitted out with tiers of cramped circular benches, one above the other up to the ceiling, and seating about a hundred men, many accompanied by their dogs. In the centre stood a square enclosure made of whitewashed boards four feet high and with a scattering of sawdust on the floor. 'I heard a squealing noise, and I saw a lad bring in a long and huge wire cage, which was swarming with gray, black and brown rats. Jumping in he opened the cage, and thrusting his forearm fearlessly through the door he drew forth, one by one, over fifty large and ferocious rats and threw them in a heap in the pit.' This exhibition was repeated until there were one hundred and five rats in the pit. The match was to be for a wager of £50 that the tavern-keeper's 'ferret-eyed little terrier', called 'Skid', could kill one hundred rats in nine minutes. Side-bets were also placed amongst the audience on the outcome. 'It was', wrote Kirwan, 'simply disgusting to witness that dreadful little terrier run at each rat, shake him for a second or two in the air and then drop him quite dead on the floor of the pit, while the roughs encouraged him to his work with shouts when the rat was destroyed quickly, but occasionally when a big and ferocious rat was attacked and showed fight in return, and when the terrier seemed to hang back for a moment, a perfect storm of curses and obscene epithets were rained on the unfortunate canine . . . When eight minutes and forty seconds had elapsed, "Skid" snapped the neck of the last rat, and now there was nothing left in the pit but a large pool of blood on which sawdust was quickly heaped, and a bleeding mass of heaving and dying rats.'[17]

The most sought-after rats for this purpose were the sewer rats rather than the house rats because 'the sewer rat will fight a terrier longer and more savagely than a house rat, and as this affords good sport, the sewer rat is at a premium in the market.' But, as a sewer inspector explained to John Hollingshead who was researching the subject for his book, 'Underground London', sewer rats 'only abound in what are called the "blood-sewers" – those under the slaughter-houses and meat-markets.'

Many more men than might be imagined made their living from London's sewers, some of them legitimately as sewer-cleansers or 'flusher-men', and others engaged in repair work, but many more illegally, known as 'Toshers' or sewer-hunters. These worked in gangs of three or four, the better to defend themselves from the rats. They collected anything saleable – copper nails, old iron, rope or bones all of which could be sold to the 'marine-store' dealers; frequently they would find coins and jewellery under the street gratings, or silver cutlery and plate accidentally washed down from the kitchens of large houses. Those interviewed by Henry Mayhew made light of the dangers inherent in their work – the choke-damp which, as one explained, could cause 'instantious death', the explosive gases, the collapse of old brick tunnels and the danger of losing oneself in the miles of warren-like sewers. Not even the Sewer Commissioners themselves knew where all the sewers for which they were responsible actually ran; as John Hollingshead commented: 'The spade and the trowel have not been idle, especially during the present century; but pen and ink have not followed close upon their footsteps. There has been a manifest stinginess in employing those recording angels – the humble clerks; and the consequence is, that the books of the sewer commissioners are very much like the accounts of a clumsy bankrupt.' One old sewer workman, 'a stout, healthy looking old man, with a face not unlike a large red potato', and who had had fifty years' experience of the south London sewers, described them to Hollingshead. "They was like warrens, you never see such shores (sewers). Some on' em was open; some was shut; an' some was covered over with litle wooden platforms, so's to make the gardings (gardens) bigger."[18]

The narrow court, known as 'New Way', in which James Mimms's family lived clearly had very defective drains, so much so that the St Thomas Vestry complained to St Thomas's Hospital about them on November 8th 1848:

> 'Gentlemen,
> The Parochial committee having reviewed and examined the several premises situate in the New Way St Thomas's, and made all the enquiries that could be made came to the unanimous opinion that the sewerage and drainage is not sufficiently deep and that in consequence thereof and of the confined state of the court there will be more or less a continued bad smell arise in that locality . . . '

The hospital authorities lost no time in responding. Their letter was dated the following day denying that the problem was their responsibility:

> '. . . the Hospital Bricklayer reports that the drains from the Houses in New Way are in a very good and efficient state, leading into the Common Sewers – but that the drain complained of in your Memorial as not being sufficiently deep, is the property of Mr Churchward to whom you have better give notice thereof.'[19]

The delicious irony of the situation, which would not have been lost on the Receiver, who was responsible for the hospital's properties, was that Richard Churchward was a prominent Vestryman of St Thomas parish, a gentleman of independent means who lived practically next door to the hospital. He was the Parochial Auditor and within five months was to be elected a junior Churchwarden. Clearly Richard Churchward owned all, or the major part of the houses in New Way and, as the whole court was private property, the responsibility for its drainage and sewerage fell to its owner until it discharged into the common sewers which were maintained by the hospital. New Way was probably drained by little more than a shallow ditch running down the middle of the 70 yard long court and, when the Vestry objected to its condition, they were obviously unaware that their complaint should more properly have been addressed to one of their own number.

London's courts and alleys, like New Way, featured prominently in John Hollingshead's other major survey, 'Ragged London in 1861'. 'Walk along the main thoroughfare from the parish church towards the city', he wrote of Shoreditch, 'and you will see a dark, damp opening in the wall, like the channel of a sewer passing under and between the houses, and leading to one of the wretched courts and alleys. You enter the passage, picking your way to the bottom, and find a little square of low, black houses, that look as if they were built as a penal settlement for dwarfs. The roofs are depressed, the doors are narrow, the windows are pinched up, and the whole square can almost be touched on each side by a full-grown man.'[20] Of Pear-tree Court in Clerkenwell, he wrote that the houses were 'very old, and chiefly made of wood, which is rotten and black with age;' and the alleys, 'with houses, dark, squeezed up, wavy in their outline, and depressed about the roof, like crushed hats.'[21] In Whitechapel he noted that 'The ashes lie in front of the houses; the drainage is thrown out of the windows to swell the heap; and the public privy is like a sentry-box stuck against the pump in a corner of the court.'[22]

St Thomas's Vestry, under the chairmanship of Richard Churchward, resolved to write to one of their Members of Parliament about the water supplied to the parish by the Southwark and Vauxhall Water Company complaining that it was 'insufficient in quantity, defective and unwholesome in quality, expensive and inconvenient in its distribution and unnecessarily high in price while a large portion of the Inhabitants are left without any conveyed supply to the injury of Comfort and health and to the imminence of risk by fire.'[23] Nothing, of course, came of it. In fact, nothing was done about London's dreadful sanitation problem, despite three severe epidemics of cholera, until what became known as 'The Year of the Great Stink' when the hot, dry summer of 1858 intensified the smell from the Thames to such a degree that even the Members of Parliament could no longer stand it. Officers standing in the corridors of the Houses of Parliament were suddenly surprised 'by members of a committee rushing out of one of the rooms in the greatest haste and confusion,' wrote The Times, 'foremost among them being the Chancellor of the Exchequer (Benjamin Disraeli) who, with a mass of papers in one hand and with his pocket handkerchief clutched in the other, and applied closely to his nose, with body half bent, hastened in dismay from the pestilential odour.'[24] This event prompted Parliament to pass the necessary Act to enable the construction of London's main drains to begin. The Bill became law within eighteen days of its first reading and, if not quite a Parliamentary record, it was a revealing example of legislative alacrity when impelled by a threat to the comfort of the legislature's own members.

The parish of St Thomas was very small indeed, about seventeen acres in extent and housing 1600 people, including the patients in the two great teaching hospitals, but it was desperately overcrowded. Some 19,000 people inhabited the St Olave's Registration District, which also covered the parishes of St Thomas and St John Horsleydown, and the 1841 census showed that in that district the average number of persons living in each house was almost exactly nine.[25] This was the first national census to record the names and occupations of the inhabitants. James Mimms was 39 years old, although the census return showed his age as '35' – all adult ages were rounded down to the nearest '5' or '0'. He and his wife, Ann had three children by then, but the house was shared with three other families; a labourer with his wife and teenage son; a porter and his wife, and a foreign couple in their 60's, Henry, a hat dyer, and Harriet Shutzback. In all twelve people, their ages ranging from over 65 down to 3 months, shared what was, in all probability, a small timber-built house and if those four families had more than one room each in which to live and sleep they could have counted themselves fortunate. In the whole of New Way there were only six houses (although James and Ann lived in what was said to be 'Number 8') and these half-dozen properties housed 54 people – an average of exactly nine each. The highest occupancy was thirteen men, women and children belonging to three labouring families. No one of any consequence lived in New Way except for James Whiting, a hat dyer, who owned a property in the parish and thus qualified as an elector entitled to vote for the two Members of Parliament for the Town and Borough of Southwark[26] but even he sublet part of his house in New Way to the three Chapman sisters, Deborah, Elizabeth and Mary, a shop assistant, a schoolmistress and a domestic servant respectively which, with his wife and three sons, made a household of eight.

Of the sixteen adult males living in that court, seven including James, were labourers, porters or warehousemen; of the rest two were brushmakers, a shoemaker and his apprentice, two hat dyers, a shopman, a carman and Joseph Downs aged 55 of no occupation, but his wife worked as a charwoman and his son as a labourer. With the exception of two schoolmistresses and a shop assistant, all the women who admitted to an occupation did casual work as laundresses, manglers, charwomen, fur workers and as shirt makers. How Mary Ellis managed to stitch shirts in a room shared with her sister and a friend, both of whom were rabbit fur pullers, must remain a mystery, but all three were unmarried and rented their part of the house from the shoemaker. Shirtmaking was one of the most exploited of women's occupations, whether they worked in a small factory or, more often, in their own homes. Occasional revelations in the press drew public attention to the desperately miserable existence of these needlewomen and led the new satirical magazine 'Punch' to print Thomas Hood's protest poem, 'The Song of the Shirt', in its Christmas edition of 1843:

'With fingers weary and worn,
With eyelids heavy and red,
A Woman sat, in unwomanly rags,
Plying her needle and thread –
Stitch! stitch! stitch!
In poverty, hunger and dirt,
And still with a voice of dolorous pitch
She sang the 'Song of the Shirt!'

Hood's poem had been prompted by a newspaper report of a young south London seamstress who had been charged with pawning material belonging to her employer and for which she had had to find a security of £2. She had recently lost her husband in an accident and her two children, one still at the breast, were starving despite earning what her employer described as a 'good living' of seven shillings a week,[27] when even the poorest labourer might earn twice that sum:

'Work – work – work!
My labour never flags;
and what are its wages? A bed of straw,
A crust of bread – and rags,
That shatter'd roof – and this naked floor –
A table – a broken chair –
And a wall so blank, my shadow I thank
For sometimes falling there.'[28]

By the time the next census was taken in 1851 the overcrowding in the St Olave District had become even worse with an average of 9.6 people to each house.[29] In New Way 50 people occupied the only 5 houses which remained standing. By then James and Ann had seven children living at 8 New Way and, even then, they sub-let rooms to Jane Piper, a widowed charwoman with two children and a couple in their '30's, George and Mary Morgan – altogether fourteen people ranging in age from a 56 year old charwoman to the one month old John Mimms, the last of James and Ann's children. In his evidence to a Parliamentary enquiry, the Southwark Water Company's engineer acknowledged that, "The poorer districts are dreadfully crowded. In many parts of it there will be more than one family in one room". When asked about the general state of those tenements, he replied, "Dreadfully filthy. There is such a closeness about the passages of the worst places, that I keep as far away from them as I can."[30]

When James Hole published 'The Homes of the Working Classes' he quoted a clergyman who had had considerable experience of death-beds in over-crowded homes. In one case the corpse of a sixteen year old boy was placed on one half of the bed, whilst his father slept on the other. On another occasion the body of a dead child was put under one of the beds at night to make room for the living and during the day-time it was replaced on the bed.[31] The Medical Officer of Health in the Southwark parish of St George the Martyr explained: 'In many of the districts of the metropolis between 60 and 70 per cent of the population are compelled to live in one overcrowded room, and in which every domestic operation has to be carried on; in it birth and death takes place; there plays the infant, there lies the corpse; it is lived in by day, and slept in by night.'[32] To emphasise his argument that London's poor were living in grossly overcrowded and thoroughly inadequate housing, James Hole quoted the words of a London magistrate: "I have often said that if empty casks were placed along the streets of Whitechapel, in a few days each of them would have a tenant . . . if you will have marshes and stagnant waters you will there have suitable animals, and the only way of getting rid of them is by draining the marshes."[33]

By the middle of the century the railway speculators and the road builders were making a considerable contribution towards 'draining the marshes' by cutting swathes through the areas which housed the poor, but very few efforts were made to provide any alternative places for them to live. London's population was growing at such a rate that speculative house builders could find tenants for as many properties as they could put up, however shoddy, believing, like the anonymous versifier, that

'The richest crop for any field
Is a crop of bricks for it to yield.
The richest crop that it can grow,
Is a crop of houses in a row.'[34]

but the required return on their investment called for higher rents than a casual labourer, earning perhaps 15s a week, could afford. With a view to catering for such tenants, philanthropists began to form charitable agencies. The earliest of these was the Metropolitan Association for Improving the Dwellings of the Industrious Classes; its stated aim was to provide 'the labouring man with an increase of the comforts and conveniences of life, with full compensation to the capitalist.' Dividends on the capital invested were to be limited to 5 per cent, with any surplus going to enhance the funds used to build 'model dwellings.'[35] The Society for Improving the Conditions of the Labouring Classes, formed two years later by Lord Shaftesbury, with Prince Albert as its President, was inspired by an evangelical spirit which sought as much to improve the morals and behaviour of its tenants as to provide them with better housing. The rules they laid down for one of their lodging houses for single men 'prohibited alcohol, smoking, gambling, card-playing, and profane language, and the Bible was read every night in the common room.'[36] Neither of these bodies expected to solve the problem alone, but, by showing that the provision of housing for labouring people could produce an acceptable profit, they hoped to encourage imitation on a much larger scale by speculators. Their hopes were never realised. Shaftesbury's experience with his Society and his philanthropic nature led him to introduce, and see passed into law, a most radical and far-seeing statute. 'Shaftesbury's Act', as the Lodging Houses Act of 1851 was known, for the first time gave permissive powers to any vestry to borrow money on the security of the rates to obtain land, build houses, and let them out at rents which should not be 'too high for the means of the labouring classes nor so low as to be an indirect means of giving relief to the poor.'[37] To bring these powers into effect required only a two-thirds majority vote of the vestry. That 'only' was one of the main reasons why the Act remained virtually a dead letter, 'Many vestrymen were either small property owners themselves or were elected to office by such men. To ask them to build houses out of the rates for the working classes was to ask them to compete with their own and their electors' interests.'[38]

The housing of London's poor population continued to worsen throughout the second half of the century, and another sixty years were to pass before any government was prepared to involve the state in the provision of decent and affordable housing.

The Baths and Washhouses Acts of the late 1840's were also permissive in that they empowered the vestries to borrow money to erect these public utilities. Unlike the response to Shaftesbury's Act, many vestries took advantage of these powers to provide such amenities to 'the great unwashed', as the poor were figuratively and literally referred to. The Acts laid down a scale of charges and the conditions for their use:

> '1. Baths for the Labouring Classes
> Every bath to be supplied with clean water for every person bathing alone, or for several children bathing together, and in either case with one clean towel for every bather.'

The maximum charge to be one penny for a cold, or twopence for a warm, bath. For up to four children under the age of eight bathing together the charges doubled.

Up to one penny could also be charged for one hour's use 'by one person of one washing tub or trough, and of a copper or boiler (if any) . . . and for the use of the conveniences for drying.'[39] Such was the pent-up demand that the first one to be provided in the dockland area attracted 35,000 customers for the baths and 49,000 for the washing and ironing facilities in its first year.[40] One would like to think that before he died, James Mimms was able to indulge himself in his first bath since he had last immersed himself in an Eynesbury horse trough.

Sixteen months after the birth of his last child, John, named after his Eynesbury grandfather, James died in St Thomas's Hospital aged only 51. His health had clearly been failing for some time. For nearly twenty years he had worked as a porter, trundling carts, sacks, bales, cases and casks along the waterfront into the Tooley Street warehouses. After that his occupation was successively described as 'warehouseman', 'light porter', and 'labourer', until his death when his widow, Ann, described him as a 'cheesemonger's warehouseman.' He must have known someone of substance to have been admitted to St Thomas's, perhaps the vicar of the small parish, or even Richard Churchward. Only a householder could authorise admission and had to guarantee the patient's removal on discharge or death.

Alternatively he could pay a guinea for the hospital to bury the corpse.[41] Once a week one or more of the Governors, together with the hospital's duty physician and surgeon selected 'the most urgent cases for admission and gave outpatient cards to the others.'[42] James would have presented himself at the Patients' Entrance, a narrow archway under the hospital Treasurer's house, just east of the parish church, on a Tuesday morning at 10 o'clock. That was the only day in the week the hospital accepted new patients[43] who knew on admission that their discharge could fall into one of only three categories, 'cured', 'incurable', or 'deceased'.

James died from kidney failure on June 11th 1852. He would not have suffered the surgeon's knife as his condition was inoperable at the time, but even had surgery been performed the end result would have been almost as certain given the knowledge which then prevailed. It had been only five years earlier that the hospital's physicians had first experimented with disinfecting fluids and the surgeons with the earliest methods of anaesthesia.[44] Nor were the nursing staff in any way trained or qualified. Ward sisters received less than 15s. a week and an annual beer allowance of £2.5s. The nurses themselves were paid between 7s.6d. and 10s.6d. a week plus their beer and were little better than drunken drudges. The Governors had recommended salary increases 'in order to attract a better class of woman', but another two years were to pass before the Crimean War revealed the appalling quality of nursing care, and prompted Florence Nightingale to recruit educated women to serve as medical orderlies. Their selfless dedication in the front line inspired donations totalling £50,000, thus enabling her to found the first training school for fifteen probationer nurses at St Thomas's four years after the war had ended.[45]

For six hundred years the hospital authorities had buried their own dead and had even paid a fee to local parishes 'for the privilege of ourselves burying those we failed to cure'[46] in the hospital's own burial ground off Snow's Fields. Today the 'Ship and Mermaid' occupies its site. James was not, however, buried by the hospital authorities, nor did he suffer the indignity of dissection by the hospital's anatomists. Somehow his widow found the money to give him a private funeral in St Olave's church nine days after his death, and he was interred in the parish burial ground which lay between Weaver's Lane and

Potter's Fields beside the river which had provided him with what had passed for his livelihood for two decades. His remains lie beneath the playground of what, today, is Tooley Street school. His body was one of the last to be laid to rest there as the burial ground, which had been in use for nearly four centuries, was closed the following year.[47]

Agitation to close parish churchyards in built-up areas had been growing for some years and given added impetus during the second cholera epidemic in the blazing hot summer of 1849 which had carried off nearly 15,000 Londoners and 72,000 victims in the whole of England and Wales. As The Times wrote in that same year, 'A whiff from a London churchyard, where the corpses of former parishioners are rotting within a few inches of the surface, is *not* acceptable even to a churchwarden. It is *not* a wise nor a salutary course for a citizen, Sunday after Sunday, to take his wife and his young children, and to sit down with them for two hours at a stretch in a close building, the atmosphere of which is infected with the gaseous influences of corpses undergoing decomposition in the vaults beneath.'[48]

St Thomas's Hospital's own burial ground was also closed in that year and for the same reason, but the hospital itself was also under threat from the expansion of the railways. By 1857, thirteen and a half million passengers a year were using London Bridge station and a Parliamentary Committee recommended that the lines which terminated there should be extended westwards to link up with the London and South Western Railway at Waterloo. At around the same time the railway companies wanted to extend their lines northwards across the Thames to Hungerford Market at Charing Cross and to the City at Cannon Street. The construction of these lines entailed an extension of the London Bridge viaduct at a height of twenty-four feet across the north-western corner of the hospital site and within only eighteen inches of its new north wing housing the women's wards. Understandably, the hospital Governors opposed the plans. They could not prevent the development, but did manage to get a clause inserted in the Charing Cross Extension Bill compelling the railway company to purchase the whole of their site, and not merely that part of it actually needed for the viaduct extension.[49]

Three years later the Governors accepted an arbitrator's award of £296,000 for the site and prepared to move away. They looked for temporary accommodation until a new hospital could be built in Lambeth. What the Governors found was a financially failing botanical and zoological park and music-hall in Newington known as 'Surrey Gardens.' The music-hall which could hold 10,000 people, was divided into three floors to hold two hundred beds, and some use was found for all the animal dens and cages: the giraffe house became a cholera ward, a pavilion housed a chemical laboratory and even the elephant house was said to have been converted into a dissecting room. The new hospital on the Albert Embankment opposite the Houses of Parliament was eventually opened by Queen Victoria in June 1871.[50]

The first of his family to migrate to London, James had survived the two great cholera epidemics. He had even survived the influx of Irish casual labourers who made for the fellmongers, glue yards and tanneries of Bermondsey and the docks and wharfs of the riverside. The 1845 potato famine had starved 700,000 Irish to death in their homeland and caused a million others to emigrate and, being largely unskilled, they looked for whatever casual, manual work might be available. So large an addition to the pool of casual labour intensified competition for jobs and consequently reduced the wages offered. A Liverpool clergyman could hardly have demonstrated the inexorable law of supply and demand more clearly when he remarked: 'In the present state of the labour market English labour would be almost unpurchasable if it were not for the competition of Irish labour. The English labourers have unfortunately been taught their rights till they have almost forgotten their duties . . . and in that case we are very frequently able to put on the screw of the Irish competition.'[51]

In nineteen years of marriage James had brought up a family of seven children on irregular earnings which could seldom have exceeded 20s. a week, and frequently fallen to nothing at all except for what he might have made by hawking firewood, or what his wife might have earned from sack-making or by taking in washing. He outlived his own father by only a year and must have wondered, in his latter days, whether he had chosen aright in leaving the land for the lure of a capital city 'paved with gold.'

References

[1] Wohl, 'Ragged London in 1861', p.59

[2] Hole, 'The Homes of the Working Classes', p.40
[3] Vallance, 'Dickens' London', p.37
[4] Thomas, 'London's First Railway', pp.79/80
[5] Myer's Universum (1841) Vol.8.p.12 : quot. in Thomas, 'London's First Railway', p.81
[6] Vallance, 'Dickens' London', p.39
[7] ibid., p.41
[8] Margetson, 'Leisure and Pleasure in the Nineteenth Century', p.178
[9] Vallance, 'Dickens' London', pp.44/5
[10] Walton, 'The English Seaside Resort', p.18 and Cunningham, H., 'Leisure in the Industrial Revolution', pp.85 and 160
[11] Cunningham, H., 'Leisure in the Industrial Revolution', p.162 and Margetson, 'Leisure and Pleasure in the Nineteenth Century', p.84
[12] Walton, 'The English Seaside Resort', p.22
[13] Margetson, 'Leisure and Pleasure in the Nineteenth Century', p.85
[14] Canning, 'The Illustrated Mayhew's London', pp.44–48
[15] Howitt, 'The Rural Life of England', pp.524/5
[16] Malcolmson, 'Popular Recreations', p.50
[17] Kirwan, 'Palace and Hovel', pp.207–209
[18] Hollingshead, 'Underground London', pp.44, 76 and 77
[19] Southwark Archives, 1664, (8 NOV 1848) Southwark Local Studies Library
[20] Wohl, 'Ragged London in 1861', p.44
[21] ibid., p.14
[22] ibid., p.25
[23] Southwark Archives, 1664, (2 APR 1850) Southwark Local Studies Library
[24] 'The Times', 3 JUL 1858
[25] Stedman-Jones, 'Outcast London', p.175
[26] P71/TMS/404, Greater London R.O.
[27] Jerrold, 'Thomas Hood', p.764
[28] ibid., pp.625/6
[29] Stedman-Jones, 'Outcast London', p.175
[30] House of Lords R.O.,(1844) XXIV – 'First Report on the State of Large Towns and Populous Districts', paras. 5878 and 5880
[31] Hole, 'The Homes of the Working Classes', pp.12/13
[32] Sheppard, 'London 1808–1870', p.289
[33] Hole, 'The Homes of the Working Classes', p.42
[34] Anon. : quot. in Tarbuck, 'Handbook of House Property'(1875)
[35] Sheppard, 'London 1808–1870', p.290
[36] Wohl, 'Ragged London in 1861', p.205
[37] Gauldie, 'Cruel Habitations', p.241
[38] Wohl, 'The Eternal Slum', p.78
[39] Hole, 'The Homes of the Working Classes', p.145
[40] Weinreb and Hibbert, 'The London Encyclopaedia', p.624
[41] Cunningham, P., 'Handbook of London', p.493
[42] Parsons, 'St. Thomas's Hospital', p.5
[43] ibid., p.78
[44] ibid., pp.112 and 118
[45] ibid., pp.102 and 149
[46] ibid., pp.130/131

[47] Boast, 'The Story of Bermondsey', p.26
[48] 'The Times', 13 NOV 1849
[49] Thomas, 'London's First Railway', p.227 and Parsons, 'St. Thomas's Hospital', p.141
[50] Parsons, 'St. Thomas's Hospital', pp.152 and 172
[51] Redford, 'Labour Migration in England', pp.154-162

CHAPTER THIRTEEN

THE SCHOOL BOARD MAN

Knock at the door! Pooh, nonsense!
They wouldn't know what it meant.
Come in and look about you;
They'll think you're a School Board gent.
Did you ever see such hovels?
Dirty and damp and small
Look at the rotten flooring
Look at the filthy wall.

– George Sims[1]

'Education meant teaching Caliban how to name the bigger light and how the less; it meant teaching Caliban the language in which to curse his master.'

– R. J. Cruikshank[2]

When James died in St. Thomas's Hospital his eldest son, William Francis, or 'Francis' as he clearly preferred to be known, was eighteen years old. On him fell the responsibility of earning for his mother and six brothers and sisters of whom only his 13 year old brother, James, might have brought in a shilling or two as an errand boy and his widowed mother, Ann, would undoubtedly have continued to earn a few shillings from mangling, charring, or, perhaps, more likely fur-pulling, sack – or paper bag-making which were the dominant home industries available to house-bound women in Southwark.[3]

Francis was employed in one of the small tin-plate factories making metal boxes and canisters for packing and re-packaging the grocery goods imported in bulk into the great warehouses along the Thames. Chests of tea from India, Ceylon and China, spices from the East Indies, and sacks of coffee from South America were repacked by wholesalers and importers for the retail trade so that metal containers were always in great demand along the riverside. It was not a skilled trade so that factory owners could employ large numbers of juveniles at low wages and then dismiss them when they reached 18 or 20 years of age, replacing them with other, younger, lads. Those displaced found it difficult to find alternative employment, having no skilled trade, and many drifted into the army in desperation.[4] Whether this is what happened to Francis we cannot know. Perhaps he was sickened with the grime and filth of Southwark and the burden of being the main support of a family of eight, so that the attraction of a smart uniform and the promise of adventure overseas proved irresistible. Whatever the immediate cause may have been, he enlisted at the Westminster recruiting office in November 1854, and, at the age of 20 years and 6 months became a private in the 8th (King's Royal Irish) Hussars. The thought of being a cavalryman may have been an added attraction, of course, but six weeks before Francis enlisted the French and British armies had landed in the Crimea in support of their Turkish allies against the Russians. The British Army had not been at war for forty years since Wellington and Blücher had defeated Napoleon at Waterloo and a new generation, which recalled only the glory and had forgotten the bloody misery, were swept up in an enthusiastic war hysteria which encouraged many young men to take the Queen's shilling a day. In the event he spent only seven months in the Crimea, surviving the mud, the disease, and the incompetence of the generals, unlike 25,000 of his fellows, most of whom succumbed to sickness and the appalling hospital conditions until Florence Nightingale and her band of dedicated nurses revolutionised the care of the sick and wounded.

Altogether, Francis served in the King's Royal Irish Hussars for 21 years, six and a half of them in India earning the Indian Mutiny Medal. In that time he was awarded the Long Service and Good Conduct Medal and achieved a second-class school certificate. Half of his service was spent as a non-commissioned officer and on his discharge he had attained the rank of Troop Sergeant Major. His discharge papers describe him as 5'7" in height with a fresh complexion, light brown hair and hazel eyes. Here then was a 41 years old ex-soldier with a commendable, if unspectacular, service record and a pension of 1s. 10½d. a day, preparing to live, at least initially, with his younger brother, James's, small family in Dockhead, Bermondsey.[5]

The winter of 1875 was not a good time for anyone seeking work, the country was entering a decade of economic depression which was to worsen dramatically before trade picked up again in the late 1880's. In any case, ex-soldiers always found it difficult to find employment. They were ill-prepared for earning a living in civilian life, they were kept on the reserve list so that potential employers were reluctant to give them a regular job as they could be recalled to the colours at short notice. Mostly they drifted into casual employment as sandwich-board men, street sellers or dock labourers.[6]

Francis was more fortunate than most or, perhaps, that second-class school certificate made all the difference to the School Board for London to whom he applied. Within three months of his discharge, whilst still unemployed, he was appointed as a 'Visitor in the Tower Hamlets Division at a salary of £80 per annum.' This curious term was employed by the London School Board to describe its fast-growing army of school attendance officers of whom about 200 had been recruited in London. The spectre of the 'School Board Man' haunted generations of school-children long after the School Boards had been abolished in the early years of the twentieth century, and he was hated and feared by parents in the poorer parts of the capital for many years after the introduction of compulsory education in London.

The job of school attendance officer had not existed five years earlier. The only education available to the majority of the population had been provided by the private benevolence of the Church and chapel congregations in the form of the 'National' or 'British and Foreign' schools, or by individuals who set up their own private acadamies for personal profit. Many of these latter were truly awful, both as regards their accommodation and the quality of education they offered. Of these private enterprise school teachers, a government report stated unequivocally, 'None are too old, too poor, too ignorant, too feeble, too sickly, too unqualified in one or every way, to regard themselves, and to be regarded by others, as unfit for school-keeping.' Amongst the previous (or even simultaneous) occupations followed by these incompetents the report listed, 'discharged barmaids, vendors of toys or lollipops, keepers of small eating-houses, of mangles . . . persons of at least doubtful temperance, outdoor paupers, men or women of seventy and even eighty years of age, persons who spell badly (mostly women, I grieve to say), who can scarcely write and who cannot cipher at all.'[7]

At the bottom of the heap were the 'Ragged Schools' designed by philanthropists to offer food, warmth and a minimal education to destitute or abandoned children, too poor to pay for any schooling. That such help was needed is clear from a later report prepared for the Charity Organisation Society: 'The masters and mistresses of ragged schools declare that the children continually cry with hunger, and frequently fall exhausted from their seats for want of food, and that it is impossible to teach them in such a state.' In that condition, 'it would be as unreasonable to expect that they should grow into healthy labourers,' added the commentator, 'as to look for grapes on thistles.'[8]

Even that level of schooling, however, was more than a large proportion of London's child population received. At least half were registered on no school roll at all, and even those who were only attended intermittently. This was not always the pupils' fault as can be seen from an entry in his school log book by Daniel Taylor, the headmaster of St John and All Saints Charity School in Southwark: 'January 7th 1863. Received a note from the father of one of the new boys, who had only been admitted last Monday, to say that "his boys didn't learn nothing". Thought he must be an excellent judge. Sent the boy home to his discriminating father.'[9]

Government had not entirely ignored education. Since 1833 it had made annual grants to the voluntary schools, provided that they were considered efficient, and in 30 years the total had grown from £20,000 to over £800,000 a year. The grant was administered by a Committee of the Privy Council, presided over by a Vice President – almost the equivalent of today's Secretary of State for Education, but successive holders of that office were not necessarily committed to the ideal of universal education. As one of them complained to Parliament:

'The object of the present system appeared to be, not to make

> ploughboys or mechanics, but to make scholars. Parents did not want that . . . If they were to pass a law to compel poor parents to send their children to school to be made scholars of, they might just as well pass another law to compel the noble lord to send his children to a school where they would be educated for becoming ploughboys or artisans. The one law would be no more absurd or tyrannical than the other.'[10]

Another Vice President, Robert Lowe, set out his views on the different educational levels he considered appropriate:

> 'The lower classes,' he wrote, 'ought to be educated to discharge the duties cast upon them. They should also be educated that they may appreciate and defer to a higher cultivation when they meet it, and the higher classes ought to be educated in a very different manner, in order that they may exhibit to the lower classes that higher education to which, if it were shown to them, they would bow down and defer.'[11]

Lowe was widely unpopular for his intellectual arrogance and his offensive manner, so much so that his epitaph was penned before his death:

> 'Here lies the body of Robert Lowe,
> Where he has gone to I don't know.
> If he has gone to the realms above,
> That's an end of peace and love.
> If he has sought a lower level,
> God have mercy on the Devil.'[12]

Even so, his view that a labourer should be educated only to the extent which suited that station in life in which the Good Lord had placed him, was widely shared. As for the proposition that any form of educational provision should be made compulsory, a highly influential Royal Commission argued that 'Independence is of a more importance than education; and if the wages of the child's labour are necessary, either to keep the parents from the poor rates, or to relieve the pressure of severe and bitter poverty, it is far better that it should go to work at the earliest age at which it can bear the physical exertion than that it should remain at school.'[13]

The conclusions of that Royal Commission, under the Chairmanship of the Duke of Newcastle, were published in 1861 and influenced schooling adversely for almost 40 years. Its terms of reference required it to report on what measures, if any, were needed 'for the extension of sound and cheap elementary instruction to all classes of people.' Economy, therefore, was to be the touchstone by which its recommendations were to be judged and the Newcastle Commission did not disappoint. In future, grants should be earned, it thought, in such a way that taxpayers and ratepayers could be satisfied that they were getting value for money. The following year, Robert Lowe, the Vice President, issued his 'Revised Code', the detailed regulations which laid down precisely how this 'payment by results' system should operate. Each child over the age of six who made at least 200 half-day attendances in the year earned a grant for the school. Additionally, eight shillings a year was earned if that child passed an examination conducted by one of Her Majesty's Inspectors in reading, writing and arithmetic. One third of that eight shillings was lost for each failure in any one of those three subjects. A total failure in all three, therefore, lost the school the whole amount. The grant thus calculated was to be paid to the school managers and the teacher was paid out of that, so it was clearly in the financial interests of the managers and the teacher not only that a high level of attendance should be achieved, but that as many children as possible should pass each of the three examined subjects. Any reduction in the grant almost inevitably led to a reduced salary for the teacher so it is scarcely surprising to find that virtually the whole of a teacher's energies were spent in preparing children to pass the Inspector's examination. There was no time to encourage a child to think for itself, to question or to experiment. Everything was subordinated to the dull monotony of parrot-learning, often so intensively that some children could 'read' their set books even when they accidentally held them upside down.

As the day of the inspector's visit grew closer, the teacher's anxiety transmitted itself to the children so that by the day itself the whole school was in a state of acute tension. So important was it to encourage every child to be present, whose attendance record qualified it, that some who were ill and even infectious were taken from bed to classroom to be examined. "To hear paroxysms of whooping-cough," reported one inspector, "to observe the pustules of small-pox, to see infants wrapped up and held in their mothers' arms, or seated on a stool by the fire, because too ill to take their proper places, are events not so rare in an inspector's experience as they ought to be."[14] Nor was the attitude of many of the inspectors calculated to lower the temperature. It may have been a tedious, repetitive and uncongenial task, but there was no excuse for bullying those who stumbled over a word or for belittling their teacher in front of a class of sixty or eighty bewildered children as many of them seemed to find a malicious satisfaction in doing. 'The fussy, the cranky, the cruel all found a perfect field for the exercise of their defects. Too often the only amusement of an otherwise barren day was a tussle with a hysterical teacher who could be baited almost to madness with perfect impunity.'[15] Those words are the judgement of a modern educational historian summarising innumerable contemporary anecdotes like Flora Thompson's recollection of the inspector who examined her village school. He was an elderly clergyman, a little man with an immense paunch and tiny grey eyes like gimlets who had the reputation of being strict: 'The very sound of his voice scattered the few wits of the less gifted, and even those who could have done better were too terrified in his presence to be able to collect their thoughts or keep their hands from trembling.'[16] Some inspectors were kindly, condemning the books provided for younger pupils as being dull and nonsensical. "Why," asked one London inspector, "should children be called upon to learn such rubbish as . . . 'Do not nod on a sod,' or 'Can a ram sit on a sod?"[17] But there were far too many who took a fiendish delight in setting incomprehensible texts for dictation or confusing problems in arithmetic. "What is the nearest number greater than 13476 which is exactly divisible by 47?"[18] was a question asked of an average 9 year old in Standard III at which level he had not yet progressed beyond using a slate and slate pencil and was expected only to be capable of calculating 'a sum in any simple rule, as far as short division.'

As the century progressed the curriculum was widened to include subjects like geography or drawing, teachers could choose specific subjects in which individual children or a whole class could be examined. But still the pernicious system of 'payment by results' underlay everything until almost the very end of the century and, even after its abolition its legacy

'The very sound of his voice scattered the few wits of the less gifted . . .'

remained a persuasive influence for years.

The year 1870 saw the beginnings of a revolution in educational provision introduced by an enlightened mill-owner with a Quaker up-bringing. W. E. Forster, the Member of Parliament for Bradford was related by marriage to Dr Arnold of Rugby and had a genuine interest in furthering educational opportunities. William Gladstone made him the Vice President of the Education Department and within two years his Elementary Education Act had become law. On introducing his Bill, Forster outlined its main purpose as being "to bring elementary education within the reach of every English home, aye, and within the reach of those children who have no homes."[19] This was to be achieved by continuing to support the voluntary, mainly Anglican and non-conformist, schools and to fill the gaps where there was no adequate provision by setting up School Boards with the power to levy a rate to enable new schools to be built. It was a compromise with the contending religious pressure groups, and even today the consequences of that compromise survive, but, in the main, it worked as a solution to a seemingly intractable problem which, simply stated, was how to provide education for that half of the child population which attended no school without antagonising the charitably -minded who, until then, had been the only providers of schooling for the poor. The Act did not abolish school fees, but those who could not afford one or two pence a week for each child could apply for a free place. Nor did it make attendance compulsory; instead, it granted each School Board the power to pass a bye-law requiring compulsory attendance in the area for which it was responsible.

Forster's reforms were later criticised, especially by those on the political left, as being both inadequate and class-based. H.G. Wells wrote, 'The Education Act of 1870 was not an Act for a common universal education, it was an Act to educate the lower classes for employment on lower-class lines' – a minimal education for those who could not afford to pay for something better.[20] R.H. Tawney claimed that 'the elementary schools were intended in the main to produce an orderly, civil, obedient population, with sufficient education to understand a command.'[21] In those criticisms both writers were echoing the sentiments of the Church of England's National Society whose sole object in providing schools for the poor at the begining of the nineteenth century was forthrightly stated to be 'to communicate to the poor such knowledge and habits, as are sufficient to guide them through life, in their proper stations . . . '[22]

Such criticism may well have been justified, as may more recent objections that the whole tenor of nineteenth century elementary education imposed the standards and moral values of middle-class England on to an unwilling working-class population. However that may be, something needed to be done to raise the standards and the hopes of a degraded urban population which had for too long been deprived of any opportunity to raise its sights from the misery of a daily existence bounded by the twin needs of finding enough to eat and shelter for the night. The supercilious Robert Lowe described the elementary education system as not being 'intended to apply to the upper or middle classes, but to those who are too poor to educate themselves.'[23] He was right, of course. Forster's Act may have been no more than a hesitant beginning, but the twentieth century should be eternally grateful for his foresight.

Forster's vision of bringing an elementary education within the reach of every English child was matched by the drive and energy displayed by the first London School Board. On the day of its first elections The Times wrote, 'No equally powerful body will exist in England, outside Parliament, if power be measured by influence for good or evil over masses of human beings.'[24] It could have added that the Board was a far more representative body than was the Parliament which had created it, in that women were allowed to stand, and two were elected on November 29th 1870, no property qualification was imposed and within a very few years working men found their place as Board members.

The Board's first task was to determine the need. An initial survey appeared to show that the number of school places required to be provided in London was in the region of 100,000, although it was later realised how great an underestimate that was: the true figure should have been nearer to a quarter of a million. The voluntary schools already provided that number of places in London so the deficiency to be met by the London School Board actually amounted to a staggering fifty per cent.[25] Such was the dedication and determination of the Board that by the time Francis Mimms was appointed as a visitor, some five years later, it had built 100 new schools with room for 100,000 pupils and it continued to expand until, by the century's end, it had provided a half-million school places or two-thirds of London's elementary schools' requirement; the voluntary schools continued to provide the rest.[26] It was a stupendous achievement. When the work of the London School Board was taken over by the London County Council after 33 years of pioneering effort, Sir George Kekewich, the secretary to the Education Board, claimed with justice that it had 'done more in a shorter time for a larger number of people than any other authority in the world.'[27]

As it was entitled to do under the Act, the London School Board swiftly adopted a bye-law requiring compulsory full-time attendance of all children between the ages of 5 and 10; those between 10 and 13 had to attend at least half-time unless they had passed Standard V which required a child to read and write from dictation from a newspaper 'or other modern narrative', and to pass an arithmetical test involving the calculation of invoices.[28] From the age of 10, therefore, a child would be employed full-time provided it had attained that level of school-learning. It was one thing to decree that children should attend school, but quite another to ensure that they did so, and to devise a system of enforcing regular attendance. To achieve this the Board appointed a School Attendance Committee to be responsible for each of the ten Divisions into which it had sub-divided the capital and recruited visitors answerable to a Superintendent to enforce the regulations.

An early recruit to the Hackney Division was John Reeves who was appointed in April 1872 but he and two colleagues were asked 'to wait for a few weeks until the sphere of our duties could be determined.' In the event it took the Board some months to decide how they should operate so that Reeves did not start work until six months later.[29] Compulsion, the Board declared, should be 'carried out especially at first with as much gentleness and consideration for the circumstances and feelings of the parents as is consistent with its effective operation.'[30] Understandably, perhaps, the authorities were anxious to avoid using too heavy a hand in imposing what many parents thought of as an unwelcome intrusion on a free-born Englishman's independence which they had long been told they possessed. John Reeves experienced that fear when he was accompanied by a Board member, the Revd. Picton, on his calls in Bethnal Green. Picton stood aside so as to overhear the conversation without being seen as Reeves enquired of a mother about her truant child. On opening the door she abused him most offensively before he could say a word. 'When she had finished,' he recalled, 'I gave a few words of earnest warning as to the attendance at school of one of her children and then left. The rev. gentleman, in a most solemn manner,cautioned me not to say anything to excite the people.'[31] The board was obviously concerned that their attendance officers should be seen not as a law enforcement agency, but rather as social workers so their choice of a title for them became important. They finally decided on 'visitor', a term widely used by religious charities whose 'District Visitors', mostly middle-class ladies, busied themselves in the slum areas. In the course of the debate it was recommended that in general they should be 'women who have had experience in similar work, as District visitors Etc.,' on the grounds that it should thereby be possible 'to secure the services of persons of a higher class than could otherwise be obtained.'[32] One title canvassed during the debate was 'Child's Beadle' which was too reminiscent of Oliver Twist for John Reeves who, after it had been rejected, observed with relief, 'I have always been thankful for the thought which preserved us from "Bumbledom" ', adding that when opening one of the new Board Schools, the author of the Act praised the work of the visitors saying that they were entitled to have 'M.P.' after their names because he regarded them as Moral Policemen.[33] However, amongst the more printable of the names popularly used to describe him was 'kid-copper', although he was most widely known and feared as 'the School Board Man.'

Each visitor was assigned to a 'block', an area of his Division containing approximately 3000 children of school age. His first task was to prepare a census of his 'block', listing for each family the name and occupation of the parent or guardian and the names and ages of all children with their dates of birth if known.[34] This 'scheduling', as it was called, was repeated annually and had to be carried out with tact and discretion, not to mention a degree of guile, as there was no legal requirement that parents should give that information and no sanction which a visitor could impose. When his schedule was completed he supplied those schools whose catchment areas were included in his 'block' with a list of children who should be attending. These they checked against their rolls. From time to time the heads provided their visitor with a list of absentees and persistent truants each one of which he had to follow up with a home visit. In the early days especially, this could be not only unpleasant but also a highly dangerous activity inviting abuse and even physical assault. Parents who objected to his enquiries 'would stand at the door and threaten and abuse me in the most dreadful language,' recalled Reeves,' and nearly all the people in the street would come out and see what was the matter and sympathise in their view. All this was very unpleasant.'[35] he concluded with praiseworthy understatement.

Parents tried to evade their responsibilities by devious means. Part of John Reeves's 'block' was the Nichol Street area, a notorious haunt of criminals and the feckless poor on the borders of Shoreditch and Bethnal Green – the locale of Arthur Morrison's horrifying novel, 'A Child of the Jago'. Enquiring after a young truant in Half Nichol Street, the boy's mother told him her son was 'dead and buried', but a few days later Reeves found him at work. In New Nichol Street a mother invited him into her room to verify that her daughter was 'ill in bed'. After leaving he waited for a few minutes and called back. 'The mother opened the door and the girl was up, fully dressed and skipping in the middle of the floor, quite well'.[36] In a Limehouse school John Jones, the headmaster, recorded in his log book: 'Mr Kerrigan, Visitor, reported that Jas. Phillips is staying at home because he was not allowed to leave the room 'when necessary' and, having diarrhoea, had twice gone home dirty.' The Head questioned his younger brother, William, 'who tells me that Jas. has not had diarrhoea as alleged but that he is at home helping his father in his business of binding up bundles of wood . . . .'[37], which is, doubtless, where brother William would have preferred to have been.

Parental objection to compulsory education was not just wilful, many often desperately needed every penny a small child could earn. . A widespread home industry available especially in London's East End was match-box making for factories such as those of Bryant and May in Poplar. The going rate for making a gross of them was twopence-farthing. A thousand separate pieces went into the manufacture of a gross and even tiny hands could contribute to the process. 'As soon as a child was old enough to stick a piece of glass paper on a box,' wrote Reeves, 'he or she was set to work to assist in this struggle for bread.'[38] Margaret Harkness described how 'the woman's hands were busy with the match boxes. Strips of magenta paper and thin pieces of wood came together with the help of a paste brush. They were then thrown on the ground to dry, forming pyramids of trays and lids which would presently be made into matchboxes, tied up with string and sent back to factories . . .'[39]. The women had to find their own paste and string and keep a fire going to dry the boxes. An industrious worker could make them at a rate of 600-700 a day which, for a seven-day week, earned her 6 to 7 shillings.[40] Little wonder then that the dexterity of a child's hands was welcomed. As one woman admitted: "Of course we cheat the School Board. It's hard on the little ones, but their fingers is so quick – they that has the most of 'em is the best off."[41]

Very shortly after his appointment as visitor, Francis Mimms married. He was a 42 year old bachelor and his wife an Irish widow, Margaret Bowman, daughter of a Chelsea builder. Although he had been living in Lucey Road, Bermondsey, south of the Thames, the School Board had posted him to the Tower Hamlets Division across the river and he had found lodgings in Stratford. It was there they were married in the parish church of St Mary, Bow, in August 1876. They settled in Limehouse where they lived for twenty years renting rooms in various houses in Acland Street.

The Tower Hamlets Division of the London School Board, together with the adjacent Hackney Division, comprised the whole of London's East End, probably the largest and most concentrated area of deprivation anywhere in England. Tower Hamlets itself was made up of five separate Poor Law Unions – Whitechapel, St. George's, Mile End Old Town, Stepney and Poplar. Its southern boundary was a seven mile stretch of the Thames waterfront from the Tower of London eastwards through Wapping, Shadwell, Limehouse and round the sweeping bend of the river which was Poplar's Isle of Dogs. Most of London's docks on the north side of the Thames – St Katherine's, the London, the Millwall and the East and West India Docks all fell within Tower Hamlets' area. Charles Booth chose the School Board Division of Tower Hamlets for his very first statistical survey of poverty in London relying, in the main, for his information upon the scheduling records supplied by the visitors. As he explained, 'The School Board visitors perform amongst them a house to house visitation; every house in every street is in their books, and details are given of every family with children of school age. They also begin their scheduling two or three years before the children attain school age, and a record remains in their books of children who have left school. Most of the visitors have been working in the same district for several years, and thus have extensive knowledge of the people . . . For this reason I have taken the information to be had from the School Board visitors as the framework of the picture I wish to give of the life and labour of the people.'[42]

The survey revealed to Charles Booth's surprise and dismay, that out of a total population of some 450,000 in Tower Hamlets no less than 160,000, or 35 per cent, of them were living in, or on the borderline of, poverty which he defined as an income of between 18 and 21 shillings a week for a moderate family.[43] In fact, those whose regular income fell between those figures he defined as 'poor' (22%), but those earning anything below that level, 'the very poor', made up no less than 13 per cent of Tower Hamlets' population, so that 59,000 people, one in every eight, were living in extreme want and some of them, said Booth, were of a class 'for whom decent life is not imaginable'.

Limehouse had been a hamlet in the parish of Stepney and at one time a thriving riverside community with a substantial ship-building industry. The collapse of ship-building on the Thames had been dramatic, its workforce reduced to one-third of its former size within five years.[44] By the time Francis and Margaret settled in Limehouse there was very little of it left, and the major source of employment was in the West India Docks close by. Charles Booth described Stepney (which included Limehouse) as 'essentially the abode of labour; here the casual labourers reach their maximum of nearly 11 per cent of the population, and have their homes in a mass of squalid streets and courts.'[45]

It was not a promising area for a newly appointed visitor, nor could he expect much sympathy from the head teachers if he failed to measure up to their expectations as they relied heavily on his efforts to maintain their attendance records. Dalgleish Street school, a third of a mile from Francis's Limehouse home had opened for business on January 5th 1880. Within a very few months the headmaster, John Jones, was confiding to his school log, 'The attendance has been bad this week, our visitor is new to the work and consequently inefficient.' During the succeeding fifteen months his complaints intensified:

June 7th	'The visitor has not given me a report since March 12th and the parents are taking advantage.'
September 10th	'I cannot get the Visitor to do his work properly – the lads seem to know that they can stop away without being visited – I find my "boy visitor" of more use than Mr Allen.'
July 18th, 1881	'The visiting has been very badly done for some twenty weeks. Today I refused to let the Visitor take away my "Duplicate Registers". I have retained them to shew to the Managers at their next meeting.'[46]

Mr Allen may well not have been a very efficient officer, but the district was a difficult one and the workload heavy. In addition to 'scheduling' and constant visiting, he was expected to attend formal hearings to which parents were called to explain a child's absence, where an application was made for school fees to be waived, or to allow a child to attend half-time. The visitor attended court to give evidence before a magistrate following a summons for persistent truancy. He had also to prepare lists of children whose attendance record seemed to justify a spell in a Truant or Industrial School, as well as constantly updating his schedule with families who moved into or out of his 'block'. The paperwork alone was a constant headache. One visitor complained that he had had 'to work till twelve, one, and even two in the mornings . . . on Saturday afternoons and on Sundays. He had even been obliged to get his children to help him in his work on the Sunday.'[47] At the very least Francis could not claim that, as he and Margaret remained childless.

One of the most arduous and least pleasant tasks which fell to the visitor's lot, especially in the early years, was the rounding up of homeless children – those who had been abandoned by parents, had run away from a violent home, or who were genuinely orphaned. They tended to congregate in gangs, living on their wits, sleeping in markets under carts, in barrels and packing cases, beneath the arches or around railway stations. Kay-Shuttleworth described the 'street-arab' as a sharp-witted, restless little creature, 'He is his own master. His powers of observation are singularly acute; his powers of decision rapid; his will energetic. He is known as 'the arab of the street'. He learns a great deal of evil. Perhaps he is an accomplished thief, or beggar, or picks up a precarious living by holding horses, sweeping a crossing, or costermongering. Such children have of late years been netted in shoals – got into schools, have been won, tamed, and in some degree taught.'[48]

These were the youngsters whom Thomas Barnardo made it his life's work to rescue. Night after night he searched them out, persuading many to come to the Homes he had set up for them. Many others seemed to prefer the street life, but even these he catered for. A short distance from Acland Street in Limehouse lay Rhodeswell Road. Here Barnardo bought what had once been one of the East End's most notorious gin-palaces, the 'Edinburgh Castle' which he refurbished as a combined temperance Mission Hall and Coffee Palace, supplying cheap meals and hot drinks for seventeen hours a day and providing entertainment, newspapers and magazines for the Stepney poor. It was at the 'Edinburgh Castle' that he held his regular 'Waifs' Suppers'. For weeks beforehand his night-searchers scoured the streets, the market-places, the riverside and common lodging-houses issuing ticket invitations to any children who appeared to be in need. On one January afternoon some 2,000 urchins toed the gutter-line of Rhodeswell Road waiting to go in; some had tramped, bare footed, six miles or more to attend. Youngsters from his Homes acted as stewards and waiters serving tray-loads of bread and butter, cake and hot tea which was followed by an entertainment from a conjuror and a troupe of performing dogs. At such gatherings Thomas Barnardo would invite his guests to come forward if they had tired of street life and were willing to work and obey his rules. From amongst those who volunteered, he selected the ones he considered the most needy and promising to join the thousands whose lives his efforts had already transformed.[49]

Thomas Barnardo's work for children was only one of many hundreds of charitable activities undertaken, one might almost say indulged in, by the comfortably off in Queen Victoria's England. By 1861 it had been calculated that there were 640 charitable agencies of all kinds operating in London alone, of which nearly a quarter had been founded only during the previous ten years.[50] The Honorary Secretary of the Metropolitan Visiting and Relief Association, the Revd. M.S.A. Walrond, claimed that in the area covered by the Poor Law

Unions of Whitechapel, St. George's-in-the-East, and Stepney 130,000 of its 200,000 inhabitants were likely to receive a home visit from one or more of about 50 'bona fide' visitors. He went on to list the many other visitors who might be expected: 8 Poor Law relieving officers, 10 or 12 School Board visitors, 3 agents of the Charity Organisation Society, about 50 Church of England clergy and dissenting ministers, 12 almoners of the Society for Relief of Distress, and what he could not quite bring himself to describe as a 'rag-bag' of 'about 100 lay agents such as City missionaries, Bible women, Scripture readers and the like, besides all sorts of religious adventurers, Gospel missioners, and quite an army of Sunday School teachers.' Little wonder then that another East End clergyman was sufficiently provoked by all this activity to remark that a court in his parish might go unvisited from one year's end to another until some calamity befell one of its inhabitants, "then there was a swoop of rival charitable eagles from all sorts of religious quarters to settle on the body."[51]

At the end of the 1860s it was estimated that whilst £2 million a year was being spent by the Poor Law authorities in legal relief in London, no less than £7 million was expended by private charity.[52] By no means all of this aid was dispensed in what the Charity Organisation Society considered to be a responsible manner. The C.O.S. was probably the most influential charitable institution in the later years of the nineteenth century. Its promoters saw the un-co-ordinated philanthropic efforts of those with kind hearts, deep pockets and time on their hands and strongly disapproved of their indiscriminate charitable handouts to the undeserving. Such irresponsible acts, the Society's supporters thought, discouraged the destitute from striving to fend for themselves resulting in 'pauperising the poor', who consequently came to rely on doles rather than on their own efforts. The Society saw itself in a co-ordinating role amongst a network of philanthropic bodies which supported local Relief Committees. When an applicant applied for help the Society's volunteer visitor completed a form with details of the names, ages, occupations and earnings of every member of the applicant's family, its present and previous addresses, any benefit clubs of which they might be members and any parish relief they might be receiving. The form was sent to the C.O.S. whose paid officer thoroughly checked every statement and sought opinions as to character and worthiness from the Poor Law relieving officer, the minister of religion and the family's past and present landlords. All this was passed back to the volunteer who then attended a weekly Relief Committee for adjudication and decision.[53] The thoroughness of their investigation was such as to reveal an applicant as of good character, thrifty, sober, hard-working, and altogether a model example of the 'deserving poor'. Once satisfied on that score, the Society's aid was always aimed at a solution which might prove to be permanently beneficial by way of a loan, for example, to purchase a workman's tools or redeem them from pawn. In the words of Octavia Hill, one of the Society's most assiduous workers: 'their aim is in every case to rouse the spirit of independence and self-help.'[54]

Of the applicants whose life histories were sifted through this fine sieve and found wanting, Octavia Hill observed that the Society's visitors 'will be encouraged to refuse such persons the pauperising doles of a merely impulsive charity, in the belief that such refusal will probably benefit the individual, and will certainly in the long run benefit the class.'[55]

It was not, however, only those who were refused aid after a long, intrusive and careful scrutiny who objected to the Society's attitude to widespread and desperate poverty. As the East London Observer, by no means a radical newspaper, commented: 'They coolly assume that it is possible for the thousands of men out of work, and unable to procure it through no fault of their own . . . to be or to become thrifty, though when they are in work they never earn enough to live on decently . . ."[56]

Thrift, of course, was one of the cardinal virtues of the Victorian age, prescribed the most strongly by those who had little need to practise it themselves. Octavia Hill included amongst her many philanthropic activities the personal supervision and management of cleaned-up slum properties. Whilst admitting that her tenants were 'of the very poor', she, nevertheless, encouraged them to save their money, adding, regretfully, 'I have never succeeded in getting them to save for old age'[57] Even her intimate knowledge of the day to day lives of her tenants, which included the running of their penny savings clubs, failed to equip her with the capacity to comprehend that 'tomorrow' was an eternity away when 'today' posed such enormous problems of sheer survival. That was something which William Booth did understand: 'how is Thrift to benefit those who have nothing?' he asked. 'What is the use of the gospel of Thrift to a man who had nothing to eat yesterday, and has not threepence to-day to pay for his lodging tonight? To live on nothing a day is difficult enough, but to save on it would beat the cleverest political economist that ever lived.'[58]

Two of the men who were prominently in the public eye at this time, both concerned with London's poor, confusingly shared the same surname: Charles Booth counted them, and William Booth fed them. Which of the two contributed most to the relief of poverty in the long term may be a moot point, but each was influential in his own, wholly different, way. Many of General William Booth's sentiments would have had the wholehearted approval of the Charity Organisation Society: 'No amount of assistance will give a jelly-fish a backbone,' he wrote, 'No outside propping will make some men stand erect. All material help from without is useful only insofar as it develops moral strength within. And some men seem to have lost even the very faculty of self-help.' And yet in the same paragraph he could express a compassion of which the C.O.S. was incapable: 'In the struggle of life the weakest will go to the wall, and there are so many weak. The fittest, in tooth and claw, will survive. All that we can do is to soften the lot of the unfit and make their suffering less horrible than it is at present.'[59] And that is what his Salvation Army had set out to do.

William Booth had no time for those 'who relieve themselves of all anxiety for the welfare of the poor by saying that in the next world all will be put right.' This he described as 'religious cant' which ignores suffering 'by drawing unnegotiable bills payable on the other side of the grave.'[60] Booth was an eminently practical man with a deep understanding of human nature and a concern for the individual driven by a desire to save his eternal soul combined with an equal determination to supply his earthly needs. He had founded his 'Blood and Fire' army in Mile End, Stepney in 1865. Within 25 years its 10,000 officers were operating from nearly 2900 centres across the world,[61] offering homes to prostitutes, a helping hand to discharged prisoners, and work for the unemployed. The Army's slum sisters lived with the poorest, helping where they could. In 1888, the year when 'Jack the Ripper' terrified the East End, Booth bought a one-time warehouse in the West India Dock Road, just half a mile from Francis and Margaret's house in Limehouse. In it he set up his first cheap food depot and within a month of opening his helpers had fed 4000 men and women.[62] Within the first three years the Army's, by then three, depots had served 3.5 million meals. They were no soup kitchens. They offered very few free handouts, soup cost ½d. a basinful or a penny a quart if the buyers brought their own jugs; potatoes, beans and baked jam roll were likewise a ½d, and a full meal of meat pudding and potatoes could be had for threepence.[63] The Army bought in bulk and sold at cost but still the C.O.S. objected. Its Secretary complained to The Times that these activities were 'a new and popular form of indiscriminate relief,' and appealed to 'Mr Booth' to reconsider his methods: 'The people, he says, are hungry; they will be hungry if he doubled his depots, and quadrupled his meals. He is adding to the number of the hungry. The hunger of the mass of the people can only be met by their own exertions; his system tends inevitably to dissuade them from exertion . . . '[64] At root the Charity Organisation Society objected because William Booth made no moral judgements. There was a need: he tried to meet it. As a modern commentator has stated simply: 'Not for the Salvationist the fashionable distinction between the deserving and the undeserving poor. For them, to be poor was to be deserving.'[65]

The warehouse in the West India Dock Road which contained William Booth's first cheap food depot also housed his first night shelter. The facilities were basic, Booth himself described the dormitory as looking like 'an endless array of packing cases,'[66] but it was warm, dry, and clean and for 4d. a night far better value than the fourpenny doss houses or common lodging houses which were the only indoor alternative. The Army shelters, moreover, offered supper, breakfast and a washhouse at that all-in price. The casual ward of the local Workhouse would not take in a man or woman for the night unless they were absolutely destitute, and when they did the Poor Law demanded that they prove their willingness to work. This 'labour test' required the overnight inmate to pick four pounds of oakum or break half a ton of stones the next morning before they could leave. The size of the task was beyond most casuals and usually meant an enforced second night in the casual ward or imprisonment as a vagabond for failure to complete the task. 'Be it remembered', wrote William Booth, 'that this is the treatment meted out to those who are supposed to be Casual poor, in temporary difficulty, walking from place to place seeking some employment.'[67]

Many more men were on the tramp in the 1880s as the whole country suffered in the depths of a long and severe trade recession. The new head of Dalgleish Street school, Limehouse, noted that, 'there is growing difficulty in gathering the School fee, the chief reason for non-payment being want of work.'[68] Across the Thames in Southwark's Farncombe Street Infants School successive log book entries record:

'Jan. 20th 1883	Numbers of children have no garments to come in, some of them are nearly naked.'
'Jan. 17th 1885	There is great want and poverty in this neighbourhood, and in consequence many are unable to attend through want of clothing.'
'June 20th 1885	We have now more children attending without boots than we have ever had in previous years.'[69]

Poverty did not excuse school attendance and help could sometimes be sought from a charity to clothe a child or provide a pair of boots. If a call on the parents by a visitor failed to procure a child's attendance, the Divisional Committee of the Board had sanctions it could use. First, it issued a written warning in the form of an 'A' Notice drawing attention to the bye-laws. If this failed to produce a satisfactory response, the more serious 'B' Notice was issued. This 'invited' the parent to attend a meeting 'to state any excuse you may have to show cause why you should not be summoned before a magistrate and fined.' A 'B' Notice meeting would take place in a room in the local school presided over by one of the members of the School Board for that Division, attended by an officer of the Board to advise on the law and the visitor. The parents waited in an outer room and were called in one by one. George Sims, the journalist, accompanied by a sketch artist, Frederick Barnard, were allowed to attend some of those meetings for a series of articles entitled 'How the Poor Live' published in 'The Pictorial World'. He gives us a vivid picture of a 'B meeting, perhaps somewhat coloured with a popular journalist's understandable exaggeration:

'"Mrs Smith," calls out the Board official, taking the next case down the list for hearing, and a young girl of about fifteen, with a baby in her arms and a child of five clinging to her skirts, enters the room and seats herself nervously on the extreme edge of the chair.

"You're not Mrs Smith, my dear," says the chairman with a smile.

"No sir; that's mother."

"Oh, you've come for her, eh? These boys, Thomas and Charles, who have been absent for three weeks, are your brothers, I suppose?"

"Yes, sir."

"Well, my dear, they ought to come you know, What's the reason?"

"Please, sir, they're at work."

"But they've not passed the Fourth Standard."

"I know, sir; but they've got a job, and it's four shillings a week each, and that's all I've got to keep us."

"All *you've* got, my dear? Where's your father?"

The girl colours a little and hesitates. The School Board officer steps forward to the table and helps her.

"It's a very painful case, sir." he says. "The father's been living with another woman – left his family. A fortnight ago the mother met him and asked him for some money. He knocked her down, and she fell and cut her head open. She's in St. Thomas's Hospital – not expected to live. The man was taken up, and he's under remand now, and this girl has to look after the entire family."

"I see," says the chairman; "and Thomas and Charles are giving you their money eh? and that's all you've got?"

"Yes, sir, I can't work myself, because I've got the baby and the others to look after." "Well, my dear," says the chairman, "I'm very sorry for you, but your brothers can only have half-time or come back to school."

The girl says nothing, she is only fifteen, and can't argue it out with the gentleman – so she curtseys and is ushered out.

I wonder if the mother dies, and the father gets a long term of imprisonment, what the fate of the family will be?'[70]

Sims then lists some of the brief details of cases applying for the remission of school fees:

> ' – Mrs Walker. 7 Children of school age, fee 2d. a week each. Total earnings of entire family 10s. Rent 5s. 6d. Husband once good mechanic, lost employment through illness and deafness.

> Parish relief none. Character good. Is now a hawker – sells oranges and fish. Children half starved. When an orange is too bad to sell they have it for breakfast, with a piece of bread.'
>
> ' – Mr Garrard. 8 children of school age; two always under doctor. No income. Pawning last rags. Rent 5s.6d. No parish relief. Starving. Declines to go into workhouse.'

On such cases George Sims comments, 'the starving children come day after day to school with feeble frames and bloodless bodies, and the law expects them to learn as readily as well-fed healthy children to attain the same standard of proficiency in a given time.'[71]

Another respondent, who deserved and received less sympathy than most, was the voluble Mrs Dash, whose son had not been to school for a fortnight. Asked why, she explained, "Well, it's all through the boots." At this the chairman reminded her that she had used that excuse the last time, and that they had arranged with a charity for her son to be provided with a pair from a local shoemaker. "I know you was kind enough to do that, but they 'urt him, and he can't wear 'em." she alleged. The visitor explained that a pair had been supplied, but Mrs Dash had taken them back demanding the best pair in stock and created such a scene that she had to be put out of the shop. "Which, beggin' your pardon," interposed the mother, "They 'urt the boy, they did, and he haves tender feet, through his father, as is dead, being a shoemaker hisself." "If he can play about the streets all day in the boots, Mrs Dash," argued the officer, "they can't hurt him very much." "My boy play about the streets! Well, of all the oudacious things as I ever 'erd!" she countered, adding the clinching argument, "As to his comin' to school, he's a beautiful little scholard now, and he ain't got no more to learn." Her protestations availed her nothing as her boy admitted that the boots didn't hurt him and Mrs Dash was, with difficulty, ushered out with a warning that the next step would be a court summons.[72]

The Charity Organisation Society, taking its usual high-minded attitude towards indiscriminate charity, warned School Board visitors against the gift of boots on the grounds that if it became widely known, a lot of parents would deliberately keep their children at home in order to obtain a pair.[73] New boots, moreover, were a saleable commodity and charity could be abused.

Sims and his artist colleague gained access to the sources on which their articles and illustrations were based by accompanying, and themselves masquerading as, School Board visitors. He paid this tribute to the men and women who undertook this work:

'The fiercest and most reckless of the lawless classes have to be bearded in their dens by the devoted ill-paid officers, who ferret out the children and insist on their coming to school. Up to the topmost garret and down to the lowest cellar, in dens and hovels given over to thieves and wantons, I have accompanied a School Board officer on his rounds, and I frankly confess that I have passed a few bad quarters of an hour.'[74]

The nature of the visitors' work, especially in the rougher areas, was such that the Board's early hopes of attracting women who had had experience as District Visitors did not materialise. It 'failed to appreciate that the difficulties which the work involved would appear intimidating to most men, let alone to ladies of refinement.' In fact a quarter of the early recruits in the Tower Hamlets Divison were women, but within six months the proportion had fallen to below 15% and within 25 years only half a dozen or so out of the 300 odd visitors in London were women, and they were often engaged on special assignments. Amongst the male recruits the non-commissioned officer featured strongly. In the two years following Francis's recruitment, 62 visitors were appointed, only two of whom were women, but 17 were former soldiers, five had been policemen and 13 others had experience as public servants – prison officers, rate collectors etc.[75] The Board offered a starting salary of £80 per annum (women were paid £50 p.a.), more than most skilled manual workers could earn, but that minimum was never raised in the whole of the London School Board's existence, and it was rigidly enforced. After nearly three years as a visitor, Francis resigned. His salary had risen to £95 p.a. by then. Perhaps the difficulties of the work had begun to affect his health, we know that he was diabetic, but whatever motive prompted his resignation, he re-applied for his old post within five weeks. The Board took him back, but offered only the starting salary of £80 p.a. From that point, by increments of five pounds a year, he advanced to £100 when, after eight years service he received his only promotion from Second to First Class visitor, which earned him a further £5 per annum rise. The Board permitted each Division to promote only one-third of its visitors to First-Class status, and to earn that promotion the Board laid down that in all cases regard had to be paid 'to the percentage of average attendance as compared with the number on the (school) roll, to the percentage of the number on the roll as compared with the School population, and to the size and difficulty of the various districts.'[76] In other words, a visitor was to be judged on the basis of his success in getting children of school age in his ' block' on to the school roll in the first place, and in maintaining the highest possible average attendance thereafter – another aspect, perhaps, of the prevailing 'payment by results' ethos.

After seventeen years in the service of the School Board, the strain of the work and the deterioration of his health had begun to tell on Francis. He had already been granted several short periods of paid absence which led the Tower Hamlets Divisional Committee to ask for a report from the Board's Medical Officers which read:

> 'I have examined Mr William Francis Mimms, Visitor, Tower Hamlets Division, and am of opinion that the tendency of his occupation is such as to aggravate the illness from which he is suffering and that he is, therefore, likely to be frequently absent from his duties.
>
> 'I have, therefore, suggested to him the advisability of his resigning his appointment so as to be free of the anxiety and risks incident to his present occupation.'

On the basis of that report the Board's School Accommodation and Attendance Committee resolved to ask that he be pensioned off. The only problem with that proposal was that the Board had so far failed to appoint a Superannuation Committee so that no proper pension arrangements were in place. Faced with that situation, the Tower Hamlets Committee asked, despairingly, 'what is to be done with Mr Mimms if he be not superannuated? . . . the Divisional Committee do not feel justified in asking him to resign, and they feel they cannot put pressure upon him in the discharge of his duty in consequence of the Medical Officer's opinion . . . .' The Board clearly had no wish to force his resignation which would deprive him of any pension he might eventually be awarded. After much wrangling he was given six months leave on half pay, followed by indefinite leave of absence without pay. Two years later Francis was awarded a provisional annual pension of £4:5:9d., the reward for twenty years' almost continuous service.[77] That 1s 7¾d. a week, added to his army pension gave Margaret and himself a weekly income of 14s 9¼d at least until Francis died in the August of the following year aged 63 from diabetic complications when both pensions, of course, ceased.

The London School Board did not long outlive Francis Mimms. The responsibility for educating the capital's children passed to the Education Committee of the London County Council in 1904, but the Board had more than fulfilled the hopes of its sponsors. Only a dozen years after its creation, George Sims felt sufficiently confident of its achievements to write, 'The children who go back to the slums from the Board Schools are themselves quietly accomplishing more than Acts of Parliament, missions, and philanthropic crusades can ever hope to do. Already the young race of mothers, the girls who had the benefit for a year or two of the Education Act, are tidy in their persons, clean in their homes, and decent in their language. Let the reader who wishes to judge for himself the physical and moral results which education has already accomplished go to any Board School recruited from the "slum" districts, and note the difference in the elder and the younger children.'[78]

Despite all that had been achieved in a generation, elementary education was still no more than that – a limited schooling in basic literacy and hygiene, with virtually no opportunity for any form of secondary or further education. Even so, there were many who thought that the state had already done more than enough. In the year of Queen Victoria's Diamond Jubilee, Sir Herbert Maxwell, Bart., M.P. boasting that the annual government grant for education, science and art exceeded £10 million, complained,

> 'Even this is not enough to satisfy some people, as was made plain by the question addressed by an elector to a candidate for a Scottish constituency at a recent election. "Is Maister Wilson," asked this enthusiast, "in favour of spending £36,000,000 a year on the Airmy, and only £12,000,000 on eddication? That's to say, twelve millions for pittin' brains into folks' heads, and thirty six millions for blawin' them oot." '[79]

References

[1] Calder-Marshall, 'George Sims', p.141.
[2] Cruikshank, 'Roaring Century', p.156.
[3] Stedman-Jones, 'Outcast London' p.86.
[4] ibid., pp.70 and 77.
[5] Public Record Office, WO97/1746/155998
[6] Stedman-Jones, 'Outcast London', pp.78/9
[7] Newcastle Commission Report, (1861), Vol.1. p.93: quot. in Curtis, 'History of Education in G.B.', p.251.
[8] Bosanquet, 'Social Work in London', p.2.
[9] LCC/EO/DIV 8/St. JOH/LB/1, Greater London R.O.
[10] Sturt, M., 'The Education of the People', p.239.
[11] Curtis, 'History of Education in G.B.' p.256.
[12] Sturt, M., 'The Education of the People', p.240.
[13] Newcastle Commission Report, (1861): quot. in Rubinstein, 'School Attendance in London', p.5.
[14] Curtis, 'History of Education in G.B.', p.267.
[15] Sturt, M., 'The Education of the People', p.348
[16] Thompson, F., 'Larkrise', pp.189/190
[17] Horn, 'The Victorian and Edwardian Schoolchild', p.47.
[18] Sturt, M., 'The Education of the People', p.353.
[19] Curtis, 'History of Education in G.B.', p.277.
[20] Wells, H.G., 'The New Machiavelli', (1911) p.93: quot. in Harrison, 'Late Victorian Britain', p.200.,
[21] Tawney, R.H., 'Education, The Socialist Policy' (1924) p.22: quot. in Harrison, 'Late Victorian Britain', p.202.
[22] First Annual Report of the National Society, London (1812): quot.in Silver, 'The Education of the Poor', pp.8/9
[23] Sturt, M., 'The Education of the People', p.255.
[24] The Times, 29 NOV 1870.
[25] Maclure, 'One Hundred Years of London Education', p.27 and Sturt, M., 'The Education of the People', p.307.
[26] Maclure, 'One Hundred Years of London Education', p.27 and Sturt, M., 'The Education of the People', p.339.
[27] Reeves, 'Recollections of a School Attendance Officer', p.65
[28] Rubinstein, 'School Attendance in London', pp.35/6.
[29] Reeves, 'Recollections of a School Attendance Officer', p.18
[30] Maclure, 'One Hundred Years of London Education', p.33.
[31] Reeves, 'Recollections of a School Attendance Officer', p.14.
[32] Rubinstein, 'School Attendance in London', p.43
[33] Reeves, 'Recollections of a School Attendance Officer', p.12.
[34] ibid., p.20.
[35] ibid., p.34/5
[36] ibid., p.50
[37] LCC/EO/DIV 5/DAL/LB/1, 16 APR 1886, Greater London R.O.
[38] Reeves, 'Recollections of a School Attendance Officer', p.46.
[39] Law, J., (pseudonym of Margaret Harkness) 'In Darkest London', (1889) p.128: quot. in Fishman, 'East End 1888', p.119.
[40] Mearns, 'The Bitter Cry of Outcast London', p.12

[41] Rubinstein, 'School Attendance in London', p.61.
[42] Booth, C., 'The Inhabitants of Tower Hamlets', p.327
[43] ibid., p.328
[44] Stedman-Jones, 'Outcast London', p.24
[45] Booth, C., 'The Inhabitants of Tower Hamlets', p.361.
[46] LCC/EO/DIV 5/DAL/LB/1, 1880/1881 Greater London R.O.
[47] Rubinstein, 'School Attendance in London', p.47.
[48] Kay-Shuttleworth, J., 'Four Periods of Education', (1862), Longmans pp.583/5: quot. in Curtis, 'History of Education in G.B.', p.266
[49] Wymer, 'Dr. Barnardo', pp.65/6 and 115, and Fishman, 'East End 1888', pp.236/7
[50] Sheppard, 'London 1808–1870', p.384
[51] Bosanquet, 'Social Work in London', pp.54/5
[52] Stedman-Jones, 'Outcast London', pp.244/5.
[53] Hill, O., 'Homes of the London Poor', p.57/58.
[54] ibid., p.62.
[55] ibid., p.72.
[56] East London Observer, 31 MAR 1888: quot. in Fishman, 'East End 1888', pp.231/2.
[57] Hill, O., 'Homes of the London Poor', pp.31/32.
[58] Booth, W., 'In Darkest England', p.78.
[59] ibid., p.44.
[60] ibid., p.80.
[61] Collier, 'The General Next to God', p.185.
[62] Fishman, 'East End 1888', p.256.
[63] Booth, W., 'In Darkest England', pp.94 and 96.
[64] Bosanquet, 'Social Work in London', p.344.
[65] Fishman, 'East End 1888', p.260.
[66] Booth, W., 'In Darkest England', p.99.
[67] ibid., p.69.
[68] LCC/EO/DIV 5/DAL/LB/1, 9 APR 1886, Greater London R.O.
[69] Riverside (previously Farncombe Sreet) School Log book.
[70] 'The Pictorial World', 23 JUN 1883.
[71] ibid.
[72] ibid.
[73] 10th Annual Report of the Charity Organisation Society (1879): quot. in Stedman-Jones, 'Outcast London', p.271.
[74] 'The Pictorial World', 30 JUN. 1883.
[75] Rubinstein, 'School Attendance in London', p.43/44
[76] School Board for London, Minutes of Proceedings, 1 AUG 1884
[77] School Board for London, Minutes of Proceedings, 7 and 14 DEC 1893, 3 MAY and 14 JUN. 1894 and 12 MAR. 1896
[78] The Daily News, 8 NOV. 1883.
[79] Maxwell, Sir H., Bt., M.P., 'Sixty Years a Queen', part-set published by Harmsworth Bros. Ltd., 1897 p.189.

CHAPTER FOURTEEN

THE THAMES ON FIRE

'See! there they come racing and tearing,
All the street with loud voices is fill'd;
Oh! it's only the firemen a-swearing,
At a man they've run over and kill'd!'
– Thomas Hood[1]

Saturday, June 22nd, was a fine, warm day. At half past four in the afternoon dockers, warehousemen and porters at Scovell's warehouses on Cotton Wharf just two hundred yards east of London Bridge, tired after a day which had started at 6 a.m., were packing up when James England, a delivery foreman, noticed smoke. He ran down to the first floor and found it rising from a pile of jute. Quickly throwing a bucket of water on it he ran down to the yard to warn Mr. Doyle the Wharf Superintendent.

Neither man could have imagined that within twelve hours all London would be watching the biggest and most spectacular fire since September 1666. Nothing like it was to be seen in the capital for another eighty years until the incendiary bombs of the Second World War blitz set London alight in the winter of 1940 – 41.

Cotton's Wharf and its warehouses stood on the south side of the Thames between the river and Tooley Street. At the western end of the street, practically on London Bridge, was the old parish church of St. Olave. Downstream from that lay Chamberlain's Wharf, then Cotton's and Depot wharves; some thirty warehouses altogether, rising five and six storeys high and packed with cargoes from all over the world – bales of hemp, hops, jute and cotton; chests of sugar, tea and silk; barrels of oil, resins, tar, saltpetre and Russian tallow, bags of rice, spices and grain. Not for nothing was Tooley Street called "London's larder".

Facing Tooley Street and backing directly on to the warehouses, with no rear entrance, were shops, houses and 'The Grapes' public house. Opposite were houses and a timber yard which were all that stood between the warehouses and London Bridge station.

There had been many large fires in this busy waterside area and Mr. Doyle, the Wharf Superintendent, would have been well aware of the danger. He immediately sent a runner three hundred yards to the nearest fire brigade station at 147 Tooley Street, near Morgan's Lane, before he and James England tackled the small fire with buckets and a handy hosepipe.

The first engine arrived from the Tooley Street Station within fifteen minutes of the discovery of smoke curling up from the bale of jute. Today that would have been an end of the matter but not so in 1861.

James Mimms was twenty-two. His father had died in St. Thomas's Hospital when he was thirteen and his mother, Ann, only nine months previously of pneumonia when they had been living at 15 Weston Street, just off Tooley Street. That house, like so many others, had been demolished to make way for an enlargement of the London Bridge terminus of the South Eastern Railway company and its extension across the river to Charing Cross. As a direct result more than 4500 of the 'labouring class' had lost their homes.[2]

During the census taken in that April one enumerator wrote with some asperity of this area:

> 'Since 1841 one Enumerator's District has been
> annihilated by railways and Termini. And
> encroachments on the dwelling houses are
> increasing by the building of large Warehouses.'

he went on to add ' . . . numbers 3 to 25 Weston Street do not exist!'

The death of their mother and the loss of their home led James and two of his younger brothers, Thomas, aged seventeen, and John, ten, to move a very short distance away to Number 8 Holcombe's Buildings, a cul-de-sac of nineteen small terraced houses built on the site of the old Black Horse Brewery. Across the narrow street its houses were dwarfed by the blank-faced brick walls of enormous hop warehouses. Behind their tiny back yards ran Snows Fields – no longer fields but rows of grimy terraces typical of the urban sprawl of South London built to accommodate the explosive growth of the population over the past fifty years.

James's family had split up. His older brother, Francis, had joined the army after an apprenticeship to a tinplate worker. Younger brother Frank had left to find his fortune as a jockey on the South Coast racecourses and sister Mary Ann had probably gone into service.

The census taker commented that two-thirds of the houses in that district took in lodgers ' . . . many are from the country and most of these remain here only a short time.' So it was at Number 8 Holcombe's Buildings. To help with the rent James made room for Ann Peach from near Croydon, her six year old fatherless son, Fred, and Sarah Lipscombe a twenty one year old milliner from Chichester.

Holcombe's Buildings were less than half a mile from Tooley Street where Dooley and England had fitted a hose to the mains water pipe but the pressure was so low that it threw the water jet less than eight feet. Instead they found a hand-worked pump in a cellar fed from a roof-top water tank supplying a private fire main. After fixing two ladders to the outside wall of the warehouse Dooley's men were able to direct two jets on to the fire.

By this time a relay of runners from one fire station to the next had crossed London Bridge and reached the Headquarters of the London Fire Engine Establishment at 68 Watling Street in the City, the house of its chief, Superintendent James Braidwood. He gave orders to turn out the engine stationed there and followed it at all speed to the fire only some two miles away. The use of runners was the only method available to alert the fire fighters. In Paris at this time an electric telegraph system linked all its stations. Even so, the news had reached Braidwood only twenty minutes after the discovery of the fire.

Braidwood headed a private fire service owned and controlled by the leading insurance companies. This was quite separate from the legal requirement that each parish had to maintain a fire engine. Each of the ninety-seven City parishes had one or sometimes two and in thirty of these parishes "parochial engineers" were appointed at a salary and rent for the engine averaging £30 per annum. No one was responsible for ensuring that they were suitable to hold the post and later investigation showed some of them to have been "aged widows". In one parish the engine was bricked up behind a blacksmith's shop and to get the engine out it would have been necessary to pull the whole building down. As an incentive to efficiency 30 shillings was paid to the first engine to reach a fire. Those parochial engineers who were capable of turning out vied aggressively to supplement their income by this means but seemed worried by little else since there was no requirement that they should actually fight the fire once they got there. Charles Dickens wrote that he had only once seen a parochial engine at a fire and said "It was unfortunately discovered, just as they were going to put the fire out, that nobody understood the process by which the engine was filled with water". The law stipulated that anyone who gave information that an engine was not in working order should receive a reward. This was, to all intents and purposes, a dead letter as cases of such a reward were unknown by 1861. It was said later "no one considered the protection afforded by these engines as being of any practical value whatever". Little wonder, therefore, that Dooley had sent his runner not to the parochial engineer but to Mr. Braidwood's outpost in Tooley Street.

It was because of the appalling state of the official fire fighting force that the insurance companies had combined all their separate brigades thirty years earlier and appointed James Braidwood, the highly regarded Master of Fire Engines at Edinburgh, as the first Superintendent of the London Fire Engine Establishment. Braidwood commanded a force of only 132 men, popularly called "Jimmy Braiders" in imitation of Sir Robert Peel's "bobbies" or "Peelers". They were distributed over nineteen land-based and two floating stations on the river at Rotherhithe and Southwark Bridge. Braidwood had been known to observe, wrily, that Paris, only half the size of London, had over 800 firemen. Nevertheless, his men were very efficient, brave and well-thought of. They were largely recruited from amongst Thames watermen and seamen but most of them were only paid on the occurrence of a fire.

The engines used were mainly manual pumps. They were operated not by the firemen but by any of the crowd which invariably gathered. These men were paid one shilling for the first hour's pumping and sixpence an hour thereafter. Firemen were trained to reach the seat of the fire in an attempt to extinguish it but as nothing resembling a smoke helmet existed they were obliged to crawl flat along the floor to keep below the noxious smoke and fumes. For the whole of Central London Braidwood had 27 large manual engines each drawn by two horses and weighing 36 hundredweights. With a long hose attached each needed 30 pumpers to deliver only 88 gallons a minute. There were also eight small manual engines drawn by hand. Additionally, two floating engines permanently moored near the London Docks and at Blackfriars were available. The larger one had only recently been fitted with a steam pump. These were, seemingly, not under Braidwood's control but under the somewhat casual direction of the watermen. Although steam was kept up and some men were always aboard, in the event of a fire a siren was sounded and eventually eighteen to twenty men crowded aboard. Sometimes twenty minutes elapsed before the fire-floats could make a start.

It was forty minutes after the discovery of the outbreak before the bigger of the two fire-floats was in attendance but this may have been partly due to the state of the tide. When it did get to work, however, it continued pumping 1400 gallons a minute from the Thames for a fortnight. Braidwood preferred manual engines but there was one large land steam engine kept at the Headquarters in Watling Street. Only four engines of this type had been seen in London up to this time. Drawn by three horses and weighing over four tons they could travel at 10 mph for short distances but once at a fire it took nearly twenty minutes from a cold boiler before steam pumping could begin.

These then were the resources at Braidwood's disposal at the start of the fire. Later, when the tide permitted, fire floats from H.M. Dockyard at Deptford and the London Docks attended and some privately owned manual engines from Lambeth Distillery and from a Mr. Roberts downstream at Millwall were also used. By the time Braidwood arrived, Dooley's men had been driven off their ladders by large sheets of flame which flared out of the loopholes in the warehouse walls and spread to the adjacent buildings. Fire-resistant iron doors had been fitted but the dense smoke had prevented the men from closing them before they were forced to back off. And the smoke forced Dooley and

England to stop pumping the hand engine in the warehouse cellar. Braidwood immediately ordered all the ships which were not aground on the low tide out into the river and brought his two fire floats into position with hoses brought ashore from them and directed on to Cotton's Wharf.

One of the ironies of the situation was that despite the Thames on its doorstep there was a chronic water shortage throughout the whole episode. The quays were about 4'9" above the high water level at Spring tides and there is a difference of almost 21 feet between high and low water at London Bridge. And the tide was out. It was impossible to draw water from the Thames except by the fire floats which were actually on the river since even the most powerful land engine could only draw up water from a maximum of fifteen feet.

The land based pumps had to rely on the Southwark and Vauxhall Water Company's mains but the supply was so poor that most of them stood idle for nearly an hour before water was available. Throughout the course of the fire many engines had to stand by and do nothing for long periods. So poor was it, in fact, that during the whole course of the fire only fifteen land engines attended. There was no point in calling any more as they could have done nothing. The water supply came from a seven inch main running the length of Tooley Street. The Water Company's turncock had closed off the branch mains to prevent water being drawn off into the side streets and had pulled out the fire plugs. These were nothing like modern fire hydrants. As the name implies they were plugs of wood hammered into sockets. The sockets fitted directly into the main and were protected by an iron plate which had first to be levered off. The plugs were steadied and protected from frost by being packed two feet deep up to the street level with what was delicately described as "horse litter or some such material". One can imagine that drawing a plug was no pleasant task on a warm summer's day. But it was worse in winter when it was not unusual for the whole pipe and plug to be frozen into a solid, compact and rigid mass. As one contemporary wrote:

> 'If water or damp penetrated the filthy stuffing it congealed into a solid block of ice with the consistency of flint which can turn the point of any crowbar and withstand all efforts made to break through it until after the time has passed at which any

> advantage could be derived from obtaining access to the water'.

Once the plug was removed a canvas cistern was placed over the socket hole and allowed to fill. Then a hose from the engine was fitted to a small hole in the cistern and pumping could begin.

In spite of these severe disadvantages Braidwood and his men tried to contain the fire. For over an hour they succeeded but it was still blazing with an intense fury. As there was a large quantity of saltpetre known to be stored nearby, Braidwood sent Alfred Tozer, one of his firemen, on to the roof of an adjoining building to direct his hose over the warehouse roofs. At about 7.15 p.m. there was a loud explosion from the cellars followed by gusts of white smoke and a great spread of the fire. Tozer was trapped on the roof. His escape down the staircase cut off, he had the great presence of mind to secure the nozzle end of his hose and slide down the outside of the building. This warehouse contained butter, lard, bacon, tallow and resins amongst other commodities and once that had ignited and fed the flames nothing was going to stop it.

Braidwood was known to be a fire chief who was always in the thick of the action, encouraging his men by example and by the concern he showed for their welfare. At about half-past seven he was passing along the cartway beside the blazing warehouse directing the hoses from the floats when he noticed Richard Henderson, a foreman of the brigade, overcome with exhaustion and the intense heat. He gave him some brandy and ordered him out of the area to recover. Shortly after there was a dull roar as the forty feet high warehouse wall collapsed into a heap of smoking rubble killing him and a companion instantly. Braidwood's death was later acknowledged as one of the greatest losses of the Tooley Street fire. The fire chief was revered by his men and his death, understandably, had a depressing effect on them. This was intensified by a sudden spread of the fire as saltpetre stored in several surrounding warehouses exploded with blasts which " . . . shook the neighbourhood and scattered clouds of burning material over the panic-stricken district".

With no television pictures, the public relied on written reports to learn about important events. There can be no better example of that skill than this magnificent piece of descriptive prose penned by the anonymous correspondent of "The Times" and published on the following Monday:

> 'It was not till night fell that the tremendous terrors of the spectacle could be appreciated in all their horrid grandeur. Never since the Fire of 1666 had such a scene been witnessed. The whole south bank of the river from London Bridge to below the Custom-house seemed one stupendous pile of fire, glowing at its core with an intensity that made it painful to look at and casting a ruddy glare above on everything far and near.
> 'There was scarcely a breath of wind, but what little there was came from the river, gently turning the blinding mass of smoke and flame across Tooley-street to the London Bridge Railway Station. Immediately between the station and the fire was a large timber-yard with some houses almost jutting into it. If these houses caught, the timber-yard and station were certain to follow, and the flames, thus spreading in two directions, might travel all over Southwark. Upon these houses, therefore, the firemen concentrated all their efforts . . . . Gradually, however, the walls began to steam, as if the houses were boiling, and little ominous curls of smoke wound through the slate roofs. Then more smoke, and the water hissed and sputtered on the roofs, and a dull increasing glow shone from all the windows, as if there were lights inside each room and the panes were filled-in with red glass.
>
> . . . 'Nothing can be seen but a town of falling ruins, with great rafters swaying about in fiery tangles before they fall headlong down – nothing heard but the roar of flames and shouts of excited thousands, which drown even the incessant dull thumpings of the engines that are working in all directions.
>
> 'Perhaps, however, the most awful view of the destruction going on was to be seen from London-bridge. Half the inhabitants of the metropolis were thronging towards this centre on Saturday night, for from the bridge was to be seen such a spectacle as we trust will never be beheld again. The north side of the Thames, with all its massive buildings, seemed red hot in the dreadful light, while on the south side the glare and heat from the blazing ruins were almost blinding. Foul and thick as are the waters of the Thames at low tide its dingy waves were nevertheless penetrated by the intense light and the river seemed almost turned to blood, but so bright and

> lurid in its deep glow that it actually appeared like a stream of fire.
>
> 'Never, probably, even when the Great Eastern left the Thames, has the river been so thronged with small boats. From far below the Custom-house to above London-bridge the stream was actually covered with them. All the roofs of the houses, the public buildings, the masts and spars of vessels, the quays and wharves, the tops of church steeples – even the gallery of the Monument – were crowded with thousands upon thousands of spectators. Looking down from one of these eminences upon the bridge, the river and the surrounding buildings, all swarming with countless multitudes, but swathed in the same deep fiery glow, it made one of the most wonderful and terrible spectacles ever witnessed in England. Probably at no time – even during the Great Fire of London – was there ever seen such a mass of flamc and heat as roared and seethed so dreadfully on Saturday night along the south side of the river'.

The London reporter of the Manchester Guardian watched the fire from a most appropriate vantage point, the Monument, which marked the outbreak of the Great Fire of 1666. He claimed that after dark the glare could be seen as far away as Epsom.

In a warehouse near to where Braidwood had fallen 600 bags of saltpetre exploded around 10.30 p.m. causing tons of molten tallow and oil to pour out of the loopholes of the waterside warehouses and on to the river almost surrounding skiffs full of spectactors. The tide swept a sailing barge which was coming up the Thames too close and the three men on board were rescued only minutes before it was engulfed in blazing oil from stem to stern. The fire floats, too, were endangered and had to sheer off to avoid being caught alight.

As the tide turned great sheets of solidifying grease were swept down the river. Watermen as far down as Millwall dragged the oily mass into their boats to sell for 2d or 2½d a pound. Four young men just down stream from the fire had almost filled their small boat when a flood of boiling oil all on fire gushed from one of the burning buildings engulfing their boat and igniting the grease it contained. They threw themselves into the river to escape it but the water itself was awash with burning oil and they were never seen again.

'from the bridge was to be seen such a spectacle as we trust will never be beheld again'

The molten tallow spread out into Tooley Street and the roads, courts and alleys which led off it. As the liquid cooled the whole area oozed ankle-deep in thick grease. Much of it was scraped up into enormous heaps but the firemen and those pumping the engines could scarcely stand upright in the congealing grey and foul-smelling mess.

> 'Dawn found London Bridge still thronged with cabs, omnibuses, carts, waggons and vehicles of every description. Peripatetic vendors of ginger beer, fruit and other cheap refreshments abounded, and were sold out half-a-dozen times over. Public houses, in defiance of the Acts of Parliament, kept open all night long, and did a roaring trade, and so, for that matter, did the pickpockets, who blended business with pleasure and had a ready hand for anything remunerative in their particular line!'

Throughout Sunday and Monday the parapets and copings of London Bridge were packed with sightseers ' . . . and all the various little alleys and by-ways into Tooley-street, even those which commanded a limited view of the blackened wall, and many from which nothing at all could be seen, were equally crowded!'

The oil and tallow which had not escaped had poured, still flaming, into the cellars. As more water was poured on it the levels rose and it threatened to flow out into the streets.

Finally the fire was extinguished two weeks later. It had destroyed all the buildings in the three wharves, part of the recently constructed Hay's Wharf to the east and of the parish church of St. Olave on its western flank.

It had consumed 1,000 tons of hemp, 3,000 tons of sugar, 500 tons of saltpetre, 5,000 tons of rice, 18,000 bales of cotton, 10,000 barrels of tallow, 1,100 tons of jute and vast quantities of bacon, tea and spices. The cost amounted to some £2m. which today would have been in excess of £100m.

We do not know what, if any, part James may have played during the fire. He was an unskilled carpenter described as a packing case maker who lived, and probably worked, in the near vicinity of Tooley Street. He and his brothers, like half London, would most certainly have been avid spectators at one of the most exciting events of their young lives and which occurred on their doorstep. They may even have volunteered to man the engines, after all four hours pumping would have paid the rent for a week. Or might they have been involved in some of the less public-spirited consequences of the fire?

Mr. Burcham, the Southwark magistrate, spent the week following the fire hearing dozens of cases of assault and theft committed near the scene.

Young William Boys was fined ten shillings or seven days imprisonment for cutting a rope stretched across Tooley Street to hold back the public. John Watts, employed at the Lambeth Distillery, received the same punishment for assaulting and obstructing the police and James Suter, a labourer at the wharf, was charged with assaulting the police officer in charge and tearing his uniform. He was fined ten shillings plus 35 shillings damages or one month in prison.

Not all the melted tallow and oil had flowed into the river. Much of it clogged up the sewers and men were employed to dig it out. It would be difficult to imagine a more unpleasant task. On Wednesday, 26th June, John Barrow was brought before the magistrates on a charge which can rarely have been heard in an English court – that of "breaking into the sewers near Tooley Street and stealing tallow". Mr. William Wilkins of the Metropolitan Board of Works gave evidence that as there were immense quantities of tallow in the sewers near the waterside he had employed men to stand guard over the manholes. As the witness was walking down Weston Street (only a hundred yards from Holcombe's Buildings) he saw '. . . several men emerge from one of the manholes, among whom was the prisoner, on whose back was a heavy sackful of tallow. Witness detained him and a mob surrounded the complainant and his men and defied their interference'. Policeman 459A stated that he took charge of the prisoner who tripped him up and kicked him severely. A mob then surrounded him and rescued the prisoner but the constable chased after them and re-arrested him. John Barrow was sentenced to one month's imprisonment with hard labour.

It would have called for a strong stomach to spend hours in a foul, brick-lined tunnel cutting and shovelling solidified lumps of melted tallow, tar and raw sewage out but, after all, at twopence a pound one hundredweight of that mixture equalled a good week's wages.

References

This chapter is based upon the following sources:
Ridley, P.E., 'The Tooley Street Fire, 22nd June 1861', (1932) Chartered Insurance Institute Journal, vol.35 The Post Magazine and Insurance Monitor, 29 JUN. 1861
The Policyholder Insurance Journal, 22 JUN.1961
'The Times', 24-27 JUN. 1861
[1] Jerrold, 'Thomas Hood', p.103
[2] Sheppard, 'London, 1808-1870', p.150

CHAPTER FIFTEEN

FISH IN A RIVER

> 'These fever dens are said to be the best-paying property in London,and owners who, if justice were done, would be on the treadmill, are drawing from 50 – 60 per. cent. on investments in tenement property in the slums.'
>
> – W.T. Stead (1883)[1]

> 'Conceal the fact as we may, it is a terrible truth that the excessive mortality among the children of the vicious and degraded alone preserves the nation from being overwhelmed by them.'
>
> – F. Peek (1883)[2]

No town in England celebrates quite like London. There are no passive onlookers; everyone gets swept up in a joyfully exuberant, laughing, cheering, waving, swaying crush, fiercely determined to enjoy itself. Sometimes the spontaneous release of pent-up tension erupts in this way and London suddenly goes wild, as on Mafeking night and VE-Day; but when a royal occasion is the focus of popular rejoicing the celebration is even further enhanced by the colour, music and unsurpassed spectacle of civic, state and military pomp and pageantry.

Such a day was promised for Saturday March 7th 1863. It was not to be a coronation nor a jubilee, not even a royal wedding, but the arrival of an eighteen years old princess from Denmark who was to marry the Queen's eldest son, Albert Edward, Prince of Wales. The Queen had decreed that the wedding should be a low key affair celebrated in St. George's Chapel at Windsor, described by a disappointed 'Punch' magazine as an obscure Berkshire village, noted only for an old castle with no sanitary arrangements.[3] Prince Albert, the Queen's Consort, had died from typhoid only fifteen months before, probably brought about by Windsor Castle's appalling sanitation. St Paul's Cathedral or Westminster Abbey would have been more fitting for a royal wedding, but Victoria was still in deep mourning and could not face the London crowds. She had not been seen in public since the death of the Prince Consort and her seclusion had begun to attract adverse comment. Edward, in contrast, was a handsome, outgoing twenty-one years old cavalry officer, a romantic figure engaged to a young foreign princess who was said to be a beauty. Denied a royal wedding by Her Majesty's selfish decree, London decided to celebrate anyway, and the people south of the river were to have the honour of being the first to welcome the princess to the capital.

The Bricklayers' Arms terminus in Bermondsey's Old Kent Road belonged to the South Eastern Railway Company and had been built twenty years earlier as a competitor to the London Bridge station after a dispute over tolls imposed by the London and Greenwich Railway Company which owned it. As a passenger terminus it was inconveniently situated and unpopular and was, by now, mainly used as a goods depot for the transport of cattle and sheep into London[4]. The directors of the South Eastern had transformed it. The old gateway became a triumphal arch, the station yard was overlaid with tons of clean gravel, the whole length of the platform covered with a crimson cloth, and a Brussels carpet placed where the royal carriage was to stop. Tier upon tier of seating was erected on the arrival platform, and anything recognisable as belonging to a railway was obscured by hundreds of flags, banners, tubs of plants and flowers, drapes, statuary, and evergreen. The company offices had been converted into an elaborate royal suite, and a sumptuous breakfast laid out by Mr Staples of the Albion Hotel.[5]

The royal yacht, 'Victoria and Albert', which had conveyed the princess from Antwerp, docked at Gravesend at 11.30 on that Saturday morning. The gales of the previous day had subsided and the Thames estuary was crowded with shipping from the ironclad warship escorts, their yardarms manned by the ships' crews, private yachts, excursion paddle steamers and rowing boats, to the grimy coal-barges and tugs, all packed with enthusiastic sightseers, and every mast and rail dressed with flags.

Very shortly after it docked, the Prince of Wales, who had travelled by rail to the North Kent Station at Gravesend, joined the royal yacht to greet his fiancee. A little over half an hour later they alighted together to receive the borough's loyal address and walk to their carriage over a carpet of primroses and violets strewn by sixty hand-picked local girls dressed in white skirts, flowing red cloaks and straw hats. Gravesend was no stranger to royal arrivals and departures and its citizens had transformed the route to the station with a forest of flags, coats of arms, shields and other heraldic devices, with banners, crests, and garlands of orange blossom and laurel. Portraits of the royal couple accompanied intricate monograms of their entwined initials, and the Prince of Wales's ostrich plume motif appeared again and again. Opposite a large grandstand, borrowed from the Epsom racecourse, stood a magnificent arch supporting mythological figures representing Neptune consigning the princess to the care of Britannia, and everywhere were mottoes and scrolls bearing legends – 'God Bless Them', 'Long Life and Happiness', and similar expressions of goodwill. Golden poles supported festoons of paper flowers and evergreens to form a canopy across the streets which led to the station.

As the royal train steamed through north Kent, crowds cheered and waved from windows, garden walls, station platforms and open fields in which every barn, cowshed and haystack sported a flag. Boys clung precariously to railings and from the branches of trees. A pair of farmhands held aloft a crude banner strung between a hayrake and a pitchfork bearing the greeting, 'Welcome to the Land of Plenty', as the royal party continued its fifty minute journey towards the capital.

At about the same time as Edward and Alexandra stepped from the royal yacht on to Gravesend pier, London's Lord Mayor was preparing to leave Guildhall for the Bricklayers' Arms depot. His welcoming procession included the masters and wardens of the City's Livery Companies, the Sheriffs, Aldermen, Common Councilmen, and City officers, accompanied by four military bands, and headed by a detachment of mounted police to clear the way. Successive City Marshals had mounted many such processions, but never had they encountered crowds like those which turned out on that March Saturday to greet the Danish princess. Two hundred years earlier, following the Great Fire, Sir Christopher Wren had proposed an entirely new and more logical plan for the Square Mile incorporating wide roads, but the City Fathers had disliked change and so the haphazard mediaeval pattern of narrow streets in a confusing maze around Guildhall had been preserved. As the carriages, the banner-bearers, the watermen, the outriders, and the military bands tried to form up the press of the crowds forced them into the side streets and back alleys from which many never escaped. 'The Daily Telegraph' reported that 'some outlying portions were quite cut off in the wilds of Coleman-street or the solitude of Aldermanbury, in which remote regions there may be, for aught we know, until this hour, whole strings of barouches full of worthy citizens in livery gowns, waiting in grim and doleful patience for the procession to "move on".'

The Lord Mayor and his immediate entourage slowly and with great difficulty headed south towards Cheapside passing other parts of the procession travelling northwards to take their appointed places. The crowds in Cheapside and Poultry were so dense that it was only with great perseverance that the mounted police and the accompanying Horse Artillery succeeded in 'digging out a temporary passage', by creating occasional gaps in the crush of people so that 'two or three carriages, a brass band and a detachment of standard-bearers' were enabled to make a brief spurt forward. Much the same conditions prevailed in King William-street where more than half the procession which had managed to accompany the Lord Mayor thus far became immoveably stuck and were obliged to suffer the frustration of having to watch, motionless, as the royal entourage approached them from the opposite direction some two hours later. In fact, three-quarters of those City worthies, who should have formed the royal reception committee, never saw the princess at all that day. The City Marshal did manage to stay close to the Lord Mayor's carriage but, according to one cynical journalist, he 'never marshsalled anything that we are aware of.' Nevertheless, the remnants of the City's welcoming party finally crossed London Bridge and managed to reach the Bricklayer's Arms railway depot shortly before the royal train arrived at twenty minutes before two o'clock.

At a brief reception ceremony more loyal addresses were presented to the couple. There was no time for them to be read, they were, instead, thrust at a gentleman usher 'who stood patiently with them under his arm, as if they had been rolls of coloured silk which the Princess Alexandra was going to choose a dress from.' The formalities were quickly over and, after some refreshment provided by Mr Staples of the Albion Hotel, the six State Carriages containing the royal party and escorted by one hundred and twenty troopers of the Royal Horse Guards (the Blues) set off for London Bridge. As they turned out of the station into the Old Kent Road the first organised gathering to greet the princess must have seemed a strange and affecting one, for immediately opposite stood the Asylum for the Deaf and Dumb Children of the Poor, of which the Prince of Wales was a governor; its three hundred children ranged on its steps mutely waved their welcome accompanied by the deafening cheers of the south Londoners lining the roadside. 'Her London reception really began', wrote the 'Telegraph', 'when she emerged . . . from the railway yard; and it was such a reception as warrants us in saying that probably no woman in this world ever experienced the like.' That reporter was impressed by the fact that even in this poor neighbourhood every house was decorated with flags or home-made paper flowers. He expressed less enthusiasm for the archway erected by the Borough at Southwark's boundary with Bermondsey:

> 'Of its chief triumphal arch,' he wrote, 'we will say nothing more than that it is solid, and no doubt strong. Perhaps, as it is not intended to last for ever, the pains expended in nailing it up so firmly might have been in part given to making it look cheerful.'

The City of London, on the other hand, had spent £40,000 on its decorations and illuminations[6] which the princess had plenty of opportunity to enjoy. At twenty-five minutes past two o'clock the procession approached London Bridge heralded by trumpet fanfares and a salute of cannon. The bridge itself had been completely cleared of people after the Lord Mayor had crossed it earlier, except for those intrepid spectators who clambered out of their boats and scaled the piers of the bridge to cling to its balustrades and parapet. The same could not be done for King William Street, however, where half the mayoral party was still marooned, surrounded by crowds even more dense than they had been two hours previously. The whole procession came to a complete standstill on the bridge for more than half an hour whilst the police and Volunteers tried to drive a path through to the Mansion House.

London Bridge was the City's gateway to the south and the authorities had taken full advantage of this one processional route into the City proper. Venetian masts carried the Danish royal emblems, the raven and castellated elephants, and a hundred tripods supporting incense burners lined the roadway leading to a seventy feet high triumphal arch at the northern end of the bridge, topped with plaster horses and depicting every known allegorical device and heathen god surrounding an enormous gold and coloured centre-piece of Britannia with a portrait of the Queen dressed in widow's weeds. The whole effect of this vast edifice was heightened by flowing crimson velvet drapes added at the very last moment before the scaffolding was dismantled just half an hour before the arrival of the royal procession. Ships and small boats filled the Pool of London, their yards, decks and rigging crowded with seamen, every window and roof of the riverside warehouses, the church towers and even the cage atop the Monument were packed with waving, cheering onlookers. The young princess, dressed simply in mauve Irish poplin, a purple velvet cloak and white bonnet edged with rosebuds, waved back impressing the crowds with her shy charm. As the procession came to a halt on the bridge the Prince of Wales stood up in his carriage with an anxious look as though aware that this first real hitch in the proceedings presaged an even worse experience to come as they approached the City's narrow streets.

Slowly the Life Guards forced a passage through the crowds in King William Street, past the beleaguered carriages of the Lord Mayor's reception party whose painfully slow progress towards Southwark had finally been abandoned. At last the six state carriages struggled to the steps of the Mansion House where the Lady Mayoress presented Alexandra with a floral bouquet in a magnificent jewelled holder, whilst all around was chaos and wild confusion. Fifty thousand people were packed into a space where five hundred might have been comfortable, surrounding the royal carriage forcing the front ranks of spectators to cling to its wheels and doors and even its side ledges, their heads practically in the princess's lap. They hung from every lamp-post and perched on every ledge and recess of the Royal Exchange and Bank of England, cheering and throwing their caps in the air with great good humour.

The procession moved slowly on forcing its way through Cheapside, St Paul's churchyard, Ludgate Hill and Fleet Street until it reached the City's western boundary at Temple Bar where, six abreast, the Metropolitan Police made a mounted charge at the crowd to create a pathway, but succeeded only in holding up the procession yet again. The distance from London Bridge to the Strand at Temple Bar is only one and a half miles, but it had taken the royal escort an hour and a half to make its halting way through the City's streets, and it was to take another hour before the procession could reach the Great Western Railway terminus at Paddington. After an hour-long train journey from there to Slough and another carriage drive through Eton, the royal couple finally arrived at Windsor as darkness fell and the rain poured down.

Alexandra had been travelling for eight hours through the densest, not to say dirtiest, crowds she can ever have witnessed, at times alarming, but always good-natured. Her demeanour throughout what was undoubtedly a severe ordeal contributed not a little to her enduring popularity with those who came to be her subjects. Whatever Edward and Alexandra's true feelings may have been as they stepped down wearily from their carriage at Windsor, London had not enjoyed itself so much since young Queen Victoria's coronation twenty-five years earlier.

A somewhat less elaborate wedding was celebrated just seven months later when the young James Mimms married Polly Wood at Trinity Church, Newington. When his elder brother, Francis, had joined the army, James had had to take on the responsibility of providing for his mother and his five brothers and sisters. He was just sixteen years old and, like Francis, employed in making containers for the Thames-side warehouse owners and importers. Whereas Francis had worked in tin-plate, James knocked-up tea-chests and packing cases from deal and plywood. Unlike his elder brother he never changed his occupation, nor lived more than a few hundred yards from the river which, indirectly, provided him with a livelihood.

James had been thirteen years old when his father had died in St Thomas's Hospital. With his brother he had probably witnessed the tumultuous scenes surrounding the execution of

Frederick and Maria Manning at Horsemonger Lane Gaol. After Francis's enlistment he would have been the sole bread-winner with his mother, Ann, until she had died from pneumonia aged 51, and he had watched a younger brother, Benjamin, decline and die at the age of 12 from a wasting disease. In this sense, at least, the family had been very fortunate: Benjamin had been the only child out of seven not to have survived into adulthood. After his mother's death James provided a home for his younger brothers in Holcombe's Buildings from where, as an unmarried adult of 22, he could not but have been caught up in some way when fire ravaged Tooley Street and set the Thames alight, and two years later he and Polly Wood must have been somewhere amongst the vast and enthusiastic crowds in Southwark or the City to welcome the princess Alexandra to London.

Polly, or Mary Ann to give her her proper names, was a daughter of George Wellington Wood – it was not only retired generals who named their children, born in 1815, after the victor of Waterloo. George Wood was in a good way of business, a contractor who employed five men and a boy to drive his small fleet of horse-drawn carts delivering goods of all descriptions around the south London streets, to and from the waterside and on every type of errand. His trade was one of the most common in that era before motorised transport drove the 'carman' out of business. If James ever worked for his new father-in-law it was not for long enough for that fact ever to be recorded. He remained a rough carpenter throughout his life, living almost within sight, and certainly within scent of the Thames along that stretch of Bermondsey's waterfront from where Tower Bridge now stands eastwards for two-thirds of a mile as far as Cherry Garden pier where Bermondsey meets Rotherhithe. This stretch of river was given over completely to granaries, ship repair yards, boat-builders, a brewery, coal and corn wharves, mills and grainstores. The only breach in the waterfront is made by St Saviour's Dock, a tidal inlet crowded with tall warehouse buildings forming a narrow 300-yard long canyon. Immediately west and running parallel to the river is Shad Thames, a long waterside street criss-crossed with iron walkways high overhead between massive warehouses which, even today, exude an elusive but definite scent of the spices they once stored. To the east of St Saviour's Dock lay Jacob's Island, cleaned up a little but not yet cleared away. At the head of the Dock and lying between Shad Thames and Jacob's Island was Dockhead. It was in the streets, courts and alleys of the area around Dockhead that James and Polly's nine children were born and brought up.[7]

When Charles Booth extended his poverty survey from Tower Hamlets to cover all of central London he calculated that the proportion of the inhabitants of this riverside area living in poverty amounted to no less than 60 per cent. 'A great number of these people are in very precarious work', he wrote, 'some at the riverside or hawking, wood cutting, fish curing, fur-pulling, or ordinary labour. One block of tenements inhabited by a very shifty lot; frequent evictions for rent. Some decent shops.'[8]

The occurrence of a desperately severe winter has, fortunately, left us with a valuable contemporary description of this area of south London. The winter of 1860/61 was one of the very worst on record. On the 17th of December the temperature dropped to 30 degrees F. and, except for just two days, stayed below freezing point for an entire month. For days on end the thermometer reading did not rise above 20° F. The Serpentine froze thirteen inches deep, strong enough to bear crowds of 50,000 people at a time, beer tents, hot chestnut stalls and charcoal braziers.[9] For six weeks all outdoor work ceased ' . . . the distress and suffering that prevail in the metropolis,' reported the Morning Star, 'particularly among the dock labourers, bricklayers, masons, and labouring classes at the East End are truly horrible.'[10] Thousands of destitute men and women crowded outside the workhouses begging for relief.

To investigate the conditions which had led to such suffering, the Morning Post commissioned John Hollingshead to write a series of ten articles between the 21st and 31st of January under the heading 'London Horrors' which Hollingshead later republished as a book entitled 'Ragged London in 1861.' In them he looked beyond the immediate impact of the severe weather to the chronic poverty which underlay the temporary distress, describing the day to day conditions of London's poor population. It is to these articles that we are indebited for a picture of riverside Southwark and Bermondsey in the 1860s:

> 'No speculator has ever been bold enough to grapple with the back streets – the human warrens – on the south side of the metropolis.' he wrote, 'start from Bermondsey, on the borders of Deptford, and wriggle through the existing miles of dirt,

vice, and crime, as far as Lambeth Marshes . . . down in the hollow of the waterside basin in London, lighted up at intervals with special markets of industry, or budding into short patches of honest trade, sinking every now and then into dark acres of crime, and covered everywhere with the vilest sores of prostitution, are something like four hundred thousand people, or one-seventh part of the whole metropolitan population.'

Anywhere between Lower Bermondsey from Rotherhithe, Jamaica Road and Dockhead westwards to London Bridge 'you can branch off on either side, and visit numerous small courts and alleys, more or less dirty, neglected, and degraded.' One he chose to describe was Magdalen Court which lay between Tooley Street and the arches of the South Eastern railway:

'It is a blind alley of small two-storied houses – close, dwarfed, foul and unwholesome; filled with the lowest order of people who prey on sailors, and curtained at intervals with patched clothes, hanging across to dry from house to house . . . There are hundreds of such courts at Wapping and Rotherhithe on both sides of the river, filled with coarse drunken women, whose thick fingers are covered with showy rings. Sometimes a crew of Malay sailors are enticed into these traps; raw spirits are sent for in basins and quart pots from the neighbouring public-houses; robbery, quarrels, and madness follow, as a matter of course; knives are drawn, a 'muck' is run, and the whole bleeding, riotous, drunken population roll out into the open thoroughfare.'[11]

In many respects Hollingshead considered this area of south London to offer a lower standard of civilization even than some of the worst parts of Whitechapel or St George's in the East:

'It has scores of streets that are rank and steaming with vice; streets where unwashed, drunken, fishy-eyed women hang by dozens out of the windows, beckoning to the passers-by . . .[12]

. . . at some of the low, dirty doors wet baskets are standing half full of a common fish called 'dabs'; in some of the wretched parlour windows, under sickly yellow curtains, a few rotten oranges are displayed on an old shutter for sale; another

> miserable front parlour seems to have been scooped out so as to form something like a shop, in which a few coals are thrown down in one corner, as a sign of trade; another parlour has been turned into a cats-meat store . . . '[13]

Those premises were actually across the river in St George's in the East, but the descriptions would serve as well for any poor quarter of London, as would:

> 'a dismal chandler's shop, with wood, tobacco, and coals mixed up with sooty lard, stale saveloys, a dry knuckle of boiled pork, and a few balls of cotton . . . '[14]

Of these, the 'lowest rank of shopkeepers' living in the greatest poverty, Charles Booth remarked that they attempted to make a living 'out of the sale of things of hardly any value to customers with hardly any money.'[15]

The quality of the goods offered in such pathetic establishments was obvious to any potential customer. The same could not be said, however, of respectable shopkeepers in a better way of business. Food adulteration was everywhere rife, most particularly in lower class areas where a customer had little money and less choice. Flour was commonly mixed with plaster of Paris, crushed bones, chalk, alum, or pipe-clay; coffee with acorns, roasted wheat and saw-dust; vinegar with sulphuric acid, and lemonade spiked with oil of vitriol. Tea leaves contaminated with chopped sloe or horse-chestnut leaves and bread mixed with mashed potato, and cocoa with fine earth dust were not uncommon tricks, and milk might be as much as 80% water:

> Little drops of water added to the milk
> Make the milkman's daughter clothe herself in silk.
> Little grains of sand in the sugar mixed
> Make the grocery man soon become well fixed.
> Little acts of meanness, little tricks of trade,
> All these pass for keenness, fortunes thus are made.[16]

Whatever its quality might have been, the provision of food for his family was a man's prime concern. Even adequate accommodation had to take second place to that. A large family would crowd into one room, subletting a second for the sake of a couple of shillings a week which might provide meat on Sunday. In protest at accusations of improvidence, waste and extravagance frequently levelled at working men, a works manager of some thirty years' experience pointed out that labourers 'were not receiving large wages, but just barely sufficient, with the most scraping and rigid economy, to make their wages last out the week'. To support his contention, he detailed a typical budget for a labourer earning 18 shillings a week with a wife and one child to maintain. Such an income bordered on Charles Booth's definition of the 'very poor' when applied to a family of 'moderate size'. Many labourers, of course, earned less and then rarely on a regular basis. Nevertheless, food and drink accounted for over sixty per cent of that weekly income:

Bread	4s. 0d.
Beer	1s. 2d.
Meat and potatoes	3s. 6d.
Butter and cheese	1s. 6d.
Tea and milk	1s. 0d.
Candles and firewood	6d.
Coals	1s. 0d.
Clothes and shoes	2s. 6d.
Rent	2s. 0d.
Soap and cleaning materials	10d.
Total	18s. 0d.[17]

The rent quoted is barely adequate for one room anywhere in central London, but, equally, a regular allowance of half a crown for clothes and shoes might be considered generous, if not wildly extravagant. In that budget there is no provision for more than one child, for any amusement or luxury, nor for sickness, seasonal unemployment, burial club or school fees; in other words any expenditure which might have made life even passably tolerable or less insecure.

By the age of 40 James had been married for fifteen years and had fathered seven children, all but one of whom had survived. Polly would have fed, clothed and sheltered her growing family on less than £1 a week. The rent for two rooms could have amounted to as much as one-third of that, and if a saving of even sixpence a week could be made a family would move to cheaper accommodation without a second thought. This undoubtedly accounted for their frequent removals. Each time they registered the birth of another child, every other year, their address had changed – Dockhead Place, Gainsford Street (behind Shad Thames), Woolf Terrace (off Dockhead), Jamaica Road – they never moved more than a few hundred yards on each occasion and often returned to the same street, but never to the same house. Charles Booth described this common phenomenon thus:

> 'In many districts the people are always on the move; they shift from one part of it to another like "fish in a river". The School Board visitors follow them as best they may, and the transfers from one visitor's book to another's are very numerous. On the whole, however, the people usually do not go far, and often cling from generation to generation to one vicinity, almost as if the set of streets which lie there were an isolated country village.'[18]

The School Board visitors of Division 8 must have been sorely tried in tracking the movements of James and Polly's family. Their eldest child was seven years of age when compulsory education was introduced and their youngest did not leave school until the middle of the 1890s. During that twenty year period we know that the family lived at at least a dozen different addresses and the total number could easily have been double that figure.

Very few admission registers for the Thames-side schools in Southwark and Bermondsey exist for this early period, but some of the head-teachers' log books have survived and present a graphic picture of life in the last quarter of the nineteenth century. Farncombe Street Board School (now Riverside School) lay between Jamaica Road and the river. Its catchment area was subject to frequent flooding: 'The attendance was unusually low on Monday owing to the High Tide. Many of the children's clothing being too wet to wear,' wrote Elizabeth Powell, the Infants' school's first head teacher. A year later she recorded that 'it had rained all the Holidays and the Thames had several times overflowed and flooded numbers of the houses . . . so that many children were very ill and are so still.'[19] Unsurprisingly, sickness and disease were endemic: ' . . . the Scarlet Fever very prevalent in the neighbourhood, several cases of deaths.' Miss Powell's use of initial capitals for this killer disease was well justified; within a month of that entry it was responsible for seven more deaths amongst her infant pupils.[20]

W.J. Peddle, the headmaster of Laxon Street Boy's school gives a much fuller account of every day school life than most of his contemporaries do, revealing an incredibly concerned and kindly school teacher in an area of the direst poverty and degradation. Laxon Street school was situate in Long Lane, Southwark, a short distance south from Guy's Hospital. This is how the area was described in the 1880s by a Congregational minister:

> 'Reeking courts, crowded public-houses, low lodging-houses and numerous brothels are to be found all around. Even the cellars are tenanted. Poverty, rags, and dirt everywhere . . . In going about these alleys and courts no stranger is safe if alone . . . a bible-woman, visiting "Kent Street", was robbed of most of her clothing. Even the police seldom venture into some parts of the district except in company.'[21]

Mr Peddle was head of the boys' school for more than twenty years. One of his early entries reads: 'I was very pained this morning on finding that two of my lads had come to school without breaking their fast; one of them having eaten only two small crusts yesterday.' He then shared his own food with them remarking that their teacher had found that they could not work as well as their fellow pupils, 'Poor lads', he commented,' How is it possible for them to work in such a starving state!' With a quite deliberate irony he added, 'It is singular that the above should casually have come to my notice on this day, when we are invited by the Board to make a Collection for the Indian Famine Fund, inaugurated by the Lord Mayor.'[22]

In the summer he organised outings, conveying four hundred boys in nine horse brakes to the London Zoo: 'During the afternoon we had sports and contests for 40 prizes consisting of bats, balls and knives. Each boy had a penny bun and a glass of milk before leaving. I collected over £15 from friends to pay the expenses.'[23] He was assiduous, too, in soliciting charities to provide his boys with free breakfasts and dinners. He was so successful in this that at one stage he had arranged for a free dinner every school day for one-fifth of his total school roll and could afford to decline further charitable offers. He also arranged country holidays for fifty of his poorest lads who, presumably, never even had the opportunity of a month's hop-picking in the summer with their families.

It was typical of Peddle that he attributed to his assistant masters the credit for a school regime to which the rough lads of Laxon Street responded:

> 'The parents of G. Stevens have left the neighbourhood for Kennington. His love for the school and his teacher, Mr Jones, induces him to walk the distance every day.'[24]

– or this,

> 'I have noted with much pleasure the special pains Mr Atwell is taking with his boys in their new work. Every day many of them bring him specimen sums worked at home on scraps of paper.'[25]

It must have been with a great sense of disappointment that within three years of writing that commendation the head was obliged to withdraw Atwell's authority to inflict corporal punishment and later to report his behaviour to the school's management committee for 'pulling little Rolls's ears, so as to make them bleed.' The Board generally disapproved of physical punishment and had laid down strict guidelines for its use. Mr Atwell's conduct eventually led them to demand his resignation for repeated infringements. Before he had worked out his notice, Atwell absented himself from school one June afternoon and committed suicide in Green Park by ingesting an irritant poison. Predictably, Mr Peddle attended the funeral, no doubt blaming himself to some extent for a tragedy indirectly arising from his deep concern for the well-being of the youngsters in his care.[26] It is pleasing to note that Her Majesty's Inspectors recognised Mr Peddle's dedication. Their reports repeatedly refer to his 'kindliness and industry'. 'This large School of very poor boys', wrote one Inspector, 'is conducted with marked integrity and a diligence deserving of high praise.'

Not all head teachers were as committed as Mr Peddle in support of the Board's policy on school discipline. The head of Dalgleish Street school in Limehouse notes with acerbity that his management committee was of the opinion that too much corporal punishment was given in the boys' department. He confided his complaint to his log in these words: 'Hitherto I have punished all sent to me by the assistants, in future I must punish myself by stopping in with the bad boys instead of giving the cane.'[27] This was the same headmaster who considered that 'The Stately Homes of England' was an appropriate song to teach his East End pupils.

A few months after Mr Atwell's resignation had been demanded by the School Board, Annie Cullen, the headmistress of a Tower Hamlets Infants' school recorded her indignation at what had followed her punishment of two sisters who had arrived very late for school one afternoon: 'I gave each child a slight stripe on the hand. The children, instead of going to their classes, went home to their mother who returned with them and gave me a severe blow in my face with her fist, in front of a class I was taking at the time. Mrs Wilkinson has been summoned.'[28]

Violence directed by parents towards teachers was certainly not unknown, and it was said that 'a knowledge of boxing was almost a necessity for a man in certain districts.' Parents who had little choice but to live in near squalour resented efforts by the schools to inculcate habits of punctuality, honesty and hygiene. One surprisingly literate mother complained in a letter to her daughter's school:

> 'I should like to know how much more spite you intend to put upon my child, for it is nothing else. First you send the Sanitary inspector and I have my home taken away; then my husband has to get rid of his few rabbits and chicken, and now you cut the few hairs that my girl was just beginning to get so nice. I think you had better hang her and be done with it.'[29]

Her home was obviously one which had been condemned by a sanitary inspector as unfit for human habitation. Sanitary inspectors worked under the direction of the local Medical Officer whose duty was to reduce death and disease which arose from overcrowding and London's insanitary conditions. The law empowered the Medical Officer to order an owner to make repairs to a property at his own expense, or, as a last resort, to demolish a house and charge the cost to its owner. There was no requirement to re-house the tenants, so that when such powers were exercised they merely contributed to the problem of overcrowding elsewhere.[30] But these powers were neither consistently nor uniformly applied. The Medical Officer for Finsbury reported the words of an old lady evicted three times for overcrowding: "Thank 'evins, now I shall 'ave a little rest, the board of 'ealth ain't so strick where I am going next."[31]

The law required a London vestry to appoint a Medical Officer, but no one said they should follow his recommendations. George Sims pointed out that 'The first thing as a rule which a man does who acquires low class and doubtful property is to try and be elected a vestryman.'[32] Many a London vestry was notorious for putting the self-interests of its property-owning members above any responsibility to its community. One newly appointed Medical Officer was greeted by his vestry chairman with the discouraging adjuration, "Now, doctor, I wish you to understand that the less you do, the better we shall like you."[33]

Overcrowding in central London worsened as the century progressed. The natural increase in population was added to by a continuing influx of immigrants from country areas and eastern Europe as street improvements, railway, warehouse, and school building, together with some slum clearance, progressively reduced the housing stock. In the district of St Olave's, which included the Dockhead area, the availability of domestic house property fell by almost two thirds in forty years from 18.29 to 6.25 houses per acre.[34] Consequently rents rose out of all proportion to income. A 'Daily News' article detailed eleven Southwark families, ranging in size from four to ten persons. Those with an average of three children were occupying a single room and paying three shillings a week in rent out of a wage of six shillings. The larger families, averaging six children, paid between 4s 6d. and 6s. for two rooms. In most cases their rent amounted to approximately half their wages, when they had any income at all to report.[35]

One- and two-room dwellings rarely had a water tap, a sink or any lavatory accommodation; those facilities were shared by all the occupants of the street or court, and a fire grate could not necessarily be guaranteed. Conditions generally in London's poorer quarters were still appalling in the 1880s despite thirty years of sanitary improvements – they were widely known about, they had been reported on often enough, but such reports achieved little more than legislative tinkering and a temporary increase in charitable giving which may have eased a conscience

'. . . their rent amounted to approximately half their wages, when they had any income at all to report.'

or two. Those who wrote and spoke about living conditions almost invariably employed emotive phrases to describe this section of the population – the degraded, the vicious, the residuum, the dregs, the submerged tenth – strongly implying that most, if not all of them, were undeserving of, or unwilling to accept, any help. They seemed conveniently to ignore the fact that the majority of the ill-housed were simply working men and women doggedly striving to maintain their families on an inadequate wage from a precarious employment in conditions of a desperate housing shortage. Sympathy for their plight generally took the form of expressions of dismay that the decent working man should risk contamination by having to live cheek by jowl with the depraved and the semi-criminal. Even George Sims could observe that, 'The constant association of the poor and the criminal also has deadened in the former nearly all sense of right and wrong.' Here he was lamenting the fact that a respectable widow did not consider it to be any of her business to interfere in drunken brawls and murderous assaults which occurred nightly in the yard outside her ground-floor tenement. She lived in one room with her six children, paying rent of 4s 6d a week. The journalist described it:

> 'the walls were mildewed and streaming with damp, the boards as you trod on them made the slushing noise of a plank spread across a mud puddle in a brickfield: foul within and foul without, these people paid the rent of it gladly, and perhaps thanked God for the luck of having it. Rooms for the poor earning precarious livelihoods are too hard to get and too much in demand now for a widow woman to give up one just because of the trifling inconvenience of overhearing a few outrages and murders.'[36]

That appeared in the second of a series of thirteen articles entitled 'How the Poor Live' which Sims wrote for 'The Pictorial World' in the summer of 1883 based, for the most part, on his wanderings through the Southwark slums, 'a dark continent that is within easy walking distance of the General Post Office', was how he described its location. Of his purpose in thus illuminating for his readers the lives and conditions of its population, he wrote that, 'the wild races who inhabit it will, I trust, gain public sympathy as easily as those savage tribes for whose benefit the Missionary Societies never cease to appeal for funds.'[37] Sims wrote with a light touch, his examples were rarely harrowing, but with the relentless accumulation of small detail he creates a composite picture of such degradation and utter hopelessness that engenders in the reader, even today, a sense of disbelief that people could have retained so tenacious a hold on life as to have survived at all in such conditions:

> 'In many houses more water comes through the roof than through a pipe, and a tub or butt in the back-yard, about half full of a black foul-smelling liquid, supplies some dozens of families with the water they drink and the water they wash in as well . . . Is it any wonder that disease is rampant, or that the Temperance folk have such trouble to persuade the masses that cold water is a good and healthy drink?'
>
> 'The accommodation which these poeple will put up with is almost incredible . . . The stairs are rotten, and here and there show where some foot has trodden too heavily. The landing above is a yawning gulf which you have to leap, and leap lightly, or the rotten boarding would break away beneath you. Open a door and look into a room. There are two women and three children at work, and the holes in the floor are patched across with bits of old boxes which the tenants have nailed down themselves.'[38]

Of his experiences during that investigation, Sims later told the readers of 'The Daily News': 'I began my task with a light heart; I finished it with a heavy one. In that two months I saw a vision of hell more terrible than the immortal Florentine's, and this was no poet's dream – it was a terrible truth, ghastly in its reality, heart-breaking in its intensity, and the doom of the imprisoned bodies in this modern Inferno was as horrible as any that Dante depicted for his tortured souls.'[39]

The public response to Sims's revelations encouraged the editor of 'The Pictorial World' to open a 'How the Poor Live' Fund, but, after twelve weeks, contributions totalled only £38.12s. It seemed as though Sims's graphic descriptions, amplified by Frederick Barnard's highly evocative illustrations, had achieved little more than to increase the journal's circulation, until a small twenty-four page penny pamphlet, subtitled 'An Inquiry into the Condition of the Abject Poor', was issued by the London Congregational Union a few weeks after the last of Sims's articles had appeared. Quite why it achieved its remarkable effect cannot easily be explained. It contained little that was new, in fact it borrowed unashamedly, but with proper attribution, from George Sims's articles. Perhaps its bold statement that the Christian community had failed in its duty to the poor, that despite praiseworthy but unco-ordinated initiatives 'only the merest edge of the great dark region of poverty, misery, squalour and immorality has been touched' struck a guilty nerve in a professedly Christian middle-class readership. Perhaps, too, the assertion that these awful discoveries had 'only quite recently' been made by the churches gave the pamphlet's readers an acceptable excuse for their earlier inaction.[40] Certainly, its title was a stroke of inspired journalism – 'The Bitter Cry of Outcast London' became an overnight best-seller. Its theme was taken up by every journal and newspaper. In the wake of its publication George Sims re-wrote parts of his 'Pictorial World' articles for 'The Daily News' generously acknowledging the profound impact of 'The Bitter Cry':

> 'The housing of the poor has long been a smouldering question; dozens of willing hands have sought to fan it into a flame, but hitherto with small results. At the last moment a little pamphlet laid modestly on the dying embers has done what all the bellows-blowing of the Press failed to accomplish.'[41]

W.T. Stead, the campaigning editor of 'The Pall Mall Gazette', asked 'Where is the leader of men who will preach a new crusade against the crying evil of our times? As for the politicians, they make no sign.'[42] That comment may not have been entirely fair, but it was near enough to the truth to help to provoke an intensified national debate on the housing question which led the government to set up a Royal Commission on the Housing of the Working Classes in the following year. The Commission's investigations were thorough, confirming the accuracy of all that had been revealed in the popular press, and substantiating it with hard evidence. It concluded that the prime cause of the terrible housing conditions was simply the poverty of the people, but it had no useful suggestion to make about how this might be remedied.[43] Any suggestion that the state might help to provide decent housing was still far ahead of its time, and smacked of 'State Socialism.' That attitude was exemplified by Lord Wemyss, the chairman of the Liberty and Property Defence League, speaking in the debate which preceded the setting up of the Royal Commission: ' . . . if they began on this system where were they going to stop?' he asked, 'If they built houses, would they furnish them? Would they put fire in the grate, or food in the cupboard? And if not, on this principle, why not?'[44]

James and Polly were probably what the Victorians would have described as 'respectable working class'. James had consistently followed the only trade he had known. A packing-case maker was, at most, semi-skilled and he would, by no means, have been categorised as belonging to the 'aristocracy of labour' – the compositors, cabinet makers and mechanics (Charles Booth's Classes 'E' and 'F') – but, equally, he was not likely to have been lumped together with the 'shiftless, work-shy residuum'. He and Polly seem to have abided by the accepted norms of decent working people: all their children's births were registered even before Parliament laid the responsibility for so doing directly upon parents, although they never seem to have bothered with baptisms, but their children married in church at a time when so many couples simply co-habited. Charles Booth would probably have placed them in his 'D' classification – 'small, regular earnings, poor' – which category he defined as 'the better end of the casual dock and waterside labour . . . .in regular work on a wage not exceeding 21s. a week', adding that 'these men have a hard struggle to make ends meet, but they are, as a body, decent steady men, paying their way and bringing up their children respectably. The work they do demands little skill or intelligence.'[45]

James and Polly's lives were spent in a poor waterside quarter of south London where they brought up a family of nine children, all but one of whom survived infancy, living in one or two extremely cramped, rented rooms. That assertion can fairly be adduced from the evidence of the 1891 census. One consequence of the housing debate of the previous decade was the decision to use that census to enquire into overcrowding. If a family lived in accommodation which comprised fewer than five rooms, the census asked how many rooms the family occupied. James by then was 52, Polly six years younger and their family had been completed eight years earlier. One daughter had married, two others were in service and the two older boys had lodgings elsewhere – one of them with his older married sister. This left James and Polly with three children aged between eight and thirteen. The family was then living at number 6, New Lane, Bermondsey, a narrow alley which crossed Shad Thames and ran down to the river at Horsleydown New Stairs. It was a house of six rooms, four of which were occupied by two other families. The remaining two rooms were shared by James's family of five and William King, a blacksmith, his wife and their two children. 'The Times' was overstating the options open to such people when it claimed that the respectable London labourer 'was faced with the choice of spending half his wages on a couple of wretched rooms, or of living like a pig in a sty.'[46] Often there was no such choice.

References

[1] Stead, W.T., 'The Pall Mall Gazette', 16 OCT 1883
[2] Peek, F., 'The Pall Mall Gazette', 19 OCT 1883
[3] Pearsall, 'The Worm in the Bud', p.198
[4] Weinreb and Hibbert, 'The London Encyclopaedia', p.86
[5] Reports of the preparations and of the procession are taken, in the main, from the special supplement to the 'Daily Telegraph', 9 MAR 1863
[6] Lorne, The Marquis of, 'V.R.I.: Her Life and Empire', Harmsworth Bros. Ltd. (part-set), 1901, p.290
[7] Elmers, and Werner, 'London's Lost Riverscape', pp.85–95
[8] Booth, C., 'Life and Labour of the People in London', Vol. 2. App.36.
[9] Wohl, 'Ragged London in 1861', p.vii.
[10] 'The Morning Star', 18 JAN 1861.
[11] Wohl, 'Ragged London in 1861', pp.85–88.
[12] ibid., p.85.
[13] ibid., p.30.
[14] ibid., p.57.
[15] Treble, 'Urban Poverty in Britain', p.49.
[16] 'The Commonwealth', 23 JUN 1888, quot. in Fishman, 'East End 1888', p.180.
[17] 'The Penny Newsman', 2 FEB 1861: quot. in Wohl, 'Ragged London in 1861', pp.159/160
[18] Fried and Elman, 'Charles Booth's London', pp.5/6
[19] Farncombe Street (now 'Riverside') School Infants' Department log, 20 NOV 1875 and 13 JAN 1877.
[20] ibid., 25 SEP – 23 OCT 1875
[21] Mearns, 'The Bitter Cry of Outcast London,' p.23
[22] LCC/EO/DIV 8/LAX/LB/1, 28 SEP 1877, Greater London R.O.
[23] ibid., 12 SEP 1890
[24] ibid., 21 FEB 1877
[25] ibid., 21 MAR 1892

[26] ibid., 18 FEB - 27 JUN 1895
[27] LCC/EO/DIV 5/DAL/LB/1, 17 OCT 1882, Greater London R.O.
[28] LCC/EO/DIV 5/HWY/LB/1, 7 OCT 1895, Greater London R.O.
[29] Sturt, M., 'The Education of the People', p.338
[30] Stedman-Jones, 'Outcast London', p.188
[31] Wohl, 'The Eternal Slum', p.118.
[32] 'The Daily News', 19 NOV 1883
[33] Wohl,'The Eternal Slum', pp.112/3
[34] Stedman-Jones, 'Outcast London', p.232
[35] 'The Daily News', 14 NOV 1883.
[36] 'The Pictorial World', 9 JUN 1883
[37] ibid., 2 JUN 1883
[38] ibid., 21 JUN 1883
[39] 'The Daily News', 8 NOV 1883
[40] Mearns, 'The Bitter Cry of Outcast London', p.3.
[41] 'The Daily News', 8 NOV 1883
[42] 'The Pall Mall Gazette', 16 OCT 1883
[43] Gauldie, 'Cruel Habitations', p.289
[44] Wohl, 'The Eternal Slum', pp.231/2
[45] Fried and Elman, 'Charles Booth's London', pp.17/18
[46] 'The Times', 9 JAN 1884

CHAPTER SIXTEEN

THE BELGRAVIA OF BERMONDSEY

'Oh! it really is a wery pretty garden,
And 'Endon to the westward could be seen;
And by clinging to the chimbley,
You could see across to Wembley
If it wasn't for the 'ouses in between.'
– Edgar Bateman (1894)[1]

'A family who have lived for years in one street are recognised up and down the length of that street as people to be helped in time of trouble. These respectable but very poor people live over a morass of such intolerable poverty that they unite instinctively to save those known to them from falling into it.'
– Maud Pember Reeves (1913)[2]

James was born in the first year of the young Queen Victoria's sixty-four year reign, and reached his seventieth birthday just three months before the very first old age pension was paid. For more than half a million people January 1st, 1909, was a day of miracles no less amazing that the manna which fell on the Israelites. Fred Willis, a south London hatter, wrote of their reaction:

'Nobody who has not lived through those years can have any notion of the profound impression old-age pensions made on the people when they came. I remember one old lady who nearly expired when she was made to understand that for the rest of her life she was to receive a Government pension, not as charity but as of right. To her, charity was anathema. It represented only humiliation and disgrace . . . When she was told that she would get it at the post office as easily as buying a postage stamp she was dumbfounded.'[3]

Elderly couples lived perpetually in the shadow of two great fears: of ending their days in the workhouse, being allowed to see each other only on a Sunday afternoon, and, at the very end, the shame of a pauper's funeral. For seventy-five years the rules of the Poor Law had laid down that bedrooms should be provided in workhouses for couples over sixty, but in practice they were almost invariably separated and sent to the male and female wards. In the whole of England and Wales only two hundred couples were accommodated together in the last decade of the nineteenth century.[4] The husband of an old couple over ninety expressed his pleasure at receiving a pension in these words:

> "Often 'ave we thought as 'ow it would be a-best for us to go, and sometimes a-most 'ave I prayed to be took; for we was only a burden to our children as kep' us; for they be good and wouldna let us go on the parish so long as they could 'elp it . . . (but) now we want to go on livin' forever.'[5]

An allowance of five shillings a week, or 7s 6d. for a couple, at the age of 70 was a quite inadequate income on which to live, but it was enough in many cases to enable the elderly to share their children's home and to feel that they were making a useful contribution, instead of being obliged, or volunteering, to go into the 'House'. As might be expected, the high-minded Charity Organisation Society objected that by receiving money they had not earned the poor would be 'pauperised' and they strongly opposed all plans for granting 'a stereotyped form of relief to large numbers of persons whose needs are very varying and only capable of being met by individual attention', as they expressed it.[6] One would have thought from that comment that they themselves were providing relief to the elderly based upon their individual needs on a very large scale indeed, but in the year the first government pensions were paid the COS was doling out a small pension to only 1371 old folk.[7] Another opponent was Henry Chaplin who raised a hearty cheer by asserting that Lloyd George's proposal 'would sap the vitality of the country by discouraging thrift in the poor', and this from a man who had already squandered two fortunes and was himself in receipt of a state pension of £2,000 a year.[8] Perhaps the exercise of thrift to which Chaplin alluded was that of an old man of 74 collecting his first pension payment and who admitted to a 'Times' reporter that for years he had had a coffin standing in his house so that the parish might not bury him. When Lloyd George claimed that by this measure the government was 'lifting the shadow of the workhouse from the homes of the poor', he could scarcely have imagined the expressions of incredulity, delight and simple gratitude displayed by those who presented themselves at the post office to collect the first payment they had ever received which was not a charitable handout, but to which they had a legal right. One old woman tried to give a Southwark postmaster a couple of rashers of bacon for helping her to complete her application form, another offered him a wing of a goose 'impressing upon him at the same time the value of the quills for pens.'[9]

By this time James and Polly had left the riverside and moved three-quarters of a mile to south Bermondsey where James had found employment as a packing-case maker with James and Sons in the Old Kent Road until he and Polly died within a year of each other at the outbreak of the Great War.

Since the turn of the century the parish vestries and district boards, which had governed London had lost those powers and local government boundaries had been re-drawn. To Bermondsey's St Mary Magdalene parish had been added St Mary, Rotherhithe and the eastern parishes of Southwark (St Olave, St Thomas and St John, Horsleydown) to form the Metropolitan Borough of Bermondsey, whose Council was given responsibility for public health, housing, the maintenance of its roads and the supervision of its markets.[10] If one excluded Rotherhithe, the new Bermondsey was still quite small, only a mile from north to south and a mile from west to east, but it housed 80,000 people in 19,000 dwellings of which only 113 had a fitted bath in 1905. Even twenty years later it was estimated that no more than another 150 baths had been installed, mainly in the houses of professional men – doctors, teachers and lawyers.[11] A tin bath hung on a nail outside the scullery door, and dragged in on bath nights to be filled from the copper or by kettle from the stove had to suffice for most folk.

Bermondsey's smells were pungent: the leather tanneries, glue-yards and curriers, sawmills, hop warehouses, breweries, distilleries, india-rubber works and pickle factories stood amongst the houses. Pink's Jam Factory and Peek Frean's biscuit works were sited in the same road not far from Atkinson's Perfumery. Many well-known names had their factories in the borough: Crosse and Blackwell, Spillers', Jacobs', Pearce Duff, Lipton, Sarsons', Hartley and Courage. Some people claimed that they could tell precisely where they were by the combination of local smells, but it was a depressing place – street upon street of two- or three-storied terrace houses, built of soot-begrimed yellow London brick topped with grey slates. Some of the more fortunate did have narrow front gardens where a few sad looking flowers struggled to survive, or where a dusty privet hedge squatted in front of a lace-curtained parlour window which framed a glossy, potted aspidistra. Of such areas of south London the Duke of York (later King George VI) remarked that they were 'a wilderness of desolation . . . miles of squalid, vulgar, ugly, shoddy stuff, without one scrap of beauty or brightness, one touch of imagination.'[12] 'Districts of this kind cover dreary acres', wrote Maud Pember Reeves, 'the same little two-story (sic) house, with or without an inconceivably drearier basement, with the same kind of baker's shop at the corner faced by the same kind of greengrocer's shop opposite. The ugly, constantly-recurring school buildings are a relief to the spirit oppressed by the awful monotony.'[13] Such areas were only really enlivened by their street markets.

Southwark Park Road served as south Bermondsey's main shopping centre, but it was busiest at weekends when two hundred stalls lined both sides of the road. The market never closed before 10pm on Saturdays, and, for the three days prior to Christmas, it stayed open all day and night. Braziers were stood along the gutters for warmth and the whole street blazed with naphthalene flares. Fish and chips (a ha'porth of each) or a basinful of saveloys and pease pudding from the pork butcher, with a quart or so of beer from the John Bull, the Blue Anchor, or the Colleen Bawn kept both customers and stallholders from flagging. Next to the John Bull a confectioner drew out lumps of hot toffee into a skein which he threw over a big hook screwed to his stall and pulled quickly into long strips before it cooled; cough candy was his speciality. Nearby, an old woman wearing a man's cap, the sleeves of her long, black dress rolled up, busily sawed away at an enormous block of cooking salt, 18 inches square and a yard high, which stood on the pavement protected by a piece of old sacking – each three-inch thick triangular piece cost a halfpenny. Fancy ladies' underclothes were briskly sold by a man dressed cheekily in his own wares, and a stallholder asking, "Who wants three pints for a bob (a shilling)?" was selling china chamber pots. Michael Manze, the fishmonger, deftly cut up live eels whilst his customers waited, and passing children cheered as one occasionally slithered free to disappear down the nearest drain. In summer an Italian ice-cream vendor offered a one and a half-inch thick mixed wafer (icecream and lemon ice with a slice of lemon on top) for a half-penny and advertised his Okey Pokey, a solid piece of pink and white ice, by crying out

> "Okey Pokey, penny a lump,
> The more you eat, the more you jump.
> – Taste before you buy!"

Street hawkers were beginning to die out in London, but until the First World War many still toured the Bermondsey streets. Apart from the common-place knife grinders, cane-chair menders, Gypsy lavender sellers and the Sunday Muffin-man, there were more exotic pedlars. Every weekday a comical, bandy-legged cats-meat man appeared, five feet tall, round, plump, rosy-faced and with a huge walrus moustache, wearing a large white apron, carrying a baker's basket bearing the legend 'PUSSIES BUTCHER', and followed by a tribe of cats. He sold a dozen pieces of horse-flesh skewered on a stick for a half-penny. Another sold comics, four for a penny. An organ-grinder and his mate toured the streets occasionally, one turned the handle and the other, who was cross-eyed, sang indistinctly out of the side of his mouth until a sufficient crowd had collected when they began to sell their song-sheets for two-pence. Two other hawkers appeared only in spring-time. One offered a four inch square card with two lambs stuck on for a penny – cotton-wool bodies and matchstick legs – drumming up custom with a mournful cry of:

> "Young lambs to sell, young lambs to sell.
> If I had as much money as I could tell,
> I wouldn't cry out, 'Young lambs to sell'!"

The other had a swarthy complexion, was dressed in a turban and flowing oriental robes and sold a medicinal purgative. His sales pitch ended with a defiantly shouted last syllable: "Turkey Rhubarb, Turkey Rhubarb, for the stomach, for the liver, for the belly-HAKE!" Less frequent, and certainly less welcome, were the Mormon missionaries. Whenever they were about mothers kept their children indoors because 'they stole children to take back to Salt Lake City.' Clothing and shoes were usually bought from Drage's, a Jewish firm which encouraged instalment payments, collected weekly by their tallyman. The ease of purchase may have been convenient, even necessary, but their delivery system was suspect. Their carter threw in all manner of parcels as soon as the front door was opened and left quickly. Not infrequently, some of the goods were found not to have been ordered, but Drage's claimed otherwise when the customer tried to return unwanted items.

St James's Road, Bermondsey, runs north for almost a mile from the Old Kent Road as far as Jamaica Road. At its southern end it crossed the Bricklayer's Arms Extension Railway lines at what was known as Mercer's Crossing. Just over the crossing Alderminster Road ran parallel to the railway westwards to the terminus itself. In St James's Road at its junction with Alderminster Road stood a row of seven three-storied houses. When those houses were built in the late 1870s, they comprised a basement and two upper storeys with their first floor front doors leading directly on to the road across the basement area. By 1880 road and rail traffic had increased to such an extent that the South Eastern Railway Company decided to build a road bridge to replace the level-crossing and its 'hideous wooden gates'. The approach roads to the bridge had to be raised to such a level that St James's Road then passed immediately in front of the top floor windows of numbers 240-252, rendering their front doors entirely redundant. The only access to that row of houses, and those opposite of course, became a flight of thirty steps down to the basement area – a cul-de-sac blocked at its far end by the side cellar wall of 'The Sultan' public house. The front doors were nailed up, the basement doors became the front doors, and the basement and first floor windows faced a solid brick wall, just eight feet away, across a gloomy canyon 15 to 20 feet below the new street level. Such was number 250 St James's Road when Jack Mimms took rooms there shortly after marrying

Elizabeth (Lil) Compton in the year of Queen Victoria's Diamond Jubilee. As their family grew, they gradually took over more rooms until they occupied them all, later letting off rooms to lodgers as their own children left home. That house was their only home until German bombers made it uninhabitable in 1940.

Jack and Lil's home fell within the parish of St Anne, Thorburn Square which Charles Booth described as 'the Belgravia of Bermondsey', and its people as 'friendly, but inaccessible, proud and poor.'[14] In the whole area from Southwark Park Road southwards to the railway lines, and from Upper Grange Road in the west as far as St James's Road, he estimated that only 19.5% of the inhabitants were living 'in poverty'. 'A very uniform block', he recorded, 'inhabited by a good working class.' The only part of that area which 'could be called at all poor' was Alderminster Road and the southern part of St James's Road where Jack and Lil lived.[15]

Housing in central London was still in short supply and expensive. 'Place a disused sentry-box upon any piece of waste ground in South or East London,' wrote one commentator, 'and in a few hours it will be occupied by a man and his wife and family, inundated by applications from would-be lodgers.'[16] Jack and Lil may well have considered themselves fortunate to have secured a couple of top storey rooms, directly overlooking the elevated roadway and with a cooker on the landing, for their first and, for many years, their only home.

Opposite Jack's house, and his second home, 'The Sultan' public house, stood Jimmy Hinson's corner shop. The Post Office directories always described number 267 St James's Road as 'Avila Tringham, Oil and Colourman', but to the locals who knew that he had worked there since boyhood and had been left the business when old Mr Tringham died, it was always known as 'Jimmy's'. The description, 'Oil and Colourman', was equally misleading. True, Jimmy sold paraffin and paint, but this did not begin to describe what his shop actually contained. Outside, it was festooned with brooms, mops, scrubbing brushes, coppersticks, wooden stools, pokers, fire-dogs, flat irons, bellows, shovels and washboards. The shop itself, no more than nine feet by ten feet six, and lit by a single oil lamp, had standing room for only two or three customers at a time. The space behind the counter allowed only one person to serve, so Jimmy's wife, a large

'the basement and first floor windows faced a solid brick wall, just eight feet away, across a gloomy canyon . . .'

red-faced, miserable woman, always stood at the top of the four steps which led to the storeroom, hands on hips, supervising and nagging at him. Jimmy was a weedy little chap with a very large droopy white moustache and a harassed expression. Hampered only by a large grubby white apron and with his shirt sleeves rolled up, he trotted everywhere, running up the steps and squeezing past his outsize wife to fetch something from the store. The smell was distinctive and almost indescribable, an amalgam of pickles, soap, jam, fish-glue, cheese, firelighters, furniture polish, treacle, linoleum and methylated spirits. An array of dozens of little drawers covered the back wall behind the counter from floor to ceiling. These held such small items as screws, buttons, reels of cotton and door handles which otherwise would have been lost amidst the clutter of boxes, sacks and tins which littered the floor. None of the drawers was labelled, but Jimmy always knew exactly what each contained. The ceiling was scarcely visible between the hardware which hung from it – kettles, saucepans, frying pans, earthenware jugs, enamel basins, colanders, galvanized buckets and baths, fenders, cheese graters and coal scuttles. Between the ironmongery a few sticky yellow fly papers, black with insects, hung down at head height. Such corner shops were everywhere in London, always called an 'Oil and Colourman' or 'Italian warehouse.' Arthur Morrison described Mr Grinder's in Bethnal Green as 'a shop ever too tight for its stock, which burst forth at every available opening, and heaped so high on the paving that the window was half buried in a bank of shining tin.'[17] Almost the only goods Jimmy didn't sell were greengrocery and sweets which could be got from George Martin's on the opposite corner.

Jack Mimms was James and Polly's eldest son who had left school at the earliest possible opportunity to work as errand-boy and porter at Meggeson's pharmaceutical works near The Star music-hall in Abbey Street, Dockhead. When he married at the age of 25 he described his occupation as 'Druggist' which meant only that he pulled the handle of a press which turned out tablets and pills. If he could be said to have had a regular trade after that it was as a carman, and for many years he drove a two-horse brewer's dray for Noakes's Brewery, delivering casks to the local public houses. London was still dominated by the horse, in fact there were thought to be at least a quarter of a million horses in daily use on the streets in the Edwardian era. C.H. Rolph, a

'The shop . . . lit by a single oil lamp, had standing room for only two or three customers.'

London policeman's son, wrote that as he walked through the narrow streets 'I was always astounded at the skill of the carmen navigating heavy pair-horsed wagons in those confined spaces: they had the advantage that they could turn in their own length, the front wheels turning right beneath the undercarriage. The stumbling horses seemed always to help intelligently and willingly in the process, and almost able to do it unaided; there was little use of the whip and not much shouting. Fallen horses were, however, a frequent sight. And once down, they were seldom able to get up while still in the shafts, and there was a general traffic hold-up while they were released from the harness, scrambled up with a clatter of irons shoes, and stood waiting patiently to be re-harnessed.'[18] London's streets in the first decade of the twentieth century were still 'rumbling with horse buses, tinkling with hansoms, and shrilling with cab-whistles,' wrote Thomas Burke, 'on wet days the roads were a morass of mud and horse-droppings . . . .Carters, bus-drivers, tram-drivers, and the few motor chauffeurs, had no protection in their vehicles against rain. They sat in the open, wearing oil-skin hats and capes, with the rain pouring off them.'[19]

Lil Compton was twenty when she married Jack, much against her father's wishes. William Compton held a position of trust, a wharf foreman, and considered the Mimms family to be 'very rough', more particularly as they hailed from the Dockhead area. Nor was a carman well paid; he was certainly fortunate if he had a regular employment and earned much above one pound a week. In the first twenty years of her marriage, Lil gave birth to ten children, five boys and five girls. When Lil's eldest son, aged 6, was dying from scarlet fever, her third child, Bert, was suffering from the same illness and she, herself, was pregnant with her fifth child who died within a few months. Margaret Llewellyn Davies shocked her readers when, in 1915, she published 160 letters from working-class women detailing their experiences of pregnancy and childbirth. A mother of eleven, whose husband earned £1 a week wrote:

> 'I had two down with the measles, one two years old with his collar-bone out, and a little girl thirteen with her arm broke. That was at the same time as I was expecting my eighth little one, and my dear husband worried out of his life.'[20]

Lil's experience was, perhaps, more akin to that of another mother who had lost four of her ten children:

> 'My husband used to lose his work through drink. I couldn't tell you exactly what my wages were, but I feel almost sure, to take the years through, they never amounted to £1 per week. I was in hopes, as soon as my boys started work, I should have got on better, but the more I got off my boys the less I got off my husband, for mine has been a miserable experience.'[21]

Altogether, three of Lil's sons died young, including her two first-born. A thirty per-cent death rate amongst poorer families was not unusual. In a study of 51 Lambeth families with less than 22s a week to live on, Maud Pember Reeves and her Fabian colleagues found that of the 276 children born to them, 85 had died – a death rate of 30.8%.[22] This she ascribed in the main to their poverty which led to a very poor diet and inadequate health care. She had by no means chosen the objects of her study from society's lowest stratum. 'They are not the poorest people of the district. Far from it!' she asserted, they were, on the contrary, 'some of the more enviable and settled inhabitants, where the father was a sober, steady man in full work', and the wives were 'quiet, decent "keep themselves-to-themselves" kind of women, and the children are the most punctual and regular scholars, the most clean-headed children of the poorer schools in Kennington and Lambeth.'[23] She admitted that the children's diet was utterly unsatisfactory but denied strongly that this was due to their mothers' ignorance or indifference. How could anyone, however educated and expert, maintain a wage-earner's strength and her children's health on the meagre house-keeping they had available? 'It would be an impossible problem if set to trained and expert people', she added with vigour, 'How much more an impossible problem when set to the saddened, weakened, over-burdened wives of London labourers?'[24] Her daughters, in later life, acknowledged Lil as an excellent cook and a wonderful manager of the scanty household finances which could have been more generous had Jack not developed into a hard and heavy drinker in the pubs to which he delivered and in the spit and sawdust public bar of 'The Sultan' public house. It was only through her unremitting efforts, and the kindness of neighbours who were no better off than herself, that Lil's surviving seven children were fed at all. She was a sweet and gentle woman who displayed much of her more respectable upbringing by defending her husband to her daughters – "Count yourselves lucky he's not violent; his bark is worse than his bite." – and by refusing to allow her children to accept anything she regarded as charity. 'These mothers lead hard, self-sacrificing lives', wrote one investigator, 'their amazing powers of endurance are only equalled by the skill with which they contrive to keep their families on about half the weekly sums found necessary in the Poor Law Schools for each child's food and clothing.'[25] That compliment might have been meant for Lil Mimms. Equally, it could have been said of Jack, as Kipling said of Tom Herodsfoot: 'He confined himself, as a rule, to beer, which is stupefying and comparatively innocuous: at least, it clogs the legs.'[26]

Just half a dozen houses away, around the corner in Alderminster Road, backing on to the railway, lived another family which was destined to become related to the Mimmses. Dick Jarman was the youngest of seventeen children, the son of a ship's carpenter, born in Greenwich. All his young adult life was spent as a merchant seaman sailing most of the world's shipping lanes, transatlantic, far eastern and antipodean. The description, 'working class Tory' fitted him perfectly: an intensely patriotic man, holding firmly to the belief that the officer class had been born to rule and with an unshakeable belief that he could do any kind of work he put his mind to – a self-confidence which stood him in good stead when he was paid off at the end of a voyage and no other berth was immediately available. The Greenwich Inlaid Linoleum Company in Blackwall Lane always took him on whenever they had enough work, but, like most seamen, he was never happy for long unless he was afloat, and signed on again as a deckhand or steward as soon as an opportunity offered. His patriotism, combined with an adventurous nature, led him to jump ship in Capetown during the Second Boer War, signing on at Pietermaritzburg in a yeomanry regiment as a trooper in the Imperial Light Horse, although he had never before ridden a cavalry horse. On his return to England with a severe bout of malaria, he was nursed back to health by Alice Jackson and her mother. Alice's parents came from Grundisburgh in the depths of Suffolk where they had been in service, but had removed to Bermondsey in the 1870s. Dick Jarman married Alice when they were both 25 and, after the birth of their first child, named after her mother but always known as 'Cis', the family was persuaded to share number 266 Alderminster Road with Alice's parents.

A strip of land some forty feet wide ran between the back gardens of Alderminster road and the railway lines, making an ideal playground for Cis Jarman and her friends where a fire could be lit to bake potatoes. Goods trucks were shunted on to the sidings when out of use and after the maintenance man had been along to fill up the axle boxes with a thick yellow grease, it could be scooped out to serve as 'butter' for playing at grocers' shops. For the same purpose, rust scraped from the underside of the street railings made a good substitute for 'tea'. In the winter it was occasionally worth while to run along beside a shunting engine shouting insults at the driver who retaliated by heaving lumps of coal from the tender to drive the children off. These made a useful addition to the coal cellar. The waste was also a valuable Tom Tiddler's ground for old bones which raised a few pence from a nearby Marine Store (fancy name for George Plummer's rag and bone shop).

Apart from the coal cart and an occasional horse-drawn delivery van, there was very little traffic in the side roads, so it was quite safe to play Alley Gobs (Five Stones) in the gutter, stretch a heavy brewer's rope right across the street for skipping or play Lurkey (Tin Can Tommy) in the roadway. 'Knock down Ginger' is a game familiar to all children, but the houses which lay well below street level in St James's Road were vulnerable to a sophisticated refinement. One child would drop a ball of string twenty feet down into the basement area, the others quietly threaded it through half a dozen door knockers taking the other end up the thirty steps before pulling the string to rattle the knockers. By lying face down, and therefore unseen, on the pavement above, the enjoyment of this game was greatly enhanced by being able to listen to the uninhibited language of the occupiers as they all appeared at their doors at the same time, generally accusing each other's children of causing the nuisance.

The little gang of ten responsible for creating this mayhem comprised Norrie Mimms, Jack and Lil's second daughter, Cis Jarman and her younger sister Doll (Doris), Gladys Gould, the daughter of a Peek Frean van driver, Ed Humphreys (whom Cis eventually married), Bill Luckings and Edie Nye, all three the children of railway workers: Doris and Daisy Timms's father was an office clerk and so quite comfortably off, but the really wealthy one was Hilda Mann, the daughter of an engine driver who, despite having eight children, was considered to be extremely well off by Bermondsey standards with a secure job which brought in four pounds every week.

Their four-week summer holiday was always devoted to the production of a pantomime. The girls, whose province this was, made the hour-long journey on foot to Marks' Penny Bazaar in Rye Lane, Peckham, to buy rolls of crepe paper. The next three weeks were spent making it into costumes, choosing the pantomime, writing the script, squabbling over casting and learning lines. The creeper-covered kitchen wall of 266 Alderminster Road and two over-arching ash trees formed the back-drop and proscenium, and stage properties were ingeniously improvised – a couple of decorated chairs became Cinderella's coach, and a spindly privet made a handy beanstalk for Jack. On the Saturday of the performance any interested adults and all the local children were charged a half-penny admission. Railwaymen at a loose end, including old Bill Maynard from the signal-box, hung over the garden fence adding to the total audience. As soon as a few pence had been collected, one of the cast ran to the nearest greengrocers to buy specked apples and oranges for interval refreshments (Ed Humphreys served there on Saturdays which guaranteed a generous bagful). At the end of the one and a half hour performance the entire cast paraded the streets in costume hoping to make a second collection from their admiring neighbours. Enthusiasm, ingenuity and imagination had to make up for more material things in that period leading up to the First World War.

Neighbours' funerals always fascinated the children who would wait by the hearse to collect any petals which fell from the wreaths for pressing into a book. At such times the street was unnaturally quiet, all the house blinds drawn, door knockers muffled, neighbours and passers-by standing still, the men's heads bared as a mark of respect as the cortege passed. The most elaborate family wreath was usually the 'Gates of Heaven', a two-feet high arch of white flowers topped by a dove and framing a set of double gates made of heavy gauge wire which were always left slightly ajar. As a final flourish, the wreath trailed a large bow of wide satin ribbon.

When Cis Jarman's grandmother died in 1919, a simple funeral was ordered with only a glass-sided hearse drawn by two horses without plumes. The parish church sent a large chaplet of laurel which was said by the neighbours to have signified that she had 'earned her laurels' as an active church worker for St Anne's, Thorburn Square. She was buried at Nunhead cemetery in a common grave. With six adults to each grave and children's coffins piled on top, there was no room for a headstone even if the family could have afforded one. That was a not untypical Bermondsey funeral, but a much more elaborate one was favoured by such as costers' families who spared no expense to put on a show rivalling that of the Lord Mayor.

Charles Booth described an East End funeral of a family of ten. The mother and her eight children had died in a tragic fire, and the father had died the same day of consumption in an infirmary. A public subscription provided a spectacular procession led by a band playing the 'Dead March'. "It's wonderful how much they think of a funeral," commented Booth's companion, "There will be many wishing they too had been burnt, to have such a turn-out as this."[27]

A death in the family was not only an occasion for grief, but brought with it severe financial hardship. A newly-born infant could be buried for thirty shillings, but when the child's body was too long to go under the driver's box -seat the price increased and could then cost between £6 and £10 for the simplest of decent burials.[28] Overriding all other considerations was the dread of having one of the family buried 'on the parish'. A pauper funeral was 'wanting in dignity and respect', and bore with it a degrading stigma on the whole family, even though one in five of the population of England and Wales could expect to be buried by the Guardians.[29] As late as 1923, the Hammersmith Guardians were pilloried for burying a pauper's dissected remains in 'a box unfit even for the carcase of a dog'. That coffin was found to have been constructed of unplaned wood, riddled with knot-holes, without handles, and with only a slip of paper glued to the lid to identify the deceased.[30] One woman expressed the feeling of many more when she told Maud Pember Reeves that she would as soon have the dust-cart call for the body of her child as that "there Black Mariar" – the Poor Law Union's hearse.[31]

Religion played little part in the lives of most of Bermondsey's residents. The church was there for weddings and funerals and the Mission Hall offered a soup kitchen or a coal ticket to the very poor, but regular attendance for worship did not feature amongst their priorities. The vicar of St James's parish displayed some insight when he wrote that, 'Religion to thousands is something associated with happier conditions of life; a luxury which goes with better food and clothing.' He could not refrain from adding, however, that 'the domestic habits of the working classes on Sunday are framed in utter disregard of the church bell.'[32] Their parents' apathy towards religious observance did not absolve their children from regular attendance at St Anne's Sunday school, nor its Band of Hope meetings on Tuesday evenings. They willingly signed the Pledge in ignorance or unconcern as to its promise 'to abstain from all intoxicating drinks as beverages', and cheerfully sang Moody and Sankey's 'Sacred Songs and Solos' – 'Hold the Fort for I am Coming', or 'Throw out the Lifeline across the dark wave/There is a brother whom someone should save', and challenging choruses like

> 'The lips that touch liquor shall never touch mine', and
> 'Dare to be a Daniel, dare to stand alone,
> Dare to pass a public house and bring your money home.'

Even more did they enjoy the highlight of the evening, a magic lantern show which featured staggering drunks and starving children, and other graphic illustrations of earnest temperance songs: accompanying a gloomy picture of a shabby garret where a barefoot boy sat sadly watching the church clock through a curtainless window, the children would sing lustily:

> 'Father, dear father, come home with me now!
> The clock in the steeple strikes one;
> You promised, dear father, that you would come home
> As soon as your day's work was done;
> Our fire has gone out – our house is all dark –
> And mother's been watching since tea,
> With poor brother Benny so sick in her arms,
> And no one to help her but me.
> Come home, come home, come home,
> Please father, dear father, come home.'[33]

The local school was, and still is, in Monnow Road, near enough for the pupils to go home to dinner, except those whose family poverty entitled them to a ticket for a free dinner: they had to assemble in the playground and be marched off in a long line to a hall in Cooper's Road, a humiliation not lost on their more fortunate fellows. The school was held in high esteem. An LCC Inspector reported a few months after the outbreak of war that 'There is an excellent spirit of work among the boys, many of whom come from very poor homes.' The work of the school, he thought, was 'really excellent'.[34] That headmaster, Mr J. Litt, had been at the school for seven years and was undoubtedly a dedicated teacher. In his first few months as head, he had arranged for a supply of spectacles for his poorer children, organised a visit to the New Cross pantomime for 1300 pupils, introduced a school badge to be awarded for special academic or athletic achievement, and persuaded the London County Councillor and popular local doctor, Alfred Salter, to distribute the school prizes. His log book rarely records a complaint, although he was unable to refrain from protesting that 'The Borough Council Election is going on today in the Girls' Dept. and the tobacco fumes are spreading through the whole buildings.'[35]

The girls' school (with its separate entrance, of course) was no less successful and caring an establishment. The girls wore a smart uniform, a brown slip over a Shantung silk blouse, were taken to Southwark Park for 'nature study', and could opt to choose a commercial (French and shorthand/typing) or an industrial course which was geared more towards factory or domestic employment (cooking, laundering and needlework). Twice a year the girls were taken to matinee performances of Shakespeare's plays directed by Ben Greet at the Old Vic theatre in the Waterloo Road, which cost each pupil sixpence. Those performances always concluded with a Harlequinade and were designed specifically for school groups. As soon as the final curtain fell, the cast in costume pranced around the auditorium chasing an actor dressed as a clown and waving a string of sausages on a stick to the great delight, and perhaps relief, of their young audience.

One of the few occasions when the girls and boys joined forces was for the celebration of Empire Day on Queen Victoria's birthday, when the piano was wheeled out to the playground, the

Union Flag run up the flagpole, and the whole assembly, the girls dressed in white with red, white and blue ribbons in their hair, marched around the flag saluting and singing 'Land of Hope and Glory.' The school log book for May 1913 contains a newspaper cutting recording that year's event which featured a 'series of tableaux illustrative of the life, customs, occupations, and dress of the people in Britain's oversea Dominions. Britannia, tall and stately, naturally led the way.' She was followed by Boy Scouts, Girl Guides and other brigades 'marching to martial music, decked and bedizened in the garb peculiar to the many and diverse possessions which go to make up the British Empire.' Following along behind were Canada's ice-maiden, an Australian gold-digger, a Maori, a South African Zulu 'whose wierd war-dance gave an air of gaiety to the proceedings.' Hong Kong was represented by a pig-tailed mandarin, and 'the maid of diminutive foot, whose mincing little gait, though amusing to the on-lookers, was a reminder of a barbarous custom in the land of the Celestial, now happily dying away . . . ' The headmaster concluded the proceedings with an uplifting homily on the duties and responsibilities of true citizenship, 'The children who belong to the English-speaking race', he asserted, 'were the inheritors of an Empire the greatest the world had known', adding that they should 'strive to live up to their inheritance.'[36] His scruffy little beneficiaries might have paused to wonder what share of that glorious inheritance had been bequeathed to them.

The 1870 Education Act and subsequent legislation up to the end of the nineteenth century provided an elementary education for every child. The Education Act of 1902 is lauded by many educational historians as another great leap forward by offering the opportunity of a secondary education for all. The Act created local education authorities empowered to co-ordinate elementary and higher education, and provided what, at the time, was described as 'the ladder from the elementary school to the university,' because it rendered possible the award of scholarships for promising pupils from the elementary schools.[37] This was all rather academic as far as Bermondsey scholars were concerned. Very few of their parents could afford to keep a child at school after the age of fourteen; they needed the income, the cost of clothing and text-books would have been prohibitive, and, it must be admitted, most youngsters preferred to earn a wage, even in a dead-end job, to more of the same chalk and blackboard and pocket-money if they were really lucky. For the most part, families which took advantage of a secondary education for their children were shopkeepers and skilled workmen earning a good, regular wage. Even a dozen years after the reform, only 2½% of those enjoying secondary schooling came from the ranks of the unskilled[38] for whom the provision of free school meals 'on the rates', and regular medical inspection were far more immediately significant. As late as 1922 the South London Mission was still serving more than 50,000 free breakfasts to Bermondsey children,[39] whilst the London School Board's medical officer had reported in 1902 that his staff had scarcely begun to reveal the numbers of children 'whose efficiency in school is damaged by dirt, parasites, chronic diseases of the ears, or impaired visual acuity . . . .'[40] The headmaster of Monnow Road boys' school noted in 1909 that 'Nurse Nash went through the school today and examined the boys' heads.'[41] The school 'nit nurse' treated head-lice, ringworm and impetigo; adenoidal children with blocked sinuses, and those with defective eyesight inhabited every classroom, and rickets, brought on by an inadequate diet, weakened and distorted many a young child's limbs. Of 119 Southwark school-children who were medically examined for the first time, more than half had decayed teeth and ear, nose and throat problems, one-third suffered from defective vision and over 10% had 'consumptive lungs.' These, moreover, were from a secondary school with an average age of fifteen whose parents would have been more than usually caring and concerned for their families' welfare.[42]

Concern that the health of the nation was beginning to deteriorate was brought forcefully to the public's attention by the army authorities who feared that they would be unable to defend the Empire with the poor quality of recruits who had volunteered to fight the Boers; 'a state of things in which no more than two out of five of the population below a certain standard of life are fit to bear arms is a national danger', warned General John Maurice.[43] To Dr Karl Pearson the fault could all be laid at the door of the feckless and improvident who bred injudiciously. 'We have two groups in the community', he claimed, 'one parasitic on the other. The latter thinks of tomorrow and is childless, the former takes no thought and multiplies.'[44] His middle-class Edwardian audience had already begun to limit the size of their families and did not need to be told who the parasites were. Professional couples who married in the last decade of the old century produced an average family of 2.8 children, whilst an unskilled labourer's family averaged 5.11.[45]

Consumption, or T.B. (pulmonary tuberculosis), caused one in seven deaths in Bermondsey, its sufferers fading away in fits of coughing and progressive weakness.[46] It was the scourge of the undernourished and overcrowded, and feared above all other illnesses by the poor as it frequently wiped out whole families. During the Great War two Alderminster Road families suffered in this way. Of the Atkins family, the father died first, followed by his wife, and then, successively, each of their five children as they reached maturity. A near neighbour's family went the same way: the survivors waiting with a resigned fatalism for the next to be struck down by what was once called the 'Captain of the Hosts of Death'. The only known treatment was good food, rest, fresh air and sunshine, none of which were much in evidence in Bermondsey.

In matters of health Bermondsey was very fortunate in one respect at least; it had been blessed with a devoted, even inspired, general practitioner. Alfred Salter had been a brilliant student at Guy's Hospital, graduating with triple first-class honours, winning scholarships, prizes and no less than three gold medals. Joseph Lister himself appointed him to the Lister Institute and before him lay what could have been an honoured academic career as a bacteriologist with a wealthy private practice. Much of Salter's training, however, had been conducted amongst the people of Bermondsey and that experience led him, instead, to choose the life of a poor man's doctor. A vacant shop in Jamaica Road served as Alfred Salter's first surgery where he attended sixty cases a night and charging only sixpence a visit – half the usual rate.

> 'It was not only his low charges which attracted patients: it was the treatment he gave and the way in which he gave it, it was the energy with which he insisted on beds in hospitals for urgent cases and on action by the public authorities in cases of bad sanitation and unhealthy accommodation.'[47]

He became a familiar figure as he did his rounds sitting bolt upright on an old-fashioned 'sit up and beg' bicycle, treating his patients with a courtesy and dignity which led the women to say, "he treats you as though you were a duchess!" Many cases he treated without charge and sent some of his patients to convalesce in the country or by the sea at his own expense. One of Cis Jarman's friends he sent to Switzerland for eight months to return completely cured of her consumptive condition. But it was not only in the field of medicine that his prodigious energy was expended. Within three years of opening his first surgery he became a borough councillor and then a member of the London County Council three years after that. He was a combative, uncompromising figure who saw poverty and injustice and perpetually battled for more and better housing, school meals, sanitation, open spaces and health provision for his constituents. As a pacifist, he espoused the cause of conscientious objectors during the war, employing them in the co-operative bakery he had helped to establish, but even his great popularity could not protect him from physical assaults by enraged 'patriotic' mobs. A convinced socialist, he organised relief for the families of men who struck work for better conditions and provided 'make work' schemes for the unemployed. Gladys Gould's father, who lived in Alderminster Road with his wife and six children, had been laid off by Peek Frean's from his job as delivery van driver and was found work with other men scraping pigeon droppings from the spire of St Anne's church by an arrangement Salter had made with the vicar; the doctor paid their wages. It sometimes irked him that people did not protest more, but, equally, he understood the reasons as he wrote in a letter to a friend, 'their work, their partial education, their neighbourhood, the exhausted atmosphere they breathe, their divorce from Nature – this environment has blunted their will to act for change.'[48] Alfred Salter protested on their behalf, holding unshakeable views on most subjects – socialism, temperance, pacifism, Christianity. He devoted every waking hour to his 'causes', and expected everyone else to be equally committed. He could not have been an easy man to work with, but he was, perhaps, the best friend the people of Bermondsey ever had.

Most wives worked if there was work available in the factories, or, if their children were young or they were too old or disabled, in some home employment. Cis Jarman's grandmother earned six shillings a week laundering for the local constabulary. Every Saturday her husband took the clean laundry to each of the eight district police stations and collected the dirty washing. Wash-day stretched into a week as each of the twenty-four men were issued with one pair of socks, one pair of long underpants, a flannel vest, an Oxford shirt, an armband and two handkerchiefs. These she would wash, mangle, dry, iron, darn and sew on buttons for just 3d. a man. All this washing blocked the copper flue with soot. The copper itself was a built-in brick affair, heated by a fire underneath the cauldron. More often than most of their neighbours, the children were sent to Jimmy Hinson's shop for a ha'porth of gun powder in a screw of paper. This was thrown in, the fire door quickly closed and firmly held shut with the yard broom held at arms-length: the resultant explosion cleared the soot as effectively, and much more cheaply, than calling in the chimney sweep.

Before she married, Alice Jarman worked as a toothpick cutter in a City backstreet for Cooper, Dennison and Walkden. Once her children came along this skill allowed her to work from home. Twice a week Alice's daughters would collect two or three circular bundles, each a foot in diameter, holding a thousand goose feathers, from Cooper, Dennison's factory beside the Surrey Canal. These, Alice cut into toothpicks and quill pens with a long thin-bladed knife, filling the room with fluff and feather fronds, but carefully preserving the feather tips which were returned to the factory to be made into tippets and hat decorations. A week's intensive work produced about 5000 picks and quills which earned her three shillings. That income, though small, was invaluable if her husband was out of work or at sea and her allowance was late.

On the night of April 18th 1910, the 'Minnehaha', returning from New York with Dick Jarman on board as steward, went aground in fog on a sandbar in the Scilly Isles. It was three weeks before the weather cleared sufficiently to allow the crew to be taken off, during which time, it was said, they drank the island dry, but for Alice and her daughters life was much less pleasant as a merchant seaman was paid off from the day after a vessel's stranding or sinking and a wife's allowance stopped. They survived on credit and with the help of neighbours until the curate of St Anne's, the Revd. Balfour, nephew of the politician, called with a gift of 30s. and the words, "That will help you with food for the children." As he walked away, he stopped and returned to hand her another £1 – a small fortune for Alice whose only other income came from her quill cutting. The 'Minnehaha' was eventually re-floated and repaired, but finally sunk by a German submarine's torpedo in 1917 off the Fastnet Rock.

At the outbreak of war Dick Jarman was at sea. On his return, Alice begged him not to go back. He volunteered for war work instead, and was directed to Woolwich Arsenal but after three days sitting at long tables with the local workhouse paupers, stamping 'W.D.' on horses' nosebags, he volunteered spending the next four years on troopships or unloading supplies around the harbour at Calais. Jack Mimms, for all his other faults, was no coward. He volunteered on the outbreak of war and served for four years in France as a Royal Army Medical Corps orderly, ending the hostilities with the rank of sergeant. That apart, very little is known of his experiences because those First World War army service records which were not destroyed by German incendiary bombs during the Second World War, were done for by the National Fire Brigade's water pumps, but until his life's end Jack's eyes sparkled at the mention of French women.

The Great War brought chronic food shortages to the civilian population even to those who, in normal times, could scarcely afford an adequate diet. A crude rationing system operated which entitled everyone to a specified weekly amount of certain foodstuffs, but without nominating any particular supplier, so that when word went round that a shop had just received a supply of margarine, meat, potatoes or butter, for example, everyone queued there hoping it would not run out before they reached the counter. Wives and children spent a good part of every day joining queue after queue for anything, rationed or unrationed, which might suddenly and unexpectedly become available.

Cis Jarman was fourteen in March 1919. Her mother had hoped she could continue her schooling for at least another year, but her father had been demobbed from the Royal Marines and could find no work whatever in the 'land fit for heroes'. There was no choice but for Cis to find a job. When the term ended the school assembled to be dismissed by the headmistress, Catherine Aggutter, who, in the course of her address, remarked, "There is one girl in this hall who is just fourteen, and she has told me that she is leaving because her father is unemployed. I imagine she thinks she is going to keep the family!" – a cruel, if thoughtless, comment which amused her audience, but left one child deeply humiliated. Miss Aggutter had, however, spoken nothing but the truth for Cis Jarman's wages of seventeen shillings a week at Peek Frean's biscuit factory had to keep her family until her father found employment again.

Her initiation into adult life at Peek Frean's meant having her head inspected for lice and, with her mother's permission, to be told the bare facts of life by a supervisor on the grounds that 'some of the girls have had a less sheltered upbringing', 'had knocked around a bit', and were 'rough and ready with their talk.' Her hours were 8am to 6pm with one hour for dinner, no other breaks and four hours on Saturday. Dressed in white cap and overalls, her first job was breaking up ginger nuts by hand. These were 'mis-shapes' and biscuits sent back to the factory by retailers to be 'processed' and returned for sale cheaply as broken biscuits. A biscuit held in each palm was cracked by snapping the fingers. The firm thoughtfully provided a set of eight finger-stalls to prevent a bleeding finger from contaminating the biscuits. Any which fell on the floor were picked up, scraped and dusted off by little old Mary, well into her 70s, for sale as dog biscuits. Peek Frean's had a staff of over 2000, a high proportion of them women, and, for those days, were considered to be enlightened employers, even providing a surgery with a nurse and doctor in constant attendance.

Atkinson's Perfume Factory in Southwark Park Road also employed many local girls. Jack and Lil's two elder daughters, Ada and Norrie, both worked there with Doll Jarman, Norrie's great childhood friend and Cis's younger sister. Atkinson's hours and wages were very similar to those of Peek Frean, but the girls' work consisted of wrapping up boxes of face powder and tablets of soap and filling perfume bottles with 'Californian Poppy', which filled the house with its sickly sweet scent when they returned home from working in that department.

With Dick unemployed in 1919, the only steady income was the 17s a week Cis earned at Peek Frean. An application for out-relief to the Poor Law Authorities produced a Relieving Officer who demanded to be allowed to inspect their home "to see what sort of a house it was, and if it was kept clean". To a proud man, this intrusion was an insult; Dick refused the demand and, in turn, was refused relief. He and Alice turned to making rag rugs from old woollen clothing bought from the rag and bone shop. Between them they could make a rug a week which would sell for £1. in the local pubs.

When no help was available from the Poor Law, short of surrendering to the workhouse, and no unemployment insurance until 1913, a long period without work drove some men to the desperate expedient of begging. Robert Tressall (the pen-name of a Hastings house-painter) described a march through the main street of 'Mugsborough' by some three hundred unemployed men bearing banners and collecting boxes:

> 'Haggard and pale, shabbily or raggedly dressed, their boots broken and down at heel, they slouched past. Some of them stared about with a dazed or half wild expression, but most of them walked with downcast eyes or staring blankly straight in front of them. They appeared utterly broken-spirited and ashamed . . . "This sort of thing does the town a lot of 'arm," remarked Slyme; "it oughtn't to be allowed; the police ought to stop it. It's enough to drive all the gentry out of the place!"[49]

In the years following the Great War, such demonstrations were supplemented by the many ex-servicemen's bands – half a dozen ill-dressed men, shuffling along but holding their heads high and their shoulders back, wearing their campaign medals, wielding a drum, an accordian, a penny whistle and a tambourine, and proffering a cocoa tin nailed to a long stick as though to distance themselves from the occupation in which they found themselves engaged.

References

Much of this chapter is owed to the written and oral memories of the author's aunt, Alice Humphreys (Cis Jarman)

[1] Bateman, E., and Le Brun, G., (1894), Francis, Day and Hunter Ltd.

[2] Pember-Reeves, 'Round About a Pound a Week' pp 39/40

[3] Willis, 'A Book of London's Yesterdays', pp.220/1

[4] Smith, F.B., 'The People's Health', p.391

[5] Aronson, H., 'Liberalism in the Village', Nation, 18 MAY 1912: quot. in Gilbert, 'The Evolution of National Insurance in G.B.', p.226.

[6] Bosanquet, 'Social Work in London', p.295

[7] ibid., p.300

[8] Cruickshank, 'Roaring Century', pp.185/6

[9] 'The Times', 2 JAN 1909.

[10] Gilbert, 'The Evolution of National Insurance in G.B.', p.49

[11] Brockway, 'Bermondsey Story', p.102
[12] Beasley, 'The Bitter Cry Heard and Heeded', p.50
[13] Pember-Reeves, 'Round About a Pound a Week', p.5
[14] Booth, C., 'Life and Labour of the People in London', Vol 4, p.127
[15] ibid., Vol 2, App.36
[16] Masterman, 'From the Abyss,' p.12
[17] Morrison, 'A Child of the Jago', p.187
[18] Rolph, 'London Particulars', p.160
[19] Burke, 'The Streets of London', p.137
[20] Davies, M.L., 'Maternity: Letters from Working Women', pp.18/19
[21] ibid. pp.90/91
[22] Pember-Reeves, 'Round About a Pound a Week', pp.26–28
[23] ibid., pp.2, 3 and 75
[24] ibid., p.145
[25] Leff and Blunden, 'Riverside Story', p.9
[26] Kipling, R., 'The Record of Badalia Herodsfoot' - Keating, 'Working Class Stories of the 1890s', p.16
[27] Fried and Elman, 'Charles Booth's London', pp.277/8
[28] Pember-Reeves, 'Round About a Pound a Week', p.69, and Rolph, 'London Particulars', p.67
[29] Treble, 'Urban Poverty in Britain', p.188
[30] Richardson, 'Death, Dissection and the Destitute', p.257/8
[31] Pember-Reeves, 'Round About a Pound a Week', p.68
[32] Booth, C., 'Life and Labour of the People in London', Vol.4. pp.130/1
[33] Turner, 'The Parlour Song Book', p.246
[34] LCC/EO/DIV8/MON/LB/2, 2 DEC 1914, Greater London R.O.
[35] LCC/EO/DIV8/MON/LB/1, 1907–9, Greater London R.O.
[36] LCC/EO/DIV8/MON/LB/2, 22 MAY 1913, Greater London R.O.
[37] Curtis, 'History of Education in G.B.', p.319
[38] Horn, 'The Victorian and Edwardian Schoolchild', p.67
[39] Leff and Blunden, 'Riverside Story', pp.19/20
[40] Newsholme, 'Fifty Years in Public Health', p.383
[41] LCC/EO/DIV8/MON/LB/1, 4 JUN 1909, Greater London R.O.
[42] Reeves, 'Recollections of a School Attendance Officer', pp.79/80
[43] Gilbert, 'The Evolution of National Insurance in G.B.', p.84.
[44] Newsholme, 'Fifty Years in Public Health', p.407
[45] Briggs, 'A Social History of England', p.249
[46] Leff and Blunden, 'Riverside Story', p.2
[47] Brockway, 'Bermondsey Story,' p.24
[48] ibid., p.45
[49] Tressall, 'The Ragged Trousered Philanthropists', pp.240/1

CHAPTER SEVENTEEN

THE NEW LEISURED CLASS

'The Means Test man came – he would be coming again next Friday – and sized you up and down to see how much food you needed and then allowed you not quite enough money to buy it.'

– Walter Brierley (1935)[1]

'You can't get much meat for threepence, but you can get a lot of fish-and-chips.'

– George Orwell (1937)[2]

The Red Flag was hoisted over Bermondsey Town Hall in November 1922. The flag, it is true, contained the Borough's arms in its top left-hand corner, but it was predominantly and defiantly red, thereby provoking an enraged outcry from the Bermondsey Labour Party's political opponents. Ten years earlier Labour had gained a single seat on the Borough Council, but Dr Alfred Salter and his wife, Ada, had led the campaign which produced a 38-16 Labour majority in that year, and Ada Salter became London's first woman mayor.

Shortly after the election, the Salters gave Fairby Grange to the corporation as a convalescent home for Bermondsey's citizens. The Grange, a modernised seventeenth century farmhouse with extensive grounds at Hartley in Kent, had been bought by the Salters five years before as a convalescent home for their patients, but now it acquired a second valuable purpose as a horticultural nursery. Its grounds produced the flowers which Ada Salter had then had planted wherever there was a churchyard or a derelict site in the borough. Within two years her 'Beautification Committee' had planted 9,000 saplings, grown at Fairby Grange, – elms, poplars, planes, acacias – in Bermondsey's soot-begrimed and featureless streets. The Council encouraged everyone to help in beautifying the borough by giving away bulbs, seeds, and bedding plants: the Horticultural Society donated window-boxes for them, and visitors came from all over Britain and abroad to marvel at the transformation. Even the Daily Telegraph was moved to describe these efforts as 'an object lesson in what can be done to beautify even the poorest neighbourhood.'[3]

The flowers and the trees were a hopeful sign that life in Bermondsey could be better. The new Council immediately embarked on an ambitious slum-clearance programme with great enthusiasm, often in the face of central government obstruction. They replaced near-derelict areas with 'village garden-style' cottages and airy flats – schemes which were widely admired by both British and foreign municipal housing authorities. Within ten years Bermondsey was said to have done 'more slum-clearance than the whole of the rest of London put together,'[4] and Ritchie Calder remarked, 'whenever I go to Bermondsey, I come away feeling that I want to take a soap-box and go round the country preaching the gospel of slum clearance with Bermondsey as my text.'[5]

Fairby Grange, the country's first municipal convalescent home, was only one of the Council's initiatives in the field of public health. To treat the scourge of tuberculosis, it established an up-to-the-minute solarium and medical centre, encouraged the supply of tuberculin-tested milk, ran health education campaigns, and even reserved six beds in a Swiss sanatorium for Bermondsey patients. A dental clinic for expectant mothers and infant welfare centres contributed to a thirty per cent reduction in infant mortality within five years, and the death rate amongst mothers in confinement became one of the lowest in London. Many other enterprises and amenities – public baths, laundries, a library, a concert hall, an orchestra – were added in the 1920s and '30s, and all these initiatives taken together came to be known as 'Bermondsey's Revolution.'[6] As this process of transformation was beginning to get under way, Alfred Salter, in typically trenchant manner, predicted that

> 'We may yet become the most beautiful as well as the most healthy borough in London. The wealthy manufacturers and wharfingers and the rich shareholders who make their dividends out of Bermondsey's grime and toil, live on the Surrey Hills and in other pleasant places of the earth. Let them . . . Well, we who *do* live here, belonging as we do for the most part to the poorest of the poor, will teach the world a lesson in citizenship and real patriotism.'[7]

Despite these challenging words and the vigorous reforms its Council had introduced, Bermondsey was still a deprived area as compared with much of London. The brief boom of the immediate post-war period was quickly followed by a slump in trade. By the summer of 1921 the total number of registered unemployed in Britain reached two millions. Jack Mimms found it difficult to find regular work and on two separate occasions he borrowed £50 from his uncle Matt and from his brother, Albert, who kept a pub in Woolwich, to set himself up in business as a carman with his own horse and cart. He also tried a barrow in Southwark Park Road market, but none of his enterprises succeeded – perhaps predictably. A decade later Jack enjoyed a brief period of unparalleled prosperity. His uncle, Matt Wood, his mother's brother, regularly organised the City of London River and Docks Regatta, an annual event which ran between Cherry Garden and Greenwich Piers. Later, Matt Wood extended his activities to the promotion of a crew of Thames watermen in a four-scull race at the Henley Regatta. Jack could display endearing characteristics and impress people with a pleasant manner. Matt employed him to visit City offices and the West End shops soliciting for prizes, in cash and in kind, for each of these regatta events. Much of it finished up at 250 St James's Road. May, his only daughter still living at home at the time, described their front parlour as an Aladdin's Cave, and on the proceeds Jack and Lil could afford two nights a week at the music hall and weekends spent with friends in the Kent countryside. But in the mid-1920's the major share of supporting his parents, his younger brother and four unmarried sisters aged between 8 and 17 fell upon Jack and Lil's eldest son, Bert.

Bert was born on Christmas Day, 1900. At the age of 3 he had survived an epidemic of scarlet fever which killed his six year old elder brother, and although he was Jack and Lil's third child to be born, he was the eldest survivor. In common with most Bermondsey children, he left school at the age of fourteen, but he was offered an indenture as an apprentice electrician, and, encouraged by his mother, he spent three evenings a week at the Borough Polytechnic in the Old Kent Road to earn his City and Guild's certificate. Towards the end of the Great War the Royal Air Force claimed him for fourteen months but, once qualified as a journeyman, he found employment at Victoria Station's Grosvenor Hotel in Buckingham Palace Road – one of London's most fashionable. In his late twenties he rose to become head electrician at the Grosvenor with a wage of £7 per week, double the average earnings of an electrical wireman.[8] With such a wage coming in to the house, Jack could devote his time to growing mushrooms and breeding chickens in the back yard of 250 St James's Road and propping up the public bar of the 'Sultan'. Even so, Bert could still afford to treat his younger sisters – chocolate Easter eggs with their names on and their first real Christmas presents which were not just an orange and a handful of nuts. It was through one of his sisters, Norrie, that Bert got to know Doll Jarman, Cis's younger sister. Although she was eight years his junior, Doll was a strong personality, determined and purposeful, traits which happily complemented Bert's quiet and gentle temperament. Doll stood out in a crowd with her black hair and flashing dark eyes, and together, often with one or more of Bert's sisters in tow, they enjoyed the West End cinemas, the Locarno ballroom, summer holidays on the Kent coast and Lilian Baylis's opera and drama productions at the Old Vic. Packing soap at Atkinson's perfume factory scarcely taxed Doll Jarman's energies, so Bert interceded with the Grosvenor's head waiter who took her on as a waitress. Her wage was miniscule, but the gratuities more than generous, so that together they were earning between £10 and £12 a week, and could comfortably contemplate marriage. The first marriage in the Jarman family, however, was Doll's elder sister, Cis, who married her childhood sweetheart, Ed Humphreys, on Christmas Day, 1929, at St Anne's, Thorburn Square, one of Bermondsey's very few architectural gems. It was celebrated in style in the Jarman's front parlour with their best Japanese tea service on display, brought home from one of Dick's Far Eastern voyages, but pride of place was given to a magnificent two-tiered wedding cake donated by Peek Frean in recognition of Cis's ten years' service.

'Her wage was miniscule, but the gratuities more than generous.'

Two days later Cis and Ed left London for good. The South Western Railway Company employed Ed as a welder and was transferring him to their maintenance depot at Exmouth Junction just outside Exeter. They were happy to go: they both knew the area from holidays spent with Ed's adoptive mother who had removed from Bermondsey a few years earlier, but it was a sad blow to the Jarmans. They were a close-knit family and there was nothing to keep them in London. Both Alice and Dick's parents were dead. Dick's brothers had mostly emigrated to America, and Alice was only too pleased to find an excuse to get away from her coarse and spiteful eldest sister, Emily Huxstep, who repeatedly hounded and bullied her two younger sisters into lending her money or clothes to pawn. Bert, in his 30th year, must have felt by then that he had discharged any duty he owed to his mother and, in any case, by the autumn of 1930 only Jack and Lil's two youngest daughters remained at home. Moreover, he and Doll had been engaged for three years, so that he had no hesitation in agreeing to join the Jarmans. It was, in many ways, the best move the six of them could have made, but with hindsight they could not have chosen a worse time to uproot themselves from dirty, smelly London for the healthy air of south Devon.

At the end of 1929, one in nine of Britain's workers was unemployed: a year later almost one in five were out of work and the level of unemployment was still rising.[9] The panic which had gripped New York's Stock Exchange on October 24th, 1929, triggered the sale of thirteen million shares on that one day alone. Businesses and individuals were ruined overnight as the bubble of frantic speculation finally burst, plunging the USA into a severe depression: American banks called in their foreign loans, creating a financial crisis of world-wide proportions. From 1931 until 1935 the number of those officially classified as unemployed in Great Britain never fell below two millions, while in the winter of 1932-3 unemployment reached its highest point when almost three million workers, a quarter of the insured working population, were out of work. The official statistics excluded large groups of workers such as agricultural labourers, the self-employed and most married women, so that the total number of unemployed was almost certainly higher than official figures revealed.[10] By adding back those who were out of work but not registered, together with the families of the unemployed, commentators have estimated that in the worst months of the slump at least six million people were living on the dole – that 'shadowy borderline between malnutrition and slow starvation', as Claud Cockburn described it.[11]

In the eyes of some, the unemployed man was to be envied as a member of the new leisured class. The Girls' Realm Guild made charitable grants for professional training to 'girls of gentle birth who are obliged to earn their living.' Its Exmouth Branch was addressed by the Revd. W. Kirk, who asked his audience to loud cries of approval,

> "Am I not justified in asking if the leisured classes of 1900 have become the deserving poor of 1930, and to go further to say that the deserving poor of 1900 have undoubtedly become the leisured classes of 1930? . . . The poor who are now our leisured classes have little or no fear of responsibility – they need have no fear of unemployment, no fear of ill-health, and no fear of loved ones being left unprovided for when they passed on. They have no fear of having to fill in those dreadful income-tax returns, because they do not have them."[12]

Exmouth was scarcely a bustling centre of industrial or commercial activity. A sleepy, somewhat smug and decorous, seaside resort which woke up only with the arrival of its summer visitors, would not be an entirely unfair description of this little town of 15,000 people spread out behind two miles of yellow, sandy beach between the estuary of the Exe and the red sandstone cliffs of Orcombe Point. By the autumn of 1930 the whole Jarman family, including Ed Humphreys and Bert Mimms, was established in a large four-bedroomed terrace house in an area of Exmouth devoted to working-men's dwellings, known locally as 'Carter's Colony'. The 'Colony', as it is still referred to in the town, had been built on land reclaimed from the Exe estuary during the previous century when it had been poorly drained and known as 'The Marsh' or 'The Green Slime' on account of its condition when each summer it dried out and exuded an appalling smell to the great annoyance of the town.[13] Its acquisition by the Carter family is a fine example of late Victorian business acumen. Alfred Augustus Carter was a man of many talents, an accountant, founder of the steamship company and building firm which bore his name and a part-time dentist.

Using a corkscrew with a hook on the end attached to a swivel, he could pull a tooth with one twist of his wrist. This devilish contrivance of his own invention earned him sixpence a tooth. A man of such enterprise soon found his way on to the Urban District Council when 'The Marsh', now properly drained, was offered to the corporation in 1895 for use as a recreation ground. The council had a reputation for indecision and, while it was dithering, Alfred Augustus Carter's son, John, learned of the opportunity and slipped in to buy up the land for cheap housing.[14]

Carter's houses in 'The Colony' were solidly built terrace properties, their baths, fireplaces and other fittings came from demolished properties of another era, but the house the Jarmans eventually rented for £1 a week in Halsdon Road had a fine view across the mile-wide estuary of the Exe, and its abundant cockle grounds, to the little village of Starcross in the distance – a far cry from Bermondsey's grimy streets and smoky factories. They could not have known that within a very few years they would be driven out by an infestation of large, black swamp cockroaches, but at the time the house suited them very well with bedrooms for the Jarmans, the Humphreys and, of course, separate rooms for Doll and Bert. They were well satisfied until they came to look for work. For some time their only income was Ed's £1.10s a week as a railway welder. Doll found part-time, casual work at Clapp's Cafe, an up-market establishment in Rolle Street, but it took months of searching before Bert was taken on by young Jim Smerdon who had a small business installing electrical wiring and servicing motors and generators. "The doorbell rang, and I saw what I thought was another commercial traveller", recalled Jim Smerdon, "He straightened his tie and stood up straight. This was Bert Mimms, a very quiet man." But Smerdon had not long started up in business and could offer only casual work at first, but even that was welcome in the early months of 1931.

Bert and Doll had been engaged for four years and now, with the prospect of, at least, part-time work they decided to marry on Boxing Day, 1931. On Christmas Eve, however, lack of work obliged Jim Smerdon to lay Bert off. Despite this blow, they went ahead with their plans, but the wedding at Withycombe parish church, which encompassed 'The Colony', was inevitably a somewhat subdued affair. Marriage 'on the dole' was not looked on with much favour in Exmouth or elsewhere. Exeter's evening paper reported that on that same Boxing Day fifty couples were married in batches of five at Pontypridd register office, 'Nearly half the bridegrooms were unemployed,' it added soberly.[15] Captain Harvie Watt, addressing the Exmouth branch of the National Citizen's Union had been less inhibited as he condemned the government for failing to stamp out 'dole abuses'. "Getting married on public money – I wish we could all do it," he commented, adding that the authorities "should see to it that no people went straight from the unemployment bureau to the marriage registry."[16]

'The dole' was a term used indiscriminately, and especially by the press, to describe any payment made to those who were unemployed. More correctly, it should only have referred to relief given to those who had lost, or had never been entitled to, benefits under the unemployment regulations. Since the 1911 National Insurance Act weekly contributions had been levied on both employers and employees to create a fund out of which an unemployed person was paid a standard rate of benefit as of right. Once he had exhausted his legal entitlement, or for some reason it had been disallowed, a workman could apply for what at different times was variously described as 'uncovenanted', 'extended', or 'transitional' payments, i.e. the dole. Any such application had to be made to the Public Assistance Committee (PAC) of the local authority and was subject to an individual means test. The PACs were the successors to the Poor Law Guardians whose functions had been abolished in 1929, but inevitably many of those who had been elected as Guardians continued in office as nominated members of PACs. More significantly, perhaps, the paid officials who served the Committees by investigating the means and needs of applicants for 'transitional' relief were the same people who, as Poor Law Relieving Officers, had previously determined the fate of those who applied to the Guardians for outdoor relief or for admission to the workhouse as destitute paupers. Not surprisingly, they carried with them into their new role the attitudes they had learned to adopt when dealing with the old and the sick, the scroungers, the work-shy and the malingerers. The Means Test investigator became the most hated and feared of men, whose attitudes and activities left a legacy of deep resentment amongst families who had never before come into contact with the Poor Law and had never expected to have to apply to anyone for a charitable handout from a body which had the right to demand admission to their house, to check their rent book, assess the value of their furniture and belongings, or require them to sell or pawn an item of jewellery. In his novel 'Means Test Man', Walter Brierley described the mental anguish of Jane Cook, whose husband had long been out of work, as she waited in trepidation and loathing for the inspector's monthly visit:

> 'It was a big thing for her to swallow the visits of the Means Test investigator; she would never have believed such a thing could come to her – never. Fancy demanding to see her rent book, insurance policies, sick-club card and bank-book. The bank-book; it showed that you weren't much while they could pry into that.'[17]

Originally, all benefit could be withheld if an applicant could be accused of 'not genuinely seeking work'. The burden of disproving the allegation lay on the claimant who was required to prove otherwise by specifying precisely when and to whom he had applied for a vacancy. This produced a senseless daily trudge from workplace to workplace enquiring after jobs which everyone knew did not exist, and the often fruitless request to the foreman to sign a chit confirming that an application for work had been made. That regulation was abolished in April 1930, but its effect lingered as evidenced two years later when an Exeter man's dole had been stopped after a Labour Exchange official had called on him one afternoon to find him pottering in his garden instead of being out in search of work.[18] Much resentment was directed at those who chose to fill their idle hours unproductively, and especially so if they sought some solace in escapist entertainment. Having noticed large queues outside Exeter's King's Hall cinema and surmised that half of them were unemployed men, the Revd. Arthur Lancefield urged Parliament to pass a law to 'prevent any person receiving the dole (from) entering a place of entertainment at the country's cost'.[19] That demand provoked a voluminous adverse correspondence in the local press which, in general, supported the views of an American researcher who asked unemployed men in Greenwich what it was that attracted them to the cinema. "The pictures help you live in another world for a little while", said one, and another answered, "Pictures are my first choice, because they make you think for a little while that life is all right."[20]

Shortly after their marriage Doll and Bert had moved away from their family in Halsdon Road to rent a couple of rooms for ten shillings a week over a shop, but still in 'The Colony'. In one respect, at least, their marriage proved to be an unwise step. Two months earlier the government, as part of a series of cost-cutting measures, introduced what it described as 'Anomalies Regulations'. The main effect of these fell upon married women and provided that unless a married woman had *since her marriage* paid a certain number of contributions she would be disallowed any unemployment benefit, no matter how many contributions she may have paid before marriage. Her benefit could only be restored if she could satisfy the authorities that she was normally employed, would seek work, and could reasonably hope to obtain such work in the district.[21] Despite having been almost continuously employed and paying contributions since leaving school ten years earlier, Doll did not qualify for unemployment insurance because the opportunities for work in her trade occurred in Exmouth only during the summer months.

Since moving from Bermondsey, Dick Jarman had been quite unable to find any regular employment. He was in his mid-fifties but his mainly outdoor life had kept him fitter than most men of that age. Above all, he was determined and resourceful. In the herring fishing season the trawlers occasionally took on a casual deck-hand, an opportunity Dick took when it was available. At other times he would borrow a hand-barrow, decorate it in the manner of a cockney coster-monger, pile it high with fruit and vegetables, and hawk it around Exmouth's streets. The summer months found him following the ebbing tide on the Exe estuary's extensive cockle grounds. Once washed, boiled, and served up on little white china plates, he would hawk his cockles from pub to pub. These and other casual enterprises kept him occupied and earning a few shillings from spring to early autumn, but by the September of 1932 his savings were exhausted and still no employment offered. His legal entitlement to unemployment benefit had long since been exhausted, since one of the government's economy measures had restricted the statutory benefit period to twentysix weeks in any one benefit year. He could, however, have applied to the local Public Assistance Committee for 'transitional relief' – the dole. This would have amounted to a maximum of 23s.3d a week – 15s.3d. for himself, plus 8s. for Alice as his only adult dependant.

In order to understand why Dick and Alice failed to qualify for any benefit whatever, not even that niggardly 23s.3d., it is necessary to go back to the government's cost-cutting exercises of the previous year. Until November 1931, the payment of 'transitional relief' had been subject to an *individual* means test. From that date, however, relief was only paid following a *family* means test. This pernicious innovation meant simply that the total income of a complete household living together was assessed against their supposed 'needs'. The household living at Halsdon Road at that time comprised Dick and Alice Jarman, Ed and Cis Humphreys and their infant daughter, Audrey. Their 'needs' would have been assessed as:

Dick	15s. 3d.
Alice	8s. 0d.
Ed.	15s. 3d.
Cis	8s. 0d.
Audrey	2s. 0d.
	48s. 6d.

and no one in that household would have been entitled to any relief whatever if the household's total income exceeded 48s. 6d. The only wage earner was Ed, but he had just left his 30s. a week job with the S.W. Railway to become the caretaker of the Exmouth Pavilion which was due to be opened the following year. His new wage was 50s a week. It was a good wage for him, but, as it exceeded the supposed needs of the whole family of five by 1s.6d. a week, it precluded Dick and Alice from receiving any benefit at all. One solution would have been for the older couple to move away and rent rooms elsewhere. In fact, many thousands of families were broken up for that very reason – old age pensioners and youngsters who had a job were almost obliged to leave the family home to enable those who remained to qualify for relief. Instead, the Jarman family closed ranks. Doll and Bert gave up their two rooms and moved back into Halsdon Road, adding their occasional earnings to the total pool to pay the rent and buy food. Cis described how they lived:

> 'You could get a breast of lamb for 2½d. so breast of lamb turned up cooked in all manner of ways. Also, you could buy

3d worth of bones from the butcher and make a stew with dumplings and vegetables, also again you could make a meatless stew, just water, Oxos, Pkt. of Edward's dessicated soup, vegetables and dumplings. Egg and chips were a treat. Also the fish man came round, he gave you 4 Dabs (small plaice) for 6d., and skimmed milk for 1½d. a pint, so there were lots of rice puddings. Tea time would be bread and jam . . . We used to go round the orchards picking up apples. And, we would steal Mangel Wurzels (like swedes) and fallen apples, so we had lots of apple pies. As for clothes, we would have one decent dress and we used to take you kiddies to the park at Exmouth, then come home and wash the dress ready for the next day. Doll would go to Woolworths and buy different coloured cotton material for 6d. a yard and she would make a child's little 2-piece suit for 6d.'

In 1934 eleven unemployed men and women broadcast their experiences of living on the dole for the BBC. One wife said:

"My husband never changes his dole money, but although he doesn't keep a halfpenny pocket money, still we can't manage. And we don't waste nothing. And there's no enjoyment comes out of our money – no pictures, no papers, no sports. Everything's patched and mended in our house. What's gone is past, but I wouldn't like to live a minute of my life over again. With all the struggling you can't manage. All the struggling is just for food."[22]

Jim Smerdon's work fell off in the summer months and Bert spent that time caring for his young son, taking him to his allotment in Phear Avenue where he grew vegetables. Clapp's Cafe was busy in the summer, but slack outside the season, so that Doll was generally employed in the summer and Bert during the winter months. Cooper Dennison in Bermondsey occasionally sent batches of quills by train to Exmouth for Alice to work on, and once the Exmouth Pavilion opened, Cis and Doll could earn 15 shillings a week as usherettes in the evenings. As a couple of cheeky, self-confident 'cockneys', they were always known as 'Gert and Daisy', and Ed, a well-built man with a commanding presence, became its commissionaire. Whenever work slackened, Alice, Cis and Doll resorted to the pawnbroker; their engagement rings spent much of the 1930s in hock, and jewellery bought in the relatively affluent '20s never was redeemed; the fines had become too expensive to repay.

Unemployment is always a desperate experience for those who want to work and are used to regular employment. The financial consequences can, to an extent, be relieved, but it is the apparent futility of a life which has no immediate purpose which is so soul-destroying. Stephen Spender expressed it well:

> 'Now they've no work, like better men
> Who sit at desks and take much pay.
> They sleep long nights and rise at ten
> To watch the hours that drain away.'[23]

Having to defer to the 'better men who sit at desks' – the Labour Exchange clerks, the Public Assistance Committee members, the means test investigators – saps a man's self-esteem and damages his pride. It may be illogical, but a sense of personal failure, even of guilt, sets in. Bert was by nature a quiet, unassertive man and his experiences in the 1930s scarred him. He never quite recovered his self-confidence in all his 83 years. Was it better, one wonders, to be unemployed with some 300 others in comfortable middle-class Exmouth where there was money about and always the chance of an odd job, but where you stood out as being on the dole in contrast to most of your neighbours, or in one of the distressed areas where, at least, everyone was in the same boat? 'It makes a great deal of difference', thought George Orwell, 'when things are the same for everybody,'[24] The Pilgrim Trust in its detailed study of 1930s unemployment considered that in areas of reasonable prosperity 'the long-unemployed man was a more isolated figure, his 'failure' more apparent to him and to others, his poverty more conspicuous when set against the affluence of his neighbours, his bitterness the greater.'[25]

Given the duration of the economic slump, the scale of unemployment it created, and the misery it caused, it is remarkable that the popular response was so subdued, even in those areas where unemployment encompassed almost the entire working population. It was as if a catastrophe of such enormity could only be regarded as an Act of God against which it was futile to resist or protest.

The only sustained campaign to bring the plight of the

workless to public attention came from the Communist-inspired National Unemployed Workers' Movement (NUWM) led by Wal Hannington. The NUWM organised protest demonstrations designed to attract publicity. Five days before Christmas two hundred unemployed men lay down across Oxford Street, eight abreast and head to toe, bringing London's West End traffic to a complete standstill for hours. A few days later, another hundred men invaded the Ritz Hotel's Grill Room in Piccadilly and demanded to be served tea for which each offered to pay twopence. On another occasion a thirty-feet long banner was unfurled from the top of the Monument as City office workers left for lunch.[26] Such newsworthy stunts gained wide public attention even though the paid-up membership of the NUWM was never large; a little over 20,000 when the total of unemployed exceeded 2 millions.[27] What really attracted widespread support, however, were the six national 'Hunger Marches' it organised with impressive thoroughness against such targets as the Means Test and the levels of unemployment benefit.

In November 1933 the government introduced a new Unemployment Bill to Parliament which, inter alia, was intended to make permanent the 'temporary' economy cuts and family Means Test introduced two years earlier. Public indignation was heightened by the Minister of Labour's admission that reductions in benefit and the strict application of the Means Test had achieved a saving to the Exchequer of £54.5m over that period.[28] This prompted the NUWM to mount another national march on the capital 'A National Hunger March is no small undertaking . . . It involves extensive planning and organising work' explained Hannington. The organisers 'not only have the job of marching men hundreds of miles to London, but of getting them safely back to their homes when the March terminates.' The route of each contingent had to be worked out so that it covered the largest number of towns; funds had to be raised to supply the marchers with boots, blankets, and overcoats; reception committees needed to ensure that food and shelter were available at each stop, and all the contingents had to arrive at their final destination on the same day. 'Weeks of marching in the dead of winter, with only the floors of workhouses and public halls for sleeping each night', wrote Hannington, 'called for physical stamina as well as courage', so that volunteers were required to undergo a medical examination, and be pronounced fit, before they were permitted to take part. The first contingent of 500 men set out from Glasgow on its 400 mile journey to London on January 24th, 1934, facing 32 days of winter weather and sore feet.[29]

Two weeks later, a small West Country contingent set off for London from Plymouth, a distance of 240 miles. At Totnes the Mayor organised a meal for them at the Temperance Hotel, but their reception at Exeter on Saturday, February 10th, was somewhat different. It had been arranged that on their arrival they would be accommodated for two nights over the weekend at the city's Poor Law Institution. Instead, they chose to sleep in their clothes and without blankets on the floor of the 'British Workman' restaurant in Waterbeer Street, close to the city's Police Station. According to its proprietor, "They could get no other accommodation, and did not desire to go into the workhouse." The reason for their refusal became clear at a meeting of the Exeter Public Assistance Committee when it was explained that the government had altered the regulations in such a way that 'casual vagrants', as the men were classified, had to stay in the Institution for two nights, instead of one. Mr Wood, the Master, had told the men that 'if they came into the Workhouse (sic) on the Sunday, they would have to stay two nights until the Tuesday and work on Monday.' The men must have objected on the grounds that their carefully arranged schedule would have been completely disrupted by leaving one day later than had been planned. Having spent one cold February night on the floor of the 'British Workman', a deputation of six of the marchers went to the Institution on the Sunday morning to appeal for the loan of blankets for that night; an appeal which the Master refused. The Clerk to the Vagrancy Committee supported the Master's ruling by claiming that, according to the regulations, they "could not allow the PAC's goods to be taken out of the Institution to goodness knows where . . . ." Had hundreds of marchers been involved that decision might not have been unreasonable, but the Plymouth party totalled just sixteen men who, joined by one more from Exeter and five from Exmouth, set out again on the Monday morning.[30]

Petty irritations such as the Plymouth marchers had endured at the hands of little local government tyrants were not uncommon, but one would not have expected such small-mindedness from a Minister of the Crown. A Member had asked that those who were taking part in the march be excused from signing on for benefit. Failure to sign on at the local Labour Exchange meant, of course, the forfeiture of any benefit. The Minister of Labour's answer, announced whilst the march was well under way, was brief: "Participation in the proposed march does not constitute such a special cause as would justify the Minister in relaxing the condition in question."[31]

The marching contingents from all over the country converged on Hyde Park on Sunday, February 25th, to be met by a welcoming demonstration, variously estimated at anywhere between fifty and one hundred and fifty thousand, despite drizzling rain. Detachments of provincial police and thousands of Special Constables had been called in to support the Metropolitan force, but, apart from acting as escort, none was needed to keep the peace. 'It was one of the most orderly demonstrations London had ever seen,' claimed one newspaper. 'When the Welshmen came in to take their place behind their appointed platform', its report continued, 'they were not smoking, because they had nothing to smoke. Suddenly, the crowd realised this and rained packets of cigarettes on them. That was typical of the crowd all the afternoon.'[32] The week which followed was taken up with a lobby of Members of Parliament and more demonstrations. The organisers had asked the government to receive a deputation, but this was refused, so they presented a Petition to the House of Commons requesting that their spokesmen be heard before the Bar of the House. In the debate prompted by that Petition the Liberal Opposition Leader denounced Ramsay Macdonald's refusal to hear the marchers in these words:

> "No one can say that the grievances of these men, who have walked to this city from many parts of this island, are trivial or imaginary. The well-to-do are suffering from a diminution of income and an increase of taxation, but no one suffers anything in comparison with those hundreds of thousands of men and women who have, month in and month out, year in and year out, to exist on 15s. 3d. a week, 8s. for a wife and 2s. for a child."[33]

Before the 'Hunger Marchers' left London they held a final rally in Trafalgar Square. The London Correspondent of the Devon and Exeter Gazette, clearly out of sympathy with the objects of the march, amused his readers with this snide little report under the heading 'MERRY MARCHERS':

> 'Whatever diverse woes and grievous wrongs may be the portion of the Hunger Marchers, it seems quite certain that hunger was not one of them. Incessant munching, between vociferous cheers, was the order of the day at Trafalgar-square last Sunday afternoon. On the paving stones of the crowded square there were sufficient bread and cake crumbs to feed an army, and so much orange peel that it was difficult to keep a footing . . . all of them have finished up a hiker's tour by making whoopee in the capital so that the grim look of the proletarian was completely missing at this demonstration.'[34]

The governments of Ramsay Macdonald, Stanley Baldwin and Neville Chamberlain all proved impotent in the face of large-scale unemployment, and George Orwell predicted in 1937: 'We may as well face the fact that several million men in England will -unless another war breaks out – never have a real job this side of the grave.'[35] He may well have been proved right. The irony of another world war solving a problem which had defeated governments and industrialists for more than a decade was not lost on Strube, the political cartoonist of the 'Daily Express'. He depicted an unemployed man in a bleak landscape staring at a brightening horizon on which appeared the shining outline of tanks, battleships and aeroplanes. Its caption read simply, 'Work at last.'

References

[1] Brierley, 'The Means Test Man', p.80
[2] Orwell, 'The Road to Wigan Pier', p.79
[3] Brockway, 'Bermondsey Story', pp.86–90
[4] 'The Daily Herald', 20 MAR 1933: quot. in Brockway, 'Bermondsey Story', p.165
[5] Brockway, 'Bermondsey Story', p.165
[6] ibid., pp 96–106
[7] ibid., pp. 111/112
[8] Branson and Heinemann, 'Britain in the Nineteen Thirties', p.135
[9] British Labour Statistics, Table 160: Department of Employment
[10] Stevenson, 'British Society 1914–45', p.266
[11] Orwell, 'The Road to Wigan Pier', p.67 and Cockburn, 'The Devil's Decade', p.27

[12] 'Exmouth Journal', 18 OCT 1930
[13] Bush, 'The Book of Exmouth', p.110
[14] Delderfield, 'Exmouth Yesterdays', pp.40 and 90
[15] 'Express and Echo', 28 DEC 1931
[16] 'Exmouth Journal', 31 JAN 1931
[17] Brierley, 'The Means Test Man', p.190
[18] 'Express and Echo', 17 FEB 1932
[19] ibid., 12 SEP, 1931
[20] Bakke, 'The Unemployed Man', p.182.
[21] Branson and Heinemann, 'Britain in the Nineteen Thirties', p.22
[22] Richards and Quick, 'Twentieth Century Britain', p.320
[23] Spender, S., 'Unemployed' (1929) – Baker, 'The Faber Book of English History in Verse'.
[24] Orwell, 'The Road to Wigan Pier', p.78
[25] Constantine, 'Unemployment in Britain between the Wars', p.38
[26] Hannington, 'Ten Lean Years', pp.222–9
[27] Laybourn, 'Britain on the Breadline', p.31
[28] Hannington, 'Ten Lean Years', pp.107–9
[29] ibid., p.53
[30] 'Express and Echo', 9,12 and 14 FEB 1934
[31] 'Devon and Exeter Gazette', 16 FEB 1934
[32] Hannington, 'Ten Lean Years', pp 112/3
[33] ibid., p.115
[34] 'Devon and Exeter Gazette', 9 MAR 1934
[35] Orwell, 'The Road to Wigan Pier', p.75

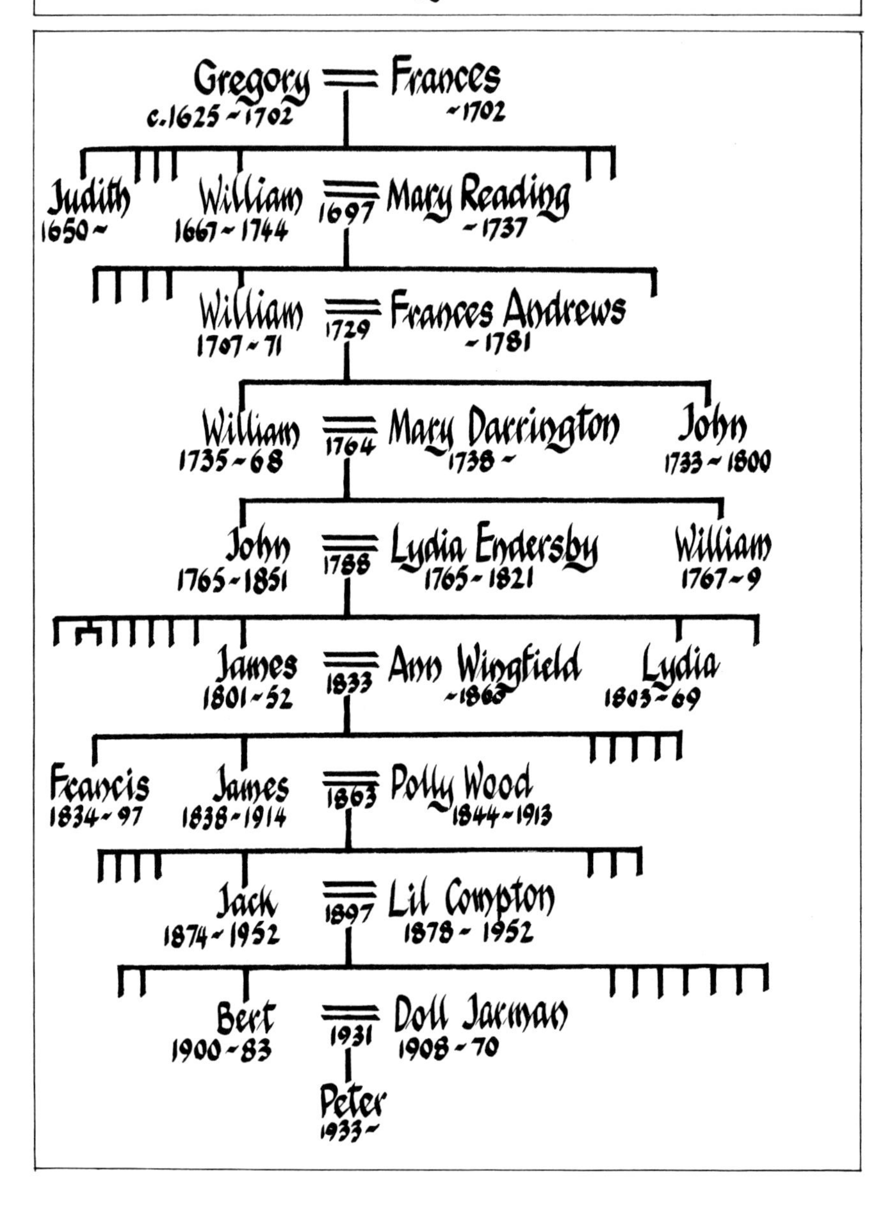
The MIMMS family, 17th - 20th centuries
Gregory c.1625 - 1702
Frances - 1702
Judith 1650 -
William 1667 - 1744
1697
Mary Reading - 1737
William 1707 - 71
1729
Frances Andrews - 1781
William 1735 - 68
1764
Mary Darrington 1738 -
John 1733 - 1800
John 1765 - 1851
1788
Lydia Endersby 1765 - 1821
William 1767 - 9
James 1801 - 52
1833
Ann Wingfield - 1863
Lydia 1803 - 69
Francis 1834 - 97
James 1838 - 1914
1863
Polly Wood 1844 - 1913
Jack 1874 - 1952
1897
Lil Compton 1878 - 1952
Bert 1900 - 83
1931
Doll Jarman 1908 - 70
Peter 1933 -

Family Tree.

BIBLIOGRAPHY

ANDREWS, C.Bruyn and F.(eds.), 'The Torrington Diaries' Eyre and Spottiswoode, (1954)

ASHBY, M.K. 'Joseph Ashby of Tysoe, 1859-1919' Merlin Press Ltd., (1974)

ASHTON, J. 'Modern Street Ballads', Chatto and Windus (1888)

AULT, W.O. 'Open-field Husbandry and the Village Community', American Philosophical Society, Philadelphia (1965)

BAKER, K.(ed.) 'The Faber Book of English History in Verse' Faber and Faber (1988)

BAKKE, E.W. 'The Unemployed Man' Nisbet (1933)

BARRELL, J. and BULL, J.,(eds.), 'English Pastoral Verse' Penguin Books (1974)

BEASLEY, J.D. 'The Bitter Cry Heard and Heeded' South London Mission (1989)

BELL, A.D. 'London in the Age of Dickens' University of Oklahoma Press (1967)

BESANT, W. 'South London' Chatto and Windus (1901)

BLOOMFIELD, R. 'The Farmer's Boy' Longman and Rees (1800) (6th edn.,1802)

BOAST, M. 'The Story of Bermondsey' The Council of the London Borough of Southwark (1984)

BOAST, M. 'The Story of the Borough' Council of the London Borough of Southwark (1982)

BOOTH, C. 'The Inhabitants of Tower Hamlets (School Board Division), their Condition and Occupations' Journal of the Royal Statistical Society. vol. L. (1887)

BOOTH, C. 'Life and Labour of the People in London' Macmillan and Co.Ltd., (1902)

BOOTH, W. 'In Darkest England and the Way Out' The Salvation Army (1890)

BOSANQUET, H. 'Social Work in London 1869-1912: A History of the Charity Organisation Society' John Murray (1914)

BRANSON, F. and HEINEMANN, M. 'Britain in the Nineteen Thirties' Weidenfeld and Nicholson (1971)

BRIERLEY, W. 'The Means Test Man' Methuen (1935)

BRIGGS, A. 'A Social History of England' Weidenfeld and Nicholson (1983) 1985 Penguin edn.

BROCKWAY, F. 'Bermondsey Story' Allen and Unwin (1949)

BROCKWAY, F. 'Britain's First Socialists' Quartet Books (1980)

BROWN, J. 'Gamblingay' Cassell (1989)

BURKE,T. 'The Streets of London' B.T.Batsford Ltd. (1940)

BUSH, R. 'The Book of Exmouth' Barracuda Books Ltd.,Buckingham (1978)

CALDER-MARSHALL, A. 'Prepare To Shed Them Now: the Ballads of George Sims.' Hutchinson (1968)

CANNING, J. 'The Illustrated Mayhew's London'. Guild Publishing (1986)

CARLTON, C. 'Going to the Wars' B.C.A. (1992)

CHAMBERS, J.D. and MINGAY, G.E. 'The Agricultural Revolution, 1750-1880' B.T. Batsford Ltd. (1966)

COBBETT, W. 'Rural Rides' (1825) Everyman Edition (1912), J.M. Dent and Sons Ltd.

COCKBURN, C. 'The Devil's Decade' Sidgwick and Jackson Ltd. (1973)

COLE, J. 'The History and Antiquities of Wellingborough' (1837)

COLLIER, R. 'The General Next to God' Collins (1965)

CONSTANTINE, S. 'Unemployment in Britain Between the Wars' Longman (1980)

CRABBE, G. 'The Borough' (1810)

CROWTHER, M.A. 'The Workhouse System, 1834-1929' Methuen (1981)

CRUIKSHANK, R.J., 'Roaring Century' Hamish Hamilton (1946)

CUNNINGHAM, H. 'Leisure in the Industrial Revolution' Croom Helm Ltd. (1980)

CUNNINGHAM, P. 'Handbook of London' (1850) 1978 reprint by E.P. Publishing Ltd., Wakefield

CURTIS, S.J. 'History of Education in Great Britain' University Tutorial Press ltd. (1957)

DAVIES, A. 'The Map of London from 1746 to the Present Day' B.C.A. (1987)

DAVIES, M.L. (ed) 'Maternity: Letters from Working Women' (1915) Virago Press Ltd. (1978)

DELDERFIELD, E.R. 'Exmouth Yesterdays' Raleigh Press, Exmouth, Devon (1952)

DICKENS, C. 'Little Dorrit' (1857) O.U.P. (1987)

DIGBY, A. 'Pauper Palaces' Routledge and Kegan Paul (1978)

EDEN, Sir F.M. 'The State of the Poor' Frank Cass and Co., (facsimile of the 1797 edn.)

ELIOT, G. 'Adam Bede' Collins Library of Classics edn. (1858)

ELMERS, C. and WERNER, A., 'London's Lost Riverscape' Penguin Books (1988)

EMMISON, F.G. 'The Relief of the Poor at Eaton Socon' Bedfordshire Historical Records Society, vol.XV (1933)

EVANS, H.A. 'Highways and Byways in Northamptonshire and Rutland.' Macmillan (1918)

FINER, S.E. 'The Life and Times of Sir Edwin Chadwick' Methuen, 1952 (1980 edn.)
FISHMAN, W.J. 'East End 1888' Duckworth (1988)
FITZGERALD, P. 'Victoria's London - The Suburbs' Alderman Press (n.d. - c.1890)
FLETCHER, G. 'The London Nobody Knows' Penguin Books (1965)
FLINN, M.W.(ed.) 'Report on the Sanitary Condition of the Labouring Population of Great Britain by Edwin Chadwick.' Edinburgh U.P. (1965)
FREEMAN, J. 'London for Everyman' J.M. Dent and Sons Ltd. (1956)
FRIED, A. and ELMAN, R.M. (eds.) 'Charles Booth's London' Hutchinson (1969)
GAULDIE, E. 'Cruel Habitations: A History of Working-Class Housing, 1780-1918.' Allen and Unwin Ltd. (1974)
GILBERT, B.B. 'The Evolution of National Insurance in Great Britain' Michael Joseph (1966)
GODBER, J. 'History of Bedfordshire' Bedfordshire County Council (Bedford) (1984)
GOLDSMITH, O. 'The Deserted Village' (1770) - The Poems and Plays of Oliver Goldsmith' J.M. Dent (Everyman edn.) (1910)
GREEN, H. 'Village Life in the Eighteenth Century' Longman (1976)
HAMMOND, J.L. and B. 'The Village Labourer, 1760 - 1832' Alan Sutton Publishing, Gloucester (1987 edn. of 1911 original)
HANNINGTON, W. 'Ten Lean Years' Victor Gollancz Ltd. (1940)
HARDY, T. 'Jude the Obscure' (1895)
HARDY, T. 'The Trumpet Major' (1880) Macmillan and Co. Ltd., (1967 pb. edn.)
HARRISON, J.F.C. 'The Common People' Fontana Press (1989)
HARRISON, J.F.C. 'Late Victorian Britain, 1875 - 1901' Fontana Press (1990)
HEY, D. 'Family History and Local History in England.' Longman (1987)
HIBBERT, C. 'The English: A Social History, 1066 - 1945' B.C.A. (1987)
HILL, C. 'Society and Puritanism in Pre-Revolutionary England' Peregrine Books (1986)
HILL, C. 'The World Turned Upside Down' Peregrine Books (1984)
HILL, O. 'Homes of the London Poor' Frank Cass and Co. Ltd. (1883)
HIMMELFARB, G. 'The Idea of Poverty: England in the Early Industrial Age.' Faber and Faber (1985 pb. edn.)
HOBSBAWM, E.J. 'Labouring Men' Weidenfeld and Nicholson (1986 pb. edn.)
HOBSBAWM, E.J. and RUDE, G. 'Captain Swing', Lawrence & Wishart Ltd., Peregrine Books (1985)
HOLE, J. 'The Homes of the Working Classes' (facsimile reprint by Garland Publishing Inc. New York, 1985) (1866)
HOLLINGSHEAD, J. 'Underground London' Groombridge and Sons (1862)
HOPKINS, H. 'The Long Affray' Macmillan (1986)
HORN, P. 'Life and Labour in Rural England, 1760-1850' Macmillan Education Ltd. (1987)
HORN, P. 'A Georgian Parson and his Village: the Story of David Davies, 1742 - 1819.' Beacon Publications, Oxford. (1981)

HORN, P. 'The Victorian and Edwardian Schoolchild' Alan Sutton Publishing, Gloucester (1989)
HOSKINS, W.G. 'The Midland Peasant' Macmillan (1965)
HOSKINS, W.G. 'Local History in England' Longman (1959)
HOWITT, W. 'The Rural Life of England' Longman, Brown, Green and Longmans (1844)
HYAMS, E. (trans.) 'Notes in England by Hippolyte Taine' Thames and Hudson (1957)
JAMES, L. 'Fiction for the Working Man, 1830-1850' Penguin University Books (1974)
JERROLD, W. (ed.) 'The Complete Poetical Works by Thomas Hood' O.U.P. (1906)
KEATING, P.J. (ed.) 'Working Class Stories of the 1890s' Routledge and Kegan Paul Ltd. (1975)
KENYON, J. 'The Civil Wars of England' Weidenfeld and Nicholson Ltd. (1989 pb.)
KERR, B. 'Bound to the Soil: A Social History of Dorset 1750-1918.' John Baker Publishers Ltd. (1968)
KIRWAN, D.J. 'Palace and Hovel' (1870) Abelard-Schuman Ltd. (1963 reprint)
KITCHEN, F. 'Brother to the Ox' J.M. Dent and Sons Ltd. (1940), 1981 edn.
KLINGBERG, F.J. and HUSTVEDT, S.B. (eds) 'The Warning Drum: Broadsides of 1803' University of California Press (1944)
LAQUEUR, T. 'Bodies, Death and Pauper Funerals' Universiy of California Representations (1983)
LAYBOURN, K. 'Britain on the Breadline' Alan Sutton Publishing Ltd., Gloucester, Glos. (1990)
LEE, L. 'Cider With Rosie' Hogarth Press (1959), Penguin Books edn. (1962)
LEFF, V. and Blunden, C.H. 'Riverside Story' City Publicity Services Ltd., (1965)
LONGMATE, N. 'The Workhouse' Temple Smith (1974)
LOW, D.A. 'Thieves' Kitchen' Alan Sutton Publishing, Gloucester. (1982)
McCANN, J. 'Clay and Cob Buildings' Shire Publications Ltd., (1983)
MACLURE, S. 'One Thousand Years of London Education, 1870 - 1970' Allen Lane, The Penguin Press (1970)
MALCOLMSON, R.W. 'Life and Labour in England, 1700-1780' Hutchinson (1981)
MALCOLMSON, R.W. 'Popular Recreations in English Society, 1700 - 1850' C.U.P. (1973)
MANNING, B. 'The English People and the English Revolution' Bookmarks (1991)
MARGETSON, S. 'Leisure and Pleasure in the Nineteenth Century' Cassell (1969)
MASTERMAN, C.F.G. 'The Condition of England' (1909) Methuen and Co. Ltd., (1960 edn.)
MASTERMAN, C.F.G. 'From the Abyss: Of its Inhabitants by One of Them' Methuen (1902)
MEARNS, A. 'The Bitter Cry of Outcast London' London Congregational Union (1883)

MORRILL, J. (ed.) 'The Impact of the English Civil War' Collins and Brown Ltd. (1991)
MORRIS, R.J. 'Cholera 1832' Croom Helm Ltd. (1976)
MORRISON, A. 'A Child of the Jago' Methuen (1897)
MULGAN, J. 'Poems of Freedom' Gollancz (1938)
NEWSHOLME, A. 'Fifty Years in Public Health' Allen and Unwin (1935)
ORWELL, G. 'The Decline of the English Murder and other Essays' Penguin Books (1983)
ORWELL, G. 'The Road to Wigan Pier' (1937) Penguin Books (1962 edn.)
OUTRAM, T.W. 'Coaching Days and Coaching Ways' Macmillan (1888)
PALMER, J. and M. 'A History of Wellingborough' Steepleprint Ltd., Earls Barton (Northants) (1972)
PALMER, R. (ed.) 'A Ballad History of England' B.T. Batsford (1979)
PARSONS, F.G. 'The History of St Thomas's Hospital' Methuen and Co. Ltd. (1936)
PEACOCK, A.J. 'Bread or Blood: A Study of the Agrarian Riots in East Anglia in 1816.' Victor Gollancz Ltd. (1965)
PEARSALL, R. 'The Worm in the Bud' Penguin Books (1983)
PEMBER-REEVES, M. 'Round About a Pound a Week' (1913) Virago Press Ltd. (1979)
PETTIT, P.A.J. 'The Royal Forests of Northamptonshire' Northamptonshire Record Society (1968)
PINTO, V. de S. and RODWAY, A.E. 'The Common Muse; Popular British Ballad Poetry' Penguin Books (1965)
POSTER, J. (ed.) 'George Crabbe, Selected Poetry' Carcanet Press, Manchester (1986)
PRETTEJOHNS, G. et al. 'Charles Dickens and Southwark' Council of the London Borough of Southwark (1974)
PUCKLE, B.S. 'Funeral Customs, Their Origins and Development' T. Werner Laurie Ltd., (1926)
REDFORD, A. 'Labour Migration in England, 1800 - 1850' Manchester U.P., (1926, 3rd edn., 1976)
REEVES, J. 'Recollections of a School Attendance Officer' (n.d. c.1912)
RICHARDS, D. and QUICK, A. 'Twentieth Century Britain' Longman & Co., (1965)
RICHARDSON, R. 'Death, Dissection and the Destitute', Routledge, Penguin Books (1988)
ROLPH, C.H. 'London Particulars' O.U.P. (1980)
RUBINSTEIN, D. 'School Attendance in London, 1870 - 1904 : A Social History' University of Hull Press (1969)
RULE. J. 'The Labouring Classes in Early Industrial England, 1750 - 1850' Longman (1986)
RUSSELL, D. and TICHELAR, M. 'Class Struggles in South London, 1850 - 1900' South Lambeth History Workshop (1980)
SABINE, G.H. 'The Works of Gerrard Winstanley' Cornell U.P. (1941)
SHERWOOD, R.E. 'Civil Strife in the Midlands, 1642 - 1651' Phillimore and Co. Ltd., Chichester. (1974)
SHEPPARD, F. 'London 1808 - 1870: The Infernal Wen' Secker and Warburg (1971)

SILVER, P. and H. 'The Education of the Poor' Routledge and Kegan Paul (1974)
SMITH, F., (ed.) 'The Band of Hope Jubilee Volume' (1897)
SMITH, F.B. 'The People's Health, 1830 - 1910' Weidenfeld and Nicholson (1979) (1990 pb. edn.)
SMITH, J.R. 'The Speckled Monster: Smallpox in England, 1670 - 1970' Essex Record Office, Chelmsford, Essex. (1987)
SNELL, K.D.M. 'Annals of the Labouring Poor: Social Change and Agrarian England, 1660 - 1900 C.U.P. (1987)
SOUTHGATE, G.W. 'English Economic History' J.M. Dent (1947)
SPEAIGHT, G. 'Bawdy Songs of the Early Music Hall' Pan Books (1977)
STEDMAN-JONES, G. 'Outcast London' Penguin Books (1984)
STEVENSON, J. 'BRITISH SOCIETY, 1914-45' (1984) Penguin Books (1990 edn.)
STEVENSON, J. 'Popular Disturbances in England, 1700-1870' Longman (1979)
STURT, G. 'Change in the Village' Gerald Duckworth and Co. Ltd. (1912) (1955 edn.)
STURT, M. 'The Education of the People' Routledge and Kegan Paul (1967)
TEBBUTT, C.F. 'Huntingdonshire Folklore' Friends of the Norris Museum, St. Ives (Cambs.) (1984)
TEBBUTT, C.F. 'St. Neots: the History of a Huntingdonshire Town' Phillimore and Co. Ltd., Chichester. (1984)
THOMAS, R.H.G. 'London's First Railway - The London & Greenwich' B.T. Batsford Ltd. (1986)
THOMPSON, E.P. 'Customs in Common' Penguin Books (1993)
THOMPSON, E.P. 'The Making of the English Working Class' Gollancz, (Pelican Books edn.) (1980)
THOMPSON, F. 'Larkrise to Candleford' Penguin Books (1979)
THOMPSON, F.M.L. 'Hampstead: Building a Borough, 1650 - 1964' Routledge and Kegan Paul (1974)
TIBBLE, J.W. and A. (eds.) 'John Clare, Selected Poems' (1979)
TONGE, W. and QUINCEY, M. 'British Social and Economic History, 1800-1900' Macmillan Education Ltd. (1980)
TREBLE, J.H. 'Urban Poverty in Britain, 1830 - 1914' B.T. Batsford Ltd. (1979)
TRESSALL, R. 'The Ragged Trousered Philanthropists' The Richards Press Ltd. (1914)
TREVELYAN, G.M. 'Illustrated English Social History - vol.3. - The Eighteenth Century.' Pelican Books (1960)
TRISTRAM, W.O. 'Coaching Days and Coaching Ways' Macmillan (1888)
TUER, A. 'Old London Cries' Field and Tuer (1885)
TURNER, M.R. 'The Parlour Song Book' Pan Books Ltd., (1972)
VALLANCE, R. (ed.) 'Dickens' London' Folio Society (1966)
VINCENT, D. (ed.) 'Testaments of Radicalism: Memoirs of Working Class Politicians, 1790 - 1885' Europa Publications Ltd. (1977)
WAKEFIELD, G. 'Swing Unmasked' (1831)
WALTON, J.K. 'The English Seaside Resort: A Social History, 1750 - 1914' Leicester U.P. (1983)

WEINREB, B. and HIBBERT, C. 'The London Encyclopaedia' B.C.A. (1983)
WILLIAMS, K. 'From Pauperism to Poverty' Routledge and Kegan Paul (1981)
WILLIS, F. 'A Book of London's Yesterdays' Phoenix House Ltd. (1960)
WILSON, F.M. 'Life in Eaton Socon, 1750 – 1850' Bedford College of Education, Bedford. (1968)
WOHL, A.S. 'The Eternal Slum: Housing and Social Policy in Victorian London.' Edward Arnold (Publishers) Ltd. (1977)
WOHL, A.S. 'Ragged London in 1861, John Hollingshead' J.M. Dent and Sons Ltd. Everyman Edn. (1986)
WRIGHTSON, K. 'English Society, 1580 – 1680' Unwin Hyman Ltd. (1982)
WYMER, N. 'Dr Barnardo' Longman (1962)

INDEX